THE PSYCHOLOGY *of*
EATING AND DRINKING

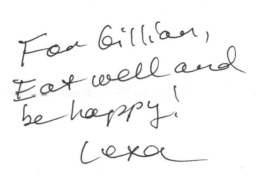

THE PSYCHOLOGY *of* EATING AND DRINKING

Third Edition

A.W. Logue

Brunner-Routledge
Taylor & Francis Group
NEW YORK AND HOVE

Published in 2004 by
Brunner-Routledge
270 Madison Avenue
New York, NY 10016
www.brunner-routledge.com

Published in Great Britain by
Brunner-Routledge
27 Church Road
Hove, East Sussex
BN3 2FA
www.brunner-routledge.co.uk

Brunner-Routledge is an imprint of the Taylor & Francis Group.
Printed in the United States of America on acid-free paper.
Typesetting: Jack Donner, BookType
Cover design: Elise Weinger
Cover photo: © Dennis Blachut/CORBIS
Back cover photo: © Jay Brady, 2005

10 9 8 7 6 5 4 3 2 1
Library of Congress Cataloging-in-Publication Data

Logue, A. W. (Alexandra W.)
    The psychology of eating and drinking / A.W. Logue.—3rd ed.
        p. cm.
    Includes bibliographical references and index.
    ISBN 0-415-95008-2 (hdbk : alk. paper) — ISBN 0-415-95009-0 (pbk : alk paper)
1. Food habits—Psychological aspects. 2. Nutrition—Psychological aspects. 3. Drinking
behavior. 4. Food preferences. I. Title
    TX357.L67 2004
    613 .2'01'9—dc 22

                                                                    2004006642

To the memory of Gaga and Dad,
both of whom understood what food and people are all about
and were incomparable people themselves

Contents

℃

Preface

𝓒

When I was a year old I stopped eating everything except bread and milk. For years my diet showed little improvement, and by 15 I was eating mostly meat, milk, potatoes, bread, orange juice, and desserts. I did *not* eat pizza, spaghetti, or any other food that I considered "foreign." I avoided soda, fresh fruit (except bananas), vegetables (except peas, carrots, and beets), and cheese (except grilled American cheese sandwiches). Fish I regarded as poison.

My parents were not alarmed; I come from a long line of people with unusual food preferences. My mother, by choice, rarely served fresh fruit or fish at our home. She never served liver, which she hates, although my father loved it. He always ate first the food he disliked most, and many times I saw him finish salad and string beans before touching baked potato and steak. When I was a child my mother frequently recounted to me how her grandfather would eat chocolate cupcakes but not cake made from the same batter; he said that the cake gave him indigestion.

At home my parents gave me vitamin pills and basically let me eat whatever I wanted. But everywhere else I had to contend with sticky social occasions in which I was served what I abhorred eating. Just imagine going to a birthday party and not being able to eat the soda and pizza that everyone else was eating.

Food aversions were not the only troubles of my youth. Food preferences also gave me problems. Although I disliked many things, when I did like a food I could eat it at any hour of the day or night. My Southern grandmother was happy to feed me fried chicken, mashed potatoes, and hot biscuits dripping with butter whenever I wished. It was not easy to keep my weight at a reasonable level. One of the most dangerous places for me was the farm of my great-aunt and great-uncle in South Carolina, where the dinner table groaned with a great many things that I loved to eat. One exception was the milk from their cows. Although I relished it when it came back from the packager, I found milk totally unacceptable when it came straight from the cow (even though my great-uncle had pasteurized it).

Two things saved me from an unhealthy preoccupation with eating and not eating certain foods: my husband and my study of experimental psychology.

My husband was known in childhood as the HGP, or human garbage pail, because of his voracious and indiscriminate eating habits. Through example, pleading, and occasional bullying over the 30 years of our marriage, he now has me regularly eating (and sometimes even liking) vegetables, fruits, and different types of ethnic food. (No one, under any circumstances, will ever get me to eat fish.)

Becoming an experimental psychologist, the other saving factor, channeled my former embarrassment into research enthusiasm. As a graduate student, I was continually drawn to research on eating and drinking behaviors. Sometimes I conducted studies that grew out of hypotheses I had about the origins of my own eating peculiarities. Only much later did I realize that a great deal of psychology focuses on eating and drinking.

As a graduate student at Harvard I was encouraged to pursue my interests wherever they led, a strategy that prepared me well for writing this book and its predecessors. As part of my studies I taught a small seminar for sophomore psychology majors. I was expected to come up with a topic for a year-long tutorial that would integrate material from many areas of psychology. I chose eating and drinking.

Later, as an assistant professor at the State University of New York at Stony Brook, I created a new lecture course: The Psychology of Eating and Drinking. Although it was an advanced, nonrequired course, it grew in popularity each year. Toward the end of my years at Stony Brook, literally hundreds of students from many different majors tried to get into the course each time I taught it. Unfortunately I could not take them all. In the first years of the course, the students read only original articles; the only textbooks that were at all relevant covered isolated topics such as hunger or alcoholism. The lack of a suitable text for my course and the enthusiasm of my teaching assistants and students finally convinced me that I should write a textbook for the course. The result was the first two editions of *The Psychology of Eating and Drinking*, and now, this third version.

The story of my path to writing *The Psychology of Eating and Drinking* would be incomplete without mention of Paul Rozin, the ultimate food psychologist. I first met Paul in 1977 at the University of Pennsylvania, where he was pursuing research on why people eat chile pepper. That first meeting with Paul and his wife, Elisabeth, cookbook writer and culinary historian, and the time we spent in their kitchen, catalyzed my interest in the psychology of eating and drinking, and the effect has not yet worn off. Liz's cookbook, *Ethnic Cuisine: The Flavor-Principle Cookbook*, has been my favorite since and I doubt if that will ever change.

This book, similar to the previous versions of *The Psychology of Eating and Drinking*, describes scientific inquiries into eating and drinking behaviors. However, the book does this in such a way that the material is completely understandable to the educated lay person. You need not have had any courses in psychology, or courses in any science for that matter, to understand what's written here. The only requirement for reading and enjoying this book is that the reader be willing to approach psychology as a science. One of my goals in writing all of my books has been to show how much can be learned by applying scientific methods to the study of behavior. Should you wish further information on any topic, the extensive references listed at the back of the book will assist you. But you can also just read the book through, or selected chapters, without being concerned with the sources of the material.

I have elected to cover only those aspects of the psychology of eating and drinking that seem well researched and interesting, and I have had to cover some of these only briefly. Complete coverage of the psychology of eating and drinking would require many, many volumes. This book is meant only as an introduction. Nevertheless, when possible I describe how the research was conducted—not just the results—so that you can judge that and other research for yourself.

This book covers the major eating and drinking disorders, but it will not tell you precisely how to diagnose or treat your own or someone else's eating and drinking problems. The book describes some of the principles for doing so, but real problem solving requires professional help. The relevant chapters list clinics and self-help organizations that may be useful in obtaining that professional help.

Acknowledgments

𝒞

Many people and organizations assisted me in preparing this book and the first two editions of *The Psychology of Eating and Drinking*. For the first edition, James Hassett gave me a great deal of valuable, general advice on how to write a psychology book. My library research assistants, Lawrence Epstein, Pilar Peña-Correal, Telmo Peña-Correal, and Michael Smith, were always ready to run to the library to find source material for me. Herbert Terrace and Columbia University kindly provided me with space and library privileges that helped me finish the book during my sabbatical. Conversations with Alex Kacelnik on foraging and Nori Geary on hunger were also very helpful. Invaluable comments were made on the manuscript by Lorraine Collins, Howard Rachlin, Monica Rodriguez, Elisabeth Rozin, Paul Rozin, Diane Shrank, Ian Shrank, Michael Smith, and Richard Thompson. Their help is greatly appreciated. In particular I thank Camille M. Logue, whose hours of insightful and witty taped comments kept me company in the lonely hours of revision; she went far beyond the requirements of sibling duty.

In preparing the second edition, the comments made in the many reviews of the first edition were extremely helpful. Several reviewers (Leann L. Birch, John P. Foreyt, Bonnie Spring, and Rudy E. Vuchinich) made many insightful, useful suggestions regarding a draft of the second edition. Many researchers put up with my seemingly endless questions about this or that aspect of eating and drinking. In particular, Kelly Brownell provided much information regarding overeating and obesity, Jasper Brener helped me to identify research on metabolic rate, and the Cuisine Group (most notably Linda Bartoshuk, Barbara Kirshenblatt-Gimblett, Rudolph Grewe, Solomon Katz, Elisabeth Rozin, and Paul Rozin) were a constant source of inspiration.

I also thank James Allison for sending me the Warm Feet. (Will the wonders of capsicum never cease?) Lori Bonvino and John Chelonis ably word processed and organized the references.

Ann Streissguth at the University of Washington generously supplied the photographs for Figure 13.2 (the children with fetal alcohol syndrome). Twentieth Century Fox provided the photograph of Marilyn Monroe from the movie *Monkey Business* for Figure 9.1a and Columbia Pictures provided the photograph of Jamie Lee Curtis from the movie *Perfect* for Figure 9.1b. Phototeque, in New York City, was of great assistance in locating these latter two photographs. Jacob Steiner of Hebrew University in Jerusalem, Israel, kindly provided the photographs of newborn infants tasting various solutions (Figures 5.3 and 5.5).

For the third and current version of this book I am indebted to John Wahlert for his many insights into and enthusiasm about chocolate, chile pepper, and computer games; David Szalda for assisting me with chemical calculations; and especially to Yenny Anderson and the librarians of Baruch College and the New York Institute of Technology, all of whom take the science of information retrieval to new heights. Yenny Anderson also prepared some of the figures. Kari Scalchunes and Joyce Mulcahy provided able office assistance and food encouragement when needed. Extremely helpful comments on the manuscript were made by Linda Bartoshuk, Amber D. Hoover, Rebecca A. Pearce, Patrice Tombline, Shawna Vogel, several anonymous reviewers, and especially Susan Brennan. My husband, Ian Shrank, and teenage son, Samuel Logue Shrank, also gave me many excellent comments on the manuscript. (The only problem with having my son read the manuscript is that he now happily recites to me the five research-based reasons why he doesn't like and won't eat certain dark vegetables or fish.) My agent, Al Zuckerman, rescued the manuscript at a critical time, George Zimmar signed it with proper gastronomic flair, and Shannon Vargo and Allison Taub ably shepherded it through the production process.

Throughout it all, the Long Island Railroad provided many, many hours of uninterrupted work time. Harvard University, the State University of New York, Baruch College of the City University of New York, the New York Institute of Technology, the United States Public Health Services Biomedical Research Support Grants, the National Institute of Mental Health, and the National Science Foundation all provided funds for research that is reported here. Many ideas and much inspiration came from the students and teaching assistants in my undergraduate and graduate courses on the psychology of eating and drinking. Finally, I want to express my deepest appreciation to Ian Shrank and Samuel Logue Shrank for their constant unquestioning encouragement and support.

CHAPTER 1

Introductions

The Essential Nutrients of the Psychology of Eating and Drinking

𝓒

SIR TOBY—
Does not our life consist of the four elements
[earth, air, fire, and water]?

SIR ANDREW—
Faith, so they say; but I think it rather consists
of eating and drinking.

SIR TOBY—
Thou art a scholar; let us therefore eat and drink.
William Shakespeare (1623/1936)[1]

Have you ever noticed just how much of your time is devoted to eating and drinking, or to thinking about eating and drinking? Pick a day and try keeping a record of the total time that you spend preparing or eating meals and snacks, as well as the time that you spend just thinking about the foods and drinks that you will or won't have. You'll likely find that far more time is devoted to these activities than to anything else, including sex. On a recent day I used a stopwatch to record how much total time I spent thinking about or touching food. My total was 4 hours and 33 minutes, and I'm not any more obsessed with food than is the average person. A great deal of the behavior of all animals consists of obtaining and consuming foods and liquids.

It doesn't take a scientist to know this. Shakespeare obviously knew it. But it does take a scientist to find out what causes these food- and drink-related behaviors. And once we understand the causes, then we may be able to change these behaviors, something that a lot of people would like to do for many different reasons.

For example, I'm sure that you've noticed that a lot of people consume so much of certain foods and drinks that bad things happen—such as weight gain from eating too much chocolate, high cholesterol from eating too many eggs, and liver damage from drinking too much alcohol. Why do people do these things? And, even more intriguing, why do some people overconsume these foods and drinks more than other people or only at certain times? Why do women tend to crave chocolate at certain points in the menstrual cycle, for instance? We need to understand the causes of behaviors such as these. Once we do, we'll have important information to guide us in modifying these behaviors.

Our fascination with such eating and drinking behaviors and their causes has resulted in a huge industry of food-related pop science. Every bookstore, every magazine stand, every grocery store checkout counter is filled with publications about how to get your child to eat vegetables, how to tell if someone has an eating disorder, or, most commonly, how to lose weight. TV programs and movies on these subjects abound. But the degree to which any of these is based on scientific research is very limited. Thus the information and advice offered is, at best, incomplete, and is often simply incorrect. Let's take as an example the advice that to eat less you should drink lots of water. Have you ever heard that? Well, it's completely untrue; people don't eat less when they drink more water. And after you read this book, you'll understand why.

This book is different from what you'll find on the newsstands or in most bookstores. It will introduce you to the scientific study of eating and drinking behavior. It will show you how scientists, particularly psychologists, conduct research on eating and drinking and what they have been able to find out so far. It will tell you many of the latest discoveries in this field. The answers aren't always simple, and they aren't always what we'd like to hear. But if you want accurate, up-to-date information about what causes our eating and drinking behavior, and about what we can and can't do to change that behavior, you'll get that information here. And while you may not always be able to use that information to change your own behavior or someone else's—serious eating and drinking problems require professional help—you will get much immediately useful information.

What's Psychology Got to Do With Eating and Drinking?

Most of the information in this book is drawn from carefully conducted psychology experiments. *Psychology* is the science of behavior, the science of "how and why organisms do what they do."[2] So if your goal is to understand the behavior of people and other animals, as opposed to, say, the reproduction of plant cells, then psychology is your field.

In this book we'll look at a certain set of behaviors—the behaviors involved in eating and drinking—using many different types of psychological approaches, from the physiological to the social. Our strategy will be to use whatever psychological science can tell us about these behaviors. We have something we want to understand—eating and drinking behaviors—and we're going to use every possible tool to gain that understanding.

Psychology is the science of behavior, and therefore the analytical method that you'll see used throughout the entire book is the scientific method. The scientific method assumes that the laws of nature govern all things and that they do so in a consistent manner for all people and other animals at all times. Without this scientific orientation it would be impossible to conduct experiments to determine the causes of behavior. In an experiment, all conditions are held constant except for one aspect of the surroundings that is manipulated by the experimenter. If this change in the surroundings is followed by a change in the behavior of the subject, the experimenter concludes that manipulating that aspect of the surroundings has the observed effect on behavior.

For example, you might take 10 people, ensure that they had eaten and drunk the exact same things for the 6 hours prior to dinner, have half of them drink a quart of water right before dinner, and then measure how much they all ate during dinner. If, on average, the people who drank the extra water ate less than the other people, you could conclude that drinking lots of water decreases how much people eat right after drinking the water. Of course, this experiment wouldn't tell you what might happen at breakfast the next morning; the water drinkers might make up for their smaller dinners by eating larger breakfasts. You would need to do another experiment, or expand your original experiment, to determine that. All psychological scientists assume a scientific orientation in their work.

The study of the psychology of eating and drinking is a huge but fascinating subject. It includes research on how you detect tastes, why you become hungry or thirsty, why you like some foods more than others, how you choose among foods, how certain foods can affect your behavior, and how and why we sometimes eat and drink in less than ideal ways. It would be impossible to cover all of the psychology of eating and drinking in one book. But I hope that this book will give you a good overview or, more appropriately, a good taste of this subject.

Getting There by Degrees: Evolution and Eating and Drinking

In doing any kind of scientific investigation, it helps if you have some conceptual framework that guides where you're going, some theory or theories that suggest how things work, so that you'll have specific ideas to test and ways to describe your findings as a whole. Psychological science, particularly psychological science as it's applied to eating and drinking behaviors, is often organized around the concepts of evolution and natural selection. The reason that the concepts of evolution and natural selection seem particularly appropriate for the psychology of eating and drinking is that every animal, including every person, must eat and drink appropriately or it will die. This means that any animal that has some genetically influenced behavior or anatomical trait that enables it to eat and drink well will be more likely to survive and will have more offspring than will other members of that species. Therefore you would expect the eating and drinking behaviors of all species to have evolved over the millennia so as to be beneficial; you would expect that, by the process of natural selection, individuals who are well adapted with regard to how they eat and drink have survived and reproduced. Repeatedly in this book you'll hear me say that some way in which a species eats or drinks is adaptive and has helped that species to survive.

At this point I hope that you're saying, "Wait a minute. You're telling me that people and other animals have evolved to eat and drink well. But we all know, and you wrote yourself earlier in this chapter, that people eat and drink in all kinds of harmful ways. If we have evolved to eat well, why is it, for example, that people eat so much chocolate that they gain weight?"

Just because natural selection is and has been in operation doesn't mean that all of the behaviors of every species will be perfectly adapted for every situation. In fact, there are several reasons why an animal's eating behavior might not be optimal. Just one such reason is that you may be observing the animal in a situation different from the one to which its species was adapted. We didn't evolve in surroundings where chocolate was easily and cheaply available around every corner, and with our advanced medical techniques, people usually don't die at young ages from overeating chocolate. Therefore, despite the harmful effects of overeating chocolate, those of us who are chocolate-obsessed are still having lots of children. In this book you'll read many explanations such as this of unhealthy eating and drinking behaviors.

Getting Down to the Subject

Now that we have our theoretical framework for experiments on the psychology of eating and drinking, let's suppose that you're a scientist thinking about an experiment that you might do to find out why people like chocolate so much. Let's assume that you've read research suggesting that a particular gene results in people loving chocolate after they've had many years of exposure to it, and you want to find out for sure if that's true. Therefore you design an experiment in which you'll take 50 people with identical genes, give half of them chocolate from birth to age 25 while preventing the others from having any contact with chocolate during those years, and then test all of the participants' preferences for chocolate when they are and aren't hungry. Sound like a great experiment? Well it is, but there are a few practical problems. To begin with, you'll never find 50 people with identical genes. Even finding two (identical twins) is hard. Second, what scientist is going to have the patience to do an experiment that lasts 25 years? Scientists are under great pressure to publish frequently in order to keep getting research grants and to get promoted at their universities. Third, where are you going to get enough money to do this experiment? The participants will expect to get paid for their time, which will be considerable. And 25 years of chocolate for 25 people will also cost quite a lot. Fourth, you might have to deprive the participants of food for a period of time in order to make sure that they're hungry. Is this ethical?

Issues such as these have resulted in scientists often using animals other than people in their experiments, something that you're going to read a lot about in this book. This should give you some concern; after all, only people behave just like people. However, in addition to the practical considerations, when you're trying to understand people's eating and drinking behaviors, there are good reasons for using animals other than people in the experiments. If I've convinced you that evolution has shaped eating and drinking behaviors, then you must also accept that different species will have at least some similar eating and drinking behaviors. One reason for this is that some species have evolved from relatively recent common origins. For example, all mammals have ancestors in common and, therefore, have some genes in common.

Thus the process of evolution ensures that, even if your primary interest is the eating and drinking behaviors of people, you can learn something of value from studying the eating and drinking behaviors of other species. Let's consider some of the advantages and disadvantages of using different species in our hypothetical chocolate experiment. As you read this material, you should be able to see many similarities in the eating and drinking behaviors of different species, while at the same time noting significant differences in the ways that these different species interact with their particular surroundings.

Let's start with the sea slug *Pleurobranchaea*. This slug is a carnivore—a meat eater. It's not much to look at; the beauty of this animal is definitely more than skin deep. *Pleurobranchaea*, similar to people, has specialized cells (known as neurons) in its body that collect information about its surroundings and cause it to move. Together these cells are known as a neuronal system. *Pleurobranchaea*'s neuronal system is less complex than ours. Therefore its neurons are relatively easily identified and manipulated. Some of *Pleurobranchaea*'s neurons, called food command neurons, are responsible for making *Pleurobranchaea* move automatically in order to eat food that it has detected. This is an example of a reflex, a specific response that occurs reliably following exposure to specific aspects of the surroundings. In such a case no learning is involved. Scientists have been able to determine that what *Pleurobranchaea* has recently eaten affects this reflex—*Pleuronbranchaea*'s motivation—by influencing how much certain inhibitory neurons decrease the activity of the food command neurons. Whether or not this slug eats can also be affected by learning—*Pleurobranchaea*'s knowledge about which events occur together. For example, if an experimenter shocks *Pleurobranchaea* whenever it eats, it will be less likely to approach and consume food.[3] Exciting as it is to be able to see the precise changes in neuronal activity that represent changes in feeding behavior, the usefulness of *Pleurobranchaea* as a model of our feeding behavior is limited due to this species' limited behavioral repertoire. To begin with, due to its carnivorous proclivities, *Pleurobranchaea* would be useless in an experiment on chocolate.

Let's consider using a mammal for our experiment. People are mammals—animals that suckle.[4] Therefore other mammalian species would seem the most likely choices for studies on the eating and drinking behaviors of people. In the early days of physiological investigations of hunger, one mammalian species—dogs—was a frequent choice for experimental subjects. Dogs, although technically considered carnivores, can consume a wide variety of foods,[5] making their eating behaviors more similar to ours than is the case for *Pleurobranchaea*. Dogs will, on occasion, eat chocolate. In addition, their social behaviors and ability to learn quickly can make them useful in studying a number of eating behaviors that are similar to behaviors seen in people. Some of the earliest and best known feeding research with dogs was conducted by one of the most famous parents of psychology, Ivan Pavlov, beginning around 1900.[6] Pavlov showed that if an attendant repeatedly gave a dog food, the dog would come to salivate simply on hearing the attendant approaching. If you have a cat, you have certainly seen something similar. (See Figure 1.1.) My pet cat, like everyone else's, goes crazy when he hears any can being opened. Pavlov's research became the foundation of one of the two major branches of learning theory, the branch concerned with learned and unlearned reflexes that is known as classical conditioning. Nevertheless, despite the fact that dogs sometimes eat chocolate, they are rarely used in current research because they are relatively large in size, take a relatively long time to reach maturity, and are popular pets.

Chimpanzees, another mammalian species, are close evolutionary relatives of people. Therefore, not surprisingly, many of their eating and drinking behaviors are similar to those of people. (See Conversation Making Fact #1.) For example, just like people, they're omnivores: they can eat fruit, leaves, insects, and meat. In addition, just as a person might use

"Zelda! Cool it! ... The Rothenbergs hear the can opener!"

Figure 1.1 Drawing by Gary Larson. Copyright 1989 FarWorks, Inc. (Reprinted with permission from Gary Larson, *Wildlife Preserves: A Far Side Collection*, Kansas City: Andrews and McMeel, 1989, p. 92.)

a hammer to crack open a nut, chimps use stones to crack open nuts, with larger stones for larger nuts.[7] Some of the most fascinating information about the eating and drinking behaviors of chimps has come from the pioneering investigations of primatologist Jane Goodall and her colleagues at the Gombe National Park in Tanzania, East Africa. Goodall was the first to discover that chimps make tools for obtaining food and water: twigs, stripped of leaves, to which termites cling when the twigs are stuck into their nests, and chewed-up leaves that can be used as sponges to obtain water from tree hollows (see Figure 1.2). Never before had a species other than ours been seen to construct tools.[8] Goodall was also the first to discover that chimpanzees hunt other animals and consume their meat. Usually males engage in these hunts and they demonstrate elements of cooperative hunting behavior. One chimp creeps toward the prey while other chimps position themselves to block the prey's escape routes. After

---

Conversation Making Fact #1

Do you sprinkle salt on your french fries or your eggs? Some monkeys also "season" their food. Travel to a small island called Kashima in Japan, and you might see a group of monkeys seasoning their sweet potatoes in saltwater using a method that Japanese scientists saw develop about 50 years ago.[9] In 1952, the scientists began giving the monkeys sweet potatoes to eat. The sweet potatoes were frequently covered with sand. In 1953, a female monkey named Imo began to wash the sweet potatoes. Imo would dip a sweet potato into the water with one hand and then brush off the sand with her other hand. By 1958, approximately 80% of the monkeys were washing sweet potatoes. During the period that most of the monkeys began to do this, the way that they washed the potatoes began to change. At first the sweet potatoes had been dipped only in fresh water. By 1961, the potatoes were being dipped primarily in salt water. Further, the monkeys would take a bite of a sweet potato, dip it, and then take another bite, "seasoning" the sweet potato—much yummier than plain sweet potato, and just like what we often do with our food.

Figure 1.2 Chimpanzee obtaining termites from a termite nest.

the hunters catch and kill the prey, they often share the food among themselves, as well as with other chimps.[10] In Gombe National Park, chimps have apparently worked together to kill almost one fifth of the red colobus monkeys in the chimps' area.[11]

The similarities between our and chimpanzees' eating and drinking behaviors are indeed remarkable. Yet it's precisely this close similarity that makes many people consider chimps an inappropriate choice for experiments. Because chimps are so similar to people, ethical constraints that would apply to using people in experiments might also apply to using chimps. There are also several practical disadvantages to using chimps in experiments. Just as with people, chimps are very expensive to maintain, can be difficult to handle, and take a long time to produce sexually mature offspring. For all of these reasons, psychologists have usually not worked with chimps—or other primates—in the investigation of eating and drinking behaviors.

This brings us, finally, to the rat (surprise!). Perhaps the rat isn't your favorite animal, but without question it's the favorite subject for experiments on the psychology of eating and drinking. There are many reasons for this. The rat's diet is diverse and very similar to that of people, which accounts for its ability to flourish for so many centuries in close association with us. Rats, for example, absolutely love chocolate. In addition, except that they can't vomit, the individual and social behaviors that rats use in avoiding poisons and identifying beneficial foods are in many ways similar to those of people. Further, laboratory rats, bred for docility, are easy to handle.[12] They're also relatively inexpensive to buy and maintain, and they reach sexual maturity only about 2 months after birth.[13] Finally, the extensive amount of information that scientists have already collected concerning rats provides a rich framework into which to place the results of any new investigations.[14]

The scientific literature lists these reasons for why the rat has become the favorite experimental subject. However, I've always wondered whether there might be other contributing factors. Having spent many years with laboratory rats, I can attest to the fact that they can be quite cuddly, even affectionate, similar to hamsters or guinea pigs. At least for me, it's a lot harder to imagine snuggling up to a slug or a chimp than to a rat.

Conclusion

In addition to justifying the liberal use of rat research in the rest of this book, I hope that this chapter has given you a sense of the rich variety and also enormous similarities among different species' eating and drinking behaviors. Similar principles govern the behaviors of many species. Yet each species has adapted to a different part of the world, a particular ecological niche. Each species obtains food and drink from its surroundings in its own particular way.[15] Therefore each species has much to tell us about the nature and origins of eating and drinking behaviors. For many reasons, rats are usually the best choice for studies in which the goal is to apply the results to people. Nevertheless, other species have provided and will provide us with much sustenance in our quest to understand the psychology of eating and drinking.

CHAPTER 2

Down the Hatch

Hunger and Satiety

ℰ

No animal can live without food. Let us then pursue the corollary
of this: namely, food is about the most important influence in
determining the organization of the brain and the behavior that
the brain organization dictates.

J. Z. Young (1968)[1]

Many of you reading this book are, I'm certain, interested in weight
control (most likely your own). In order to modify one's weight, it's
extremely helpful to understand the basic factors responsible for the starting
and stopping of eating. In other words, you need to understand the basic
factors responsible for hunger and satiety. This information will help you
understand what might be wrong if someone is eating too much or too little,
and will also give you ideas about how to change the amount that someone
eats. Perhaps most interestingly, this information will tell you what will *not*
affect the amount that someone eats. This chapter will explain why filling
up with water won't decrease how many calories you eat, something that
anyone familiar with the basic laboratory research on eating knows.

Given that the focus of this chapter is on hunger and satiety, its material
is more closely related to physiology than that of most of the other chapters.
However, particularly toward the end of this chapter, I'll also discuss the relationships of hunger and satiety to aspects of our surroundings. Think of this
chapter as providing you with the psychophysiological framework in which
to place much of the social and cultural information on eating that you'll
read about in later chapters.

The story of the scientific investigation of hunger and satiety reads like
a minihistory of psychology laboratory technique. For each time period, the

hot theories about what was responsible for hunger and satiety were very much a function of what laboratory techniques had been developed at that time. So, in the early 20th century, scientists investigated the relationship of stomach contractions to hunger because they had a way to measure those contractions. Later, in the 1940s and 1950s, as surgical techniques advanced, the effects on hunger of different types of substances in the stomach, substances that had or had not arrived there via the mouth, were investigated. Also around this time, investigations of the brain's effects on eating began, investigations that still continue and use ever more specific methods to determine which part or aspect of the brain affects which precise type of behavior. Most recently, techniques have advanced to the degree that scientists can show how specific parts of the brain and chemicals elsewhere in the body work together to influence hunger. Now, in the 21st century, the number of different aspects of the body shown to affect hunger and satiety is dazzling and still growing. In this chapter I'll organize all of the major findings so that you'll get an idea of the results and the significance of hunger and satiety research over the past 100 years.

As we progress through these experiments and their results, it'll be helpful for you to keep a few principles in mind. First, many animals, including people, don't eat continuously. Instead, there are periods of time—meals—during which food consumption occurs frequently and periods of time during which there's little food consumption. So this chapter will be looking at what's responsible for a meal starting and stopping. Note that all else being equal, more food will be consumed during a long meal than during a short meal. Therefore, investigations of what causes hunger and satiety are also investigations of what determines how much is eaten. (See Conversation Making Fact #2.)

Second, investigations of how much is eaten have traditionally been classified into two types: investigations of short-term regulation and long-term regulation, that is, animals' abilities to consume both what will satisfy their short-term energy needs and their abilities to maintain fairly constant body weight over long periods of time. Before you scoff at your ability to maintain body weight over a long period, consider this: Suppose every day you eat 2% more calories than you need, approximately the number of calories in one extra pat of butter or margarine. After 1 year, this would be equivalent to a 5-pound weight gain. So, even if you find yourself gaining 2 or 3 pounds each year, you're still doing a pretty good job of eating very close to the amount that your body needs to maintain its current weight.

In both short- and long-term regulation, our bodies have been thought to behave in a way that is similar to a household thermostat. A thermostat is set for a particular temperature, and if the temperature becomes too warm

---

Conversation Making Fact #2

In the United States we all eat three meals per day, correct? Not exactly. Scientists Matthew P. Longnecker, Janice M. Harper, and Seonhee Kim studied thousands of people and found that, if small snacks were excluded, on average these people ate 3.1 meals per day. This sounds like just what we were expecting. But this average was based on a lot of variation. About one third of the people studied ate less than 2.4 or more than 3.9 meals per day. In addition, there was more variation in how many meals one person ate on different days than among different people.[2] In other words, although on average the people in this study ate 3.1 meals per day, on many days they ate significantly fewer meals than that and on many other days they ate significantly more. The stereotype of the American "three squares" per day is just not accurate.

---

or too cold, air conditioning or heat kicks in to bring the temperature back to the ideal level. Many theories of hunger have postulated that, in our bodies, there's a physiological characteristic (for example, available energy or stored fat) that has an optimal level, the set point, and whenever there's a deviation from that optimal level, something in the body happens so that the optimal level is restored. Walter B. Cannon, an early 20th-century American physiologist who is mentioned several times in this chapter, coined the term *homeostasis* to describe processes such as these.[3] In the sections that follow, see if you can identify the theories of hunger and satiety that incorporate the concept of homeostasis, as well as the complications for such theories.

One final caution is in order here. In some of the experiments described in this chapter and in subsequent chapters, people are asked to report how hungry they are or what they have eaten. There has been some controversy about how meaningful such statements are.[4] Do people's hunger ratings correlate closely with how much they eat, and do people report accurately how much they eat? What people say they felt and what they say they ate don't necessarily correspond to their actual behaviors. For example, sometimes people report eating significantly less than they really ate, and sometimes they can be quite accurate. As long as there are at least some situations in which people's self-reports help us predict their eating behaviors, experimenters will continue to use self-report data.

The number of different factors that have been shown to influence hunger and satiety is truly mind-boggling. To make your comprehension of this material easier, I'm going to divide it into two major categories: investigations of peripheral factors and investigations of central factors. However, as we go along, you'll see that researchers have increasingly looked at the relationships between these two types of factors.

Out of Your Mind (and Brain): Peripheral Factors

Peripheral factors that influence hunger and satiety are those factors involving parts of the body other than the central nervous system (the brain and the spinal cord). Let's follow a piece of chocolate cake as it wends its way from your refrigerator into your mouth, down into your stomach and intestine, to see what peripheral factors might contribute to making you hungry or satiated.

Getting From the Living Room to the Kitchen

You're in your living room watching TV. What are some of the factors that might make you start thinking about going into the kitchen to eat the piece of chocolate cake on the table? Thinking about it enough to get up from your nice comfy couch?

Let's suppose that your stomach growls, and it feels as if it's contracting like crazy. Many people believe that a rumbling stomach is synonymous with hunger and a nonrumbling stomach is synonymous with satiation. Such beliefs led scientists to formulate the stomach contraction theory of hunger, which says that the initiation and termination of eating can be predicted on the basis of stomach contractions. Someone whose stomach has been contracting might be more likely to eat and vice versa.

Cannon's 1912 work on this theory with A. L. Washburn was one of the first experimental studies of hunger.[5] Cannon and Washburn developed a technique for measuring stomach contractions, and Washburn was the first lucky person to experience it. First, Washburn had to become accustomed to having a long tube inserted down his throat into his stomach and left there for several hours each day. One end of the tube was in his stomach, and the other end was outside his mouth. During the experiment, air was passed into the outer end of the tube to inflate partially a balloon attached to the end of the tube that was in Washburn's stomach. (Washburn must have been a very dedicated scientist!) Stomach contractions were measured by monitoring changes in air pressure in the balloon. Washburn pressed a telegraph key whenever he felt hungry. His stomach contractions were closely associated with his reports of hunger. Apparently, Washburn would report hunger at the height of a contraction, not at the beginning, which suggested that the stomach contractions caused the feelings of hunger and not the other way around. When Washburn wasn't hungry there were no contractions. Follow-up studies with additional subjects obtained similar results.[6] The stomach contraction theory was the first peripheral theory of hunger to receive experimental support, and it was the dominant peripheral theory for many years.

However, subsequent studies showed that neither stomach contractions nor even a stomach are necessary prerequisites for reports of hunger.[7] Further, as more sophisticated methods of measuring stomach contractions have been developed, the relationship between hunger and stomach contractions has been found to be extremely weak.[8] Therefore the stomach contraction theory of hunger now appears to be primarily of historical interest.

You've still got to get from that living room into the kitchen. If stomach contractions won't get you moving, what might? Suppose, in flipping channels, you happen upon a cooking show about how to make the perfect chocolate cake. All of a sudden you're dying for that piece of chocolate cake on your kitchen table. Have you ever noticed that smelling food, hearing cooking noises, or just looking at food makes you feel hungry? You're not imagining this. What's happening to you is related to what happened to Pavlov's dogs. As you will recall, Pavlov showed that dogs would salivate when they heard or saw something that had previously been associated with food. Similar to the dogs, you also salivate when you hear or see or smell things that have been associated with food. And salivation isn't the only response that your body has to these situations. Even if you haven't yet touched the food, your pancreas may secrete insulin, a chemical involved in the metabolism of sugar. The insulin lowers your blood sugar level, which makes you feel hungry. There are several such reflexes that are related to the ingestion and digestion of food and that occur immediately upon—or, with experience, even prior to—our contact with food.[9]

Understanding how these salivation and insulin responses occur can help in understanding the differences in hunger between Muslim men and women during Ramadan. Ramadan is the month during which devout Muslims fast from sunrise to sunset. Researchers have shown that, during the initial days of Ramadan, women report being significantly more hungry than men. However, during the latter days of Ramadan, women and men report approximately equal levels of hunger. As it turns out, during Ramadan, the men aren't usually at home during the fasting periods. In contrast, the women are at home and are involved in preparing food for the children to eat during the day and food for the adults to eat after sunset. Thus, during the fasting periods, the women are probably exposed to far more odors, sounds, and sights that are associated with food than are the men. However, as the month of Ramadan proceeds, the food-related phenomena to which the women are exposed during the day are never accompanied by the women ingesting food. Therefore those phenomena are no longer associated with food ingestion.[10] This may stop salivation or insulin release and result in decreased hunger.

Getting the Cake Into Your Mouth

You've taken the big step and entered the kitchen. Now, with that cake staring you in the face, you're releasing more insulin and are feeling hungrier. But the kitchen's window air conditioner breaks, and because it's July and 95°F outside, the kitchen quickly becomes unpleasantly hot and stuffy. Suddenly, you're no longer so interested in that chocolate cake.

The surrounding air temperature is well known to affect hunger. If your kitchen is hot, it's likely that you'll eat less than when your kitchen is a little chilly. One explanation for this influence of the surrounding temperature on the amount eaten is that in cold weather the body needs more fuel to keep itself heated to 98.6°F, and a major source of heat for any animal is the food it consumes. Therefore it's possible that initiation and termination of feeding are related to the maintenance of a specific, optimally efficient body temperature. If this sounds to you like a homeostatic process, you're exactly right! The temperature theory of hunger was proposed in the late 1940s.[11] Since then, experiments with rats and people have supported it—animals do consume more in cold surroundings. Experiments have also shown that exposure to cold surroundings speeds the movement of previously consumed food from the stomach into the intestine. Such a process would, of course, decrease whatever it is about food in the stomach that normally inhibits feeding,[12] and thus this finding helps to explain why animals eat more in the cold.

Cake in the Mouth

Let's suppose that you felt hungry enough that you've now put the chocolate cake into your mouth. Does the food's stimulation of your mouth affect your hunger and satiety?

In order to determine whether oral factors by themselves contribute to hunger and satiety, over 50 years ago researchers developed a particular type of surgery called an esophagostomy. You may find the description of this surgery difficult and unpleasant to read. Performing an esophagostomy was one of the few then-available techniques that could be used to separate the influence of oral and gastric factors on hunger and satiety. This surgery involves first bringing the subject's esophagus—the tube through which food passes from the mouth to the stomach—out through the neck. The esophagus is then cut, forming an upper and a lower piece. If an animal that has had this operation eats, the food consumed passes out through the animal's neck instead of continuing to its stomach. This is known as sham feeding. An animal that is sham fed has all of the usual oral experiences that accompany feeding but none of the sensations that originate in the stomach. The subject tastes, chews, and swallows the food, but the stomach never receives it.

Scientists Henry D. Janowitz and M. I. Grossman were among the first researchers to use this surgical technique. They reported that sham fed dogs eventually stop eating, but before they stop they consume much more food than usual.[13] Over many sham feedings, the amount of food eaten increases.[14] Once the animals learn that food in the mouth is no longer associated with food reaching the stomach, the satiating ability of food in the mouth ceases. Thus, oral factors can contribute to the cessation of eating, but by themselves oral factors don't precisely regulate food intake.

Assuming that you're not engaging in sham feeding, what characteristics of that piece of food in your mouth might affect whether or not you feel hungry? One food characteristic that has been widely investigated in this regard is whether the food is sweet. Both rats and people eat more of sweet than nonsweet foods, even if the number of calories in these foods is equal. In other words, even if a food is made sweet using a noncaloric sweetener, animals will eat more of it than had it not been sweet. One possible explanation of these findings is that the presence of a sweet taste causes more insulin to be released than if there's no sweet taste, thus lowering blood sugar to a greater degree and making someone feel hungrier. Another possible explanation is that when we eat food that is sweet, the body makes less of what's eaten available for immediate use and stores more of it than if what was eaten weren't sweet. Therefore, when we eat sweet food, in order to have enough energy for our immediate needs, we have to eat relatively large amounts. There may be similar explanations for the fact that we eat lots of any good-tasting food.[15]

The Cake in the Gastrointestinal Tract

You've chewed up and swallowed that piece of cake and now it's in your stomach, on its way to the small and large intestines. What effects does the presence of food within the gastrointestinal (GI) tract have on your feeling hungry or full? In a survey of college students, most said that the reason they stop eating is because they feel full.[16] But what's responsible for that feeling? What can increase or decrease it?

Investigation of GI effects is complicated because, ordinarily, food gets to the GI tract by way of the mouth. Therefore, effects of food in the GI tract could be due to either the oral or the GI stimulation provided by the food, or both. Nevertheless, just as with oral factors, researchers have come up with ways to isolate the effects of GI factors. For example, researchers can insert food directly into the lower portion of the esophagus following an esophagostomy, thus bypassing oral factors. Alternatively, they can make a hole by which food or an undigestible substance such as an inflated balloon can be inserted directly into the stomach from outside the body. When what's inserted is food, this process is known as intragastric feeding.

Several scientists, including sham feeding researchers Janowitz and Grossman, have investigated the effects of intragastric feeding on dogs' eating behaviors. These researchers have put different amounts of food and other substances directly into the stomach. For example, they have studied the effects of inserting an inflated balloon into the stomach. One finding from this research is that intragastric feeding decreases sham feeding only when that feeding is large and occurs at the same time as sham feeding. Further, a balloon has no effect on feeding unless the balloon is so inflated that it causes nausea and retching. Finally, dogs with holes directly into the stomach or with esophagostomies can eventually learn to eat less when they have been fed intragastrically.[17]

In addition, we now know that foods that are very viscous or that have a lot of fiber are more satiating. The precise reasons for this increased satiety aren't known. It may be that a food's viscosity or amount of fiber affects absorption of that food's nutrients or the speed with which that food passes through the GI tract.[18] Further, even with the total number of calories consumed held constant, higher volumes of food are more satiating than lower volumes if the foods contain at least some calories.[19]

If you're a good detective you'll have put all of these pieces of evidence together into a fairly consistent story. Here's my version. Putting something in the stomach so that the stomach stretches isn't very influential in getting us to stop eating unless the stretching is extreme or is accompanied by nutrients in the GI tract.[20] This explains why drinking lots of water or inserting an inflated balloon into the stomach aren't very effective in decreasing food consumption. Although these substances stretch the stomach, they contain no nutrients, and thus they won't increase satiety effectively.

Effects of Digestion and Storage of the Cake

You've eaten the cake. Now it'll be digested, and some of it may be stored as fat. What effects might these processes have on hunger and satiety?

When you digest food, including chocolate cake, the amounts of certain chemicals in your body increase. Some of these chemicals are the products of the digestion of food. Others are the chemicals produced by the body to aid in the digestion of food. The presence of high levels of chemicals in either group can act as a signal to your body that food has been consumed and so eating should stop. Conversely, when the levels of these chemicals are low, this can signal your body to start eating. A large number of such possible signals have been investigated.

A good chemical signal of currently available energy would be one that increases quickly following feeding and slowly decreases with time until the next feeding. Internationally known physiologist and nutritionist Jean Mayer realized that there was such a signal when he formulated the glucostatic theory of hunger in 1953.[21] The glucostatic theory postulates that hunger is related to blood sugar level and that information about the energy available to an animal is indicated by the level of sugar in the blood. In addition to rising quickly and then decreasing slowly following feeding, blood sugar is known to be the primary energy source for the central nervous system. Therefore, you would expect animals to have evolved so as to use eating to ensure that adequate levels of blood sugar are maintained.

As a refinement to his model, Mayer proposed that it wasn't the absolute level of blood sugar that was important in the initiation and termination of feeding, but the difference between the levels in the arteries and veins. Arteries take blood to the body's tissues, and veins return blood from those same tissues. If the blood sugar level is high in the arteries but low in the veins, sugar is being removed from the blood as it passes from the arteries through various tissues and then into the veins. In such cases the body is receiving a fair amount of sugar. If the blood sugar level in both the arteries and veins is low, then the body isn't receiving much sugar. In support of his theory, Mayer found that the difference between the blood sugar levels in the arteries and veins correlated well with people's reports of hunger.[22]

Mayer realized that his glucostatic mechanism would make errors on a daily basis and that some long-term mechanism would be needed to correct those errors. A mechanism related to the fat stores in the body was the obvious choice. Our bodies store excess energy as fat. One pound of fat is equivalent to 3,500 calories. In order to use this storage system to correct errors made by the glucostatic mechanism, the body must have a way of detecting the extent of its energy stores. Lipostatic theories propose that a circulating chemical related to the amount of the body's stored fat is responsible for long-term regulation of stored fat; when the chemical indicates that fat stores are low or decreasing, eating should increase, and vice versa. In this way, the glucostatic and lipostatic mechanisms could work together to regulate the body's food intake on both a daily and a long-term basis. Mayer was among the first to propose a lipostatic theory of long-term regulation.[23]

Over the years since lipostatic theories were first developed, researchers have proposed several candidates for the chemical that signals the amount of stored fat, including free fatty acids, which are the products of the metabolism of stored fat, and leptin, a hormone found in the blood and manufactured by the cells that store fat. The level of each of these chemicals in the body is related to the amount of stored fat.[24] I hope that you're not bemoaning the complexity of all of this because, chances are, this complexity will only increase. My guess is that, as we learn more about fat metabolism and storage, even more candidates for the chemical signals in lipostatic theories will emerge—and this isn't surprising. Your body should have several, redundant mechanisms to help ensure that you have adequate stored fat. Then if one mechanism doesn't work properly, another can get the job done.

In the meantime, while lipostatic theories have been proliferating, the glucostatic theory of hunger has been encountering some bumps in its progress toward making eternal scientific history. Unfortunately, there hasn't been extensive evidence supporting the difference in blood sugar between the arteries and veins as a primary determinant of hunger.[25] Therefore, researchers have proposed alternatives to this difference as the indicators for the body's short-term energy level. These alternatives include the body's level of a form of carbohydrate that is stored in cells, particularly in the liver and muscles,[26] and the level of metabolism in the liver.[27] Scientists L. Arthur Campfield and Francoise J. Smith proposed a somewhat different version of the glucostatic theory of hunger. They have shown that the insulin release that occurs in response to odors, sounds, sights, and the like previously associated with food causes a brief fall and then a rise in blood sugar level. This fall and rise in blood sugar level is highly likely to be soon followed by the initiation of a meal. In other words, this pattern of blood sugar level change appears to be associated with hunger. Campfield and Smith's research is very exciting because it shows us that the temporal pattern of a chemical's level in the body may be important in hunger and satiation. But what a daunting thought. Now we need to investigate the temporal patterns of many other chemicals affected by food consumption to determine if these patterns also predict well when we will start and stop eating.[28]

Among the chemicals produced by the body to aid in food digestion, three of the most investigated in terms of their import for hunger and satiety are insulin, cholecystokinin (CCK), and glucagon. There is a great deal of evidence that insulin outside of the central nervous system is a satiating agent—insulin produced by the pancreas during the digestion of food does reduce subsequent food intake.[29] Experiments also suggest that CCK, which is produced in the small intestine during digestion, may help to terminate feeding.[30] In one experiment, rat pups were first administered a chemical that causes the release of CCK from the small intestine. These experimental rats subsequently ate less than untreated rats.[31] Similar to insulin, glucagon is produced in the pancreas. One experiment gave small doses of glucagon (like the levels that occur naturally after food consumption) intravenously to people. These people subsequently ate less food than if they had not been given glucagon.[32] Therefore glucagon may be another naturally occurring substance that plays an influential role in satiety.

Types of Foods

By this point, you're probably pretty well satiated with the effects on hunger and satiation of different levels of your body's different chemicals. So let's turn to something else. What sorts of foods increase and decrease hunger? For example, does a food's caloric density affect how much we eat? A gram of one food can have a lot more, or a lot fewer, calories than a gram of another food. Consider our infamous piece of chocolate cake. The cake could be made with a high proportion of fat (which contains 9 calories per gram) or with a high proportion of sugar (which contains 4 calories per gram). Will we eat different amounts of chocolate cake (or other food) depending on the relative proportions of fat and sugar in it? This is a question to which I would personally like an answer because a few hours ago I bought and ate a piece of a low-fat, low-calorie chocolate truffle cake.

A great many experiments have been conducted to answer this question. In general, these experiments find that, when single meals are examined, eating a high-calorie food can cause us to eat less soon afterward.[33] Similarly, over the long term and many meals, if animals are fed foods that are relatively low in caloric density as part of their regular diet, they will eat more so that their total caloric intake remains the same.[34] This is disappointing news— after all, what's the point of buying that low-calorie chocolate truffle cake? But this news shouldn't be that surprising. When we were evolving, in order to maintain adequate fat stores, our bodies had to be able to compensate by eating more when food supplies were relatively poor in calories.

Nevertheless, psychologists repeatedly tantalize us with experiments showing that certain foods under certain conditions result in more short-term satiation than other foods. For example, with calories held constant, eating a meal of meatballs is more satiating that eating a meal of pasta; tomato soup is more satiating than crackers with cheese or than melon; protein is more satiating than carbohydrates; and eating the exact same meal in liquid form isn't as satiating as eating it in solid form.[35] But before you rush to your kitchen and start preparing meals of dehydrated tomato soup and meatballs, I think it would be wise to await further laboratory results that can help us understand the general principles behind these seemingly unrelated findings.

Conclusion to Peripheral Factors

I hope that, by learning about the many different factors that contribute to our starting and ending meals, you're also learning to appreciate how exquisitely constructed our bodies are. Eating the right amount of food is absolutely essential to survival. Therefore it's not surprising that our bodies have apparently evolved with a number of different, sometimes redundant, mechanisms that each help to ensure that the correct amount of food is consumed. Should one of these mechanisms fail for any reason, another will still be in effect so that we are unlikely to starve or eat ourselves to death. These different mechanisms work together to guarantee that eating is basically within normal limits. You'll see more examples of our bodies' exquisite construction and redundancy as we now turn to the central nervous system factors that are involved in hunger and satiety.[36]

Food on Your Mind: Central Factors

Ever since scientists began investigating the influence of the central nervous system on the initiation and termination of feeding, they have viewed the brain as first receiving information about what's going on inside and outside of the body and then causing the body to take some action. The initial experiments tried to identify the many individual parts of the brain, each made up of millions of neurons, that were responsible for these sorts of central functions. In recent years, investigations of the role of the central nervous system in hunger and satiety have grown far more complex. These more recent investigations include examinations of the combined effects of activity in several parts of the brain, as well as examinations of the effects of a variety of chemical substances present in the brain. What follows is a semihistorical review of the highlights of the research on central factors.

Hunger and Satiety Centers

This story begins with a now famous case of obesity in an adolescent boy with a large tumor of the pituitary gland around 1900:

> R. D., a boy, was born in 1887. . . . Since March 1899 the patient, who previously had been slim, had been rapidly gaining weight. In January 1901 he complained about diminishing eyesight on the left. . . . Later, vision in the right eye also began to fail. . . . Since the patient suffered from severe headaches and his eyesight was rapidly decreasing, an operative procedure appeared justified. The operation by the nasal route was performed by von Eiselsberg on June 21 [1907]. In the depth of the sphenoid sinus the whitish membrane of a cyst the size of a hazelnut was encountered. After incision in the midline, several spoonfuls of a fluid resembling old blood drained out. By measuring with the finger and comparison with the roentgenogram, it could be ascertained that the cyst which contained this

fluid corresponded to the hypophysis [the pituitary gland, connected to and near the hypothalamus]. The walls of the cavity were cut away as far as could be done without damaging the optic chiasm and the carotid arteries.... The postoperative course was favorable.... There was considerable improvement in the general condition.[37]

Information such as this suggested that the hypothalamus might be involved in satiety; interference with the hypothalamus apparently resulted in overeating and obesity.

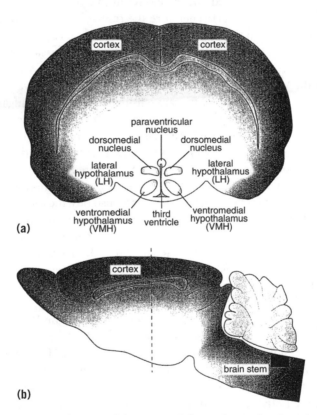

(a)

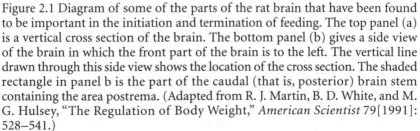

(b)

Figure 2.1 Diagram of some of the parts of the rat brain that have been found to be important in the initiation and termination of feeding. The top panel (a) is a vertical cross section of the brain. The bottom panel (b) gives a side view of the brain in which the front part of the brain is to the left. The vertical line drawn through this side view shows the location of the cross section. The shaded rectangle in panel b is the part of the caudal (that is, posterior) brain stem containing the area postrema. (Adapted from R. J. Martin, B. D. White, and M. G. Hulsey, "The Regulation of Body Weight," *American Scientist* 79[1991]: 528–541.)

By 1940 science had advanced far enough that scientists A. W. Hethington and S. W. Ranson were able to conduct a detailed physiological study of the brain and the control of feeding.[38] They inserted small electrodes into the brains of anesthetized rats, more specifically, into the area of the hypothalamus. When an electrode was in the proper place, electrical current was passed through it, thereby destroying the surrounding cells. Several such small lesions were made in each rat's brain. The rats subjected to this procedure usually recovered after the operation and appeared fairly normal. However, they ate excessively and became obese, behavior known as hyperphagia. The most likely place, if lesioned, that would result in obesity was the ventromedial hypothalamus (VMH). Therefore the researchers concluded that the VMH was involved in the control of satiety. Additional research showed that stimulation of the VMH (activating the cells with an electrical current, rather than destroying them with lesions) inhibits eating,[39] which seemed to confirm that the VMH functions as a satiety center. Further, it was discovered that there are cells in the VMH that are sensitive to one kind of sugar, glucose, and that destroying these cells caused rats to behave similarly to VMH-lesioned rats.[40] This suggested that the VMH receives information about blood sugar levels, thus allowing it to serve as a central collection center for information about the body energy level. (See Figure 2.1.)

During the next decade, scientists reasoned that if there were a location in the VMH that controls satiety, there might also be a location in the hypothalamus that's involved in hunger. Physiologists Bal K. Anand and John R. Brobeck's 1951 report[41] identified such a location as the lateral hypothalamus (LH). Their research seemed to show that destruction of this specific area of the hypothalamus resulted in rats that would never eat again, rats that eventually die of starvation. Further, it was shown that stimulation of the LH induced rats to eat.[42]

Together, the data that had been collected through the 1950s seemed to form a tidy package, as indicated in Table 2.1. Based on this evidence, in 1954 psychologist Eliot Stellar formally proposed that the VMH is the brain's satiety center and the LH is its hunger center.[43] According to Stellar, these centers, essentially little brains within a larger brain, gather information about, for example, the body's temperature and blood sugar level using a variety of

Table 2.1 Summary of Findings Involving the Hypothalamus in the Mid-1950s

Area of Hypothalamus	Lesion	Stimulation
Ventromedial hypothalamus	Increases eating	Decreases eating
Lateral hypothalamus	Decreases eating	Increases eating

sensory receptors in the hypothalamus; synthesize this information; and then may cause the body to do something, such as eat. Stellar saw brain centers as major locations in the brain that integrate information. However, he stated specifically that areas of the brain other than the hypothalamus are probably involved in the initiation and termination of feeding. Note that Stellar's concept of brain centers did not eliminate the peripheral theories that we talked about earlier. Instead, Stellar's concept of brain centers integrated peripheral theories with central theories of hunger. The brain centers theory dominated study of the initiation and termination of feeding for many years.

Unfortunately, in the 45 years since Stellar first proposed the hunger and satiety centers hypothesis, a number of research findings have revealed problems with it. One major problem concerns the methods that were used to collect much of the data on which the hypothesis was based. These experiments used lesions or stimulation of particular parts of the brain. It can be very difficult to be precisely certain about what particular behavior has been affected by lesions or stimulation. Every action consists of many component actions. The act of eating a forkful of peas after being instructed to do so by one of your parents involves hearing and understanding the instruction, seeing the peas, bringing the fork to the peas, balancing the peas on the tines of the fork, bringing the fork to your mouth, scooping the peas into your mouth, chewing the peas, swallowing them, and in some way finding this act worth doing (if only to avoid your parent's wrath). A brain lesion or brain stimulation that interfered with eating peas might do so by interfering with any one or several of these components of the act of pea eating. Psychologists are now aware that interfering with what seems to be a very small part of the brain can have profound effects on general arousal or on complex sensory functions.[44] Thus, with regard to the brain centers theory of hunger, it's possible that the brain lesions and/or stimulation affected motor or sensory behavior instead of interfering with hunger and satiety.

Another major difficulty with the hunger and satiety centers hypothesis is the degree to which the lesions and stimulation were actually limited to the parts of the brain where they were supposed to be. These manipulations may have affected larger areas than were intended. In part this may have been due to the shape of neurons; a neuron can have a central part (the cell body) and extensions (fibers) as long as 1 meter. As a result, the lesions and stimulation may have affected neuronal fibers passing through the lesion/stimulation areas, and not just cell bodies at those locations. There seems to be some validity to such criticisms. For example, it appears that lesions strictly confined to the VMH are less effective at inducing the VMH syndrome than lesions not strictly confined to the VMH.[45]

Still another problem with the hunger and satiety centers hypothesis is that experiments have shown that other parts of the brain, including all of those named in Figure 2.1, are also very important in detecting aspects of the surroundings and initiating behaviors related to feeding.[46] Research has shown how these areas of the brain work together in starting and stopping eating. For example, it's now believed that areas of the brain, such as the paraventricular nucleus, monitor and regulate what's going on in the body and then pass their information to the lateral hypothalamus. The LH then influences the brain's frontal cortex, which then affects how the animal plans and performs specific behaviors.[47]

Not all recent experimental results have been incompatible with the hunger and satiety centers hypothesis. For example, data from one study[48] showed that putting food in the small intestine quickly results in less activity in the LH and more activity in the VMH. These changes in brain activity were probably the result of information conveyed by the vagus nerve, which projects between the intestine and the part of the brain containing the hypothalamus.

The hypothalamus is one of the major integrators of information about what's going on inside and outside of the body, and of activity from higher and lower brain structures.[49] However, the little brains within a brain that would have so neatly explained the initiation and termination of eating simply don't exist.

Chemical Substances in the Brain

It's not just the anatomy of the brain that influences the initiation and termination of feeding; the chemical substances present in the brain are also very important. In fact, the effects of brain chemistry on feeding may be particularly intriguing because a thorough understanding of the influence of brain chemistry on feeding might allow us to develop drugs that would be highly effective in treating anorexia or overeating. One group of brain chemicals that has received intense scrutiny is the neurotransmitters, the chemical substances released in the small gaps between two adjoining neurons. These chemicals are necessary for the occurrence of the electrical impulses by which neurons communicate. Two types of neurotransmitters that have been extensively investigated are dopamine and serotonin. It has been known for many years that both of these neurotransmitters inhibit feeding.[50] Recent experiments have examined how these two neurotransmitters might work together in this regard. For example, a review of data from several studies indicated that the interaction of dopamine and serotonin within the LH affects the size of the meals that an animal eats, and that the dopamine and serotonin within the VMH affect the frequency with which an animal eats. These aren't the only mechanisms by which meal size and meal frequency are determined, but they're important ones.[51]

Other chemical substances present in the brain can also affect the initiation and termination of feeding. One example is neuropeptide Y. This substance modulates the effects of neurotransmitters. Ultimately, it increases eating, primarily by affecting the hypothalamus. Research suggests that when excess neuropeptide Y is present for extended periods, significant overeating and obesity can result. In contrast, inactivation of neuropeptide Y inhibits eating.[52] A second example is a substance called intracerebral corticotrophin releasing hormone—its concentration in the brain appears to influence the set point for body weight.[53] A final example is a protein called apolipoprotein A-IV, which is naturally present in the fluid within the central nervous system. When this protein is infused by an experimenter into the third ventricle of the brain, eating decreases.[54] These are just some of the great many chemical substances involved in the initiation and termination of feeding within the central nervous system.

Putting It All Together: Combinations and Interactions of Different Factors

We've spent most of this chapter pulling apart and examining separately the various peripheral and central factors that affect hunger and satiety. Now it's time to try to put things back together. How do different mechanisms work as a team to determine when we start and stop eating? The answers are complex, and much of the research on these combinations and interactions is very recent. It's extremely exciting research because we can finally see how influences inside and outside of the body combine in determining how much and how frequently we eat.

Combinations of Peripheral and Central Factors

You've already been given some hints about how peripheral and central factors can work together. One such case was when we discussed how the hypothalamus detects the presence of blood sugar, thus integrating the glucostatic (peripheral) and the VMH (central) theories of hunger. Lots of other similar connections have recently been investigated.

For example, several researchers now believe that insulin links both peripheral and central control of feeding (see Figure 2.2a). As you'll recall, the level of insulin released by the pancreas increases either when an animal eats food or experiences things, such as the smell of chocolate, that have been previously associated with food consumption. An additional fact is that, when nothing associated with food is present, insulin levels are higher in individuals with more body fat. Finally, insulin circulating in the peripheral blood supply can enter the brain, and the more insulin that enters the brain, the less the central nervous system causes eating, and body weight decreases.

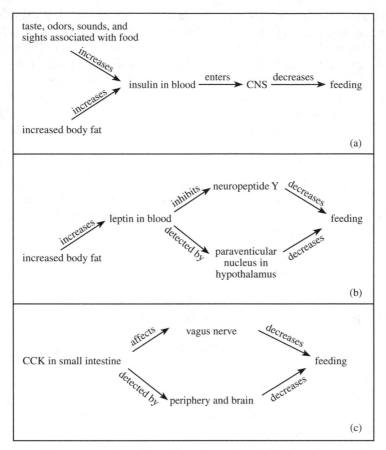

Figure 2.2 Three examples of combinations of peripheral and central factors. (a) Insulin. (b) Leptin. (c) CCK.

Together, all of this information indicates that insulin level is an important factor in the short-term initiation and termination of feeding as well as in the long-term control of body weight, with both peripheral and central mechanisms at work.[55]

Figure 2.2b shows another pathway that links peripheral and central controls of feeding. The more fat someone has, the higher the level of leptin in that person's bloodstream. It's believed that special cells in the brain (for example, in the paraventricular nucleus in the hypothalamus) detect these leptin levels. Further, leptin inhibits the production of neuropeptide Y. Therefore, when leptin levels are high, levels of neuropeptide Y decrease, causing decreased eating.[56]

Finally, let's consider the example of CCK (Figure 2.2c). When first we met CCK in this chapter, it was described as an intestinal chemical involved in the peripheral control of hunger and satiety. We now also know that there are special cells both in the periphery and in the brain that are sensitive to—in other words, behave differently in—the presence of CCK. Further, it appears that CCK released in the periphery affects the vagus nerve, which then sends information to the brain that results in the termination of feeding.[57]

The Effects of Our Surroundings, Memory, and Learning

It's essential, in all of this discussion of anatomy and chemicals, not to forget the influence of our surroundings on eating behavior. The presence or absence of food and things associated with food ultimately cause all of the bodily reactions that we've been discussing. Furthermore, the act of eating, or of not eating, is by definition an act that involves interaction with the world around us. At least partly for these reasons, it has been argued that the only way to determine an animal's homeostatic set point is to know what's going on around that animal. For example, even though hens eat 20% less than usual when they're incubating eggs, we shouldn't describe this behavior as nonhomeostatic. There are so many ways in which our surroundings affect what should be considered homeostatic behavior that it has been suggested that the whole concept of homeostasis be abandoned.[58]

Not only current surroundings, but experience with past surroundings (memory and learning), greatly influence hunger and satiety. In fact, similar memory and learning processes that operate in other contexts also affect when we start and stop eating. For example, reminders of the previous meal—of how much and what was eaten—influence the next meal.[59] Brain-damaged patients with no memory for events more than 1 minute ago will eat a second lunch 10 minutes after a first lunch, but people with no brain damage won't.[60]

As another example, I've already explained how odors, sounds, and sights previously associated with food can affect what goes on in the body concerning hunger and satiety. More specifically, you'll recall that just as food you've eaten will cause insulin to be released, so will aspects of your surroundings that have been previously associated with food. Such an explanation can help us understand the differences between men's and women's hunger levels during Ramadan. These learned reactions of the body to upcoming meals have been described as the body's way of anticipating and decreasing the large, potentially harmful, ups and downs in homeostatic functions that are caused by eating food.[61]

As a third example, if rats have learned to associate a particular odor such as almond or violet with the later stages of a meal of a highly caloric carbohydrate solution, they will drink less of another carbohydrate solution if that odor is present than if a novel odor is present.[62] The rats apparently learn that the odor indicates that they have consumed a lot of calories. Thus learning associated with an odor can help to control meal volume.

As a fourth example, psychologist Leann Birch and her colleagues first repeatedly gave preschool children snacks in a specific location where they could see a rotating red light and hear a certain song, but not in another location with other sights and sounds. Later, even if the children had been recently fed, they were more likely to eat in the presence of the sights and sounds that had been associated with eating in the past than in the presence of cues that had not.[63]

Some psychologists, known as psychodynamic theorists, believe that although hunger has a physiological basis, it's immediately affected by learning. They believe that an animal learns how to regulate its intake properly according to its energy needs based on its early eating experiences.[64] As a result of learning, eating can become associated in early life with experiences that usually accompany feeding, such as a parent's attention and warmth. It's therefore easy to see how "love" could become associated with food ("the way to a man's heart is through his stomach"), although love and food might have originally been independent. Psychodynamic theories postulate that eating can come to stand for many things and thus can occur inappropriately. According to this view, it's understandable that a child might come to eat when frightened or lonely, since he or she has associated feeding with security and a mother's love.[65] Alternatively, if early caregivers are wise in feeding a child and respond well to the child's biological needs, they can teach the child to consume food only when it's really needed. Although the psychodynamic approach seems an eminently reasonable one, we have little in the way of research findings to make its conclusions significant for experimental psychologists.

Some psychologists have tried to use learning and memory principles, descriptions of specific aspects of the surroundings, and descriptions of animals' responses to explain the starting and stopping of eating without any reference to physiology whatsoever.[66] These psychologists believe that at least some aspects of eating can be understood and predicted solely on the basis of what's happening around us. Such approaches are useful because they remind researchers of how important it is to consider current surroundings, as well as experience with past surroundings, when trying to predict when an animal will start and stop eating. Nevertheless, there's a great deal of information to be gained from physiological investigations, information that cannot be obtained solely from the study of behavior.

Conclusion

Now you should have a pretty good idea about many of the factors involved in your wanting to eat that piece of chocolate cake, and about how chewing and swallowing that cake affects your wanting to eat more of it. Although, contrary to what was originally thought, stomach contractions and stomach distention per se don't appear to play a leading role in the starting and stopping of eating, many other factors do. These include peripheral factors such as the surrounding air temperature, oral factors, food volume, and blood sugar level changes. You've also learned about the influences of the levels of certain chemicals in the GI tract and in the central nervous system, as well as the importance of certain parts of the central nervous system. You've even learned how peripheral factors and the central nervous system might work together. Finally, you've learned about how important it is to know what's going on in an animal's surroundings, and to know what experiences an animal has had with its surroundings, if you want to do a good job predicting whether or not it will start or stop eating. In sum, there has been ample opportunity for you to see how beautifully people and other animals have evolved—with multiple mechanisms designed to ensure that the right amounts of food are consumed.

The challenge for the future is to continue to investigate the initiation and termination of feeding on many different levels and to show how the results of those different investigations interrelate.[67] The world around us and many different parts of our bodies work together in determining whether or not we eat, and, therefore, so should our investigations. Such research will require the efforts of scientists whose work is interdisciplinary or who are skilled in more than one area. What's so exciting is that many scientists are capable of rising to this challenge.

CHAPTER 3

"You Never Miss the Water Till the Well Runs Dry"[1]

Thirst

℃

> Paul swallowed, suddenly aware of the moisture in his mouth,
> remembering a dream of thirst. That people could want so for
> water they had to recycle their body moisture struck him with a
> feeling of desolation. "Water's precious there," he said.
> From the novel *Dune* by F. Herbert (1965)[2]

Just as an animal can't live without food, so too can it not live without water,
a fact that Frank Herbert used to enormous effect in his classic work of
science fiction, *Dune*. When I first read this book and journeyed with Paul
and the other characters across the sands of the desert planet of Arrakis, I
repeatedly felt thirsty. Gradually, through Herbert's absorbing prose, I
became aware of the enormous role that water and thirst play in our lives.

There are several reasons that we may not always be aware of the prominent role of water and thirst. First, for most of us most of the time, water is
easily and abundantly available. Schools, businesses, and public parks have
water fountains; grocery stores and street vendors sell bottled water and
other thirst-quenching beverages; restaurants serve water; and virtually every
house and apartment contains a water faucet. Second, because many foods
contain at least some water, eating can help to satisfy thirst. For example, a
person is unlikely to feel thirsty after eating large amounts of lettuce—
lettuce is 96% water.[3] Thus we may not always be aware of how much
water we need or of how powerful thirst can be; we rarely reach a state of
extreme thirst.

Nevertheless, loss of water can occur very quickly. For example, when
sweating, people typically lose about 1 quart of fluid per hour, which is about
2% of the total fluid contained in our bodies.[4] Given this fact, and given that

water is essential to life and isn't always available in nature, you would expect that people have evolved powerful mechanisms to ensure that we drink appropriate amounts of water. You would also expect that people have evolved multiple, redundant mechanisms responsible for drinking water appropriately, similar to what seems to have evolved for hunger. This chapter will tell you about some of these mechanisms. But first, when do you and other animals drink because you really need water, and when do you drink for other reasons? What are the drinking behaviors that any theory of thirst needs to explain?

How We Drink·

In some ways thirst is easier to study than hunger because it involves the intake of only one substance: water. Despite this simplicity, an astonishing number of different types of drinking behaviors can be observed. These behaviors can be divided into two major categories: homeostatic and nonhomeostatic drinking. Homeostatic drinking restores an animal's water balance when the amount of water in the animal's body isn't optimal. Nonhomeostatic drinking encompasses all other types of drinking. Both categories of drinking are common, as you've probably observed. A truly comprehensive theory of thirst needs to address both homeostatic and nonhomeostatic drinking.

Homeostatic Drinking

The concept behind homeostatic drinking, just as for homeostatic eating, is that there's an optimal physical state (the set point) and when there's a deviation from this state, the body does something to restore the set point. There are several different types of drinking behaviors that seem to occur according to a homeostatic model.

For example, one type of homeostatic drinking is the drinking that occurs when you eat. Deprived of food, an animal consumes less water.[5] Similarly, an animal deprived of water consumes less food.[6] This interdependency of food and water consumption may be due to animals' needing to keep a certain ratio of the weight of food to the weight of water in their gastrointestinal (GI) tracts. In rats this ratio is approximately 1 to 1 in their stomachs, and approximately 1 to 3 in their intestines.[7] Maintenance of these ratios is optimal for digestion and absorption of nutrients. Therefore animals, including us, that haven't eaten will drink relatively little, and animals that have eaten a great deal will drink a lot. This helps to maintain the set point, the optimal physical state, for the ratio of food and water in the GI tract.

Much other homeostatic drinking involves the maintenance, within fairly narrow limits, of the overall volume of the blood plasma and of the plasma's concentration of certain substances, such as salt. When the volume is less than optimal and/or the concentration of these substances is greater than normal, drinking will increase in order to restore the optimal states, and vice versa.[8]

These sorts of set point deviations can be caused by loss of water in either of the two main fluid compartments of the body: the water inside cells and the water outside cells. The latter consists of the water between the cells and in the blood plasma.[9] The two types of water loss can occur alone or together. For example, a hemorrhage, such as the sudden loss of blood following a car accident, causes loss of the fluid only outside the cells. When this happens, medical personnel usually administer fluids intravenously. If this isn't done, and if the blood loss is 10% or more, thirst will develop.[10] As another example, if there's a high concentration of salt in the fluid outside the cells, which can occur if salty food is eaten, water will be drawn out of the cells, causing a loss of the fluid only inside the cells.[11] A loss of only 1–2% of the water inside cells is enough for thirst to occur.[12] Finally, simply being deprived of water causes loss of water both from inside and outside the cells and again causes thirst. Drinking water restores water both inside and outside cells.[13]

However, it's important to remember that water won't be restored by the drinking of just any fluid. For example, fluids containing alcohol or caffeine cause the kidneys to increase their manufacture of urine. Therefore, drinking such beverages isn't the best way to counter water deprivation.[14]

Nonhomeostatic Drinking

Despite these many examples of homeostatic drinking, much drinking that people and other animals do does not alleviate a water deficit. For example, the amount that rats drink depends greatly on the time of day, independent of when the water is actually needed. Rats receiving 50% of their food during the day drink only about 25% of their water during that time; they drink most of their water at night even though they aren't getting most of their food then.[15]

Let's consider an example that you may be able to relate to more directly. If you keep a record, you'll see that you do most of your drinking while you're eating a meal.[16] Why do you think that's the case? One possible reason might be that you need the water to help digest your food, to maintain the optimal food to water ratio in your GI tract, as was already discussed. Another possible reason might be that you need the water because the food is salty and you need to replenish the water that the salt draws out of your cells. Both reasons are, however, only partly correct. You don't actually need the water until several hours after you eat. When you drink during a meal, you're anticipating a need for water and taking advantage of available water to prevent a deficit.[17] Animals drink, as well as eat, before there's any actual need for doing so, following the maxim, "Dig a well before you are thirsty."[18] This is an excellent way to prevent any serious deficits from occurring.

There are many other examples of anticipatory drinking. People traveling in the desert with no means of carrying water will consume as much water as possible at each water hole before moving on. In general, when water is scarce, animals drink when it's available, as opposed to drinking only when they're thirsty.[19]

There's another kind of nonhomeostatic drinking that's quite intriguing. It's called schedule-induced polydipsia (SIP). It's the excessive drinking that results from delivering rewards according to certain schedules. For example, a rat that had been deprived of food but not water, that is then given food once per minute for 3 hours, and that has continuous access to water, will consume a reasonable amount of food but will consume half its body weight in water[20] (just imagine the effect on the shavings in the rat's cage). This is far more water than the rat could possibly need.

SIP isn't seen just in the laboratory. Here's an example I saw some years ago. I was walking in New York City's Chinatown and went into an arcade. In one game, the customer could play tic-tac-toe with a chicken in a box (see Figure 3.1). Each customer put money in a slot in the box and then selected a square for the first X. The chicken pecked to place its O. As the game continued, the chicken received a little bit of food after each peck. In the back of the chicken's cage was a cup of water. Each time the chicken received food, it ran over to the cup and drank large amounts. I heard people watching this say that the chicken must be very thirsty, that the poor chicken must not get enough to drink. But the chicken had had plenty of water; what we were seeing was SIP. By the way, the game was fixed so that the chicken always won.

SIP can also be seen in people. When people in the laboratory were given money from a slot machine every 90 seconds, they consumed about 1.2 cups of water in a 30-minute period. These people had no water deficit and there was no food available, yet they still consumed a large amount of water.[21]

Theories of Thirst

Now you should have a pretty good idea of the many types of drinking that a good theory must explain—a difficult task. The rest of this chapter will tell you about some attempts to construct such theories. As was the case

Figure 3.1 Diagram of a tic-tac-toe game played by a chicken inside of a box. Each time a human opponent marks an X on an outside tic-tac-toe grid, the X appears on both the inside and the outside grid, and the chicken pecks at the round button on the right wall of the chamber. An O then appears in a square of both grids, and the chicken receives a reward of food through the opening at the bottom of the box's right wall. Water is continuously available in the cup on the left of the chamber.

with theories of hunger, theories focusing on peripheral physiological cues generally developed before theories focusing on central physiological mechanisms. And, as was the case with theories of hunger, the most recent theories are quite complex.

The Dry Mouth Theory

I'm sure that you remember physiologist Walter B. Cannon's stomach contraction theory of hunger, described in Chapter 2. Around 1920, Cannon also constructed a theory of thirst based on peripheral cues. The result, the dry mouth theory of thirst, dominated research on thirst for many years.[22] According to this theory, animals drink when their mouths feel dry and don't drink when their mouths feel wet. A large amount of evidence has been amassed both supporting and attacking this theory.

You've probably experienced yourself the strongest evidence in support of the dry mouth theory. Have you ever noticed that when you're greatly in need of water, you have less saliva? Perhaps your mouth feels rather gummy? Salivary flow correlates closely with water deprivation. If someone's water deprivation increases, their salivary flow decreases.[23] I remember one time in junior high school when I had to go to the dentist right after playing several hours of field hockey in the hot sun without anything to drink. The dentist's hand practically stuck to the inside of my mouth and he said that I had the thickest saliva he'd ever seen. Although proud of having exceeded the dentist's expectations, I realized that he wasn't exactly giving me a compliment.

There's more evidence that supports the dry mouth theory. Many ways of removing the sensation of a dry mouth also remove the sensation of thirst. For example, hospital patients awaiting surgery aren't permitted to drink, but their thirst can be decreased if they simply rinse their mouths with a liquid. As another example, applying cocaine to the mouth of a person or a dog anesthetizes the mouth and also decreases thirst. People in the desert provide a final example. They sometimes increase their salivation and thus decrease their thirst by putting small amounts of acidic fruit juices or insoluble objects such as rocks in their mouths[24] (this probably isn't good for their teeth, but their overriding immediate concern is thirst).

Some additional evidence supporting the dry mouth theory comes from studies of both rats and camels. When half an ounce of water is put directly into a rat's stomach, the rat will subsequently drink almost as much as if no water had been put directly into its stomach. In contrast, if a rat is allowed to drink the half ounce of water normally and is subsequently permitted to drink as much as it wants, it will drink much less than if the initial water had been put directly into its stomach or than if there had been no initial water at all.[25] When camels have been severely deprived of water, they can consume the amount that they need, more than 30% of their body weight, in a scant 10 minutes. They stop drinking before much of this water could possibly be absorbed from the gastrointestinal tract.[26] Together these findings suggest that water passing through the mouth does help to slake thirst. Therefore it's possible that a sensation of a very wet mouth is necessary in order for thirst to decrease.

But before you become too enamored of Cannon's dry mouth theory of thirst, there's also a great deal of evidence that seems contrary to it. First consider an incident described by psychologists Barbara J. Rolls and Edmund T. Rolls in their book on thirst. Apparently, in 1925, a man tried to commit suicide by cutting his neck. However, he missed his arteries and veins and instead managed to cut his esophagus, thus giving himself what was, in essence, an esophagostomy. Consequently, when he drank water through his mouth, the water didn't reach his stomach and he remained extremely thirsty. However, if he put water into the lower half of his esophagus, his thirst decreased.[27] This appears to be clear evidence against the dry mouth theory.

The incident described by Rolls and Rolls is a real-life example of the phenomenon known as sham drinking. Sham drinking is similar to the sham feeding described in Chapter 2. In a sham drinking procedure, the water consumed by the experiment's participants is prevented from reaching the participants' stomachs, for example by means of an esophagostomy. Experiments using esophagostomies usually find that, similar to sham feeding, sham drinking isn't very effective in suppressing future drinking. The experiments' participants drink much larger amounts of water than they would ordinarily.[28] Thus, even though the mouth is continually moistened, thirst isn't satisfied.

Additional evidence against the dry mouth theory comes from cases in which animals, including people, have no salivary glands. These animals still consume relatively normal amounts of water. This has been shown both in experiments in which the salivary glands of a member of a nonhuman species were removed and in clinical cases of people who have had no salivary glands since infancy.[29] In all of these cases the mouth is never moistened, but thirst functions fairly normally.

Further, I should point out that an increase in thirst as a result of a dry mouth or a decrease in thirst as a result of a moistened one would apply mainly to homeostatic drinking. The dry mouth theory has little to say about nonhomeostatic drinking. For example, the dry mouth theory cannot explain the nonhomeostatic anticipatory drinking that occurs when you eat. And, when you see or smell food you salivate,[30] just like Pavlov's dogs. Yet, despite your mouth being moistened, you still drink significant amounts when you eat. Thus, the drinking that occurs with eating isn't only not needed, as explained previously, but occurs despite the presence of a moist mouth, in contradiction to the dry mouth theory. (See Conversation Making Fact #3.)

Conversation Making Fact #3

We all tend to drink cold beverages when we're really thirsty. But do cold beverages really quench your thirst better than warm ones? The dry mouth theory has nothing to say about this. As it turns out, drinking cold water decreases thirst significantly more than drinking warm water, although this effect apparently lasts for only a few minutes. After that point, thirst is most affected by how much water has been drunk.[31] So if you're one of the people who thinks that a cold drink is the best way to quench your thirst, that's only true for a very short period of time after you drink. Over the long term, the best way to quench your thirst is to drink more water.

In general, scientists now agree that a dry mouth is a signal of thirst but not a cause. When the mouth is moistened, there's an immediate but temporary decrease in thirst. For a lasting decrease in thirst, it's necessary to drink fluids that reach the stomach.[32]

Once More Into the Brain: The Lateral Hypothalamus

Because the dry mouth theory has proved unsatisfactory, researchers have sought more central, neural mechanisms as the causes of thirst. Using a strategy similar to that used in the research on hunger, researchers have looked for a particular location in the brain that satisfies two criteria. First, the location should collect and integrate information about how much fluid there is in the animal. Second, using this integrated information, the location should then be responsible for the animal starting or stopping drinking.

There's a fair amount of evidence supporting the lateral hypothalamus as the part of the brain best satisfying these criteria. For example, B. Andersson showed in the early 1950s that injections of salt water into the hypothalamus initiated drinking in goats.[33] Apparently, cells in the hypothalamus are sensitive to salt water, a substance that causes loss of liquid from within cells. Andersson also showed that electrical stimulation of cells in the same area cause drinking.[34] Other researchers have shown that lesions in the lateral hypothalamus interfere with drinking behavior.[35]

A further indication that the hypothalamus is the central area for regulation of the amount of water in the body is the hypothalamus' role in the release of a substance called antidiuretic hormone (ADH). When the hypothalamus releases ADH, water is retained by the kidneys, thus helping to compensate for any water deficit. The hypothalamus releases ADH under two types of conditions. First, ADH is released when pressure sensors in the hypothalamus indicate a loss of fluid from within the cells. Second, ADH is released when pressure sensors in the blood vessels indicate that there has been a decrease in blood pressure, which can be caused by a loss of fluid from outside of the cells.[36] Further, when the hypothalamus detects a decrease in blood pressure, thirst and drinking result.[37] In general, blood pressure is kept very close to optimal through neural as well as hormonal mechanisms, mechanisms in which the amount of fluid excreted by the kidneys plays a significant role.[38]

Together, all of these results seem to suggest that a location within the hypothalamus is responsible for thirst and for the regulation of the amount of water in the body. This conclusion, however, is subject to many of the same criticisms that have been made of the brain centers theory of hunger and satiety, discussed in the previous chapter. These criticisms have pointed to the possibility that neither the experimental manipulations of the brain nor the modified behavior that results from them are specific enough to prove the theory. For example, a lesion in the hypothalamus may appear to affect drinking but may actually affect some other aspect of motivation or behavior.

Angiotensin

It's also possible to explain some types of drinking behavior using physiological mechanisms that aren't completely focused on the central nervous system. One such major contribution to the understanding of drinking behavior was the discovery of the role of the hormone angiotensin around 30 years ago.[39] (See Figure 3.2.)

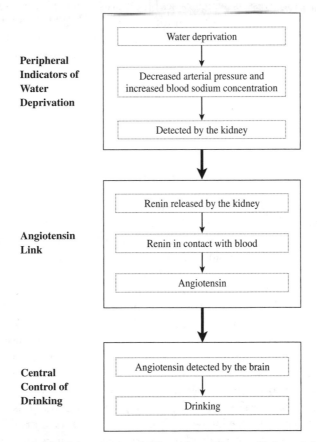

Figure 3.2 A model of the way in which angiotensin may link peripheral indicators of water deprivation with central control of drinking.

As indicated previously, water deprivation causes physiological changes in the body outside of the central nervous system, such as decreased arterial blood pressure and increased salt concentration in the blood. These changes in the fluid outside of the cells are detected by specialized cells in the kidney, which then secretes an enzyme called renin. When renin comes into contact with blood, angiotensin is produced. Therefore the concentration of angiotensin in the blood is greater under conditions of greater water deprivation.[40] Experiments have shown that the presence of angiotensin in the brain increases drinking.[41] Similar to the way that blood sugar level affects eating, the level of angiotensin in the blood may increase drinking by acting on centrally located sensory receptor cells. Thus angiotensin may function as the link between peripheral indicators of water deprivation and central control of drinking. Angiotensin also helps compensate for fluid loss using three additional physiological mechanisms: (1) It causes constriction of the blood vessels, which raises blood pressure; (2) it causes increased release of a hormone important in the regulation of sodium reabsorption by the kidney; and (3) it causes increased release of ADH.[42] The renin-angiotensin system appears to be quite similar across all mammalian species, probably reflecting the fact that all species need water and that need is relatively independent of individual species' particular diets.[43]

Explanations of Nonhomeostatic Drinking

The theories of thirst that I've discussed so far can basically account only for homeostatic drinking behavior. For example, the hypothalamic theory proposes that thirst is caused when a specific part of the brain detects inadequate fluid levels in the body. But, as you know, much drinking is nonhomeostatic; animals often drink even though they have no water deficit. Therefore we need to consider some alternative theories.

Remember the tic-tac-toe chicken? What might explain its behavior and the behavior of other animals (including people) that demonstrate SIP? One explanation that's widely accepted makes no reference whatsoever to specific physiological factors. According to psychologist John L. Falk,[44] animals exhibit SIP when they're motivated to eat but cannot do so. Their motivation to eat is displaced to another drive, another motivational system, whose satisfaction is available—in this case, thirst. Falk suggests that such displacement increases the probability that animals in the wild will take advantage of whatever rewards are available. However, under laboratory conditions, SIP results in quite unadaptive behavior—greatly excessive amounts of drinking.

What about anticipatory drinking? Scientists don't know for certain what causes all anticipatory drinking. One explanation relates to a substance called histamine that is produced by the vagus nerve. Histamine is produced during mealtimes prior to food's being absorbed or even entering the stomach, and it elicits drinking.[45] There's also some research indicating that the insulin that's released during a meal and its associated decrease in blood sugar can elicit thirst.[46] Thus the body may have several mechanisms by which anticipatory drinking occurs as an automatic reflex. However, some other cases of anticipatory drinking, such as people who drink a great deal before crossing a desert, are clearly the result of learning. This has been shown in the laboratory by exposing animals to sights, sounds, and odors that normally elicit no response but, after having been paired with a subsequent need for water, come to elicit drinking.[47] In all of these cases, animals consume water before they're seriously impaired by water deprivation, which is very adaptive behavior. This is a useful illustration of the fact that examples of behaviors that appear similar and have the same function can arise from very different causes.

There is as of yet no unified theory of nonhomeostatic drinking, or of homeostatic drinking for that matter. One way that scientists might overcome this lack would be for them to cease constructing theories for particular kinds of homeostatic or nonhomeostatic drinking behaviors and instead construct complex models incorporating a variety of physiological and nonphysiological factors that influence drinking behavior, similar to recent trends in attempts to explain hunger and eating behaviors.[48]

Thirst and Water Regulation in Specific Groups of People

Thirst and water regulation aren't identical in all groups of people. For example, many elderly people don't drink enough water to compensate for the amounts they lose following water deprivation, or as a result of exposure to heat, or as is needed with accompanying food ingestion. They can therefore develop potentially dangerous water deficits.[49] Even without water deprivation, the total amount of water in the body decreases with age. Therefore when elderly people don't drink sufficient amounts of water it's more serious than when younger people fail to do so. The result can be a higher than intended, possibly toxic, concentration in the body of any medication that the elderly person is taking; a decreased ability to withstand changes in the surrounding temperature; and impaired memory and decision making.[50] It's for reasons such as these that I worry more than I used to about my mother when she drinks alcohol; the concentration of alcohol in her body may be higher than would have occurred years ago when she drank the same amount of alcohol.

Another group of people about whom there's been concern with respect to water regulation is African Americans. Approximately 35% of black

Americans develop chronic high blood pressure at some point during their lives. The high prevalence of this disorder in black Americans contributes to about 500,000 deaths per year as a result of heart disease, stroke, and kidney failure. Recent research has shown that the prevalence of high blood pressure among African Americans corresponds very closely to the prevalence of obesity in this population. For this reason, in the United States, where every nonnative group, including African Americans, tends to be more obese than elsewhere, black Americans tend to have significantly higher blood pressure than blacks residing in other countries. Further, it has been hypothesized that obesity enhances the activity of the renin-angiotensin system discussed earlier, thereby increasing blood pressure.[51] In other words, obesity affects the body's water regulation and, therefore, blood pressure. What this line of reasoning suggests is that a decrease in the prevalence of obesity among African Americans should result in a decrease in chronic high blood pressure. However, losing weight is easier said than done, as will be explained in depressing detail in Chapter 10.

Thus, research on thirst is of more than laboratory interest. Thirst research can benefit our health, as well as inform basic theories of thirst.[52]

Conclusion

Using an approach similar to that taken in investigating hunger, scientists began by trying to explain thirst according first to peripheral, and then to more central, physiological factors. Although these peripheral and central factors clearly are influential in the initiation and termination of drinking, much drinking is nonhomeostatic and therefore isn't fully explained by this type of approach. More recently, researchers have turned to models that include the many different factors that influence drinking behavior, such as an animal's interaction with its surroundings.

I hope that you were able to get through this whole chapter without repeatedly feeling that you had to have something to drink. My typist was apparently not so lucky. When he was midway through the manuscript for this chapter, I heard him announce that he had to take a break to get some juice, that he was very thirsty. He never made the connection to the chapter, but I did.

CHAPTER 4

The Nose Knows
(and So Does the Tongue)

℃

When it comes to food tastes, we all speak in different tongues.... People inhabit separate taste worlds.

L. Bartoshuk (1980)[1]

"Every time I smell her perfume I think of the day we met and all our many days to come." If a picture is worth a thousand words, then your sense of smell is worth a million.

From a 1995 advertisement
by The Fragrance Foundation[2]

You're at a restaurant that serves an enormous buffet dinner and you're starving. Does that mean that you stuff yourself on whatever food is first in line? Probably not. You'll try to choose the best foods from the buffet. This chapter is the first of several to consider how we choose which foods or drinks to consume. In order to make such choices, you have to be able to tell the difference between various foods and drinks. In making these discriminations, you use the senses of taste and smell. In fact, taste and smell are the two senses most involved in eating and drinking. The present chapter will tell you what scientists have learned about how taste and smell work. You may be surprised to learn that not everyone tastes and smells in the same way. It's for this reason that, in the first quotation at the beginning of this chapter, psychologist Linda Bartoshuk states that we "inhabit separate taste worlds." You may also be surprised to learn about some of the many different ways that taste and smell enrich our daily lives, as expressed so ably by the Fragrance Foundation in the other quotation. We are creatures greatly influenced by what enters our noses and mouths.

The Chemistry of Survival

Both taste and smell are what we call chemical senses. They operate by detecting minute amounts (molecules) of chemical substances. The sense of taste, also known as gustation, operates by detecting molecules dissolved in liquids, and the sense of smell, also known as olfaction, operates by detecting molecules in the air. Both taste and smell function in ways designed to help us survive.

Although you may be quick to acknowledge dogs' powerful sense of smell or toddlers' sometimes too-discriminating sense of taste, you may not realize that men and women also have extremely sensitive senses of taste and smell. The average person can detect as little as 1/3 teaspoon of salt in 1 gallon of water.[3] This average person can also detect the scent of perfume when as little as one drop is diffused into the air of the average-size house.[4] People can also detect extremely small amounts of chemicals.

When we are enjoying a food, such as a hamburger, we usually don't think about the taste and smell of the food as separate entities. Instead, we tend to think about the flavor of the food, a sensation that combines taste and smell, as well as the touch, temperature, and any pain provided by the food.[5] To some degree, this makes sense. Taste and smell aren't necessarily independent. Chemicals that affect taste can also affect smell, and vice versa. For example, chemicals in the air from chewed food can reach the nose via the back of the mouth. As another example, everyone has experienced the tastelessness of food that comes with a cold. However, taste and smell don't operate identically, and they serve and protect the body in overlapping, but somewhat different, ways.

In nature, an essential task for any omnivore is determining which foods and drinks are not only safe but good to consume. Omnivores have the difficult job of avoiding poisonous substances and finding the foods and drinks that nourish them best. Taste and smell play very important roles in this effort, both in terms of identifying and promoting the ingestion of nourishing substances and in terms of helping us to reject poisonous substances. Jean M. Auel described some of this process in her 1980 book of historical fiction, *The Clan of the Cave Bear*:

> Part of every woman's heredity was the knowledge of how to test unfamiliar vegetation, and like the rest, Iza experimented on herself.... The procedure for testing was simple. She took a small bite. If the taste was unpleasant she spit it out immediately. If it was agreeable, she held the tiny portion in her mouth, carefully noting any tingling or burning sensations or any changes in taste. If there were none, she swallowed it and waited to see if she could detect any effects. The following day, she took a larger

bite and went through the same procedure. If no ill effects were noticed after a third trial, the new food was considered edible, in small portions at first.[6]

Once a food or drink has entered the stomach, removing it from the body may be difficult or impossible. People can vomit if they swallow something poisonous, but even so, some of the poison may remain in the body, particularly if the poison is a slow-acting one. Rats are worse off; they lack the muscles necessary for vomiting,[7] so once they've swallowed something poisonous, they're stuck with it. Rather than dealing with poison in the stomach, it would be better if a poisonous substance could be ejected from the mouth before it's swallowed. That's where the sense of taste becomes helpful. The fact that the taste receptors are located on the tongue helps prevent any undesirable items from reaching the stomach. In addition, in most species, including people, the sense of taste is linked to the gag and vomit reflexes.[8] It's for this reason that when someone eats something that tastes really bad, such as a piece of horseradish hidden in a dish of ice cream, that person is likely to immediately eject the offending item from his or her mouth.

Tastes can also be good and rewarding. These sorts of tastes cause the occurrence of certain reflexes that aid in digestion, such as salivation.[9]

Let's turn back to poisonous substances. Even better than ejecting them from the mouth before they get to the stomach would be detecting them before they enter the mouth, so that there's no possibility of any effect of the poison on the body whatsoever. This is where the sense of smell becomes helpful. Similar to the sense of taste, the sense of smell is also linked to ejection reflexes and helps to identify desirable and undesirable foods and drinks.[10] You can avoid tasting a bad bottle of wine by smelling the cork the waiter gives you; and who hasn't turned away from spoiled milk because of its distinctive odor?

Our bodies have evolved in such a way that any substance must pass several tests before we judge it acceptable and ingest it. The senses of taste and smell are both part of this testing process, with smell being an earlier line of defense and taste being a later line of defense.

Finding the "Secret" Code for Taste and Smell

Now you should have a pretty good understanding about why taste and smell are important to us and the harm that their malfunctioning could cause. In order to prevent or remove any such harm, we need to know precisely how taste and smell work. We need to know how chemicals in the air and chemicals in liquids get perceived by us as particular odors and tastes, what happens when they come into contact with our bodies, and how messages concerning them reach our brains. Scientists call this process coding, and although this type of coding may not be exactly secret, it hasn't been at all easy to decipher.

Several factors have made quick progress in understanding taste and smell coding difficult. One is that it's hard to deliver a taste or an odor in isolation, without any other contaminating tastes or odors. A second factor is that the chemicals that constitute specific tastes and odors vary in a myriad of different ways. For example, there are many different chemicals that taste sweet. For these reasons it can be very difficult to figure out which aspects of which chemicals are responsible for a particular substance having a specific smell or taste.

Ever since the beginning of scientific investigations of taste and smell coding, researchers have tried to identify what are called the taste and odor primaries. These are the smallest number of tastes and odors that could be used to describe all other tastes and odors. For example, if the primaries for taste consisted of sweet, sour, salt, and bitter, as many scientists believe is indeed the case, then it would be possible to describe the taste of, for example, a hamburger, as a combination of various proportions of only these four tastes. Don't confuse the way these primaries work with the way that color primaries work. Scientists aren't proposing that any taste could actually be made from different combinations of substances having one of the primary tastes, only that any taste could be described as consisting of different proportions of the primary tastes.

Scientists have hoped that, if they could identify the taste and odor primaries, they would then be able to see what chemical characteristics distinguish substances that have those tastes or smells. This information would then give scientists significant clues about what sort of physical processes are involved in taste and smell coding. Now let's see how successful scientists have been in this coding investigation, first concerning taste, and then smell.

Taste Coding

Investigations of the four taste primaries of sweet, sour, salt, and bitter began almost a century ago. Because these primaries described most tastes fairly well,[11] scientists reasoned that the physiological coding of taste must somehow be organized according to these primaries. Bolstering this view was the fact that many substances tasting mainly like one of the four taste primaries have distinctive chemical properties. For example, substances that taste sweet often contain a certain configuration of the elements oxygen or nitrogen bonded to hydrogen, those that taste bitter can often be dissolved in fats, those that taste salty usually ionize easily, and those that taste sour are often acids.[12] Scientists also realized that at least three of the four taste primaries are critical to the survival of omnivores. A sweet taste such as the taste of an apple often indicates a good source of carbohydrates. In other words, foods that taste sweet are usually good sources of energy. Poisonous foods are sometimes bitter. Salt is necessary for maintaining the body's proper physiological functioning.[13] Thus it would make sense that the body would have evolved to give special attention to these tastes. Given all of this evidence, scientists reasoned that taste coding must be directly related to the taste primaries of sweet, sour, salt, and bitter.

One hypothesis about the nature of this relationship was that there are four types of sensory cells on the tongue, with each type being maximally sensitive to one of the four taste primaries. Even before there were microscopes, it was easy to see that there are four types of bumps—the taste papillae—on the surface of the tongue: the foliate, filiform, circumvallate, and fungiform papillae (see Figure 4.1). If you've got a mirror or a friend handy, you can check this out yourself.

However, until the techniques developed to allow investigations of the responses of single neurons, it wasn't possible to determine what role these four types of papillae had in taste coding, including whether they were or were not related to the four taste primaries.

And there was still another coding question whose answer awaited the technology for investigating the responses of individual neurons. Suppose that there are four types of taste primaries that are somehow associated with

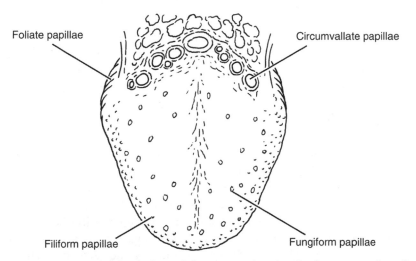

Figure 4.1 Diagram of the surface of the tongue, showing the four types of papillae and their locations. (Adapted from P. L. Williams and R. Warwick, *Gray's Anatomy*, Philadelphia: W.B. Saunders, 1980.)

four different types of sensory cells on the tongue. How would the information from these cells proceed from the tongue to the brain? One possibility is that each type of sensory cell is connected to different neurons, and the brain distinguishes different tastes by determining which of the four types of neurons are most active. This is what's called a labeled line theory, because it postulates that there are specific lines (i.e., neurons) that are labeled for specific tastes. The other possibility is that there aren't separate neurons for each of the taste primaries, and that the different tastes are coded by a complex pattern of response of many different neurons. The overall frequency of response of the neurons indicates the concentration, or intensity, of the substance that is being tasted. This is what's called a pattern theory.[14]

About 60 years ago, scientists developed the techniques to start investigating precisely how taste coding works. Here's one example of the sort of experiment that can now be done. Kristina Arvidson and Ulf Friberg used suction to draw individual fungiform papillae into tiny tubes. (Please don't try this at home!) The researchers then stimulated these papillae, one at a time, with various chemical substances. Next, each papilla was cut off the tongue (don't worry; they're very small, so the pain is minimal). Then the papillae were examined under a microscope to see how many taste cells were located in each one. The results showed that a papilla containing a single taste cell could be sensitive to more than one of the four primary tastes. Further, the number of primary tastes that a papilla could sense was greater in proportion to the number of taste cells located in it.[15]

Based on a great many experiments, including this one, we now know that the parts of the tongue that actually sense tastes aren't necessarily cells associated with papillae. Fungiform papillae do have taste cells located on their top surfaces. However, the filiform papillae aren't associated with sensory cells in any way. Circumvallate papillae have taste cells located in the trenches around their sides, and taste cells are located in the folds between foliate papillae.[16]

In addition, we now know that the taste cells don't simply sit on the topmost surface of the tongue. The tongue has openings on its surface that are known as taste pores. Underneath a taste pore is the taste bud made up of many different types of cells, including taste cells (see Figure 4.2). Each taste cell is connected to one of the neurons that make up the chorda tympani nerve. This nerve is the first stage in transmission of information from the tongue to the brain. Individual neurons that make up the chorda tympani nerve can be connected to one or more taste cells.[17]

When chemicals dissolved in liquid on the tongue come into contact with the surface of the taste cells, various chemical changes occur in the taste cells. The nature of these chemical changes depends on the particular nature of the chemical substance, which is, as you would imagine, related to how that substance tastes.[18] In other words, substances that taste salty result in

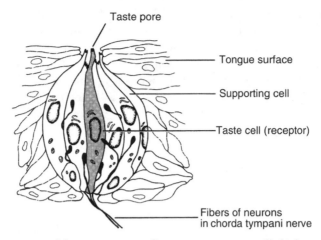

Taste pore

Tongue surface

Supporting cell

Taste cell (receptor)

Fibers of neurons
in chorda tympani nerve

Figure 4.2 Anatomy of the area surrounding a taste receptor cell. (Adapted from V. F. Castellucci, "The Chemical Senses: Taste and Smell," in *Principles of Neural Science*, 2nd ed., eds. E. R. Kandel and J. H. Schwartz, New York: Elsevier, 1985.)

one sort of chemical change in the taste cells, sour another kind of chemical change, and so on. As a result of one or more of these types of chemical changes, certain taste cells respond and, ultimately, so do the neurons in the chorda tympani nerve that are connected to those taste cells.

Most taste cells in mammals will respond to a wide variety of chemical substances. Such data support the pattern theory of taste coding.[19] However, it's also the case that individual neurons in the chorda tympani nerve and in the brain tend to respond more to one of the taste primaries than to the others, which would tend to support the labeled line theory.[20] For example, in an experiment with monkeys, many of their brain neurons that were tested showed some response to sweet, sour, salty, and bitter solutions when these solutions were placed on the monkeys' tongues. However, most of the tested neurons clearly responded the greatest to one of the four types of solutions.[21] It appears that taste coding does not operate strictly according to a single method. The monkey tastes a sweet banana, and many of its neurons increase their activity, but some—the sweet detection neurons—do so more than others.

Detecting Specific Tastes

To figure out more about how taste coding works, let's consider some very specific, unusual cases. For example, consider what happens when a substance called gymnemic acid is applied to the surface of the tongue.

Gymnemic acid is a chemical derived from the leaves of a plant native to India. Its effects were first noted in the scientific literature in 1847 when a British officer, Captain Edgeworth, told the Linnaean Society that if he chewed some leaves from this plant, his tea tasted as usual except that he could not taste the sugar that he had put in the tea. Apparently, when gymnemic acid is applied to the tongue, the chorda tympani nerve no longer responds to sweet substances on the tongue, although it continues to react to other tastes.[22] The fact that the reaction to only sweet substances is affected by gymnemic acid is part of the evidence indicating that the tongue has a specialized mechanism for the detection of sweet. Gymnemic acid somehow blocks these receptors.[23] The idea that a chemical in leaves could selectively decrease the enjoyment of dessert while leaving intact enjoyment of the rest of the meal is quite appealing.

On the flip side we have the aptly named West African miracle fruit, a berry about the size of a small grape. This fruit was first brought to scientists' attention by an American named David Fairchild who explored West Africa in the 1930s. Miracle fruit has the opposite effect of gymnemic acid. Although this berry does not have a particularly wonderful taste itself, after it has been eaten, sour foods (such as lemons and rhubarb) taste sweet. The active substance in miracle fruit is named miraculin[24]—and miraculous it is. When placed on the tongue, this substance, similar to gymnemic acid, selectively affects the taste of sweet, again suggesting that the tongue has a specialized mechanism for detecting sweet. But just think how attractive all foods would be to someone who had been "miraculinized." Miraculin is something that I definitely want to stay away from; there could be heavy consequences for encountering it!

Let's turn to the detection of bitter, beginning with a very simple experiment that you've probably done yourself without knowing it. Have you ever tasted distilled water? Some irons and machines can only operate with distilled water, which has absolutely nothing in it except H_2O. Distilled water often tastes bitter. The reason for this is that your saliva contains various substances such as sodium, a component of table salt.[25] Your tongue adapts to those substances in the sense that, because they're continuously present, it reacts less to them. As a result, when you fill your mouth with distilled water, water that contains nothing but H_2O, and taste it, that adaptation is not in effect and your response to bitter is much stronger than when your saliva is continuously present (see Conversation Making Fact #4). The effects on bitter taste when switching between liquids with different concentrations of minerals suggest that the tongue has a specialized mechanism for detecting bitter. Very recently, scientists have been making significant progress in determining precisely how the taste cells detect bitter tastes. Their evidence suggests that there may actually be many different types of bitter taste.[26]

So far in this chapter we've assumed that there are only four taste

---

Conversation Making Fact #4

The adaptation of your tongue to the substances in your saliva explains why the "pure" designer waters that you drink aren't really so pure. Even the most expensive brands must contain small amounts of minerals such as sodium. Otherwise the water would taste bitter.

---

primaries. But not everyone agrees with that. Some very recent evidence suggests that there's a fifth, which scientists have called *umami*, a Japanese word meaning meaty or savory. Umami is the taste of glutamate, an amino acid present in many foods, including monosodium glutamate (MSG). Some researchers believe that the particular taste cell mechanisms for detecting the umami taste have been identified, but this is controversial.[27] This is an area of research that will undoubtedly receive further attention in the next few years.

Recent evidence also suggests that taste cells may respond in a particular way to free fatty acids (one of the products of the metabolism of fat that you read about previously). However, such responses aren't the only way that our bodies detect the presence of fat in food. Odor and texture cues are also very important in the detection of fat.[28] Isn't it wonderful that we have all kinds of cues to detect fat, making it easy for us to find it and eat it?

Odor Coding

Just as they did with taste coding, scientists have tried to identify the odor primaries, which they hoped would provide cues regarding how odor coding works. However, unlike the outcome for taste, it has not proved possible to identify a small set of odor primaries.

Scientist John E. Amoore, who has been one of the most active researchers in this area, has tried to identify the odor primaries by looking for what are known as specific anosmias. A specific anosmia is the inability to smell a particular odor when all other odors can be smelled normally. Specific anosmias can be due to genetic effects, infection, or exposure to certain types of chemicals. The existence of a specific anosmia suggests that the nose has a special way of detecting that particular odor, and therefore that odor is a primary. Using this approach, Amoore has identified what he believes are eight odor primaries: sweaty, spermous, fishy, malty, urinous, musky, minty, and camphoraceous. (I certainly would never volunteer for one of his experiments!) In any case, Amoore believes that these eight are only a starting point, that many more odor primaries will be found.[29]

Some researchers believe that there may be as many as 1,000 different types of cells that are at the front line detecting odors.[30] These cells are located on what's called the olfactory epithelium, the tissue up inside your nose that detects odors. Chemicals in the air come into contact with the olfactory epithelium, more specifically with the tiny hairlike entities on the olfactory epithelium, and this causes the special odor receptor cells to respond. The different types of receptor cells seem to be randomly distributed within different regions of the olfactory epithelium.[31]

But what of that wonderful mucus with which your nose is often filled? This mucus covers the olfactory epithelium. Only certain chemicals can pass through the mucus, and some chemicals change as a result of this passage.[32] So your mucus is actually an important part of odor coding.

Turning to the receptor cells, these are essentially neurons that can each extend 3 to 4 centimeters in length toward the brain. The projections from some 10 million of these neurons converge in an area of the brain called the olfactory bulb. In the olfactory bulb, these neurons form groups of about 10,000 neurons each. The neurons within each group tend to be most sensitive to the same small set of molecular features, and particular odors are coded by the spatial pattern of activation of the neuron groups. Finally, the receptor cell neurons in the olfactory bulb are connected with the rest of the brain by additional neurons.[33]

Thus, the olfactory system, similar to the gustatory system, seems to contain elements of both the labeled line and the pattern theories of coding. There are a great many different types of odor receptor cells, so that there can be almost one type of cell for each odor that we can detect, as would be the case with a labeled line theory. However, within the olfactory bulb, it appears that odors are coded by the pattern of activity of the neuron groups, consistent with a pattern theory.

As you can see, both odor detection and taste detection are exceedingly complicated. For this reason, construction of electronic devices that will detect tastes or odors—in other words, artificial tongues and noses—has proved very difficult. This is unfortunate because such devices could be employed, for example, to detect smoke or gas to see if a location such as a mine shaft were safe for people to enter. Although artificial noses are now being constructed, so far they can distinguish among only a very limited set of odors.[34]

We're Not All the Same

Up until now, everything that I've told you about the senses of taste and smell applies to pretty much everybody, including most mammals. But, as I indicated at the beginning of this chapter, we're not all the same when it comes to smelling and tasting. To begin with, species differ in terms of how sensitive they are to different tastes and smells. These differences help enable more than one species to exist in the same geographical area, with the different species consuming different foods in that area.[35] For example, consider the seabirds that obtain their food as they fly back and forth over the ocean. You may have assumed that those birds were using their excellent vision to spot food near the water's surface, and that assumption would often be correct. However, it appears that some seabirds—notably albatrosses, petrels, and shearwaters—are actually using their very sensitive sense of smell to identify certain parts of the seascape that, given their odor, are likely to have significant concentrations of food (squid, fish, and krill). Not all birds can do this, but these particular species have very highly developed olfactory systems and are usually attracted to fish-related odors. Therefore, although you and I look at the ocean and perceive one uniform surface, these birds perceive the ocean's surface as the odor equivalent of hills and valleys, deserts and forests, with greater and lesser amounts of different kinds of food in different parts of the seascape.[36] So the next time that you watch seabirds wheeling and diving over the surface of the ocean, consider the possibility that they're smelling for their supper.

In addition to there being differences in taste and smell sensitivity among different species, there can also be differences in taste and smell sensitivity among individuals of the same species. You already had a hint of that when I discussed Amoore's investigations of specific anosmias. Only some people have these specific anosmias.

It has been difficult to get a handle on just how much variation in taste and smell sensitivity there is among people. A now famous, truly mammoth attempt was the 1986 smell survey conducted by *National Geographic*. This magazine inserted into one of its issues a scratch-and-sniff smell test. Readers of the magazine were asked to scratch and sniff each odor patch and answer several questions about each odor. A total of about 1.5 million people participated from many different countries, although by far the largest number were from the United States, suggesting that the results would have been even more varied if a truly global sample of people had been obtained. The survey revealed some significant differences in odor sensitivity and odor preferences between men and women, and among people from different countries. For example, on average, women, no matter what the country, rated odors as more intense than did men. And although odors such as banana, peppermint, lemon, and vanilla were preferred by everyone, preference for other odors differed according to the country in which a study participant currently resided. For example, the scent of cloves was much less preferred by people living in Asia than by people living in the United States.[37]

In the following sections we'll consider additional ways in which people differ in terms of how they taste and smell, beginning with material about my own peculiarities.

The Taste of Bitter

Now we come to what is my most favorite subject in all of the psychology of eating and drinking—the subject that may very well have been responsible for my interest in psychology and food in the first place, although I didn't realize it until well into my adulthood. This is the study of sensitivity to the taste of phenylthiocarbamide, otherwise known as PTC, and its chemical relative 6-*N*-propylthiouracil, otherwise known as PROP. I'm sure you're saying, "phenyl-what? 6-*N*-prop-what? How can they be relevant to anything?" Well, some people taste very low concentrations of PTC and PROP as bitter, and those same people—adults and children—also tend to taste as bitter substances such as saccharin, caffeine, beer, grapefruit juice, and dark green vegetables including brussels sprouts, among others.[38] Perhaps you can see where I'm going with this.

To be more specific, people seem to divide roughly into three groups—those who can taste very low concentrations of PTC and PROP, those who need a somewhat higher concentration of PTC or PROP in order to taste them, and those who can taste PTC or PROP only if the concentrations are very high. These three groups are known as supertasters, tasters, and nontasters, respectively. Whether you're a supertaster, taster, or nontaster is determined by your genes.[39] About one third of Northern Europeans are nontasters. The proportion of nontasters in other groups is much smaller.[40] For example, among university students in China it's about 10%.[41]

If you've read this book's preface, you should have a pretty good guess as to which group I fall into. Yes, I'm a supertaster. This may very well explain why I've never liked vegetables, beer, coffee (even coffee ice cream), grapefruit juice, or saccharin. I abhor brussels sprouts. Apparently many things taste bitter to me that don't taste bitter to many other people. Recent research has also shown that supertasters seem to be more sensitive to pain in the mouth.[42] This may explain why I've never liked soda—from the time I was a child I felt that the bubbles hurt my mouth. Similarly, especially as a child, I never liked raw fruit because I felt that it was just too acidic and hurt my mouth. The one exception was bananas, which I've always liked (similar to other primates). I also prefer my water to be room temperature, not ice cold as most Americans do. Finally, the findings on pain and supertasting can also explain why I've never been able to eat food that contains a great deal of chile pepper.

How I discovered my supertaster status is a story that warrants telling. In the late 1980s I was part of something called the Cuisine Group, a small informal group of psychologists, historians, anthropologists, and the like who were interested in food and cuisine. The group was organized by the food psychologist nonpareil, Paul Rozin, a professor at the University of Pennsylvania. About one Saturday a month, we would meet in the Manhattan loft apartment of Barbara Kirshenblatt-Gimblett, a professor at New York University. At a typical meeting, we would gather at noon, each having brought something interesting to share for lunch. Usually the other members of the group, who were all interested in food because they liked to eat everything (and I do mean everything), would bring all kinds of strange things for lunch. Much of lunch would be spent by the other attendees trying to get me to eat whatever strange things they had brought (they were never successful). Then we would have discussions and perhaps a lecture during the afternoon, during which we would snack. As the afternoon drew to a close, we would all go out to dinner at some interesting place.

Each meeting had a theme. At one meeting, psychologist Linda Bartoshuk—an otolaryngology professor at Yale University, Cuisine Group regular, and the top expert on taste in the world—brought her little taste-testing papers. These are very small squares of what look like plain white paper. One in particular was doused with PROP. She asked each of us to taste a PROP paper. The other Cuisine Group members were chomping down happily on theirs. I touched my tongue to the tip of one corner of the PROP paper and *bam*! It was incredibly bitter. Linda dubbed me a supertaster on the spot. I asked for an extra paper to take home to test my husband, who, as a child, as you may remember from the preface, was known as the HGP (human garbage pail). That night I gave him the paper to taste. He tasted one corner and said, "It tastes like paper." "Put the whole thing in your mouth," I growled. He complied and said again, "It tastes like paper." This was definitely not a match made in heaven. I had managed to pair myself with someone who was as different from me in food preferences as possible—a nontaster! Well, at least now I knew it was genetic, and so all of my husband's nasty comments about how supposedly intelligent people don't turn up their noses at delicious vegetables could be deflected with a quite authoritative statement that they *really* do not taste so delicious to *me*. Facilitating détente, we were glad to discover recently that our son is a taster, occupying the middle ground between the extremely different taste worlds inhabited by my husband and me.

Some years ago I was able to put the information on PTC tasting to a very practical use. Two friends of mine, Liz and Rich, had been going out together for years. It wasn't a smooth courtship, to put it mildly. One complaint that Liz had about Rich was that he was a very picky eater—he didn't like to eat vegetables and many other foods. Liz thought that this pickiness was evidence of Rich being egocentric. Liz's opinions made Rich very angry. One night, when we were all out to dinner together, I questioned Rich about his food preferences and realized that they fit the PTC/PROP supertaster pattern. I explained this to both Liz and Rich, and it was as if a light went on in Liz's head. She immediately stopped being upset with him about his food preferences, and it wasn't too long after that they decided to get married. They now have three children and live happily together in New Jersey.

Being a supertaster has increasingly become a public matter. In 1991, Linda Bartoshuk was president of the Eastern Psychological Association (EPA), and she gave her presidential address at EPA's annual meeting. The subject was my favorite—PTC/PROP tasting. As Linda discussed the latest information on supertasters, she repeatedly used me as an example, pointing me out in the audience. In 2002, the music group They Might Be Giants immortalized supertasters in their song "John Lee Supertaster." The Web site www.pickyeatingadults.com contains information about supertasters, as well as other causes of picky eating. Finally, Paul McFedries's Web site, The Word Spy (www.wordspy.com), a site devoted to "recently coined words and phrases, and to old words that are being used in new ways," lists the word *supertaster* as one of its entries. After quoting Linda Bartoshuk, the entry goes on to state that the earliest citation of the word *supertaster* is contained in a 1989 *New York Times* article written by Lawrence Kutner about my being a picky eater. Who would ever have predicted that my eating habits would become part of a dictionary?

Memory

One way in which people vary significantly is in their ability to recognize an odor or a taste and to identify its source correctly. This ability seems to depend on the experiences that people have had. How well you can remember an odor or a taste depends on the circumstances under which you previously experienced that odor or taste, as Marcel Proust realized so well:

> And once I had recognized the taste of the crumb of madeleine soaked in her decoction of lime-flowers which my aunt used to give me ... immediately the old grey house upon the street, where my room was, rose up like the scenery of a theatre ... and with the house the town, from morning to night and in all weathers, the Square where I was sent before luncheon, the streets along which I used to run errands, the country roads we took when it was fine ... so in that moment all the flowers in our garden and in M. Swann's park, and the water-lilies on the Vivonne and the good folk of the village and their little dwellings and the parish church and the whole of Combray and of its surroundings, taking their proper shapes and growing solid, sprang into being, town and gardens alike, from my cup of tea.[43]

When people try to learn to identify the odors of many different chemicals, such as pyridine, butanol, and acetone, even if they're given a great deal of practice and feedback, they can learn to identify at most 22 odors. However, if, instead of consisting of chemicals with little significance for ordinary people, the odors consist of those likely to occur frequently in everyone's daily lives—substances such as chocolate, meats, bandages, and baby powder—then people on average can identify 36 substances.[44] In general it appears that it's easier for people to identify an odor if it has been encountered frequently, if they have associated that odor with a particular brand name for a long period of time, and if they're given feedback when they try to identify an odor. These principles may help explain why we sometimes recognize an odor but cannot recall the circumstances in which we smelled it before. Such odors are usually ones for which we had no names when we smelled them previously.

Memory for odors may have some special characteristics. For example, it may take longer to forget an odor than it takes to forget something else that we experienced in our surroundings.[45] As another example, odors can help you to remember all kinds of past events. If someone gives you an unexpected present while you're in a room that smells of roses, then smelling roses again will tend to remind you of the gift. This is particularly true if you were under stress at the time at which you smelled the roses and got the gift.[46] Thus, odors can greatly enhance our memories and they contribute to our living rich, complex mental lives.

Memory for tastes can also be influenced by emotion. Suppose a college student is in a good mood and is given several baby foods to taste, some that taste good and others that don't. Suppose further that the college student is then told to identify which baby foods from among a large set were tasted previously. In this situation, the college student will have an easier time picking out the good-tasting previously tasted baby foods than the bad-tasting previously tasted baby foods. On the other hand, if the college student is in a bad mood when originally tasting the baby foods, that student will subsequently have an easier time picking out the bad-tasting previously tasted baby foods than the good-tasting previously tasted baby foods.[47] In other words, it's easier to remember good tastes when you've experienced them in a good mood, and it's easier to remember bad tastes when you've experienced them in a bad mood. Something to think about the next time you're contemplating checking the temperature of your crying child's baby food by taking a little taste.

Age and Health

Our abilities to taste and smell are affected by how old we are. As we age, our abilities to taste and smell low concentrations of chemicals and to discriminate among various chemicals decrease. More than 75% of people over age 80 have a major olfactory impairment.[48] Further, people in their 70s and 80s are less able to taste salt in their food than are young adults and middle-aged people.[49] Age-related decreases in olfactory sensitivity may explain why older people, on average, are more willing to try new or unpleasant-smelling foods than younger people.[50]

However, the age-related decrease in the ability to taste and smell does not appear to occur identically for these two senses. First, when problems develop with taste, they usually involve problems in detecting specific tastes, whereas problems that develop with smell are more often problems in detecting all smells.[51] The other way that age affects taste and smell differently is that decreases in odor sensitivity are more likely to occur with age than are decreases in taste sensitivity. In fact, there is evidence that the ability to smell starts to decline when people are in their 50s.[52] However, it's important to keep in mind that there are many people of advanced age who show no diminution whatsoever in the ability to smell.

We don't know what causes the decreases in taste and smell ability with age. They could be an inevitable part of the aging process; or they could be due to the fact that people, as they age, are more likely to have experienced some physical trauma, some disease, or some toxic substance in their surroundings that has damaged the ability to taste or smell.[53] One thing that we are sure of is that these age-related decreases in the ability to taste and smell have strong implications for the health of elderly people. Elderly people who can't taste and smell well don't enjoy their food as much as they used to and are less likely to eat a nutritionally balanced diet. They're also less likely to show the reflex responses such as salivation that normally accompany eating. These reflexes aid in digestion; impairment of such reflexes can therefore impair digestion.[54] In addition, elderly people who can't taste and smell well are less likely to detect the odors of smoke and gas, making them more likely to succumb in a fire or when there is a gas leak.[55] Family members and health professionals need to be aware of these potential dangers so that they can take steps to help the elderly avoid them. For example, family members can ensure that their elderly relatives have working smoke and gas alarms. Extra flavorings can be added to their elderly relatives' meals, but such a strategy can backfire in the case of food tasting salty. One study showed that, as compared to people aged 18–30 years, a group of adults aged 69–87 years needed more than two times as much salt in their tomato soup in order to experience its taste as slightly salty.[56] Therefore, problems in the ability of the elderly to taste salt could result in an excessive, unhealthy intake of salt.

It's not just diseases associated with aging that can take their toll on taste and smell. As you surely know without my telling you, a simple cold can decrease the ability to smell. But you probably don't know the whole story. T. Hummel and colleagues examined the ability of men and women to smell during a cold. As expected, smelling was impaired. Then each participant used a nose spray containing the decongestant oxymetazoline, the active ingredient in the over-the-counter nasal decongestant Afrin®. Unexpectedly, although mucus secretion was greatly decreased, the participants still couldn't smell as well as when they didn't have a cold. This suggests that having a cold can adversely affect smell independent of any nasal congestion that may be present.[57] So even if you use a decongestant while you have a cold, you may not be in tip-top shape when it comes to detecting odors.

One case of taste disability that got some publicity was the temporary inability to taste of Raymond D. Fowler, the chief executive officer of the American Psychological Association. In 1997 he suddenly was unable to taste. Food not only didn't taste good, it seemed to be foreign matter, something that he didn't want to put in his mouth. As a result, he ate very little. His regular physician didn't have a clue as to what was going on. Finally, Fowler went to see Linda Bartoshuk, taste expert extraordinaire. She gave him every possible test, including painting his tongue bright blue and videotaping it, and anesthetizing various parts of his mouth while taste tests were done. After conducting the tests, Bartoshuk was able to diagnose Fowler's problem as a respiratory virus that had gotten into his inner ear and attacked the chorda tympani nerve. Luckily, Fowler soon spontaneously recovered from his very debilitating taste problem.[58]

There are several places to which someone with a possible taste or smell abnormality might turn in addition to contacting Dr. Bartoshuk. One is the Monell Chemical Senses Center in Philadelphia, and another is the Smell and Taste Center of the University of Pennsylvania. Both of these centers will evaluate patients who are having difficulties with taste or smell.

Conclusion

If there's one concept that you should take away from this chapter it's that we live in a world richly populated by food tastes and odors, a world that isn't the same for everybody. Our individual abilities to taste and smell play extremely important roles in eating and drinking; it's these senses that largely determine which foods and drinks we will consume, or whether anything will be consumed at all. Taste and smell provide critical information that the body needs in order to distinguish among various foods and drinks.[59] Food preferences and aversions are often based on this information, as we will see in the next two chapters.

CHAPTER 5

Genes Rule—Or Do They?

℮

"I used to drink milk all the time when I was young, but now I hardly ever do. Why did I change?"

"Why can my wife never seem to get enough sweet or salty snacks, even though she knows they're bad for her?"

"Five years ago I ate a hot dog and a few hours later got really sick to my stomach. I still can't stand even the thought of hot dogs. Will this ever go away?"

"Our son won't eat vegetables, but the rest of the family eats them. How did this happen? What can we do?"

Do any of these questions sound familiar? It seems that almost everyone has a food preference or food aversion of mysterious origin, or one that he or she would like to change. Parents worry about what their children like to eat and what they refuse to eat, and for good reason. (See Figure 5.1.) Not only is a balanced diet synonymous with good nutrition, but what you eat is known to influence the incidence and course of many diseases. For example, cutting down on saturated fats and increasing the proportion of fiber in our diets may decrease the risk of heart disease and some types of cancer.[1] Food preferences and aversions clearly have medical as well as social consequences.

The previous chapter explained how people and other animals tell one food and drink from another. Given that animals can tell foods and drinks apart, and assuming the foods and drinks are all equally and easily available, which ones do animals prefer and which ones do they dislike and why? This chapter and the next one will tell you what scientists have discovered about the nature and causes of food aversions and food preferences.

"Let's review the whole picture, Janine. You don't like milk. You don't like chicken. You don't like anything green. Now, you tell me, Janine—what does that leave us with?"

Figure 5.1 Drawing by Saxon. Copyright 1981 The New Yorker Magazine, Inc. (Reprinted with permission from *The New Yorker* [August 10, 1981]: 37.)

There's a huge amount of research on this topic. Therefore, to make it more comprehensible, I've divided up the discussion. This chapter focuses on the contributions that genes make to food preferences and aversions. The next chapter focuses on the contributions that our experiences make to food preferences and aversions. Nevertheless, as you read this material, please remember that no trait is entirely determined by your genes or your experience. For example, if I asked you what determines whether someone is male or female, you'd say it was entirely due to the person's genes, wouldn't you? But it turns out that if the necessary amount of male hormone isn't present at the appropriate time during pregnancy, a genetic male can develop into a person who is, to all outer appearances, female.[2] In other words, what happens during fetal development can affect whether someone has a male or female body. Consider another example. If I asked you what determines whether someone can sing a particular song, you'd probably say it was entirely due to the person's experiences. But without vocal cords and a mouth, which are genetically determined, singing that song would be impossible.

Knowing the extent to which food preferences and aversions are genetically influenced can help us understand how to change them. If an animal's food preference or aversion is determined primarily by the genes, it will be difficult to change it by manipulating the animal's surroundings. If an animal's food preference or aversion is determined primarily by experience, it will be much less difficult to change it by manipulating the animal's surroundings.

This chapter begins with discussion of three specific food preferences: the preferences for sweet foods, salty foods, and milk. Describing them will introduce you to many of the themes and problems common to all studies of food preferences. These three food preferences were chosen because, at least to some degree, most people prefer them at some point in their lives. The fact that these preferences are virtually universal, despite the varied circumstances in which people grow and mature, suggests that they're substantially genetically determined and that possession of these preferences has helped animals to survive. The last section of this chapter presents more general information about how genes contribute to food aversions and food preferences. You're about to discover that what you like to eat is controlled a lot more by your genes than you thought.

Our Sweet Teeth

The preference for sweet is stronger and more prevalent than the preference for any other taste. No matter who you are, no matter what your origins, you usually can find room for almost anything that is sweet, even after a satisfying dinner. In addition to people, many species (including horses, bears, and ants) are likely to pick sweet foods over others.[3] Common laboratory lore holds that if you're having trouble training your rat to press a lever, smearing a little milk chocolate on the lever will solve the problem.

It's not surprising that many species seek out sweets. Sweet foods and drinks tend to have a high concentration of sugar and, therefore, of calories. Calories provide energy for the body and are necessary for the body to function. In the natural surroundings of most species, including people, digestible calories are frequently not freely available in sufficient amounts. Therefore a preference for a concentrated source of calories is likely to help animals to survive.[4] One example of such a source would be ripe fruit, which, in addition to providing sugar, provides many vitamins and minerals necessary for body function and growth. It was very advantageous for our ancestors to prefer the taste of sweet, thus ensuring that they consumed ripe fruit whenever it was available.[5]

Now, thanks to advanced industrial technology, most people in developed countries can count on having a huge variety of cheap, readily available foods and drinks that contain sugar but very little else. From cupcakes to cola, candy to Cocoa Pebbles® (46% sugar by dry weight), we are confronted at every turn with foods whose main nutritive value consists of the calories they provide. As a result, we tend to consume these foods and drinks instead of others. For example, the preference for cheap, easily available, sweet soft drinks is blamed, in large part, for the huge numbers of calories that Americans now consume in the form of sugar—an average of 760 calories per person per day. These many hundreds of daily empty, sweet calories promote obesity and substitute for calories from more healthy foods such as milk, which contains the important nutrients protein and calcium.[6] In addition, the excess sugar we now consume can increase the incidence of medical problems such as cavities and heart disease.[7] It's essential for our health that we understand what causes our preference for sweet foods and drinks and what factors do and can affect that preference. (For an example of how soft drinks affect our nutrient consumption, see Figure 5.2.)

At Face Value

One way that you might be able to tell if the preference for sweet is primarily due to genes or to experience is to see how people react when they first encounter a sweet taste. One such approach has involved examining the reactions of newborn babies to a sweet taste. For example, Teresa R. Maone and her colleagues gave newborn infants two kinds of nipples to suck: gelatin-based nipples that had sugar embedded in them and standard latex nipples. As an infant sucked the sugar nipple, very small amounts of the sugar—just enough to provide a sweet taste—were released into the infant's mouth. The results showed that even premature babies who never before had food in their mouths sucked more often and stronger when there was sugar in the nipple.[8] These findings provide strong evidence that the preference for sweet is inborn and isn't dependent on experience with sweet foods or drinks.

Another similar approach that has been used to see if the preference for sweet is inborn is to examine the facial expressions of newborn babies' reactions to sweet and other substances. Scientist Jacob E. Steiner has shown that when babies, tested before any breast or bottle feeding, taste a sweet liquid, they show a facial expression very similar to that of adults when they taste something sweet (see Figure 5.3):

> The sweet stimulus leads to a marked relaxation of the face, resembling an expression of "satisfaction." This expression is often accompanied by a slight smile and was almost always followed by an eager licking of the upper lip, and sucking movements. This licking and sucking is almost

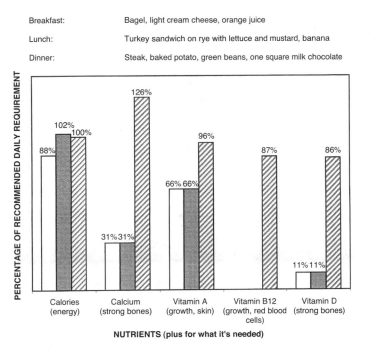

Breakfast: Bagel, light cream cheese, orange juice

Lunch: Turkey sandwich on rye with lettuce and mustard, banana

Dinner: Steak, baked potato, green beans, one square milk chocolate

□ Above meals

▨ Above meals plus 2 cans (24 ounces) cola

☑ Above meals plus 24 ounces fortified skim milk

Figure 5.2 Intake of various nutrients when given meals are consumed with two cans of cola versus the equivalent volume of fortified skim milk. The top part of the figure shows what foods someone who was eating in a very healthy way (for an American) might consume in a typical day. Note the absence of snacks, fried foods, alcohol, and sweets (except for one square of chocolate after dinner). The bottom part of the figure shows what percentage of the recommended daily requirements these foods would constitute for five important nutrients, as well as the percentages when, in addition to these foods, the person consumed two cans of cola or the equivalent volume of fortified skim milk. Note the inadequate daily intakes of calcium, vitamin A, vitamin B_{12}, and vitamin D when the cola, as opposed to the milk, is consumed. The calculations are for an adult who needs 2,000 calories per day to maintain his or her current weight. The cola provides 40 calories more than the milk. This would translate into a weight gain of approximately 4 pounds in 1 year. Note that children usually consume much less than 2,000 calories per day. Therefore, assuming no weight gain, two cans of cola would leave very few calories to be consumed as nutritious foods.

"aloud" sucking. The facial play elicited by the sucrose stimulus was labeled by the observers of the films and pictures as an expression of appreciation, liking or enjoyment.[9]

Rats also make facial expressions of satisfaction when a sweet substance is placed on their tongues, and both normal rats and rats missing the upper portions of their brains do this.[10] Note that these characteristic responses to a sweet taste, as described by Steiner, result in the sweet substance being taken into the mouth and swallowed. It appears that the acceptance and

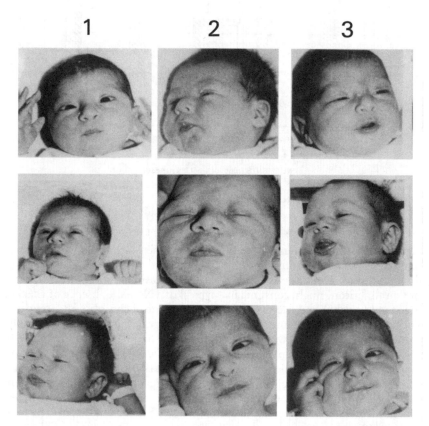

Figure 5.3 Facial expressions of newborn infants in reaction to sweet liquid. Typical facial expressions of newborn babies between birth and the first feeding: 1: Resting face. 2: Reaction to distilled water. 3: Response to sweet liquid. (Reprinted by permission from J. E. Steiner, "Facial Expressions of the Neonate Infant Indicating the Hedonics of Food-Related Chemical Stimuli," in *Taste and Development*, ed. J. M. Weiffenbach, Bethesda, MD: U.S. Department of Health, Education, and Welfare, 1977.)

consumption of sweet substances is, in many cases, an inborn reflex that can occur without conscious awareness.

It's also possible to look at the first experience with sweet of men and women. There have been several documented cases in which a culture that lacked sweet foods and drinks (with the exception of milk, which is slightly sweet) came into contact with a culture that regularly consumed sweet foods and drinks. In these cases none of the cultures previously without sugar rejected the sugar-containing foods and drinks of the other culture.[11] The Eskimos of northern Alaska are an example of such a sugar-adapting culture.[12] Once again, these findings seem to point to the preference for sweet being inborn, and not the result of experience.

Age and Sex

Let's take another tack in our investigation into the origins of the preference for sweet by seeing what happens to that preference as people age and become sexually mature.

Some people have speculated that exposing babies to a sweet taste very early in their lives would predispose them to preferring sweets later in life. Early exposure to a sweet taste happens in many cultures in the form of what's called prelacteal feeding, a feeding that is given to a newborn infant before that infant begins to consume milk. Prelacteal feeding usually consists of a solution of sugar and water[13] and is much sweeter than breast or cow's milk. Does prelacteal feeding predispose people to prefer sweet later in life? We know that 6-month-old babies who are being fed sweetened water prefer that water more than 6-month-olds who aren't being fed sweetened water,[14] but this could be due to a number of reasons. For example, perhaps the 6-month-old babies who are being fed sweetened water like it more simply because they're more familiar with it.

Some helpful information comes from an experiment with rats performed by Judith J. Wurtman and Richard J. Wurtman. They fed rat pups, 16 to 30 days of age, one of three nutritionally equivalent types of food containing either 0, 12, or 48% sugar. Between 31 and 63 days of age, the rats were given simultaneous access to all three types of food. During this period of simultaneous access, the rats' total consumption of sugar was unrelated to their previous exposure to sweet.[15] Therefore it appears that, at least for rats, early exposure to sweet does not influence later preference for sweet.

Let's consider still another approach to finding out whether experience can modify sweet preference. If exposure to sweet increases the subsequent preference for sweetness, then you would expect people's preference for sweetness to increase as they age. However, the opposite appears to be true.

Many studies have found a greater preference for the taste of sweet among younger, as opposed to older, people and rats.[16] Given that it's not clear how this change could be due to experience, other explanations must be sought. One possibility, although it has not yet been proven, is that younger animals prefer sweet substances because these animals are growing and thus have larger caloric requirements.[17]

Most of the studies examining the change in the preference for sweet from young to older ages have compared people and rats pre- and postpuberty. Therefore, perhaps the change in the preference for sweet due to age has something to do with the hormones of puberty. If this were true, then you might expect to find differences between men and women in their preferences for sweet. I'm sure you've heard people say that women like sweets more than men. As it turns out, there are no such clear differences. Among the studies that have been done, some have found a greater preference for sweet foods in men, and others in women.[18] Because the methods of all of these studies were so different, it's difficult to say whether their results are contradictory. The only firm conclusion that can be drawn regarding sex differences in the preference for sweet is that, as yet, no consistent, striking differences have been demonstrated.

Body Basics

Given that there doesn't seem to be anything about people's sweet preferences that clearly supports the effects of experience, let's look at some more physiological aspects of consuming sweet foods and drinks to see what they might tell us about the causes of the preference for sweet tastes.

You'll recall from the previous chapter that there's fairly substantial evidence that the tongue has special mechanisms for detecting the taste of sweet. In fact, we now know that there is genetic determination of several taste receptors important in the preference for sweet. In addition, as it turns out, in many species, including people, the chorda tympani nerve, the nerve that relays taste sensations from the tongue to the brain, contains more fibers maximally sensitive to the taste of sweet than to any other taste.[19] These findings suggest that the taste of sweet is more important to the body than any other taste, providing additional support for the hypothesis that the preference for sweet has a substantial genetic component.

However, it's still possible that early exposure to the taste of sweet could permanently increase the sensitivity of the chorda tympani fibers to sweet and thus be responsible for there being more chorda tympani fibers maximally sensitive to sweet than to other tastes. In rats, early exposure to an odor has been shown to increase neural responses to that odor.[20] To eliminate this possibility for the taste of sweet, experiments are needed that investigate the sensitivity of the chorda tympani nerve in either newborn babies or older people who have no previous exposure to the taste of sweet.

There's another physiological aspect of the consumption of sweet foods and drinks that can be used to explore whether the preference for a sweet taste is largely determined by the genes or by experience. Some people are unable to digest a particular kind of sugar called fructose, a sugar that is found in fruit and honey. If they consume it, they become nauseated and pale, vomit, develop diarrhea, and may even lose consciousness (other than that, they enjoy the experience). Such people are referred to as fructose intolerant. Because one of the products of the digestion of sucrose (table sugar) is fructose, people who are fructose intolerant can eat neither table sugar nor fruit. Just imagine becoming seriously ill each time you ate a cookie or even an apple. People who are fructose intolerant learn to decrease their consumption of sucrose and fructose. Nevertheless, some fructose-intolerant individuals persist in eating small amounts of fructose and sucrose and risking the consequences.[21] Apparently, in at least some cases, although being fructose intolerant can decrease the consumption of sweet foods and drinks, it doesn't decrease liking for the taste of sweet. The inborn preference for sweet may be so strong that even though tasting sweet is associated with severe illness, people may still prefer to ingest sweet foods and drinks.

The Role of Experience

Surely there are some experiences that can at least modify people's preferences for sweet foods and drinks. As is discussed in detail in the next chapter, we know that, in general, rats learn to prefer the foods that other rats prefer, and young children learn to prefer the foods that other people, including both children and adults, prefer. In addition, we know that young children develop an increased preference for foods that are given as rewards or that are accompanied by attention from adults.[22] Couldn't some of these influences be at least partly responsible for the preference for sweet? How many times have you heard a parent say to a child, "If you're really good you can have some candy"? However, none of this past research has been specifically directed at the preference for sweet. We don't know whether these sorts of manipulations of rats' and young children's experiences can modify their preferences for sweet. It may very well be the case that the preference for sweet is so strong to begin with that nothing can make it stronger.

We do know that, as the economy of a country develops, per capita consumption of sugar increases.[23] This would seem clear evidence of the effects of our surroundings on the preference for sweet. However, such an increase in sugar consumption might not be due to an increase in the liking for sugar. If more people can afford foods and beverages with a high sugar content as the economy of a country develops, those foods and drinks would probably be consumed more. But this change in consumption doesn't have anything to do with how much the people in that country actually like sweet foods and drinks.

Some scientists think that the greatest influence of experience on the preference for sweet isn't on the preference for sweet itself, but on the particular foods that we prefer to be sweetened.[24] We adults don't want a sugar coating added to our pot roast or fried eggs, but we would often prefer to eat ice cream or cake rather than pot roast or fried eggs. Our culinary experiences, which may be very different for different cultures, determine which foods we expect to be sweet. For example, in the United States, chocolate is usually sweetened, but in traditional Mexican cuisine it is not. As adults, it's by means of our preferences for commonly sweetened foods that we demonstrate our preferences for sweet.

When my son was young, I tried really hard to decrease his preference for sweet foods and drinks by controlling his contact with them. Basically, from the time he was born, I tried to keep him away from sweet foods and drinks, even when we were out and about, and I kept this up as long as possible. Until he was old enough to have learned on his own what cookies, ice cream, cake, candy, and soda were, I never let him have these foods or drinks, and I never talked about them. It has never been clear to me why parents often go out of their way to give their children these foods and drinks, particularly when the children are too young even to know what they really are. Although the children may look happy eating them, their health may, as a result, be compromised. Wouldn't it be much better if parents made their children happy just by playing with them? Though perhaps this early exposure has something to do with the fact that infants can be calmed by consuming sugar.[25]

Getting back to my son, restricting his access to high-sugar foods and drinks at home wasn't much of a problem when it came to soda, because neither my husband nor I like it and so we never have it in the house. However, I love cookies, ice cream, cake, and candy and allow myself one of these most days. For example, I usually have a box of cookies in the house and frequently I'll have a couple after dinner (my favorites are chocolate chip and oatmeal). At about age 2, my son began to notice that I was eating things after dinner that he wasn't eating. He'd watch me take the cookies out of the cabinet and eat them. Once he had learned to ask questions, he began asking me what I was eating. "Brown things," I'd say. "Oh," he'd reply. This worked for a year or two until, thanks to *Sesame Street* and Cookie Monster, he figured out that there was another name for the brown things I was eating. Then I started hiding them on a high shelf, and only taking some when I thought he wasn't watching. Unfortunately, in recent years, he's grown taller than I am, is very inquisitive, is determined to have whatever dessert I'm having, and navigates New York City on his own with money in his pocket. I'm afraid the days of my restricting his access to sweets are over, and he seems to like them as much as any other child. So much for that grand experiment!

Siblings and Other Relatives

Given that this chapter hasn't been doing too well at finding evidence that the preference for sweet foods and drinks can be modified by experience, let's consider some direct examinations of the contribution of genes to the preference for sweet tastes.

One way to do this is to try to breed animals that have different levels of preference for sweet. This has been done successfully with rats by selectively breeding together those rats that have the greatest and least preferences for sweet.[26] These findings suggest that genes can play a role in the preference for sweet in rats. But these results don't, of course, indicate that genes must play a role in the sweet preferences of other rats or, for that matter, in the sweet preferences of people.

The most traditional way of assessing the contribution of people's genes to some trait is to do twin studies. Twin studies look at how similar the members of fraternal twin pairs are, as compared to the members of identical twin pairs. Fraternal twins arise from two eggs, each fertilized by a different sperm. Thus, on average, they have half of their genes in common, just as any two siblings. Identical twins, on the other hand, arise from a single egg and sperm that split into two developing embryos very soon after conception. Thus, identical twins have identical genes. This means that if a trait has a substantial genetic component you would, on average, expect a pair of identical twins to be more similar with regard to this trait than a pair of fraternal twins would be. Twin studies that have looked at the preference for sweet have consistently failed to find greater similarity in sweet preferences for identical twin pairs than for fraternal twin pairs.[27] However, if you were to say that this means that the preference for sweet isn't largely due to genes, you would be jumping to conclusions.

Consider the study done by Lawrence S. Greene, J. A. Desor, and Owen Maller. In this study, both identical and fraternal twins ranked their preferences for different concentrations of sugar. As I previously indicated, the identical twins were no more similar in their rankings than the fraternal twins. But let's look at the ratings themselves. All of the twins tended to give very similar ratings for the different sugars.[28] I hope you can see that, if everyone gives the same ratings, it isn't possible for some pairs to be more similar in their ratings than other pairs. Thus, Greene and his colleagues' failure to find greater similarity in sweet preference for identical versus fraternal twin pairs doesn't necessarily mean that genes have little to do with the preference for sweet tastes. Greene and his colleagues' data could still be explained by saying that everyone easily learns a similar preference for sweet tastes. However, the virtual universality of this preference suggests a strong genetic component in the preference for sweet tastes. It's the weight added to this point by Greene and his colleagues' study that makes their research important.

All of the findings on the preference for sweet, including those of the twin studies, most strongly suggest that the preference for sweet is largely genetically influenced, and that, unlike some other largely genetic traits, it shows little variation among people. This lack of variation is actually not that surprising. As I previously mentioned, the taste of sweet is often a good indicator of available calories. Therefore you would expect evolution to result in a preference for sweet tastes that is strongly influenced by genes and that shows little variation. And what this means is that it's going to be very difficult for you, or anyone else, to decrease your preferences for sweet foods and drinks.

Salt Licks

The preference for salty tastes is, similar to the preference for sweet tastes, extremely strong and prevalent. With the exception of newborn babies, all people, and many other species, prefer salt. What's more, animals—including people—show a strong preference for salt the first time that they taste it.[29] Newborn babies appear not to be able to detect salt, possibly due to the taste mechanism for salt not yet being mature. However, after 4 months of age, the story is very different, and these babies, similar to older people and to other species, show a preference for salty water over plain water.[30]

It wouldn't be surprising for natural selection to result in an innate preference for salt in most species. Similar to calories, salt is essential for the body to function properly, in people as well as many other species. Many bodily functions depend on the presence of salt and even on a particular concentration of salt.[31] For example, the concentration of salt in the blood must be kept at a specific level. However, small amounts of salt are lost continually through sweat and through the action of the kidneys. If someone ceased to ingest salt, eventually the body would excrete water in an attempt to keep the concentration of salt in the blood at the optimal level, and that person would die of dehydration.[32]

Salt isn't easily available in the wild. Prior to industrialization, people sometimes had great difficulty obtaining enough salt. Many species must constantly seek salt in order to have sufficient amounts. In such situations, an inborn preference for salt would be extremely useful.[33] In the following sections we'll consider more direct evidence regarding the extent to which the preference for salt is due to genetic factors.

When Salt Is Really Needed

There has been a great deal of research concerning how animals, including people, seek out salt when they're deprived of it. Under such conditions, the preference for salt is increased (see Conversation Making Fact #5).[34] One factor that may be involved in this increased preference is the release of angiotensin,[35] which you learned earlier in this book occurs during conditions of water deprivation and has several consequences that increase drinking. Recall that, when an animal is salt deprived, the body of that animal will excrete water in an attempt to keep the concentration of salt in the animal's blood at optimal levels. This essentially deprives the animal of sufficient water, and therefore should result in the release of angiotensin. The

---

Conversation Making Fact #5

Have you ever wondered why, at certain times of the year, you often see small animals by the sides of rural roads—alive or dead? For example, the summer presence of porcupines near roads in the Catskill Mountains in New York state appears to be due to a need for salt. These porcupines must maintain approximately equal amounts of the chemicals potassium and sodium (a component of table salt) in their bodies in order to remain healthy. However, the summer vegetation in the Catskills generally contains at least a 300 to 1 ratio of potassium to sodium. As the porcupine's body works to remove the excess potassium, it also removes the sodium, and the porcupines cannot keep sufficient amounts of sodium in their bodies. Therefore the porcupines seek out sources of salt, which contain sodium but no potassium. The locations of two such sources are the salt left on the sides of roads from the previous winter and the wood on the sides of barns. Seeking out salt in either of these two locations is extremely dangerous for the porcupines, because in the one case they're likely to get run over and in the other they're likely to get shot by an angry farmer. Yet the majority of porcupines are driven to areas of human habitation by their need for sodium.[36]

possibility that angiotensin increases the preference for salt is based entirely on automatic physiological processes that are independent of an animal's experiences.

Psychologists Robert J. Contreras and Marion Frank did an experiment investigating another reason why the preference for salt increases when animals are salt deprived. These researchers first deprived rats of salt for 10 days, so that the rats' preferences for salt increased. They then measured the responses of various neuronal fibers in the chorda tympani nerve to different concentrations of salt. They found that, although the lowest concentration of salt that would induce a response in the nerve did not change, a higher concentration of salt was necessary to make the nerve respond as vigorously as before deprivation.[37] Similarly, neurons in the brain that respond to the presence of salt respond much less after salt deprivation.[38] Both of these findings suggest that, after deprivation, the rat would perceive a particular concentration of salt as equivalent to a lower concentration prior to deprivation and would therefore prefer foods with a relatively higher concentration of salt. Once again, these mechanisms for increasing the preference for salt seem to be based entirely on automatic physiological processes that are independent of an animal's experiences.

However, unlike any findings that have been obtained with regard to the preference for sweet, experience can modify a salt-deficient rat's salt-seeking behavior. A salt-deficient rat will eat less of a salt-enriched diet if it has recently interacted with other rats that aren't salt deprived.[39] In other words, social interaction can affect a rat's food preferences. Any rat that can use another rat's experiences to shape its own food preferences, rather than experimenting itself, is going to increase its chances of survival.

Evidence for the influence of physiological state on the preference for salt has also been seen in people. For example, in 1940 L. Wilkins and C. P. Richter published a letter written to them by the parents of a boy who had an unusual preference for salt due to a tumor in his adrenal gland:

> When he was around a year old he started licking all the salt off the crackers and always asked for more. He didn't say any words at this time, but he had a certain sound for everything and a way of letting us know what he wanted. . . . [H]e started chewing the crackers; but he only chewed them until he got the salt off, then he would spit them out. He did the same with bacon, but he didn't swallow the pieces. . . . In an effort to try to find a food that he would like well enough to chew up and swallow, we gave him a taste of practically everything. So, one evening during supper, when he was about eighteen months old, we used some salt out of the shaker on some food. He wanted some, too. We gave him just a few grains to taste, thinking he wouldn't like it; but he ate it and asked for more. . . . [T]his one time was all it took for him to learn what was in the shaker. For

a few days after that, when I would feed him his dinner at noon, he would keep crying for something that wasn't on the table and always pointed to the cupboard. I didn't think of the salt, so I held him up in front of the cupboard to see what he wanted. He picked out the salt at once; and in order to see what he would do with it, I let him have it. He poured some out and ate it by dipping his finger in it. After this he wouldn't eat any food without the salt, too. I would purposely let it off the table and even hide it from him until I could ask the doctor about it.... But when I asked Dr. [ ] about it, he said, "Let him have it. It won't hurt him." So we gave it to him and never tried to stop it altogether.... [B]ut he wouldn't eat his breakfast or supper without it. He really cried for it and acted like he had to have it.... At eighteen months he was just starting to say a few words, and salt was among the first ones. We had found that practically everything he liked real well was salty, such as crackers, pretzels, potato chips, olives, pickles, fresh fish, salt mackerel, crisp bacon and most foods and vegetables if I added more salt.[40]

Tragically, the boy had died in a hospital because the hospital diet did not give him the salt that he craved and his body needed.

There are several special situations in which the body's needs may increase the preference for salt. For example, similar to what has been found with the taste of sweet, 9- to 15-year-old children prefer saltier liquids more than do adults.[41] We can speculate, as with sweet, that these findings are related to the evolutionary history of humans. If, during this history, there was generally an increased need for salt by younger, growing people, some automatic mechanism that results in relatively higher preferences for salt among young people might have increased their chances of survival and therefore have been passed on to future generations.

It has also been shown that when mice live in cold surroundings (45–48°F), 6 hours per day for 4 days, their preferences for salty liquid increases. The authors of this research speculate that taking increased salt under such conditions helps the mice to survive better in the cold. The increased salt intake may increase blood pressure, which can help decrease the chances of frostbite in people.[42] Therefore, perhaps mice (and people) evolved such that they prefer salt more when they are cold. These findings make me wonder if people attending fall football games in cold climates would be well advised to take along plenty of salty foods, such as potato chips and pretzels. But keep in mind that there is as yet no research indicating that the findings with mice would also apply to people.

And finally there's a very recent study that I find particularly intriguing. I'm a big fan of physical fitness and sweat quite a bit when exercising. I've always wondered whether the resulting lost salt affects my preference for salt. Psychologists M. Leshem, A. Abutbul, and R. Eilon have shown that, immediately after exercising for 1 hour, male university students preferred a higher concentration of salt in tomato soup than did students who had not exercised. The students were allowed to add as much salt as they wanted to the soup, and the exercisers added 50% more than the nonexercisers. In fact, even 12 hours after exercising, the exercisers still preferred a higher concentration of salt in their soup than the nonexercisers.[43] It appears that people, and not just other species, are quite good at finding ways of obtaining extra salt when some of their bodies' salt content has been lost.

How Much Is Too Much?

Salt isn't just consumed when people and other animals are deprived of it; it's also consumed when there's no need for it whatsoever.[44] Similar to sweet foods, salty foods are more easily and inexpensively available now than when people first evolved. Consequently, the preference for salt has resulted in consumption of salt in amounts far exceeding the body's needs—an average among U.S. adults of 10 g per day, in comparison to the recommended 6 g per day.[45] Many scientists believe that this excess salt consumption contributes to high blood pressure, although other scientists dispute this.[46]

No matter what you think about this controversy, it has sparked much interest about whether it's possible to modify people's preferences for salt so that they eat less of it. We've known for many years that, similar to the preference for sweet, after the age of 2 years, children learn which foods are supposed to be salty and reject foods that don't contain the customary degree of saltiness. But can adults' preferences for the amount of salt in a food be modified?

In fact, in contrast to findings with sweet, there is some evidence that the preference for salt can be directly modified in adults. For example, if adults are put on a low-salt diet for several weeks, they will begin to prefer foods that have less salt.[47] Similarly, men and women on a low-salt diet given salt tablets to swallow subsequently add less salt to unsalted tomato juice.[48] Other evidence of modified salt preference seems related to very recent experience with low or high amounts of salt. For example, if men and women are first given lunch and then, immediately afterward, are given vegetable broth to eat, they prefer the broth to have a lower concentration of salt if the lunch has been high-salt (cheese sandwich plus high-salt chicken noodle soup) as opposed to if the lunch has been low-salt (low-salt chicken sandwich and low-salt chicken noodle soup).[49] Thus there have been several experiments showing that experience can modify the preference for salt. And, unlike the situation for sweet, there's some possibility that you might be able to decrease your preference for salt.

Beyond Mother's Milk

Milk contains calcium, essential to building and maintaining strong bones. Nearly every newborn baby avidly consumes milk—not surprisingly given that milk contains a type of sugar, lactose. However, this isn't the case for every adult. Some groups of people, such as Northern Europeans, drink a lot of milk and also eat a great deal of milk products, such as cheese. Other groups, such as the Chinese, consume neither milk nor its products. Still other groups, such as the Hausa-Fulani of Nigeria, eat yogurt but don't drink milk.

It turns out that these groups differ not only in terms of how much milk they drink, but also in what's called lactose intolerance, the inability to digest the sugar present in milk. Whether someone is lactose intolerant depends on whether his or her body has sufficient lactase, a chemical that breaks down lactose during digestion. When people without lactase drink milk, the result is diarrhea and enough flatulence to be unpleasant to those nearby.[50] I was much relieved when I figured out that my husband, who is of Eastern European descent, was lactose intolerant, and when he then stopped drinking milk. Lactose intolerant people can, however, eat cheese and yogurt because bacteria in these milk products have already largely broken down the lactose.

Many groups of adults tend to be lactose intolerant, including many groups in the United States (see Figure 5.4). In fact, by 1.5 to 3 years of age, most people around the world become largely unable to manufacture lactase, a loss that is shared with all adults of all other species. In other words, men and women who can digest milk are the exception in the adult animal world.[51] This means you shouldn't give your cat milk! Men and women who can digest milk are such a glaring exception in the animal kingdom that it raises the question as to how such people could have come to exist.

One possibility is that, if you always drink milk from the time you're born, your body adapts by continuing to produce lactase beyond early childhood.[52] No other species could be in such a situation because, in other species, young animals are weaned to make way for subsequent offspring. But people have kept cows and goats for thousands of years and so can continue to drink milk into adulthood without jeopardizing the nutrition of their younger siblings. If this explanation of lactose tolerance in adults were correct, you would predict that intolerant adults given milk to drink over a period of time would start to manufacture lactase and be more able to digest milk. However, such experiments have shown very little, if any, increases in lactase activity.[53]

Therefore we must look elsewhere to explain lactose tolerance in adult humans. Given the title of this chapter, you won't be surprised to learn that that explanation lies in the genes. Whether someone can manufacture lactase as an adult is genetically determined.[54] But why did people, but not other species, evolve this ability?

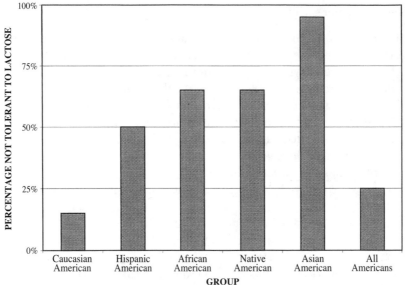

Figure 5.4 Percentage of various groups who are not tolerant to lactose. (Adapted from D. France, "Groups Debate Role of Milk in Building a Better Pyramid," *The New York Times* [June 29, 1999]: F7.

The most popular theory is that people first domesticated cattle for their meat and for the work they could do. Then, during periods of famine, people who could successfully consume the milk from these cattle were more likely to survive and reproduce than other people. In this way people who were lactose tolerant became more common in the population. This evolutionary process would have been particularly likely to occur with people living far from the equator. There's more cloud cover and less sunlight away from the equator than near it. Sunlight on the skin of people results in the synthesis of vitamin D, a vitamin that assists in the necessary absorption of calcium into the body.[55] Therefore, people living far from the equator aren't able to synthesize lots of vitamin D. Because the digestion of lactose by lactase also assists with the absorption of calcium, consumption of lactose accompanied by lactase manufacture may have been important in the survival of human adults living away from the equator. Consistent with this explanation, most groups of people who possess large amounts of lactase tend to keep cattle, drink milk from those cattle, and live far from the equator.[56]

Once again, please keep in mind that even though lactose intolerance may result in certain men and women not drinking milk, this doesn't necessarily mean that these people don't like milk; many of them would drink it if a magic pill would just prevent the diarrhea and flatulence (and such pills do, in fact, exist). We have here another case in which genes seem to affect the frequency with which a food or drink is consumed, but not the actual liking for that food or drink.

Because milk contains so many important nutrients, such as calcium, the U.S. Department of Agriculture and the U.S. Department of Health and Human Services recommend that adults consume two to three servings per day of milk and milk products.[57] But such recommendations can obviously be a problem for many people. For example, governmental recommendations concerning which foods should be eaten form the basis of many public school lunch and food assistance programs. Given that many of the people participating in these programs are from groups that are mostly lactose intolerant, are the government's recommendations good for people's health? Or do the government's recommendations just support the dairy industry's "Got milk?" campaign? Not all milk products contain significant amounts of lactose, therefore, perhaps people should be advised to focus on consuming those products. Such issues have resulted in much acrimonious debate that may or may not cause changes in the U.S. government's recommendations regarding milk consumption.[58] This is just one example of how the psychology of eating and drinking can help to inform federal policy.

The Bitter End and Other Points for the Genes

Several other areas of research implicate genes as important contributors to food preferences. First, as you'll recall from the previous chapter, the ability to taste very low concentrations of phenylthiocarbamide (PTC) and 6-N-propylthiouracil (PROP) is determined by genes. And, as you also know, PTC/PROP supertasters are more likely than other people to taste food as bitter and therefore dislike substances such as saccharin, caffeine, beer, grapefruit juice, and dark green vegetables. However, these aren't the only food preferences related to PTC/PROP tasting. For example, psychologists Jean Ann Anliker, Linda Bartoshuk, and their colleagues examined the relationships between sensitivity to PROP and preferences for various foods and drinks in 5- to 7-year-old boys and girls. Children who were PROP tasters liked cheese relatively less and milk relatively more than nontasters.[59] (I could have told them that's what they would find.)

The influence of genes on the aversion to bitter tastes has had implications beyond what we and other species like to eat. It appears that the aversion to bitter tastes may have resulted in some species evolving so that their bodies themselves taste bitter, so that people and other animals wouldn't eat these species. For example, you may know that some birds and their eggs are good to eat and some are not. In fact, people's rankings of how good various birds are to eat correspond well with the preferences of various species that prey on birds, species such as rats, cats, and ferrets. One of the most famous bad-tasting birds is the New Guinean Pitohui (just guess what people say when they taste it!). It turns out that there's a chemical in the skin and feathers of this bird that makes it taste bad. In general, birds and their eggs that are easy to see and thus relatively likely to be attacked are more likely to taste bad—particularly bitter—and vice versa. This helps keep predators away from the easy-to-see species.[60]

Before we leave evidence concerning the taste of bitter, look at the pictures of the babies in Figure 5.5. This figure shows what babies' faces look like when they taste bitter. This expression has been described as follows:

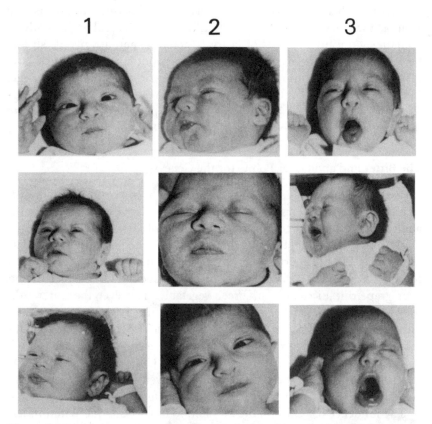

Figure 5.5 Facial expressions of newborn infants to bitter liquid: 1: Resting Face. 2: Reaction to distilled water. 3: Response to bitter liquid. (Reprinted by permission from J. E. Steiner, "Facial Expressions of the Neonate Infant Indicating the Hedonics of Food-Related Chemical Stimuli," in *Taste and Development*, ed. J. M. Weiffenbach, Bethesda, MD: U.S. Department of Health, Education, and Welfare, 1977.)

Stimulation with the bitter fluid leads to a typical arch form opening of the mouth with the upper lip elevated, the mouth angles depressed, and the tongue protruded in a flat position. This expression involves primarily the mouth region of the face and ... was typically followed by spitting or even by the preparatory movements of vomiting.[61]

When adults watched babies making this expression they described it as a rejection response.[62] This facial expression is similar to the rejection response that rats make when they're given an aversive substance to taste.[63] This information, together with that on the characteristic facial response to sweet, suggests that there are two distinct inborn taste response systems: an acceptance system and a rejection system. These two systems are apparently universally present in at least two species (people and rats) and probably other species as well, and they appear to be genetically linked to certain tastes—the acceptance system to the taste of sweet and the rejection system to the taste of bitter. These two systems increase the chances that newborn babies without taste experience, or animals experiencing new foods, will take in substances that provide calories but won't take in substances that could be poisonous.[64]

Let's turn now to more general evidence indicating innate systems of food preference. You already know that being deprived of certain nutrients such as salt can automatically, without any previous experience, increase preference for that substance. In fact, in general, being hungry makes people rate foods—including specific odors and tastes—as more pleasant. Hungry people aren't better at detecting low concentrations of chemicals; they're just more likely to say that they like a given food, particularly a high-calorie food.[65] It would be hard to see how people could have survived all of these thousands of years if this weren't the case. But it does make you wonder if it's such a good idea to go grocery shopping when you're hungry.

A related, but more controversial, area of research has focused on whether eating certain nutrients at one meal will make it more likely that you'll eat different nutrients at the next meal. Judith J. Wurtman and Richard J. Wurtman believe, based on their research, that food intake modifies chemical transmission among neurons in the brain. This modification, they feel, then changes the probability of what will subsequently be eaten. For example, if breakfast consisted mostly of carbohydrates, people tend to eat more proteins at lunch, and vice versa.[66] However, there has been disagreement over the degree to which Wurtman and Wurtman's results apply to daily eating situations outside of the laboratory.[67]

Finally, I would like to tell you a little bit about a personality trait called sensation seeking and its relationships with food preferences. Research on sensation seeking was pioneered by psychologist Marvin Zuckerman, who has described sensation seeking as the tendency to seek out new or unusual experiences.[68] How much of a sensation seeker someone is can be measured by asking that person to choose between such statements as "I like 'wild' uninhibited parties" and "I prefer quiet parties with good conversation."

Several studies have shown strong relationships between sensation seeking and certain food preferences. Michael E. Smith and I found that people who scored high on sensation seeking tended to report a greater preference for spicy foods, and people who scored low on sensation seeking tended to report a greater preference for bland and sweet foods. We also noted that people who scored high on sensation seeking tended to prefer items such as alcohol and shellfish, foods that are often reputed to cause illness; but people who scored low on sensation seeking tended to prefer items such as bread and corn, foods that are rarely reputed to cause illness.[69]

Because there appear to be many relationships between sensation seeking and food preferences, there may be a common basis for some aspects of sensation seeking and some food preferences. Further, based on studies examining sensation seeking and food preferences among identical and fraternal twins, Zuckerman has argued that there's a genetic component to sensation seeking.[70] Therefore Zuckerman's research raises the possibility that there may be genetic influence on whether someone likes strong-tasting foods.

You'll remember that I used to belong to the Cuisine Group described in the previous chapter. At one meeting, I gave everyone a sensation seeking questionnaire. I got one of the lowest scores possible, and everyone else (these people who would eat *anything*) got among the highest scores possible. So it appears that I have at least two factors with genetic input that have contributed to my food finickiness: I'm a PTC/PROP supertaster and I'm unusually low in sensation seeking, an unfortunate double whammy.

Conclusion

In the world in which we evolved, eating sweet things and salty things was virtually always good for us, as was drinking milk, if we could digest it. Therefore it would have helped people to survive if they liked to consume these things the first time that they encountered them, with no learning period, particularly if they were hungry. Under such conditions, survival is more likely if preferences for these substances are strongly influenced by the genes. Now we live in a world where there's too much of these substances, a world in which advertisers try to get us to buy and then consume things that we shouldn't, and our genetic tendencies can get us into deep trouble. Unfortunately, even when food preferences and food aversions can be modified by experience, this doesn't necessarily mean that the resulting eating is ideal, as you'll see in the next chapter.

CHAPTER 6

One Person's Meat
Is Another Person's Poison

The Effects of Experience on Food Preferences

ℰ

> No other fundamental aspect of our behavior as a species except
> sexuality is so encumbered by *ideas* as eating; the entanglements
> of food with religion, with both belief and sociality, are particu-
> larly striking.
>
> Sidney W. Mintz (1996)[1]

The previous chapter may have convinced you that much of what you do
and don't like to eat has a strong genetic basis, but that's by no means the
whole story. There's a great deal of variation in what people like to eat that
clearly has no genetic basis. Take entomophagy (insect eating). Many insects
are highly nutritious and are widely consumed. For example, caterpillars
consist of 30–80% protein, and dozens of different species are eaten in
Cameroon, Mexico, and Zaire. In the United States, the government officially
approves of entomophagy: the Food and Drug Administration permits as
many as 56 insect parts in every peanut butter and jelly sandwich. Nevertheless, in the United States most people, no matter where they immi-
grated from, think eating insects is disgusting.[2] Why are there such huge
differences in food preferences? Do these differences in food preferences help
us and other animals to survive?

Suppose you must live in the wild without any of the benefits of civilization, under the sort of conditions in which people evolved. Think about
how many food choices you would have. There would be many different
kinds of plants and animals that you could conceivably put into your mouth
and swallow. Which ones will taste good to eat and which ones won't? Which
ones will keep you healthy and which ones won't? Which combination of
foods will give you all of the nutrients that you need? And if you move from,

say, an open savanna to a shady woodland, the food choices available to you will completely change. How do you decide what to eat in your new surroundings?

When people are born, they consume only milk. But usually by the time a child can walk, the child is eating a large variety of foods. How do young children and other animals learn what foods they should be eating when their parents are no longer around?[3]

For omnivores such as us, our genes just can't preprogram all of our food preferences. There are too many choices and the choices change too much. Somehow, omnivores have to learn what foods are good to eat and what foods aren't, and they had best do that as quickly and efficiently as possible and as often as necessary. Eat the wrong thing and you'll die; there are plenty of poisonous plants and animals.

Fortunately, we and other omnivores figure out pretty well what is and isn't good to eat under changing conditions. In the laboratory, psychologist Paul Rozin showed that thiamine (vitamin B_1)–deficient rats preferred a food with thiamine over a food without thiamine.[4] Moose on Isle Royale in Lake Superior consume large amounts of aquatic vegetation each summer in order to obtain the sodium they need and that is missing from the land vegetation.[5] In classic research known as the cafeteria experiments, psychologist Curt P. Richter showed that rats given a wide choice of nutritive substances—such as sugar, olive oil, cod liver oil, and baker's yeast—did quite well at selecting all of the nutrients that they needed.[6]

But what about people? Do our preferences also result in our eating a balanced diet? If you've raised a child, some well-meaning person probably told you at some point not to worry about your child's finicky eating, that over a period of time children choose to eat the nutrients that they need. My own parents were convinced that, as long as they gave me vitamin pills, I'd be fine. Many people, including some pediatricians, believe this because of famous research done in the 1920s and 1930s by physician Clara M. Davis. Davis's research used 15 healthy babies between the ages of 6 and 11 months who, at the time the experiment began, had little experience with foods other than milk. All of the babies lived in a hospital for the 6 months to 4.5 years that they participated in the experiment. (Such an experiment would never be permitted now.) At meal times a nurse presented each child with a tray containing a variety of foods, such as different meats, cereals, eggs, milk, fruits, and vegetables. The nurse would give the child any item to which the child pointed. The children sometimes went on binges during which they consumed large amounts of particular foods for extended periods, but these binges eventually stopped. Over long periods of time the children ate fairly well-balanced diets and grew well.[7]

So parents should just stay out of it and let babies choose their own foods, correct? Unfortunately, it isn't that simple. There were two major problems with Davis's experiment. First, even though they were told not to, it's possible that the nurses who were giving the foods to the babies unconsciously—or perhaps even consciously—affected the babies' choices. Suppose a baby you were taking care of ate nothing but beets for five meals in a row. Could you just ignore this and not nudge the baby to eat something else? Second, the sweetest choices available to the babies were milk and fruit and, not surprisingly, those items were also the ones chosen most often. These babies showed the sweet tooth described in the previous chapter. Luckily the sweetest choices available to them, milk and fruit, were also quite nutritious. It seems unlikely that Davis's subjects would have chosen an equally nutritious diet if candy and soda had been available.

This all means that, unfortunately, unless you remove the nonnutritious foods from your child's surroundings, you can't rely on your child to choose a nutritious diet. And as a parent, I can testify to how difficult ensuring a healthy food world for your child can be. Since he started visiting friends' homes, my son (who is now 18) has been repeatedly offered candy, soda, chips, and other wonderful but nonnutritious foods, which most of our culture seems to think appropriate to have available for children at all times of the day or night. This gave my husband and me three choices: (1) call the relevant parents and nicely ask them to change their ways (what do you think is the probability of an enthusiastic response to a call like that?); (2) tell our son that he can't go places where unhealthy food is available, thereby isolating him from just about everybody; or (3) try to educate our son about what foods he should eat, and then grin and bear the situation. You can guess which one we picked.

Nevertheless, in many situations, people, similar to rats, choose fairly balanced diets. But we still need to know how they do that and what's responsible for the huge variety in our food preferences. How do our experiences influence these preferences? Why is it that some people learn to like eating insects and others don't? Perhaps if we knew the answers to these questions we could help our children to eat healthier foods. The rest of this chapter will tell you what scientists have learned about the effects of experience on food preferences.

Tried and True: Experience With Particular Foods

There are many ways in which experience with a particular food can increase or decrease your subsequent preference for that food. At least in the world in which people evolved, most of these food preference changes helped people to survive.

Familiarity With a Food

You're at a dinner party and your hosts serve you a plate of what is supposedly food, but there's nothing on the plate that you recognize. There's a mound of something green and squishy and some things shaped like sticks that are purple, complemented by a pile of small orange ovoids. Most likely you wouldn't feel terribly enthusiastic about eating this dinner. Such feelings have been immortalized in college students' description of certain cafeteria dishes as "mystery meat." Our disinclination to like and eat foods with which we are unfamiliar isn't unique. In general, people and other animals have a fear of new things, which is known in the scientific literature as neophobia.[8] In general we prefer foods and situations that are familiar.[9]

Some people are more neophobic than others. When it comes to food, neophobic people don't just avoid trying new foods. If they're persuaded to try them, they tend to rate them lower than do neophilics (people who enjoy trying new foods).[10]

If we are afraid of new foods and prefer familiar ones, then simply exposing someone to a new food should increase that person's preference for the food. Many experiments have shown that this is indeed the case. For example, psychologist Patricia Pliner gave male college students between 0 and 20 tastes of individual novel fruit juices, such as guava, mango, and soursop. Juices that had been tasted more frequently received higher preference ratings.[11] As another example, psychologist Leann L. Birch and her colleagues repeatedly asked 2- to 5-year-old children to just look at some fruits and to both taste and look at other fruits. All of the fruits that they used were novel ones such as kiwi, papaya, lychee, and sugar palm. Preference for a fruit's appearance was greater the more times that a child had seen that fruit. Preference for a fruit's taste was increased only if a child had tasted that fruit. Therefore, Birch and her colleagues concluded that in order to increase preference for the taste of a food, experience with the actual taste of the food is necessary.[12]

If familiarity increases preference for a food, then why do we not end up eating, say, bananas, day after day, year after year? The more you eat them, the more you should like them as compared to something else, until finally you're eating nothing but bananas. This wouldn't be very adaptive because no natural food contains all of the nutrition that a grown person should have. Fortunately, after we eat something, there's a short-lived decrease in preference for that particular food. In other words, exposure to a food appears to cause a temporary, short-term decrease in preference for that food, as well as a long-term increase in preference for that food.[13]

A number of experiments on food preferences have demonstrated this phenomenon. In psychologist David J. Stang's experiment, women repeatedly tasted 15 spices, including chile powder, mustard, cloves, and marjoram. The preference ratings for the spices decreased with repeated tastings but recovered after a week without tastings.[14] In another experiment, psychologist Barbara J. Rolls and her colleagues showed that female student nurses would consume more sandwiches if the available sandwiches had four different fillings (cheese, egg, ham, and tomato) as compared to if the available sandwiches had only one of these fillings.[15]

This tendency of people and other animals to prefer familiar foods coexists with a tendency to avoid recently consumed foods. For omnivores such as us, this combination of strategies is very useful, ensuring that a variety of familiar foods, and thus a variety of nutrients, is eaten.[16] When it comes to food preferences, familiarity does appear to breed (some) contempt, while absence makes the heart grow (somewhat) fonder.

It's Good and Good for You!

At the beginning of this chapter you learned that rats, and sometimes even people, are fairly good at selecting foods that have the nutrients that they need. When an animal that needs a particular nutrient shows a preference for a food containing that nutrient this is called a specific hunger.[17] (See Conversation Making Fact #6.) Researchers have some good ideas about what causes specific hungers.

Rozin's experiments with thiamine-deficient rats, which were described at the start of this chapter, give us some clues. The rats spilled the thiamine-deficient food from their dish, the same way that they treated a food to which quinine, a very bitter substance, had been added. Even when no longer thiamine deficient, the rats preferred to eat nothing when they were hungry

---

Conversation Making Fact #6

One type of specific hunger has been of particular concern to physicians. Some children and pregnant women repeatedly consume nonnutritive substances such as paint, plaster, and dirt. Because such food cravings are most likely to appear in people who need a lot of nutrients, it has been proposed that these cravings are the result of specific hungers for minerals such as iron.[18]

if the only choice was the old, deficient food.[19] Thus the rats appeared to have an aversion to the thiamine-deficient food.

Based on evidence such as this, a good explanation for specific hungers is that animals develop aversions to nutritionally deficient foods.[20] In other words, animals may appear to like a nutritional food solely because they don't like the other deficient food that is available, and the nutritional food is all that is left. This is similar to when I eat broccoli because the only other available vegetable is brussels sprouts; this does not mean that I *like* broccoli. However, there's also evidence that animals can learn a preference for a particular food that makes them healthier, a food tasted right before an animal recovers from illness. Such a learned preference is known as the medicine effect.[21]

Nevertheless, before you think that the existence of specific hungers will allow all animals to select a perfect set of foods to eat, there are two cautions. First, it has been very difficult to demonstrate specific hungers in rats fed diets deficient in certain nutrients, such as vitamins A and D.[22] Second, the experiments on specific hungers give the subjects a very limited choice of foods. In situations more similar to real life, when there are lots of foods available, it might be quite difficult for people and other animals to choose the nutritionally best foods. Once again, we can't count on having great bodily wisdom.

Often what you need to eat isn't a particular nutrient but simply calories. Every animal needs a certain number of calories to fuel its activity. In the world in which people evolved, calories were much more scarce than they are now. So it's not surprising that we and other animals have evolved to learn to prefer foods that are dense in calories. A great many experiments support this conclusion. As just one example, E. L. Gibson and J. Wardle showed that the best way to predict how much 4- to 5-year-old children would prefer different fruits and vegetables was not how sweet they were, or how much protein they had, or whether the children had tried them, but how dense in calories they were. When I read this study I was fascinated by the fact that the most calorie-dense fruits and vegetables turned out to be, in order, bananas, potatoes, peas, and grapes,[23] very similar to my fruit and vegetable preference order when I was growing up.

But, you might say, always preferring foods that have lots of calories isn't always the best goal. In order to consume an appropriate number of calories, you should show a large preference for a high-calorie food when your body needs calories, and a small preference for a high-calorie food when your body does not need calories. This does happen sometimes. Psychologist D. A. Booth and his colleagues showed that if men and women are hungry when they eat meals containing a lot of disguised high-calorie starch, their preference for these meals increases. However, if people are full when they eat these meals, they later show less preference for them. Further, people will even learn to eat smaller meals when they contain a lot of disguised high-calorie starch.[24] Psychologists Leann L. Birch and Mary Deysher got similar results with preschool children. The preschoolers learned to eat smaller amounts of cookies or crackers following a snack (vanilla or chocolate pudding) that had regularly contained a large number of calories, and larger amounts of cookies or crackers following a snack (vanilla or chocolate pudding) that had regularly contained a smaller number of calories.[25]

I can hear your puzzlement. If people adjust their meal size depending on how many calories they have eaten or are eating, why does anyone become overweight? Keep in mind that the research shows that people eat fewer, not necessarily few, calories when they're full or when they're consuming other calories. Someone could be eating fewer calories when full than when hungry, but enough calories to gain weight in both situations.

Now that you understand how our preferences for foods are affected by their caloric densities, you should also understand our obsession with foods that are high in fat, for example, french fries, ice cream, fried chicken, scrambled eggs, butter—the list goes on and on. Fat is much denser in calories than are protein or carbohydrate; fat contains 9 calories per gram, but protein and carbohydrate each contain only 4 calories per gram. Therefore we have a learned strong preference for high-fat foods. Because of this preference, and because, for most people in the United States, high-fat food is easily available, many of us end up consuming much more fat than is recommended.[26] This tendency to learn to prefer high-fat foods, combined with our largely genetic preferences for sweet and salty foods, though originally useful, gets us into a lot of trouble in our current environment.

When Eating a Food Makes You Sick (or Seems to)

Have you ever eaten something, become sick, and then did not want to eat that food again? Perhaps one time you drank too much champagne, became sick, and now you cannot stand the thought of even tasting champagne? If so, you're not alone. A questionnaire given by Iris Ophir, Kerry E. Strauss, and myself to over 500 college students[27] found that, on average, each student reported one food aversion of this sort. In general the aversions were strong and had persisted a long time; 62% of the aversive foods had never been eaten again, even though the aversions had been acquired an average of about 5 years previously. Many of the students wrote quite explicit derogatory comments about the aversive food in the margins of the questionnaire. For example, one student wrote that hot dogs, a food that popped up relatively frequently on the questionnaire, "are 100 percent s_ _ _!"

This type of learning, known in the research literature as taste aversion learning, is extremely powerful. Usually, a person has to get sick only once after eating a particular food in order for a taste aversion to form, and taste aversions can last an extremely long time. The illness needs to be gastrointestinal in order for this type of learning to occur. Taste aversions are more likely to form to novel, as opposed to familiar, foods. Taste aversion learning occurs similarly in a huge variety of different species, including people and rats. In fact, the food aversions described in the previous section, the aversions to nutritionally deficient foods that make it appear that animals have specific hungers, are thought to be taste aversions.[28]

Taste aversions were first observed by farmers trying to get rid of rats. The farmers found it was difficult to kill rats by putting out poisoned bait. The rats would take only small samples of any new food, in this case the bait, and if they then became ill, they would subsequently avoid the bait. For this reason, farmers called the taste aversion learning phenomenon bait shyness.[29]

Another report of taste aversion learning in nature came from a well-known psychologist at the University of Pennsylvania, Martin E. P. Seligman (president of the American Psychological Association in 1998). In 1972 Seligman described how he ate sauce béarnaise on steak and subsequently became ill with what was definitely stomach flu: his work colleague who had not eaten the steak came down with the same affliction, and his wife who had eaten the steak did not. Yet, even though he was absolutely convinced that the sauce béarnaise did not cause his illness, Seligman acquired an aversion to it. Because of this famous story, taste aversion learning has also been called the sauce béarnaise phenomenon.[30]

Psychologist John Garcia and his colleagues were the first to study taste aversion learning in the laboratory. Garcia noticed that his rats ate less after being irradiated. Apparently the irradiation made the rats gastrointestinally ill and they associated the illness with the food, resulting in a taste aversion to the food.[31] Since Garcia's original discovery, most of the research on taste aversion learning in rats has made the subjects sick by means of injection.[32]

You may wonder how taste aversion experiments are done with people—how are people made sick? It's obviously difficult because researchers don't want to inject people unless there's an extremely good reason. Therefore a variety of other techniques have been used. One consists of putting the participant in a rotating chair. There's a big problem with this, however. If the procedure is very successful, there can be quite a mess for the experimenter to clean up. For this reason, and also for the participants' safety, researchers have learned which symptoms indicate that someone is about to vomit (forewarned is forearmed); with this information, they can stop the chair before the participant vomits.[33] Possibly a more practical means for making people ill for taste aversion experiments uses a large rotating cylinder whose inside is painted with vertical stripes. The participant sits inside the cylinder and, while it rotates, tilts his or her head to the right and then to the left. This procedure really works, and if vomiting seems imminent, a participant can simply close his or her eyes.[34] If you're wondering why anyone would volunteer for such an experiment, the participants tend to be neophilic and/or sensation seekers (I'd never be in one of these experiments).

By far the most famous paper on taste aversion learning was published in 1966 by psychologists John Garcia and Robert A. Koelling. The design of their experiment, shown in Figure 6.1, was very clever. In the first part of the

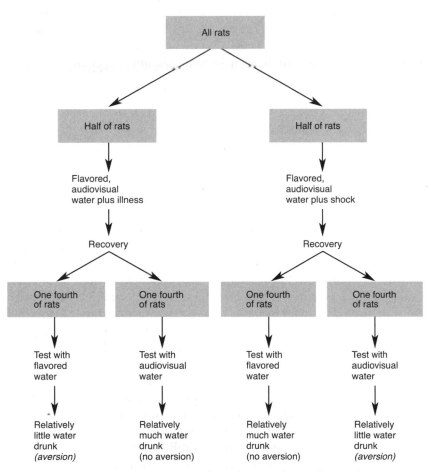

Figure 6.1 Garcia and Koelling's procedure showing the tendency of rats to associate taste with illness and audiovisual stimuli with shock. (Adapted from J. Garcia and R. A. Koelling, "Relation of Cue to Consequence in Avoidance Learning," *Psychonomic Science* 4[1966]:123–124.)

experiment, Garcia and Koelling allowed thirsty rats to lick at a spout. With each lick, all of the rats got flavored water and there was a light flash and a click. Half of these rats were shocked whenever they licked. The other half, while licking, were made ill, either by irradiation or injection. Several days later, in the second part of the experiment, after all of the rats had recovered, the rats were again allowed to drink from a spout. But this time, for half of the rats, the water was flavored but there were no light flashes or clicks. For the other half of the rats, there were light flashes and clicks after each lick, but the water was unflavored. The results showed that the rats that had been shocked in the first part of the experiment drank very little of the water that was accompanied by light flashes and clicks in the second part of the experiment, but the rats that had been made ill in the first part of the experiment drank very little of the water that was flavored in the second part of the experiment. Garcia and Koelling concluded that it's easier for rats to associate taste with illness and audiovisual events with shock than vice versa.[35] Due to results such as these, the term *taste aversion learning* has been more popular in the research literature than *bait shyness* or *the sauce béarnaise phenomenon.* Subsequent experiments have suggested that, in addition to tastes, odors may also play an important role in food aversions linked to illness,[36] yet the term *taste aversion learning* has persisted. The fact that tastes and odors are more easily associated with illness than with other sorts of events helps us to survive. The presence of a poison is more likely to be indicated by a particular odor or taste than by a particular appearance or sound.

Many subsequent experiments have found that taste aversion learning has some other unusual properties that may help animals to survive. For example, taste aversions can be acquired within and up to 24 hours between consumption of the food and illness.[37] This is helpful because it may take hours before a poison will result in illness. In addition, in taste aversion learning, the taste actually seems to acquire aversive properties.[38] Remember how the rats treated the thiamine-deficient food in Rozin's experiments on specific hungers, overturning the food dish and in general behaving toward the thiamine-deficient food as they would to a bitter, aversive food? Remember how some of my participants felt about hot dogs? This charac- teristic of taste aversion learning helps us to survive because a poison should be avoided no matter under what circumstances it's encountered. Finally, the fact that taste aversions are more likely to form to novel foods, and often form after just one pairing of a taste with illness, helps to ensure that, as much as possible, we stay away from foods that are likely to make us sick.

Lest you think that the only current interest in taste aversion learning is by laboratory researchers, I should point out that taste aversion learning has been used to help understand and treat many eating and drinking disorders.

Understanding how taste aversion learning works may have other practical implications as well. For example, Carl R. Gustavson and his colleagues tried to use taste aversion learning to prevent coyotes from attacking sheep on sheep ranches in the western United States. Many ranchers choose simply to kill the coyotes. Coyotes are a valuable part of the ecosystem, however. For example, they help to keep the rabbit population under control. Gustavson and his colleagues reasoned that if they could train the coyotes to avoid sheep but not rabbits, this would disrupt the ecosystem much less than killing the coyotes. Gustavson and his colleagues therefore placed lamb bait laced with an illness-inducing drug on the range in areas frequented by wild coyotes. The coyotes appeared to acquire an aversion to eating or even approaching sheep.[39] In fact, after the aversion training, coyotes behaved submissively toward sheep, running the other way when a sheep approached. I've seen this amazing sight myself on film. The coyote in the film actually cowered when the sheep was near.

A final practical application of research on taste aversion learning might be to help us understand people's food aversions that seem of unknown origin. Young children frequently eat novel foods, and young children also frequently become ill; therefore, it seems possible that people could acquire many aversions at young ages and later not be able to recall the origins of those aversions. Further, adults might acquire a taste aversion, possibly after only a mild illness, and never be aware of what caused the aversion, or forget the cause after only a short time.

"You Can Have Candy Only if You Eat Your Spinach"

There are a number of other interesting ways that you can increase or decrease a preference for a taste by pairing it with something. One way is to pair a taste with a better or worse taste, which will increase or decrease the preference for the first taste, respectively.[40]

Psychologists believe that this type of learning is responsible for our learning to like initially aversive substances such as coffee and tea. Think back to the first time that you tasted coffee or tea. If there was nothing added to it, most likely you did not particularly enjoy the experience. A new coffee or tea drinker usually adds sugar or milk. Gradually, as the taste of the coffee or tea becomes associated with the taste of the sugar or the milk, the coffee or tea can be drunk with less, and finally no, sugar or milk. Psychologist Debra A. Zellner and her colleagues did an experiment demonstrating this. They varied the numbers of times that college students (both men and women) drank several different types of sweetened herbal teas. The more times that a student drank a particular sweetened tea, the more the student's preference for that tea increased.[41]

A recent experiment by psychologists Karen Ackroff and Anthony Sclafani showed that not all sweet tastes are equally effective at increasing preference when they're paired with another taste. Ackroff and Sclafani's experiment used rats and two types of sugar: glucose (one of the products of the digestion of table sugar) and fructose. When almond- or vanilla-flavored laboratory chow was paired with unflavored glucose or fructose, preference for a particular flavor of chow increased more when it was paired with glucose than when it was paired with fructose (yes, there really is laboratory chow for laboratory animals, not just dog chow and cat chow). Also, although the rats initially preferred the fructose, with experience they came to prefer the glucose. Therefore something about the postingestion physiological effects of the glucose must have been relatively more positive for the rat than was the case with fructose. Two possible explanations are that glucose remains in the stomach longer than fructose and that glucose produces a greater increase in insulin after it has been absorbed than fructose.[42] One conclusion that you might draw from Ackroff and Sclafani's experiment is that, at least for rats, regular table sugar is in some way more pleasurable to eat than fruit. Most people would probably agree with the rats!

Let's consider situations in which a taste is paired with doing something rather than with another taste. L. L. Birch and colleagues have conducted ground-breaking experiments with children in this area. For example, Birch let preschool children engage in a specific play activity, such as drawing or tricycle riding, only if they drank a specific type of fruit juice, such as apple or grape. This decreased the child's subsequent preference for the fruit juice.[43] The flip side of this phenomenon, also demonstrated by Birch, is that if you give children a particular snack only if they behave well in the classroom, preference for that snack can increase.[44]

Think what this means for parents. If they want their children to eat more spinach and not to eat so much candy, they may be doing exactly the wrong thing if they tell the children that they can have candy only if they eat spinach. According to Birch's research, this would decrease the preference for spinach and increase the preference for candy, making it even more difficult to get the children to eat spinach and to stop eating candy. How many parents do you know who tell their children that they can have dessert only if they eat their dinner? Just about everybody.

Nevertheless, it seems doubtful that telling children that they can eat spinach if they first eat their ice cream would result in the consumption of more spinach and less ice cream. The bitterness of spinach (for some people) and the sweetness of ice cream (for practically everyone) would make it difficult to use such methods to change people's extreme feelings about spinach and ice cream. Birch did not use highly liked or highly disliked foods in her experiments. Even so, parents may want to keep Birch's findings in mind when setting guidelines for their children's eating behaviors.

A final experiment conducted by Jennifer Orlet Fisher and Birch also has a sobering message for parents. If day care workers restricted 3- to 6-year-old children's access to snack foods such as fruit bar cookies and fish-shaped crackers, the children later tried harder to get those snacks as opposed to other snacks.[45] In other words, my attempts to keep my son away from unhealthy snacks when he was young may have backfired.

Perhaps the proper tactic to help children eat the right foods is to have them experience surroundings in which unhealthy foods simply aren't present, as opposed to present but unobtainable. However, although this may work at home, it's unlikely to work when visiting other people's houses or even walking in the street. Unhealthy foods abound in such places. I'm afraid that there's no easy strategy for parents to use.

"I'm Not Sure What to Order for Dinner.... What Are You Having?"

The fact that animals' experiences with food can modify their food preferences clearly helps us to survive. But wouldn't it be much more efficient, not to mention safer, for animals to share their information about which foods are good to eat and which are not? Wouldn't it make great sense for animals to eat what they see other members of their species eating safely?

Perhaps you remember the commercials for Life® cereal some years ago. Three brothers are in their kitchen faced with a box of cereal that they have never seen before. The youngest brother is named Mikey. "Let's get Mikey to try it!" the two older brothers exclaim. If he eats it and likes it, then they will eat it too. This is a very smart move on the part of the older brothers. If the cereal is deadly poisonous, only Mikey will die.

As it turns out, there are many different ways in which members of a species influence one anothers' food preferences. We have all had the experience in a restaurant of getting advice from our table companions or the waiter before ordering. There has been increasing awareness among researchers that it's important to study such effects. Sometimes these sorts of effects involve one animal directly influencing the food preferences of another member of the same species. There are also more indirect ways in which people influence the food preferences of other people through the effects of our culture.

"Are You Telling Me What to Eat?"

Sibylle K. Escalona was one of the first to record observations of changes in people's food preferences due to social interactions. She worked as a psychologist in the Massachusetts Reformatory for Women during the 1940s. The women then incarcerated in that institution were often permitted to keep their children in the institution if the children were under 3 years of age. The children lived in the prison nursery, and their mothers could frequently visit and care for them. Other inmates as well as reformatory employees also cared for the children in the nursery.[46]

On many occasions Escalona observed what she believed to be cases in which the caretakers influenced the children's food preferences subconsciously. For example

> It came to attention accidentally that many of the babies under four months of age showed a consistent dislike for either orange or tomato juice. (These juices were offered on alternate days with equal frequency.) The number preferring each kind of juice was about equal. Furthermore, such preferences seemed to change and a baby who had refused orange juice for about three weeks occasionally would reverse his preference within two or three days, accepting orange juice and refusing tomato henceforth. A checkup revealed that where there was a sudden change in preference the baby's feedings had been re-assigned from one person to another. Next we determined the preference of the students who took care of these babies in such a way that they could not know why the question had been asked, in fact, were not aware of its having been asked. In the fifteen cases we were able to investigate in this matter, the student in charge of a baby showing a decided preference had the same preference, or rather the same dislike, as the baby. That is, babies who refused tomato juice were found to be fed by adults who also expressed a dislike for tomato juice. In three cases we were able to establish the fact that a baby reversing a preference had been changed to a student who possessed the dislike acquired by the baby subsequent to the change in personnel.[47]

These are sobering observations, especially for parents. Perhaps parents can influence their children's food preferences without any awareness whatsoever that they're doing so.

But how might this happen? What unconscious signal could a parent give a child about whether a food is good to eat? One possibility is related to the acceptance and rejection responses shown by many species, including people, discussed earlier in this book. These responses are present at birth.[48] In addition, babies as young as 36 hours are apparently able to imitate the facial expressions of adults.[49] Perhaps adults who are feeding young children consciously or unconsciously make faces of acceptance or rejection, depending on their own preferences for the food being fed, and the children then imitate the expressions and consume more or less food accordingly. This could explain why people feeding babies so often intone "open the hangar" while simultaneously opening their own mouths and directing a spoonful of food at the babies' mouths.

Escalona's research wasn't a controlled experiment, so her results and her interpretations of them aren't conclusive. For many years, very little properly controlled research was done to find out to a high degree of certainty whether someone's facial expression when eating a food could influence someone else's preference for that food. However, a recent experiment showed that primary school children's preferences for a drink with a particular flavor could be decreased by watching a boy make a facial (and sometimes an oral) expression of disgust after tasting the same drink.[50]

Birch has done several intriguing experiments showing other ways in which social context can affect children's food preferences. For example, she has shown that if an adult repeatedly gives a child a snack food such as canned unsweetened pineapple or cashews while being very friendly to the child, the child's preference for the food will increase.[51]

In perhaps her best-known experiment, Birch arranged for certain 3- to 5-year-old children (called the target children) to eat lunch repeatedly with other children the same age. They ate in groups of four or five (one target child and three or four other children) that did not change during the experiment. Adults came by with serving plates to each group's table. The adults asked the children to choose between a vegetable preferred only by the target child at a given table and a vegetable preferred only by the other three children at the same table. The same pair of vegetables was served to each table for the 4 days of the experiment. On the first day the target child chose first, but on days 2, 3, and 4, the other children chose first. Not only did the target children increase their choices of their nonpreferred vegetables during the latter days of the experiment, but their reported preferences for those vegetables also increased. These effects were stronger for the younger children.[52] Peer pressure doesn't just affect such matters as wearing the latest styles and drinking too much beer!

Laboratory research has also demonstrated that young children are more willing to try something new if they first see an adult try it (similar to what happened in the Mikey commercial).[53] Along the same lines, the likelihood that a college student will eat a new, as opposed to a familiar, food depends on what the student sees someone else do. For example, if the other person, faced with a choice between potato chips and cassava chips, picks the cassava chips, then the student will be more likely to pick the cassava chips, and vice versa.[54]

These experiments with people illustrate some of the fascinating ways in which we influence one another's food preferences. Experiments with rats have investigated these sorts of effects in much more detail. By far the most accomplished at conducting such experiments has been psychologist Bennett G. Galef. He has performed a great many ingenious experiments designed to identify the mechanisms that are involved in the social transmission of food preferences among rats. We don't know to what degree these mechanisms also operate in people; few similar experiments have yet been done with people. But Galef's research certainly points to some intriguing possibilities.

For example, Galef has shown that rat pups learn to choose adult rats' preferred food. Further, he has identified three ways in which this preference is transmitted: odor or taste cues at the feeding site, such as might be contained in feces, which attract pups to the site; the presence of adult rats at the feeding site, which attracts pups to the site; and a particular odor or taste cue, specific to a mother rat's preferred food, which is present in her milk and which increases the preference for that food in her nursing pups.[55]

Apparently, then, there are at least three ways in which food preferences can be transmitted from adult rats to rat pups. This means that if rat pups don't learn appropriate food preferences one way, they will learn them another way. It's clearly safer for rat pups to learn food preferences by these multiple, redundant mechanisms of social transmission rather than by their own trial and error.

In other species, the young also learn to eat what the adults of their species eat. Preferences of young cats, chickens, and monkeys can be acquired simply by observing adult animals.[56]

Galef and his colleagues have also shown that long-lasting food preferences can also be transmitted between adult rats. Preference for Food A is increased in an "observer" rat after the observer interacts with a "demonstrator" rat that has previously eaten Food A.[57] This interaction need last only 2 minutes, but during that time mouth-to-mouth contact between the observer and the demonstrator must occur. The resulting increase in the observer's preference for the food appears to depend on the presence of food taste and/or odor on the fur or emerging from the digestive tract of the demonstrator rat[58] (yes, what you have in your stomach can affect your breath). In addition, when it accompanies the food taste and odor, carbon disulfide, a chemical compound present in rat breath, enhances rats' subsequent preference for the food.[59] What all this means is that if an observer rat encounters a dead demonstrator rat or a demonstrator rat with deodorized fur and breath, the observer rat's food preferences won't change, no matter what the demonstrator ate. On the flip side, a rat can acquire a taste aversion if it eats a food and is then exposed to a sick rat.[60]

Apparently there are a large number of different mechanisms by which rats and other species, including people, learn food preferences and food aversions from members of their own species. However, we haven't yet discussed the origins of one major food aversion: the aversion to eating members of your own species. What's responsible for this particular food aversion? If you thought this chapter's section on techniques for inducing nausea and vomiting was fascinating, just read on.

It's hard even to imagine someone doing experiments on this subject with people. However, the relevant research has been done with rats.[61] Demonstrating yet another similarity to people, rats rarely eat members of their own species. Although a hungry adult rat will easily eat an unattended, live, newborn rat pup of its own species, the older the rat pup is, the lower the probability that the adult rat will eat it. Further, adult rats are more likely to eat dead adult rats of another species, or dead adult mice, than dead adult rats of their own species. However, rats raised next to a mouse are as unlikely to eat a mouse of that species as a member of their own species. The likelihood that an adult rat will feed on a member of its own species increases when the consumer rat is hungry or can't smell, when the carcass has been covered with the urine of another species, or when the carcass has been skinned. Finally, an adult rat's readiness to feed on a member of its own species can be increased when that rat observes another adult rat eating a member of its own species. Observational learning appears to be important here as well as in the transmission of other food aversions and preferences.

Yet how does a rat know that another animal is or isn't a member of its own species? The results of the experiments described above all seem to point to taste or odor cues present in fur, cues with which rats become familiar through experience with either their own or other animals' bodies.

It's not known whether similar mechanisms are involved in the tendency of people to avoid eating other people. However, the descriptive information given in Piers Paul Read's book *Alive* (from which a movie of the same name was made) suggests that at least some of the same mechanisms may be involved.[62] In *Alive*, survivors of a plane crash in the Andes quickly ran out of food. The only way that they could survive was to eat the bodies of the people who were killed by the crash. As with rats, increased hunger contributed to them eating the corpses. In addition, some people were unable to do it until they saw someone else do it (a possible example of observational learning). Keeping the bodies covered, so that the meat did not look as if it came from a person, helped other survivors to eat them. Some people finally began to eat the corpses only after they conceived of the process as similar to Holy Communion, a sacrament in which Christians symbolically consume some of the body of Jesus Christ.

When in Rome, Eat as the Romans Do

You've already learned a great deal about how one person can influence another person's food preferences. Given this information, you would expect that a culture's attitudes toward certain foods would also influence people's food preferences. After all, a culture consists basically of the views held by and the practices of a group of individual people. There appear to be many ways in which our culture influences our food preferences.

For example, consider television advertising, a ubiquitous part of our culture. Most of the research in this area has been concerned with the effects of television advertising on children. Many studies have shown that children in the United States spend more time watching television than they do engaging in any other activity.[63] American children view an average of some 10 food commercials per hour of TV watching, and the huge majority of these commercials advertise foods that are poor in nutrition.[64] Good nutrition is critical to good health. Therefore, if children are influenced by commercials, these commercials could be seriously harming their health.

Those of us with children have all had the experience of their asking for some totally nonnutritious food that they saw advertised on TV. For my son it has usually been some revolting cereal that is about 95% sugar. Therefore it will also not surprise you that several experiments have indeed shown that when children were exposed to commercials for foods poor in nutrition, the children said that they liked those foods more and they were more likely to eat them.[65] On the other hand, other reports have shown that when children saw commercials that present nutritional information, their preference for nutritious foods did not change. The differences in the results for nutritious and nonnutritious foods may have been at least partly due to the greater amounts of effort and money put into producing commercials for nonnutritious foods.[66] This means that the TV our children are watching is very likely teaching them to prefer foods that are poor in nutrition.

Another way that our culture can affect our food preferences is by affecting the types of things that are considered appropriate to eat. As you learned in the previous chapter, this can include such preferences as which foods should have salt or sugar added to them (after all, why shouldn't we sprinkle salt on our ice cream and sugar on our fried eggs?), the temperature at which certain foods should be served (warm soda is considered good only for upset stomachs), which foods should be eaten at certain times of the day (we don't eat green beans at breakfast or Danish at dinner), and which foods are considered ethical or moral to eat. People learn through their culture to prefer foods with certain characteristics.[67] Cultures exert these effects by means of the sorts of food preference mechanisms described earlier in this chapter, for example food familiarity and observational learning.

Our culture also repeatedly tries to tell us what's healthy to eat; these days the relative health benefits of eating different types of foods is a popular subject in the media. This information does appear to be having some effect on our food preferences. For example, American consumption of eggs and other high-cholesterol foods has decreased since the health problems associated with a high-cholesterol diet began receiving publicity.[68] Women and older people are more likely than men and younger people, respectively, to report that health factors are important in their food choices.[69] But if you're one of the many people who no longer eats eggs because they can increase your cholesterol, does this mean that you no longer like eggs? Often that isn't the case. Several people I know, after starting to take medication that dramatically lowers your cholesterol no matter what you eat, immediately began consuming large amounts of eggs and other high-cholesterol foods. Information about foods' convenience and nutrition may primarily affect the amount eaten of a food, but not the degree to which that food is liked; food liking may be more affected by emotional statements such as how the food reminds you of your childhood.[70]

Finally, let's consider the effects of religion. Many religions have rules about what may or may not be eaten, and these rules may be consistent with the food preferences of the members of the religion. For example, many Jews don't enjoy the taste of pork.[71] This lack of a preference for eating pork is probably due to members of the religion influencing one another in the ways described earlier in this chapter. Some people have also claimed that a religion's beliefs about what should and should not be eaten may have helped the members of that religion to survive. You'll hear more about that in a later chapter.

Classifying Different Types of Our Food Aversions: How Much Can You Stomach?

By now you've heard a lot about what causes people to like and dislike certain foods. Much of the information on food preferences and aversions can be summarized using psychologists Paul Rozin and April E. Fallon's classification of the four different types of food aversions shown by people: foods that are rejected because they're distasteful, dangerous, inappropriate, or disgusting.[72] (See Table 6.1.) Some of these types of aversions seem to be due to contact with other people, and others seem to be due to experience with the food itself. While I describe each of them in the following paragraphs, see if you can figure out how to classify my aversion to eating seafood (or your own favorite food aversion).

Distasteful foods are those that most people would not mind eating if the taste of the food were covered up by another taste or if they only discovered what they had been eating after they had finished. An example of a distasteful food is warm milk, whose fulsome aroma and taste many people find quite unpleasant. Taste aversion learning, in which the taste of a food is

Table 6.1 Classification of Food Aversions in People

Type of Aversive Food	Description	Example	Possible Origins
Distasteful	Not aversive if cannot be tasted	Warm milk	Aversive taste, smell, or texture; consumption of the food may have been followed by gastrointestinal illness
Dangerous	Could cause physical harm if eaten	Poisonous mushrooms	Consumption of the food has been followed by, or has been reputed to be followed by, a non-gastrointestinal illness
Inappropriate	Not considered to be food	Tree bark	Genetically based aversive taste, or direct experience with food or information from other people indicates that food cannot be consumed and/or digested
Disgusting	Aversive even if cannot be tasted or if in very small quantities; substances paired with a disgusting food also become disgusting (i.e., contamination occurs)	Urine	Direct or indirect contact with other people who consider the food disgusting, or contact with another disgusting food, or similarity to another disgusting food

paired with gastrointestinal illness (principally nausea), usually results in a distaste for the food. A genetically based reaction to the taste of a food (for example, if a food is very bitter) may also result in a food aversion that is categorized as a distaste.

On the other hand, if eating a food is paired with another type of illness, such as difficulty breathing, as can happen with an allergic reaction, this will result in a food aversion in which the food is classified as dangerous. Dangerous foods are those that could cause physical harm if eaten. With this sort of food aversion, someone would be glad to eat the food again if a magic pill would just prevent the illness. An example of a dangerous food is a poisonous mushroom. Someone may consider a food dangerous because of direct experience with the food or because of information received from other people.

Inappropriate foods are those items that aren't considered food. An example is tree bark (and for me, items such as lettuce, which seems very similar to grass). Someone may consider a food inappropriate due to a genetically based reaction to the food's taste, due to direct experience with the food (have you ever tried to chew tree bark?), or due to information from other people.

And now we come to by far my favorite category: disgusting foods. These are foods that most people would never want in their stomach no matter how the foods were disguised and no matter how small the amount. Some examples are urine and feces. Disgust has been described as an emotion that helps to maintain and emphasize the distinction between people and other animals. It's certainly the case that foods become disgusting in large part because of direct and indirect contact with the reactions to these foods by other people. Thus as children age and acquire increased experience with adults' reactions to certain potential foods that adults tend to treat as disgusting, such as insects, the children themselves come increasingly to treat those potential foods as disgusting. Foods may also be classified as disgusting because they have come into contact with something disgusting, or because their appearance is similar to that of something disgusting. For example, a milkshake that once had, but no longer has, a cockroach floating in it is disgusting, as is fudge shaped to look like dog feces. This makes sense according to traditional learning theory, which says that we tend to associate events or aspects of our surroundings that have been paired together or that are similar to each other.[73]

Now take a guess into which category my aversion to eating seafood falls? If you guessed "disgusting" you were correct! I cannot stand the thought of touching seafood nor of having even the tiniest particle of seafood in what I eat. Once, on a trip to a friend's house in Martha's Vineyard off of Cape Cod, Massachusetts, I was served lobster and had no choice but to try and eat it. I managed to get down a small amount. That night, in bed, I kept tasting the lobster, and it was horrible. Finally, I got up, went to the bathroom, and put a huge amount of toothpaste into my mouth—that helped some. Paul Rozin, the world's leading expert on food aversions, has tried mightily to figure out what's responsible for my aversion to seafood. The fact that it's classified as a disgust has puzzled him; he would have expected it to be a distaste.

What Rozin did not know, and what I learned only recently, is what my early food surroundings were like when it came to fish. A few years ago, my mother uncovered a set of instructions the pediatrician wrote out for her concerning how I should be fed when I was 9 1/2 months old: "Offer baked and broiled fish—cod, flounder, halibut. Shred well to avoid bones. Try tuna fish and salmon." I asked my mother if she could remember if she did this. "Oh, I'm sure I didn't," she said. "I can't stand the smell of cooking fish." Further interrogation of my mother revealed that, at the time, she herself ate only lobster and shrimp. She had no tuna fish in the house. She never, ever cooked fish at home with the exception of, when I was child, steaming shrimp. She says that this odor seems different to her than the odor of cooking fish, that the shrimp odor does not bother her. On the other hand, I can remember vividly as a child the odor of her steaming shrimp and finding it so horrible that I had to retreat to my room next to the attic.

Thus it appears that, similar to me, my mother is extremely sensitive to the odors of fish and seafood. As it turns out, my father did not like these odors either. So I probably got my fish-odor sensitivity from my parents' genes. However, in addition, my parents never exposed me to the taste of fish when I was young, so it did not become a familiar, preferred food. Further, it's possible that I may have observed my mother's aversive reactions to the taste or smell of fish, thus resulting in my disgust for fish.

Conclusion

Armed with this chapter's and the previous chapter's scientific information about the origins of various food preferences and aversions, we can now try to answer the questions posed about various food-preference and food-aversion problems at the beginning of the previous chapter. Some of these problems, for example the decreased preference for milk with age and the extreme preferences for sweet foods and for salty foods, are probably due largely to the effects of genes. In most people milk becomes largely indigestible after the age of 3, and people show a genetic preference for sweet and salty foods. However, the degree to which an animal (including a person) prefers to eat sweet foods, salty foods, and milk can be modified by experience.

The acquired aversion to hot dogs after hot dog consumption has been followed by illness probably is due primarily to the effects of experience. Animals associate food consumption with subsequent nausea, resulting in eating that food less.

Finally, a child's—and my—aversion to eating vegetables may result from a number of different factors. Some people (such as me) may find some vegetables bitter tasting because of a genetically based taste sensitivity to certain chemicals. In addition, vegetables, when eaten by themselves, are low in salt and sugar (both of which are innately preferred) and are also low in fat (which we learn to prefer due to its high concentration of calories). Finally, as Birch's research has shown, children can learn to prefer certain vegetables by observing other children eating them. If someone does not see other people eating vegetables, or sees people eating them although clearly not liking them (and I always saw my father eat his vegetables first, knowing full well that he ate the food on his plate in reverse order of preference), then a preference for eating vegetables is unlikely.

Therefore it would probably be easier to change, for example, the hot dog aversion than the sweet preference. In the case of the hot dog, research indicates that preference is likely to be changed by repeated consumption of the food in a familiar, good-tasting sauce, under pleasant circumstances, and in the company of others who apparently enjoy hot dogs. Gradually, the sauce can be eliminated.

To a large degree, the ways in which our food preferences and aversions arise and change reflect our evolutionary heritage. Not only have we evolved to like certain tastes and to dislike others, but we have evolved to learn to like certain foods under certain conditions and to learn to dislike them under other conditions. All of this greatly helped us to survive in our original surroundings in which calories and salt were scarce and nutritious, nonpoisonous food sources had to be identified. That world no longer exists, but our preferences for salty, sweet, caloric food and our aversions to foods associated with illness continue. This legacy of our past can cause serious problems.

Now that you've read this chapter and the previous ones, you may enjoy an exercise involving Figure 6.2. For each of the panels, see if you can explain why the different people feel the way they do about the various foods. In addition, you probably now understand the national obsession with fast food such as McDonald's; many of the foods served at such locations are high in fat and calories and are very familiar. An article in *The New York Times Magazine* provided the following description of McDonald's, which made $30 billion in 1995: "McDonald's has no bad tables, there's no tipping and the French fries are always a quarter-inch square. The customer wants no surprises, and there aren't any. . . . People talk thin and eat fat."[74] Finally, you won't be surprised by *Time* magazine's report of what various executed criminals chose for their last meals: "TED BUNDY: Serial killer; electrocuted Jan. 24, 1989; Starke, Florida. Last meal: steak, eggs, hashed brown potatoes, coffee. GARY MARK GILMORE: Murderer; shot by firing squad Jan. 17, 1977; Point of the Mountain, Utah. Last meal: hamburgers, eggs, potatoes, coffee, whiskey. PERRY SMITH AND RICHARD HICKOCK: Murderers; hanged April 14, 1965; Lansing, Kansas. Last meal: shrimp, French fries, garlic bread, ice cream, strawberries and whipped cream."[75]

The Generation Gap

Figure 6.2 Drawing by Lynda Barry. Copyright 1996. Reprinted with permission from *The New York Times Magazine* [March 10, 1996] 55.)

CHAPTER 7

This or That

Choosing What We Eat and Drink

℮

I t's early Saturday morning, you're lying in bed, and you realize that there's no food in your house. You've got to go to the grocery store. You've also got to visit your elderly parents and take your teenage children to soccer practice that afternoon, so you have limited time for grocery shopping. You decide to do the grocery shopping right away because, although you'll be able to spend less time lying in bed, the really good grocery deals sell out by 10 AM on Saturdays, so in the long run, you'll be able to buy more food if you get out of bed now. And, because you spent all but $30 of your cash last night playing bingo and you've maxed out your credit card, there's a limited amount of food that you can buy; you'll need to get as much food as you can per dollar. It needs to be enough to provide dinner for your children and a few of your nephews and nieces who will be coming over after soccer practice, absolutely starving. Although $30 probably won't buy enough food to stuff all of them, it will buy enough so that your children and their cousins won't die before morning.

So you drive to the grocery store and race down the aisles. You, your children, and their cousins eat all kinds of things, so choosing what to buy is more complicated than if, for example, you were koala bears eating only eucalyptus leaves. And you can't just buy what you and your children like best (caviar and lobster) because $30 won't buy enough of that. You also can't buy just foods or just drinks; consuming food without drink, or vice versa, isn't at all appealing. You have to figure out the right combination. In addition to these problems, you wish that you could remember which aisle the soda is in so that you wouldn't have to spend your precious time looking for it. While you're looking for the soda, it occurs to you that maybe you should just spend the whole $30 on food for yourself. After all, you're the one who earned it in the first place, not your children and their cousins. And $30 doesn't buy a whole lot of food these days. But then you remember how much you love your children and their cousins and you decide to buy food for everybody.

There are just a few other shoppers this morning. Suddenly, there's a loudspeaker announcement: There are marketing demonstrations in aisles B and F. In aisle B, the demonstrator is making miniature waffles with a new type of waffle iron that does a great job, but takes about 5 minutes to make each waffle. In aisle F, another demonstrator is making hors d'oeuvres on a new type of cracker, averaging one per minute. Given that there was no food in your house when you woke up, you haven't had breakfast, and you really like both miniature waffles and hors d'oeuvres, so these demonstrations sound great. But you've got limited time—which demonstration do you go to? And if you have time to get some more free food while you're grocery shopping, do you keep going to the same or a different demonstration? Maybe you should go to aisle F five times as often as aisle B, because the hors d'oeuvres are ready five times as often as the miniature waffles. Or maybe you should calculate the time for each trip to aisles B or F, as well as calculating when the next waffle and hors d'oeuvre will be ready, and visit the two demonstrations in such a pattern as to get the most total food.

Is this all sounding really complicated? Well, maybe you don't consciously think about all of these issues when you go grocery shopping. However, whether you're aware of them or not, psychologists would contend that it's just these sorts of factors that are involved any time you choose one food or another to eat, and that very similar factors were involved when our ancestors foraged for food in jungles and savannahs and are still involved in the food choices of other animals in the wide world.

What you actually choose to eat and drink is the ultimate focus of the psychology of eating and drinking. So far, this book has provided a lot of information about how we distinguish among different foods and what causes us to like or dislike certain foods. But knowing all of that won't tell you everything you need to know to predict whether someone will consume a particular food or drink at a particular point in time. You need to know what else is available, how hungry the person is, what else is going on in the person's surroundings, and how much work, time, and money it's going to take to get a particular food or drink as compared to something else.[1] This chapter will tell you about some of these other factors and how they influence eating and drinking.

Choosing to Survive

What can help us understand how and why people and other animals choose certain foods? You've already heard a lot about how eating behaviors have evolved in ways that, at least originally, helped us all to survive, such as the innate preferences for sweet and salty foods. Perhaps thinking about the relationships among food choice, survival, and evolution can increase our understanding of the factors involved in animals'—including people's—choosing different foods.

It shouldn't surprise us if animals choose foods or drinks in ways that appear to help them survive. Think about the major food problem facing an animal living in the wild: It has to find and consume enough food and water to meet its energy needs and reproduce. And this animal must do this no matter in what surroundings it finds itself. A uniform, steady food supply is unusual in the animal kingdom. Things change, both over time and through space, and therefore the best food choices for an animal also change.[1] Even grocery stores that are members of the same chain can carry different items in different locations.

Given that animals' surroundings aren't fixed and uniform, one particular set of choices of what to eat and drink won't, in the long run, be best for an animal. Instead we would expect that evolution has resulted in various strategies that animals employ to make their choices, strategies that would, over time, best help the animals to survive. Thus the most important questions for this chapter are what sorts of choice strategies will best help us to survive? and do we and other animals follow those best strategies?

It's important to remember that evolution of food choice strategies is multifaceted and continuous. Not only do choice strategies per se evolve, but so do the cognitive abilities needed for those choice strategies—abilities such as memory. Here's one example.

Two species of monkey, golden lion tamarins and Wied's marmosets, perform differently on memory tasks in the laboratory. The marmosets do better than the tamarins when they have to remember something for only 5 minutes, but the tamarins do better than the marmosets when they have to remember something for 24 or 48 hours. As it turns out, the marmosets, but not the tamarins, obtain a lot of their food in the form of gum from trees, which they gouge with their teeth. The gum is rapidly replaced by the tree, sometimes in less than an hour. Therefore the marmosets confine their food search to a small area involving a few trees to which they return several times in a day. In order not to waste time going to a tree without much gum, the marmosets need to remember well where they have been for only a few minutes or hours. In contrast, the tamarins eat little tree gum. Instead, they eat small animals (primarily insects) and plant parts such as ripe fruit. These foods are widely spread out over a large area. In order to locate good food sources, tamarins need to remember well over large distances and periods of time.[2] In a nutshell, these monkeys' cognitive abilities and their food choices have evolved to be well suited to each other.

Now let's consider how food choice strategies and cognitive abilities might have evolved together in people. Some scientists believe that the excellent cognitive abilities of people are actually a result of food-related evolution. Scientist Katharine Milton has speculated that, when people were evolving, they were caught in a sort of dietary squeeze because specialized carnivores and herbivores were evolving at the same time, increasing the competition for certain foods. To survive, omnivorous humans had to become good at finding all kinds of different food sources in different locations at different times. They needed to remember well and to learn quickly, contributing to the evolution of a large brain. In fact, according to Milton, "Overall, I would say that the collected evidence justifiably casts the evolutionary history of primates in largely dietary terms."[3] Milton believes that in addition to people's cognitive abilities, certain physical abilities, such as our highly manipulative hands, evolved to serve food choice needs. Our hands allow us to obtain and consume all kinds of food items that we otherwise could not.[4]

Before we leave the topic of evolution and food choice, there's one particular aspect of food choice that has occupied the attention of many researchers interested in evolution: food sharing. If evolution results in individuals choosing foods that maximize their survival, why would anyone ever share food? Particularly in times of food scarcity, such behavior would make it less, not more, likely that you would survive. Nevertheless, there have been several documented instances of food sharing in species other than people. For example, when a young raven finds a good food source such as a dead moose, it will leave to find other young ravens, and then they will all return to the carcass and eat it together. As another example, vampire bats will regurgitate blood that they have eaten and give some to a roostmate. There may be very good reasons for the individual young ravens and bats to share food. In the case of the young ravens, ravens must eat on a fairly regular basis to survive, and one young raven by itself cannot gain access to a carcass in the territory of older ravens. By inviting many other young ravens to share, the finder ensures that it will get something to eat.[5] In the case of the bats, bats that go two nights without consuming blood will die. Bats that roost together tend to be related to one another. This means that when bats share food they ensure that their relatives, and thus other copies of their genes, will survive.[6] Therefore food sharing in bats helps to ensure that the genes of the sharer will be multiplied in the future, a factor that may also be at work when we feed our children and other relatives.

Model Choice Behavior

The previous material should have given you a fairly good idea of the general strategies that animals, including people, use to choose among different foods, and the general relationships between those strategies and evolution.

This section examines more extensively particular food choice strategies that different scientists believe animals use.

Some scientists have tried to specify in great detail the strategies that animals use in choosing among different foods—such detail, in fact, that it's possible to predict exactly how much time or energy an animal will devote to choosing one food versus another food. These scientists believe that if you know everything about an animal's history and current surroundings, and if you have a good idea of what choices will best help an animal to survive, then you'll be able to predict those choices very closely. Such predictions could be extremely useful in helping us find ways to modify undesirable eating behaviors. But scientists have disagreed over what strategy they think that animals are most likely to use in making their food choices. So they construct elaborate mathematical models of these strategies and then test to see how closely animals' actual food choice behaviors do or don't conform to these models. Here we'll look at two of the most popular models of animals' food choice behaviors: the matching law and optimal foraging theory. We'll look at each of these models' advantages and shortcomings to see what each can contribute. You've already had an introduction to each of these models at the beginning of this chapter when I described two possible strategies that you might use in choosing between the two free sources of food in the grocery store: visiting the hors d'oeuvre source five times as often as the miniature-waffle source (the matching law) or calculating which source will get you the most energy consumed for the least energy expended (optimal foraging theory).

The Matching Law

The matching law assumes that animals follow one simple rule that often results in maximizing the total amount of food that they obtain. If you're mathematically inclined, it's possible to learn a great deal about the matching law in the form of equations. However, given that some readers of this book may not be particularly enamored of equations, I'm going to describe this law without resorting to any mathematical intricacies. Let's go back to the free food available in the grocery store and see what the matching law has to say about it.

The question is how should you, during the limited time that you have to get food in the grocery store, choose to distribute your time between the miniature-waffle and hors d'oeuvre demonstrations? What strategy will result in your obtaining the most free food? When you first hear the announcement about the two demonstrations you should choose the hors d'oeuvre demonstration, because food is available there more frequently. However, if it has been at least 5 minutes since you've been to the miniature-waffle demonstration, then you should go there, because a waffle is likely to be available. If you then spend 1 minute at the waffle demonstration, obtaining any waffles available there, you should return to the hors d'oeuvre demonstration, because another completed hors d'oeuvre is likely to be waiting there for you, and so on.

The matching law, first formulated by Harvard University psychologist Richard Herrnstein, states that, on average, animals, including people, distribute their choices in proportion to the distribution of the foods available.[7] They "match" the distribution of their choices of foods to the distribution of those foods. Thus, according to the matching law, you should choose to spend five times as much time at the hors d'oeuvre demonstration as at the miniature-waffle demonstration because hors d'oeuvres are available five times as often as waffles.

Scientists have tested the matching law in many different species, including cows, people, pigeons, and rats. These experiments have used many different kinds of food, including hay, snack foods, grain, and laboratory rat chow. The results have shown that, in general, the behavior of all of these species conforms well to the matching law.[8] The matching law has even described well the food choice behavior of a flock of wild pigeons: The total number of choices the members of a flock of wild pigeons made of each of two food sources matched the frequency with which food was available at those two food sources.[9] There are very few psychological principles that can predict precisely how someone will behave. Most of my own research for the past 30 years has made use of the matching law in one way or another.

The Matching Law and Self-Control

One of the most important uses of the matching law in the psychology of eating and drinking is the matching law's explanation of self-control—the choice of a larger or better piece of delayed food over a smaller or worse piece of immediate food—and its explanation of the opposite, impulsiveness.[10] One of the most famous psychologists of the 20th century, B. F. Skinner, gave the following example of self-control involving food: "A principle of self-control: In looking at a menu, ask not what will taste good but what will feel good an hour or so from now."[11]

Consider now the following example:

Suppose a child's mother tells him on a Tuesday evening that if he eats all of his vegetables at dinner that night he can have three cookies for dessert. [I know you learned in the last chapter that this would only make the child like cookies more and vegetables less, but remember I'm trying to give an example similar to what people actually do, not what they should do.] He eats his vegetables, but then the mother discovers that there's only one cookie in the cookie jar. (The father secretly eats the cookies in the cookie jar, always leaving one cookie because he thinks that way no one will notice what he's been doing.) Because she believes that it's important to keep promises to children, and because she feels bad that she does not have the cookies immediately available, she tells the child that he has two choices. He can either have the one cookie after 1 hour or he can wait until tomorrow, Wednesday, and when she goes to the store she will get him three cookies for dessert after tomorrow night's dinner. But he cannot have both.

If the child chooses the one cookie Tuesday evening, this would be an example of impulsiveness; a choice of the three cookies Wednesday evening would be an example of self-control. In order to get the most cookies, the child should show self-control. However, we all know that many people, adults as well as children, would show impulsiveness in such a situation. What does the matching law predict?

The matching law states that the greater the amount of food, the more you should choose it, and the more a food is delayed, the less you should choose it. The delay decreases the value of the food—the greater the delay, the more the value of the food is decreased. In the above example, one choice offers 3 times as many cookies as the other, but 24 times as much delay. Therefore, the overall value of the choice of three more delayed cookies is less than the overall value of the choice of one less delayed cookie, and the matching law predicts that the child will be impulsive and choose the one cookie. In the laboratory, people as well as other animals are frequently impulsive when choosing among foods of differing amounts and delays.[12]

Scientists don't yet know precisely the physiological basis of self-control and impulsiveness, but we have some clues. For example, the neurotransmitter serotonin seems to play a role. In one experiment, the level of serotonin was decreased in various parts of the brains of some rats, including the hypothalamus. When compared with other rats that hadn't had this treatment, the treated rats were less likely to wait for delayed food.[13] In people, it has long been observed that patients with damage to the frontal parts of their brain cortex are very likely to behave impulsively.[14] Similarly, activity in the frontal parts of the brain cortex increases when sated men make choices from highly-valued menus.[15] Thus we seem to have some idea of the anatomical and chemical elements of the brain that are important in demonstrating self-control.

You may be saying to yourself, "Well, all of this information is fine and good for explaining self-control, but can it help us to increase self-control?" The matching law analysis of self-control and impulsiveness actually suggests a number of different ways that self-control can be increased. Many of these self-control techniques are used in treating eating and drinking disorders, as you'll learn about in Chapters 10 and 11. For now, let's just go over some of the techniques that have been demonstrated in basic research laboratories, and you can begin thinking about how these techniques might be used to increase or decrease food and alcohol consumption.

One way to increase self-control is for the choice to be made as early as possible before any food can be obtained. In the cookie choice example described earlier, if the choice is modified so that the child can have one cookie tomorrow evening or three cookies the evening after, he will be more likely to choose the three cookies than with the original choice between one cookie in an hour and three cookies tomorrow evening. With the modified choice, in addition to discounting the value of the three cookies a great deal because of their delay, the child also discounts the value of the one cookie because of its extended delay, and so the three cookies are worth more to the child than the one cookie.

But what happens as time marches forward? Gradually, as time passes, the child, if allowed to, will change his choice to the one cookie; he will reverse his preference. This occurs because, as time passes, the choice becomes the original one between the one cookie delayed 1 hour and the three cookies delayed 24 hours. Therefore, to make sure that self-control is maintained, the child's early choice must be irrevocable; the child must not have a way to change his choice. For example, once the child makes his choice, he could ask his mother to write a big note and put it on the refrigerator stating that choice and that nobody (father, babysitter, grandparents, etc.) is to let him change his mind. When people do something to prevent themselves from changing from self-control to impulsiveness, that act is known as a precommitment device.[16] Precommitment devices are perhaps the most useful of all methods for enhancing self-control. I use them all the time, such as when I take to work a lunch that I packed the night before and am thus stuck eating a lunch consisting of yogurt, crackers, and fruit, as opposed to the leftover chocolate cake that I might have been tempted to eat if it were near me at lunchtime.

Describing how the child's choice might change suggests another way in which self-control might be increased. Suppose the child were first given the choice between one cookie tomorrow evening and three cookies tomorrow evening, and the child chooses the three cookies. Suppose further that the choice is irrevocable and the child gets and eats the three cookies. Now suppose that the child is given a similar choice twice a week, each week for 26 years, and that with each subsequent choice, the delay to the one cookie is decreased by 30 seconds. Finally, after 26 years, the child is choosing between an immediate cookie and three cookies delayed until tomorrow evening. Experience with such a procedure, in which the delay to the small reinforcer very gradually fades away, results in both pigeons and impulsive children showing far more self-control than if they had not been exposed to this pro-cedure.[17]

What goes on during the delay periods also affects self-control. You've probably noticed yourself that if you're hungry and you focus on how good something tastes, it's harder to wait for it. But if you're hungry and you distract yourself with some absorbing non-food-related task, it's easier to wait for a good-tasting food. Columbia University psychologist Walter Mischel and his colleagues, in their experiments with children, collected much evidence showing that thinking about the motivating qualities of foods, such as how good cookies taste, makes it harder to maintain self-control. But thinking about other characteristics of foods, such as cookies' round shape and the little specks in them, makes it easier to maintain self-control. These types of thoughts can be termed *hot* and *cool thoughts*, respectively.[18] Playing games during the delay period or even falling asleep, both of which presumably decrease hot thoughts, increase self-control in children.[19] Performing the equivalent of distracting behaviors during the delay of a food item may also help pigeons maintain self-control.[20] The effects on self-control of reminders present during the delay periods have also been studied. For example, when colored lights are present during food delays for pigeons, and the color of the lights indicates whether a self-control or an impulsive choice has been made (when the pigeons have a "reminder" of which choice they have made and thus which food item they're waiting for), they show more self-control.[21]

It's possible that there may be a single physiological explanation for the effects of hot and cool thoughts, reminders and distracting behaviors. Recall that Chapter 2 showed that some aspects of our surroundings that are associated with food cause the release of insulin and increase hunger. Given that increased hunger can increase people's impulsiveness, perhaps the hot and cool thoughts are equivalent to events that do or don't result in the release of insulin. You see yummy chocolate cake in front of you, you release insulin, and, despite having just finished lunch and being on a diet, you can't resist eating some of the cake. Additional evidence seems to support the hypothesis that insulin release is related to self-control and hot and cool thoughts. For example, both dieters and pigeons seem better at self-control for food in the laboratory when they can't always see the food .[22]

B. F. Skinner obviously had an inkling about the role of visual cues in self-control for food and how to control those cues when he wrote his provoca-tive, prescient, and amusing 1948 novel *Walden Two* about a utopian community founded on psychological principles:

"Take the principle of 'Get thee behind me, Satan,' for example," Frazier continued. "It's a special case of self-control by altering the environment. Subclass A 3, I believe. We give each child a lollipop which has been dipped in powdered sugar so that a single touch of the tongue can be detected. We tell him he may eat the lollipop later in the day, provided it hasn't already been licked. Since the child is only three or four, it is a fairly diff—"

"Three or four!" Castle exclaimed.

"All our ethical training is completed by the age of six," said Frazier quietly. "A simple principle like putting temptation out of sight would be acquired before four. But at such an early age the problem of not licking the lollipop isn't easy. Now, what would you do, Mr. Castle, in a similar situation?"

"Put the lollipop out of sight as quickly as possible."

"Exactly. I can see you've been well trained. Or perhaps you discovered the principle for yourself. We're in favor of original inquiry wherever possible, but in this case we have a more important goal and we don't hesitate to give verbal help. First of all, the children are urged to examine their own behavior while looking at the lollipops. This helps them to recognize the need for self-control. Then the lollipops are concealed, and the children are asked to notice any gain in happiness or any reduction in tension. Then a strong distraction is arranged—say, an interesting game. Later the children are reminded of the candy and encouraged to examine their reaction. The value of the distraction is generally obvious. Well, need I go on? When the experiment is repeated a day or so later, the children all run with the lollipops to their lockers and do exactly what Mr. Castle would do—a sufficient indication of the success of our training."[23]

There is additional support for the hypothesis that insulin release is related to self-control. Both people and pigeons do better at self-control in the laboratory when they're working for tokens that can be exchanged for food after many choices have been made, rather than when they're working for food that they get before they make their next choice.[24] We could easily surmise that more insulin is released—with the animals becoming hungrier and therefore more impulsive—when food is always visible or is available after every choice, rather than when food isn't always visible or when it's available only after many choices have been completed.

Finally, research suggests that the passage of time by itself can affect self-control. For example, if you fall asleep while you're waiting for the three cookies, time will pass very quickly for you. If time seems to pass very quickly, then you'll discount the value of the three cookies very little due to their delay. Thus, anything that makes time seem to go faster should increase self-control. Doing something fun, taking certain drugs, having certain reminders present, as well as falling asleep, might all make time seem to pass quickly and thus increase self-control. The afternoon before I was to go to Europe the first time and was terribly excited and felt that I couldn't wait to leave for the airport, my now husband took me to see the movie *The Godfather*. The time waiting to leave for the airport flew by while we were in the theater. In contrast, being hungry, staring at good food, taking certain other drugs, or doing something that isn't fun might all make time seem to pass less quickly and thus decrease self-control. The matching law has ways of mathematically expressing, and even predicting, the differences in individual animals' sensitivities to the passage of time that result from these sorts of factors.[25] I hope that you can see that research on self-control within the context of the matching law suggests many different ways for increasing and decreasing food and alcohol consumption. Now we should give optimal foraging theory a chance to make its case.

Optimal Foraging Theory

To *forage* means to "wander or rove in search of food or other provisions."[26] Therefore optimal foraging theory, also known as optimization or maximization,[27] refers to a set of theories about the best way to find food. Most likely, if you had to forage in nature, and food was scarce, you would try to find the most food you could while expending as few calories as possible. Such a strategy would best enable you to survive. Not surprisingly, one version of optimal foraging theory assumes that evolution has shaped us to behave in this way;[28] animals that follow such a strategy would be likely to reproduce successfully.

Similar to the matching law, optimal foraging theories are often expressed in the form of extremely complicated mathematical equations. Once again, although I personally enjoy such equations, I'm not going to present them here; the equations aren't necessary for you to understand the basic concepts of optimal foraging theory. The optimal foraging theory equations calculate everything in terms of energy—energy consumed via foraging and energy expended via movement and metabolic processes. They essentially treat optimal foraging as analogous to the earning and spending of money. Consumed food can be thought of as income, and energy expended in order to obtain that food can be thought of as cost. As you might therefore guess, many scientists draw parallels between optimal foraging research and the theoretical framework for economics.[29]

Using the framework of economics to understand eating and drinking choice behavior can be very helpful in a number of ways. One way is that it can help scientists to understand the consumption of different food and drink combinations. For example, consider a typical meal in which an animal both eats food and drinks water. If you try to figure out separately how much food and water an animal will consume, you'll have trouble because each depends on the other. In Chapter 3 you learned that most animals require food and water in specific combinations of so much food and so much water. Therefore food is worth little to a hungry and thirsty animal unless water is also available. This is why, when you go to the grocery store, you're unlikely to buy just food or just drinks. The matching law has no way to describe or predict such findings. However, the economics framework of optimal foraging theory can help us to understand such situations because economics contains concepts for items whose worth is affected by the presence and absence of other items.

But perhaps you've realized that animals can't always do everything optimally. There are limits—constraints—on animals' physical and cognitive abilities. All animals' foraging behaviors are constrained to at least some degree.[30] One example is when you're in the grocery store and can't remember which aisle the soda is in and, as a result, you don't take the route to the soda involving the least steps and the least energy expenditure.

Micro- and Macroapproaches

You may have heard of microeconomics and macroeconomics. These areas of study involve applying the principles of economics to individual people and to groups of people, respectively. These two types of economics are both used in studies of optimal foraging.

For an example of foraging and the microapproach, let's consider first experiments conducted by biologist Graham H. Pyke.[31] If you like to watch birds, perhaps you've wondered why, in obtaining food, some birds hover but other birds perch. Pyke investigated this question with two bird species that both obtain nectar from flowers: hummingbirds, which hover, and honeyeaters, which perch. He conducted three types of studies. One type involved observing the birds' behaviors under natural conditions, measuring as many of the relevant aspects of the birds' surroundings as possible. For example, he measured the distance the birds traveled between flowers, the time they spent at each flower, and the birds' body weights. Pyke conducted the second type of study in an aviary. He constructed artificial "flowers" consisting of surgical needles filled with sugar water so that he could control the exact amount and spacing of available food. For the third type of study, Pyke fed into a computer information about the birds' actual foraging behaviors as well as certain assumptions about how the birds foraged. Together, these three types of studies showed that the actual foraging behaviors of the two species of birds— hovering for the hummingbird and perching for the honeyeater, as well as the birds' patterns of movement between the flowers and the amount of time that they spent at each flower—was approximately optimal. For example, hovering allows a bird to move more quickly and easily between flowers, but hovering requires more energy than does perching. Thus, hovering is more suited to a smaller bird that requires less energy to hover, such as the hummingbird, than to a larger bird that requires more energy to hover, such as the honeyeater. (See Conversation Making Fact #7.)

> ## Conversation Making Fact #7
>
> *Optimal foraging theory and the microapproach can give you a new perspective on your favorite couch potato. Consider what happens to an animal's behavior when it has to expend increased energy to obtain food. Psychologists Suzanne H. Mitchell and Jasper Brener have shown that rats pressing levers for food will press the levers harder if it's the only way to get food. However, while pressing the levers harder in order to get food, the rats will expend less energy on other activities so as not to increase their total energy expenditure.[32] Similarly, couch potatoes, and all of us from time to time, will take advantage of opportunities to expend little energy. (Hence the success of the TV remote control!) This would have been adaptive when we were evolving in surroundings containing limited food, but now can result in some people being labeled as lazy. As you can now see, the word lazy may not be the most accurate way to describe such behavior.*

A little closer to home are two clever experiments conducted with university students by Herbert L. Meiselman and his colleagues. These scientists manipulated the difficulty of obtaining candy and potato chips in a university cafeteria that served a full range of foods. In the first part of each experiment, large displays of candy (Experiment 1) or potato chips (Experiment 2) were placed at each of the four main locations that students paid for their meals. In the second part of each experiment, the candy or potato chips were available only at a location that was some distance away from where the students usually paid for their meals, and the students had to stand in another line and pay separately for anything bought at that location. The cafeteria cashiers told the students the new candy or potato chips location only if the students asked about it. The experimenters found that when it was harder to get candy or potato chips, the students were much less likely to buy these items. Under these conditions, the students tended to buy foods such as fruit and other desserts instead of candy and other starches instead of potato chips.[33] Apparently it's possible to use effort—the amount of energy required to obtain a certain food—to influence what sorts of food someone chooses. Just imagine the effects on the eating behaviors of all of the office workers of America if vending machines containing junk food were banished to the basement instead of being right down the hall.

Now let's consider some examples of the macroapproach—using economic principles to describe the food choice behavior of groups of animals, including people. Using the macroapproach makes sense if you believe, as many scientists do, that the behaviors of groups of individuals, in addition to the behaviors of individuals, follow the principles of economics. Another reason that the macroapproach is often used is that group data are often the only data available.[34]

Do you remember reading in the section on sweet preference that when the price of sugar products went down and the availability of these products went up, consumption of sugar products increased? That's an example of how economics and a macroapproach can explain choice of sweet foods and drinks. Increasing sugar consumption is a common pattern as countries industrialize.[35]

The macroapproach has also been used frequently in anthropological studies of different cultures. For example, it has been used to explain how groups of people forage together and the degree to which they share food.[36] As a more specific example, the Ache foragers in Paraguay and the Hiwi foragers in Venezuela work together to obtain food from a particular source only when that food will provide them with more energy than they will use to obtain that food.[37] As another example, the relatively low amount of energy involved in obtaining calories and protein from insects may explain the popularity around the world of insects as a food source.[38]

Optimal Foraging Theory, Risk, and Self-Control

What does optimal foraging theory have to say about choosing between events that can occur only some time in the future? About self-control and impulsiveness? First let's think about what might happen when you're waiting for food, such as the free miniature waffles in the grocery store. During the delay period, you might be interrupted and never get any waffles because (a) you got a call on your cell phone that your child just tried to wash the family dog using laundry detergent, (b) you collapsed with a heart attack, (c) the waffle iron was opened by some ravenous children who ate all the half-cooked waffles, or (d) a waffle iron malfunction caused the waffles to burn up. This example shows that waiting for food can be a risky proposition; for many different reasons, you may or may not end up getting the food. As psychologist Edmund Fantino put it, "The future is uncertain; eat dessert first."[39]

Most species, including people, evolved in surroundings in which food was scattered and not reliable. In such surroundings, taking any immediately available food could give an animal a definite survival advantage, particularly if the animal is hungry. In nature, if you're hungry, and if there aren't lots of reliable food sources, the most sensible thing you can do is to eat anything that you can get your hands or paws or beak on right now; to do otherwise is to risk not having enough energy to find better food, and even to risk death.[40]

Therefore, particularly if an animal needs some food quickly in order to survive, the optimal choice, the choice that would be predicted by optimal foraging theory, may be for an animal to choose a smaller, immediate food item (impulsiveness) over a larger, delayed food item (self-control). And the advantages of immediate food aren't limited to the jungle and the savanna, as illustrated by this section of the play *Annie*:

> WARBUCKS: The New Deal, in my opinion, is badly planned, badly organized and badly administered. You don't think your programs through, Franklin, you don't think of what they're going to do to the economy in the long run.
> FDR: People don't eat in the long run.[41]

Work on the constraints that prevent animals from foraging optimally provides another explanation for the tendency of some animals to be impulsive. Many scientists have observed that species such as pigeons and rats will work for food even though free food will be given to them some time later. There's little advantage to these animals doing this work, but they work anyway. These results have been interpreted as indicating that some species under some conditions integrate events over a fairly brief period of time; their time window is relatively short.[42] In fact, one explanation of the greater self-control shown by people in the laboratory (as compared to pigeons) has been that people have a greater time window than do pigeons. People can count how many events occur and can time the durations of events, and this allows them to integrate events over entire laboratory sessions.[43] Nevertheless, as I've already discussed, people are still often impulsive with food. And although that may have benefited us greatly in the unpredictable surroundings in which we evolved, it doesn't do much for us now when eating any immediately available food results in our eating far more frequently than is good for our health.

Conclusion

You've seen many examples of how studying choice behavior can help us to understand why we consume particular foods and drinks. In particular, you've seen how two very specific models of choice behavior—the matching law and optimal foraging theory—try to describe and predict choice behavior. The matching law postulates that animals rely on a (relatively) simple rule of thumb when choosing among different foods, a rule of thumb that sometimes, but not always, coincides with choosing so as to maximize food or drink intake.[44] In contrast, optimal foraging theory postulates that animals choose in accordance with many different aspects of their surroundings, assessing energy output and energy input, in order to determine which choices will result in maximizing food or drink intake. Thus the focus of optimal foraging theory is on energy input and output and survival. Nevertheless, under some conditions, the matching law and optimal foraging theory make the same predictions. For example, both predict that when you go to the grocery store with the free demonstrations you should choose to get the hors d'oeuvres five times as much as the miniature waffles. Although many scientists have conducted tests to see if the matching law or optimal foraging theory is better at describing animals' food choice behaviors,[45] it's important to realize that there may not be one single correct model of food choice behavior. For example, both models have particular contributions to make to our knowledge about self-control. This is helpful because the study of self-control is of paramount importance to understanding and modifying eating and drinking behavior. You'll learn lots more about this in future chapters.

CHAPTER 8

You Are What You Eat and Drink

$\mathscr{C}$

A full belly counsels well.
French proverb

CAESAR:
Let me have men about me that are fat;
Sleek-headed men and such as sleep o' nights;
Yond Cassius has a lean and hungry look;
He thinks too much: such men are dangerous.
William Shakespeare (1599/1936)[1]

We've spent a lot of time so far in this book examining the factors that affect what we eat and drink. Now we're going to turn things around—how does what we eat and drink affect our behavior? In the extreme case, when someone eats or drinks nothing for a long period of time, all behavior ceases and the person dies. But what about situations in which at least some food and drink are being consumed? Under such circumstances can what is or isn't consumed affect specific aspects of a person's behavior? And what sorts of effects occur? Clearly the French, as well as Shakespeare, have expressed the opinion that eating well makes people easier to live with. Are opinions such as this correct?

Consider the fact that every single part of our bodies originated as some sort of nutrient that we or our mothers consumed. As with other mammals, the nutrients might have come to us through our umbilical cords or through our mouths. If everything about our bodies has originated as consumed nutrients, and if our behavior is entirely a function of our bodies (as opposed to some nonphysical entity or entities), then what we do must be affected by what we have eaten and drunk. As stated by Alice in what's perhaps the best-known published work on how you can be affected by what you eat or drink *(Alice's Adventures in Wonderland)*, "I know *something* interesting is sure to happen ... whenever I eat or drink anything."[2]

In this chapter we'll be looking at two basic types of situations: situations in which something missing from an animal's usual intake causes it to behave abnormally, and situations in which something present in an animal's usual intake causes it to behave in specific ways. One example of the latter that we won't cover in the present chapter is alcohol, because that subject is covered extensively in Chapter 11.

I'm sure that you've heard or read that it's okay to take such and such pill or drink for some illness or psychological problem because the pill or drink is "all natural." Such beliefs are part of our awareness that what we eat and drink can affect our behaviors, that foods and drinks can function as drugs or medicines. Foods and drinks that can prevent disease and increase health are known as functional foods. Functional foods have been used by many cultures for millennia. For example, one traditional Chinese belief is that diabetes can be treated with stewed duck egg and green tea. Functional foods represent a growing part of the United States food industry.[3] But what many people don't seem to realize is that just because something is "natural," it isn't necessarily good for you. In fact, although there are plenty of foods in our natural surroundings that can ameliorate symptoms of illness, our surroundings also contain plenty of poisons and toxins, substances that can cause abnormal behavior.

Because there has been so much hype and pop psychology about the effects of natural substances on our behaviors, I'll be spending some time in this chapter trying to show you how scientists investigate these effects and whether these effects really exist. I hope that by the time that you finish reading this chapter you'll have a new respect for how what you put in your mouth can affect your behavior and that, at the same time, you'll be better prepared to evaluate what you hear others say those effects may be.

Garbage in, Garbage out: Effects of Missing Nutrients

Some nutritional deficiencies affect virtually everyone, but other deficiencies cause problems in only some people's behaviors. We'll discuss both of these types of cases.

Effects Seen in Everyone

There are a number of different ways that we can look at how deprivation of certain nutrients affects behavior—deprivation of all nutrients versus just one nutrient, deprivation for a short or a long period of time, and deprivation of nutrients during pregnancy and early childhood or later. Let's start with early general malnutrition, beginning before or soon after birth. Malnutrition during infancy and early childhood can hinder children's cognitive development with accompanying brain abnormalities. However, nutritional supplements, if begun early, can eliminate some of these effects.[4]

Some scientists now believe that there isn't a simple relationship between malnutrition in children and subsequent impairments in their cognitive development. Instead, scientists believe that a child's nutritional status interacts with other aspects of the child's surroundings and that interaction can impair cognitive development. Adequate nutrition by itself isn't enough for a child to develop well intellectually—a child needs both adequate nutrition and intellectually stimulating surroundings.

Tufts University nutritionist Ernesto Pollitt and his colleagues examined such interactions among poor children in a village in Guatemala. For 8 years, beginning in 1969, children in two villages were given Atole, a high-calorie, high-protein nutritional supplement, while children in two other villages we were given Fresco, a relatively low-calorie, sweet drink that contains no protein. Some 20 years later, Pollitt showed that the children (now adults) who had received Atole performed significantly better on most cognitive tests than the children who had received Fresco. Pollitt also showed that the differences between the Atole and the Fresco children increased the greater the amount of education that these children had had. It was as if the better nutrition provided by the Atole allowed the children to take advantage of the educational opportunities available to them.[5] Malnutrition may decrease children's energy levels, curiosity, or responsiveness to changes in their surroundings, all effects that can inhibit their ability to learn.[6]

Now let's consider malnutrition in older adults. For many reasons, people of advanced age are relatively more likely to suffer from nutritional deficiencies than younger adults. One of these reasons, as you read about in Chapter 4, is that elderly people often have impaired senses of taste and smell and consequently don't eat well. The resulting nutrient deficiencies can impair memory, as well as cause other psychological problems. Therefore nutritional supplements can be extremely important for elderly people.[7]

The absence or presence of a single meal can also affect the cognitive abilities of children, as well as of adults. The usual nighttime fast, followed by missing breakfast, can cause both children and adults to perform worse on memory tests.[8] Similarly, college men who had a calorie-containing sweet snack in the afternoon did better on memory tests, made quicker responses, and solved more arithmetic problems than college men who had a snack with no calories (decaffeinated lemon-lime flavored diet soda).[9] In another experiment, psychologist Andrew Smith and his colleagues showed that there were no differences in the number of errors that women made on tasks requiring focused attention if the women had a lunch sized appropriately for their caloric needs or if they had a lunch 40% smaller than that. In other words, eating a little was as good cognitively as eating a normal amount. In contrast, if the women had a lunch 40% larger in calories than what they needed, they made significantly more errors on the focused attention tasks.[10] It therefore seems that if you want to work well in the afternoon, you need to eat just a small amount and should stay away from those big business lunches.

Now let's consider the effects of depriving children or adults of specific nutrients over long periods of time. Can such situations affect people's behaviors? In many cases, the answer is yes. For example, studies have shown that children with deficiencies in iron, iodine, or chloride do worse on cognitive tasks. Luckily, in many such cases, providing children with sufficient amounts of the previously inadequate nutrient will remove the cognitive deficiency.[11] In adults, deficiencies in folate have been associated with depression.[12] Perhaps of more concern given our present obsession with low-cholesterol diets, recent research has suggested that eating a very low cholesterol diet can make people more likely to engage in suicide or violent behavior.[13] Is this was what Caesar was thinking when he was speaking about Cassius? I've always known that trying to eat a low-fat diet makes me feel cranky, but I've never thought that I might go so far as to kill myself or someone else!

Effects Seen in Some People

Some researchers believe that, for a variety of reasons, some people, even though their intake is considered normal, have bodies that are deficient in one or more nutrients. These researchers reason that such deficiencies can cause the nutrient-deficient people to behave abnormally, and that the abnormal behavior can be treated or prevented by removing the deficiencies. The Nobel Prize–winning scientist Linus Pauling has called this approach orthomolecular psychiatry.[14]

One example of such a deficiency has been known for quite some time— the irreversible memory disorder that has been called Wernicke-Korsakoff syndrome. People who suffer from this disease have difficulty remembering recent events. The syndrome is caused by two factors. One factor is a genetic abnormality in the activity of a particular chemical substance in our bodies that normally, among other actions, helps us to digest glucose. The other factor is food intake that is deficient in thiamine. When both of these factors are present, the syndrome will develop. This syndrome tends to be seen in alcoholics because they're frequently malnourished, but it can also occur in nonalcoholics if they have the genetic abnormality and a thiamine deficiency.[15]

The symptoms of Wernicke-Korsakoff syndrome were dramatically demonstrated to me when I was only 17 years old. For my high school senior project I worked as a nurse's aide in a psychiatric hospital in Philadelphia. During one of my first days at the hospital, a nurse asked me to take a middle-aged woman patient for a walk. The patient was attractive looking and well dressed. The hospital grounds were quite nice and it was a beautiful day. I didn't know my way around very well and the patient repeatedly told me she was new there also and had no idea which way to go. We walked to the greenhouse and the patient said that she was delighted to find out that this hospital had a greenhouse. We also passed an old tree with huge, twisting roots, which the patient said looked like snakes. We had a very pleasant conversation during our walk and I kept trying to figure out why she was in the hospital—could it be related to her thinking that the roots looked like snakes? When we got back to the ward, I checked her chart. She had been there for many weeks and had been to the greenhouse many times. She was an alcoholic and had been diagnosed with Wernicke-Korsakoff syndrome. She could not remember that she had seen the grounds and the greenhouse before. I was told that, even if she stopped drinking alcohol, her memory would never improve.

Pauling conceived of orthomolecular psychiatry as much more than disorders such as Wernicke-Korsakoff syndrome. According to Pauling, many people are suffering from nutrient deficiencies that can be cured by changing what they eat. For example, he contended that schizophrenics suffer from a deficiency of vitamin C and that schizophrenia can be successfully treated by giving large doses of vitamin C. However, firm scientific results for such beliefs, as well as the belief that large doses of vitamin C help to cure or prevent other diseases, have not been forthcoming.[16]

Some researchers have claimed that the amounts of some neurotransmitters such as serotonin are deficient in some people with resulting psychological abnormalities. Researchers have repeatedly shown that low levels of serotonin in people as well as other animals are associated with high levels of impulsive behavior, including aggression and suicide.[17] In fact, it's believed that low levels of cholesterol in the body may decrease the level of serotonin, and that is why, as you just read, low cholesterol levels are associated with violent behavior in some people.[18] Other researchers believe that low levels of serotonin cause depression in some people.[19] Now how does this relate to what you eat? Amino acids, the building blocks of proteins, are also important building blocks of neurotransmitters. You get amino acids into your body by eating protein. Behavior is influenced by the levels of the neurotransmitters, which in turn are influenced by the levels of amino acids, which in turn may be influenced by what you eat each day.[20]

If all of this is correct, then increasing the levels of serotonin in people who are impulsive, violent, and depressed should decrease their problem behaviors. There have been attempts to do this using medication as well as by modifying what people eat. The latter, although somewhat more speculative, is of greater interest to us here. We know that, theoretically, it should be possible to affect serotonin levels by manipulating people's food intake. Serotonin is made in the body from its precursor tryptophan, which is an amino acid. As it turns out, the concentration of tryptophan in the blood can be increased by eating a high-carbohydrate meal. Note that I didn't say that you increase tryptophan in the blood by eating a high-protein meal. If you've been following this section closely, you should be saying, "How can that be? Tryptophan is a component of protein, not carbohydrate." Let me explain.

Protein foods contain very little tryptophan, although they do contain a great many of the other amino acids. After an animal, such as you, has eaten a high-protein meal, the tryptophan and the other amino acids that you've eaten enter your blood. From there, they compete to enter your brain. Also present in your blood at this time is insulin, because you've probably also eaten at least some carbohydrate, and the body produces insulin to digest the carbohydrate. The insulin transports some of these other amino acids (but not tryptophan) to the muscles that move your bones. Yet there will still be enough of these other amino acids left to compete with the tryptophan in the blood around the brain so that many more of these other amino acids will enter the brain than will tryptophan. (See Figure 8.1.) On the other hand, if you eat a high-carbohydrate meal, the amounts of tryptophan, other amino acids, and insulin in your body are such that there end up being very few amino acids other than tryptophan competing to enter the brain, and so much more tryptophan enters the brain.[21] This should then increase the levels of serotonin in the brain. I say *should* because this last part is somewhat controversial. Many experiments haven't directly measured levels of brain serotonin, or at least not in people, so the researchers don't know for sure that what they were doing affected the brain.

Let's take an example of all of this in people. Dutch scientists C. R. Markus, G. Panhuysen, A. Tuiten, and colleagues did an experiment to examine people who were and weren't prone to stress. The researchers were specifically interested in finding out whether stress-prone people would be less likely to get depressed in performing a stressful task if they ate a food rich in carbohydrates prior to doing the task. These researchers assumed that people more prone to stress reactions would have deficient levels of serotonin in their brains, and therefore eating significant amounts of carbohydrate would increase their brain serotonin levels and make them less likely to demonstrate stress reactions.

During the experiment, in addition to measuring the participants' mood levels, the researchers measured the participants' stress levels (for example, by measuring pulse rate) and blood levels of tryptophan and other amino acids. The stressful task that the participants were asked to perform consisted of doing mental arithmetic—arithmetic without the benefit of pencil, calculator, or computer. Further, during the mental arithmetic, loud noise was

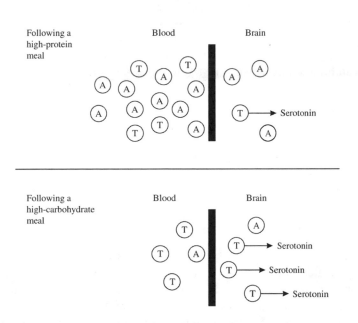

Figure 8.1 Conceptual diagram of how tryptophan may enter the brain and thus affect behavior. Tryptophan (T) in the blood competes with other amino acids (A) for access from the blood to the brain. After a high-protein meal is eaten, many amino acids enter the bloodstream; few of these are tryptophan. Therefore, because of competition, relatively little tryptophan enters the brain, and therefore tryptophan does not affect behavior. However, after a high-carbohydrate meal, very few amino acids enter the bloodstream. In addition, insulin is released. Insulin transports most of the amino acids, but not tryptophan, to the muscles that move your bones. Therefore, because there's little competition, a relatively great amount of tryptophan enters the brain. In the brain tryptophan increases serotonin, which may affect behavior. (Adapted from H. R. Lieberman, S. Corkin, B. J. Spring, J. H. Growdon, and R. J. Wurtman, "Mood, Performance, and Pain Sensitivity: Changes Induced by Food Constituents," *Journal of Psychiatric Research* 17[1982/1983]:135–145.)

present, and the participants were led to believe that they were repeatedly getting the questions wrong (sounds pretty stressful to me!). Participants were tested on the task both after eating food that was rich in carbohydrate and after eating food that was rich in protein. The number of calories and the amount of fat were kept constant. Thus, there were two kinds of participants (stress-prone and non-stress-prone participants) and two kinds of meals (rich in carbohydrate and rich in protein); everything else was kept constant. The results showed that, for the stress-prone participants only, there was less of a stress response, including no increase in depression, when they performed the task after eating the carbohydrate-rich food. Also, the ratio of tryptophan to other amino acids in the participants' blood after they had eaten the carbohydrate-rich food was significantly higher than after they had eaten the protein-rich food. These results suggest that, if you've a tendency to get stressed out, you may do better if you eat mostly carbohydrates, and that effect may be due to increased serotonin in your brain.[22]

"One Side [of the Mushroom] Will Make You Grow Taller, and the Other Side Will Make You Grow Shorter"[23]

But what about people who have no demonstrable nutritional or neurotransmitter deficits? Can what such people eat affect their behavior? There's a lot of good evidence indicating that, at least in some cases, it can.

Effects Seen in Everyone

A large number of experiments have demonstrated that eating a meal or even just drinking water can affect your level of activity, mood, performance of a task, and the speed with which you think time is passing. Sometimes eating a meal increases these aspects of behavior and sometimes it decreases them, depending on the time of day that the meal is eaten and what it contains. For example, a high-carbohydrate meal, which, you'll remember, increases tryptophan and therefore probably also serotonin, can make you feel more tired, improve your mood, and make time seem to pass more slowly.[24]

As a more specific example, in an experiment performed by psychologist Bonnie Spring and her colleagues, women reported feeling tired after a single high-carbohydrate meal, but not after a single high-protein meal or a single meal containing both carbohydrate and protein. In addition, Spring and her colleagues showed that the fatigue following the high-carbohydrate meal wasn't related to blood sugar level; instead, the onset of fatigue coincided with the elevation of tryptophan in the blood.[25] This is interesting because serotonin is important in the regulation of sleep, and many studies have shown that direct administration of tryptophan improves sleep in adult and newborn humans.[26] Spring and her colleagues have also shown that people tend to perform worse on a task requiring sustained attention following a high-carbohydrate meal than following a high-protein meal.[27]

What all of this says to me is that, if I'm having trouble sleeping, my dinner should consist of nothing but carbohydrates. And if I want to be alert, it's a good idea to eat some protein, as opposed to snacking on cookies and crackers, or even on vegetables and fruit (all of which consist of nothing but carbohydrates). But my reading of this literature has probably resulted in an even larger impact on my teenage son's life than on mine. Whenever he describes what he ate for lunch at school, he has to listen to me intone, "Where was the protein?" (His favorite lunch is pasta with meatless tomato sauce washed down by juice, a meal containing virtually no protein.) At every breakfast, ever since my son started attending preschool at age 2, I've obsessed about his having some protein—be it in the form of milk in his cereal, yogurt, or cheese (all of which contain the calcium that I also insist that he have). If none of these are available or are, heaven forbid, refused, I'll even resort to giving him his favorite leftover—takeout sesame chicken. Anything, as long as he has some protein in his stomach for his morning classes.

But if protein makes you relatively more alert, and carbohydrate makes you feel more tired, what about the sugar high that everyone talks about, especially in kids? Sugar is 100% carbohydrate, but kids go crazy when they eat lots of candy, correct? This is one of the most cherished beliefs of American parents and teachers: When kids are wild, it's not them or how they're treated; it's the sugar they ate. Yet carefully conducted experiments have repeatedly failed to show that sugar significantly affects children's behavior.

For example, pediatrician Mark L. Wolraich and his colleagues published an analysis of a group of 16 previously published studies of the effects of eating sugar on children's behavior. To be included in the examined group of studies, a study had to have several characteristics. First, it had to give children a specific, measured amount of sugar. Second, it had to compare the effects of giving sugar to giving an artificial sweetener. Third, in order to ensure that whatever behavioral changes were seen were due only to the actual effects of the sugar, and not due just to what someone thought the sugar should do, the children, their parents, and the researchers monitoring the children's behavior could not know when sugar (as opposed to artificial sweetener) was given. After the sweet substance was given to a child, and the child's behavior measured, only then could a qualifying study have revealed to the participants when a child had been given sugar or an artificial sweetener. The analysis of all of the studies meeting these criteria showed that, no matter what aspect of the children's behavior was measured, be it activity level or performance on a learning task, there was no significant change in the children's behavior due to sugar. The authors do admit, though, that there may be some children whose behavior is somewhat affected by sugar. However, there's no question that the behavior of at least the large majority of children isn't affected by sugar.[28] So, all those times when your kids seem to go crazy at Halloween, it's probably the holiday that's exciting them, not the candy that they've eaten.

Performance isn't just improved by eating a little protein; pleasant odors may also have this effect. Psychologists Robert A. Baron and Marna I. Bronfen investigated how male and female undergraduates at Rensselaer Polytechnic Institute performed on a word task in which they had to use one letter and a six-letter word to make a new seven-letter word. Some of the participants were placed under stress while they performed the task. The experimenter watched them, a timer was used, and they were told that most people could complete more words in the time allotted than was really the case. In addition, for some participants Glade® Powder Fresh air freshener was sprayed in the room where the participants worked, for other participants Glade Spiced Apple was used, and for the remaining participants no air freshener was used. Both of the air fresheners had been previously judged by undergraduates to be very pleasant and attractive. The results showed that the air fresheners significantly enhanced performance in the high-stress conditions.[29] Reading this experiment has made me seriously consider spraying some air freshener around my office staff (to whom I undoubtedly cause stress) for my own version of aromatherapy. But I'm afraid that the staff might be so surprised to see me spraying the office that their astonishment would counteract any positive effect of the air fresheners!

Let's consider the effects on behavior when you eat a very different substance: MSG, otherwise known as monosodium glutamate. MSG is a form of an amino acid that is frequently added to foods, presumably as a flavor enhancer. Nevertheless, taste researchers have known for many years that MSG does not enhance flavors already present in food; instead it adds its own taste.[30] As you probably already know, eating MSG gives many adults what's known as the Chinese restaurant syndrome, or, to be more accurate, Kwok's disease. This is a fairly immediate, short-lived reaction frequently characterized by a tightening of the muscles of the face and neck, headache, nausea, giddiness, and sweating.[31] In the brain, MSG acts as a neurotransmitter, one that increases neuronal activity. When MSG is present in excessive amounts, it becomes an excitotoxin, literally a substance that excites neurons to death.[32] MSG given in high doses to rat pups can cause brain lesions and later difficulties in learning, even when the MSG is part of what the pups normally eat. The effects of lower doses aren't known.[33]

Because of these findings, MSG has been removed from baby food, and for many years there has been controversy about whether the Food and Drug Administration should ban it from all food.[34] But so far the concerns about MSG haven't resulted in much change in what's in prepared foods. For example, I challenge you to go to the supermarket and try to find canned soup without MSG—it can be done, but it's not easy.

Finally, what about that well-known plant extract, ginkgo biloba? There have been many claims that taking this herbal supplement enhances memory. However, experiments have shown that any positive effects on memory that may result from consuming ginkgo biloba are no greater than the relatively small improvement in memory resulting from eating sugar, a cheap and easily available alternative.[35]

Effects Seen in Some People

Some scientists have contended that some people's bodies are sensitive to particular nutritive substances present in normal food, and that if these sensitive people eat these particular substances, they will behave abnormally. The study of these food sensitivities is part of what's called clinical ecology, the study and treatment of animals' reactions to what's present in their surroundings.[36]

A well-documented food sensitivity that results in psychological symptoms is shown by children with PKU (phenylketonuria). Approximately 1 in every 20,000 children born in the United States has this disease. These children are born missing the gene that plays an important role in the metabolism of the amino acid phenylalanine. Phenylalanine therefore accumulates in the body, resulting in very severe and permanent retardation. Luckily, in the United States, newborns are now tested for PKU. If an infant with PKU is given only low-phenylalanine foods immediately after birth, he or she will usually develop normally.[37] However, this dietary treatment may need to continue indefinitely. In fact, continuing the treatment may be particularly important if a woman with PKU becomes pregnant. If treatment isn't continued throughout pregnancy, the resulting baby may have low IQ, low birth weight, and brain and heart abnormalities.[38]

Experiments are scanty on more subtle food sensitivities. One study was conducted by scientist David S. King.[39] He examined participants' reactions to substances to which they were likely to be sensitive. First he asked the participants how frequently they ate various substances, how much they craved them, and how they felt after they ate them. Based on those reports, he selected for his study the substances to which he thought his participants would be most likely to be sensitive: extracts of wheat, beef, milk, cane sugar, and tobacco smoke. King placed these extracts under the participants' tongues and compared the subjects' reactions to when a placebo (distilled water) was used instead. He took many precautions to make sure that participants' responses were solely a function of the actual substances under their tongues and weren't affected by what they believed was under their tongues. For example, he didn't tell the participants which extract he was using when or even that sometimes a placebo was used. The participants reported significantly more cognitive-emotional symptoms (such as depression and irritability) following administration of the extracts than following administration of the placebo. However, they did not report significantly more bodily symptoms (such as nasal congestion and flushing) following the extracts. Therefore King's results appear to provide support for the hypothesis that some food substances can cause psychological reactions in people. But it isn't clear to what extent these reactions are characteristic of only some people, as opposed to the general population. Also, it's important to keep in mind that King used food extracts, not natural foods, and so his results might not apply to natural eating conditions.

Put a Tiger in Your Tank: The Effects of Nonnutritive Substances in Foods

What we eat and drink often contains substances that don't provide any nutrition. These substances include artificial colors, flavorings, and preservatives, as well as unintended contaminants and toxins. (See Conversation Making Fact #8.) To the extent that these substances affect our behavior, they're of concern to us here. I'll be discussing three examples: caffeine, lead, and the food additives that some people believe make some children hyperactive.

Caffeine

One nonnutritive substance that can strongly affect behavior and that many Americans consume frequently is caffeine. Caffeine is present in chocolate, many soft drinks, coffee-flavored yogurt, and, of course, tea and coffee (see Table 8.1). Among people in the United States who are at least 18 years of age, the average consumption of caffeine per day is equivalent to the amount in about two cups of regular coffee (200 mg),[40] but keep in mind that some people never consume any and other people regularly consume a great deal more that 200 mg. It's also important to remember that many Americans, including children, currently get their caffeine in the form of soft drinks. In fact, the marketing of the soft drink Jolt is based on its high caffeine content— one 12-ounce can has almost as much caffeine as a cup of coffee.

> ### Conversation Making Fact #8
>
> *History is replete with examples of nonnutritive substances that have been present in food and that have contributed to events of major historical significance. Let's consider two examples. First, some researchers believe that a type of food poisoning, ergotism, was responsible for the 1692 Salem witch trials. The symptoms of ergotism include temporary deafness or blindness, sensations of pinching or of ants crawling under the skin, and convulsions. Ergotism is caused by ergot, a fungus that grows on grains, particularly rye. It's likely that a great deal of rye contaminated with ergot was eaten in Salem around 1692, and, probably not coincidentally, those accused of being bewitched in the Salem witch trials complained of symptoms almost identical with ergotism.[41] As another historical example, if you're a Van Gogh fan, you should know that his paintings may have been influenced by his addiction to a pale green liqueur called absinthe. Absinthe was popular in France in the late 19th and early 20th centuries and was contaminated with a toxin called thujone. Thujone causes hallucinations, mental impairment, and, eventually, irreversible brain damage. Some people believe that Van Gogh's addiction to absinthe contributed to his psychosis and suicide.[42] Van Gogh was so enamored with absinthe that in 1887 he even created a still life painting entitled* A Glass of Absinthe and a Carafe.

As you certainly know yourself if you've ever drunk a cup of coffee, consumption of caffeine, in moderate doses, increases feelings of alertness and energy, as well as increases attention and sociability. It can even enhance memory in older adults.[43] Many people find these effects pleasant, so that they're willing to expend effort to obtain caffeine. For example, in the laboratory, psychologist Suzanne H. Mitchell and her colleagues showed that habitual coffee drinkers, whether or not they were caffeine deprived, would repeatedly move a computer mouse and click it at specific locations in order to obtain points exchangeable for coffee.[44] In another experiment, scientists Nicola J. Richardson and her colleagues compared people who regularly did and didn't consume a caffeinated beverage after lunch. Only those who did showed greater increased preference for a novel-flavored fruit juice after drinking it with a caffeine

Table 8.1 The Amount of Caffeine in Some Foods and Drinks

Food/Drink	Amount of Caffeine
Starbucks coffee, 12 ounces	190 mg
Brewed coffee, 6 ounces	100 mg
Jolt Cola, 12 ounces	72 mg
Mountain Dew, 12 ounces	56 mg
Dannon coffee yogurt, 8 ounces	45 mg
Tea, 6 ounces	40 mg
Hershey chocolate bar	20 mg

Sources: American Psychiatric Association, *Diagnostic and Statistical Manual of Mental Disorders* (Rev. ed.), 4th ed., Washington, DC: APA, 1994; E. O'Connor, "A Sip into Dangerous Territory," *Monitor on Psychology* (June 2001):60–62.

capsule as compared to if the capsule were a placebo. Such findings can help us understand why some people who have decided to stop consuming caffeine will still drink black decaffeinated coffee, a bitter substance. They have previously associated the positive effects of caffeine with the taste of coffee, resulting in an enduring preference for the taste of black coffee.[45]

There has been much discussion regarding whether caffeine can be considered an addictive drug. It's certainly true that some aspects of caffeine consumption are similar to consumption of well-known addictive drugs. For example, at least sometimes, people develop tolerance to caffeine so that, with increasing experience with caffeine, larger doses are needed in order to get the same effects. In addition, at least sometimes, removing caffeine from regular consumers results in adverse consequences such as headaches and feelings of lethargy. In other words, removal of caffeine from regular caffeine consumers results in withdrawal symptoms, which is a hallmark of addiction. Nevertheless, caffeine does not appear to affect the brain as do other addictive drugs,[46] and, for a variety of reasons, some people may be reluctant to classify caffeine with such dangerous drugs as heroin.

There has also been some controversy as to whether caffeine can have adverse health effects. Certainly in high doses it can. For example, high doses can cause panic attacks and palpitations, as well as aggravate stomach ulcers and disturb sleep.[47] Caffeine can also increase metabolic rate, so that more calories are burned, which sounds like a good thing if you're concerned about your weight. However, that possible benefit may be counteracted by the decrease in blood sugar level caused by caffeine, which in turn increases hunger.[48] In addition, in some people consumption of as little as one cup of coffee can result in a disorder called caffeine intoxication, which is marked by "restlessness ... nervousness ... excitement ... insomnia ... flushed face ... diuresis [excessive discharge of urine] ... [and] gastrointestinal disturbance."[49]

Lead

Lead is a toxin that has often been present in what we've eaten or drunk, and whose effects have been extensively investigated. There is much evidence that ingesting lead can cause behavioral problems. In one experiment, a group of rats began consuming lead-containing liquids as soon as they were weaned. The liquids given to another group of rats contained no lead. Then as adults, all of the rats, while hungry, were tested on a task in which a fixed number of lever presses would result in the rats getting a food pellet. In addition, if a rat waited a specified amount of time after receiving a pellet before beginning to press the lever again, that rat would receive extra pellets. As it turned out, the lead-exposed rats responded more quickly on the lever and were less likely to wait after receiving a pellet. Thus, although they still received a lot of pellets, they ended up making many more lever presses per pellet.[50] These results seem to suggest that lead exposure can increase nonefficient, impulsive behavior.

We also know that large doses of dietary lead hinder children's learning and even cause retardation.[51] Further, there are indications that children whose bodies contain significant amounts of lead may be more likely to have decreased attention and be aggressive[52]—tendencies that can be described as impulsive.

Lead poisoning has been affecting our behavior for much of history. Because lead has a sweet taste, people, since the time of the Roman Empire and continuing through the 18th century, added various lead-containing substances to wine to preserve or sweeten it. In the 18th century, the powder used to whiten wigs contained lead.[53] Just imagine how much of that got on people's hands and in their food! Another example of how, in the past, lead entered the food supply concerns the 134-member Franklin expedition of 1845. This expedition left England for the Arctic with the task of mapping the Northwest Passage. During the course of the expedition, many of the expedition's members began to behave strangely, and all of them died before they could complete their mission. Examinations of their bodies have indicated that their deaths were caused by lead in the expedition's food supply. The recovered bodies contained high amounts of lead, and the cans that contained the expedition's food supply were probably made with large amounts of lead.[54]

We know enough now to make our food cans without lead and to keep lead out of our wine, and, thank goodness, we no longer wear powdered wigs. In fact, knowledge about the damaging effects of lead poisoning has resulted in the United States banning lead from house paint and gasoline for the past several decades.[55] However, there is still lead-based paint in many older buildings, and particles or chips of lead-based paint may be generated when an older building is renovated. Then people who get the paint particles on their hands and then put their hands in their mouths are at risk. Remember that lead is sweet. Therefore it's possible that lead-based paint particles may be particularly attractive to children. Further, it has been shown that inner cities that have exposed soil (such as Philadelphia, but not Manhattan), have greater frequencies of lead poisoning in the children who live in those areas. Scientists believe that lead has gotten into those cities' soil from such sources as gasoline fumes (when gas contained lead) and from renovations of older houses. Once the lead is in the soil, it stays there for decades, ready to cling to the hands of children who play in it.[56] Unfortunately, children are particularly susceptible to lead poisoning, and lead, once in the body, remains there for a great many years.[57] For all of these reasons it's particularly important to keep children away from all possible sources of lead.

Before ending this section on lead I should note that there has been a great deal of controversy concerning precisely how much lead exposure will noticeably compromise the cognitive abilities of a child. Psychiatrist Herbert L. Needleman believes that even low exposure can decrease IQ.[58] Based at least partly on his findings, the U.S. Centers for Disease Control lowered the amount of lead in children's blood deemed indicative of lead poisoning.[59] However, other scientists have contended that there were serious problems with Needleman's research, even to the point of falsification of data. However, ultimately, Needleman was cleared of charges of scientific misconduct.[60]

Hyperactivity

There have been many claims that food additives cause psychological abnormalities in some people. The most thoroughly investigated as well as the most controversial claim of this nature concerns attention-deficit/hyperactivity disorder (ADHD). This disorder is characterized by "a persistent pattern of inattention and/or hyperactivity-impulsivity that is more frequent and severe than is typically observed in individuals at a comparable level of development." Examples of inattention are "makes careless mistakes in schoolwork, work, or other activities [or] does not follow through on instructions"; and examples of hyperactivity-impulsivity are "often talks excessively [or] often interrupts or intrudes on others." Before you get too upset thinking, "But I do that!" keep in mind that all of us, particularly children, engage in these sorts of behaviors some of the time. In order to be diagnosed with ADHD, someone must show many of these behaviors in several settings, and these behaviors must clearly interfere with the person's ability to lead a successful life. Please also keep in mind that no one description characterizes all people diagnosed with ADHD. There are a number of different subtypes, and even within one subtype the same symptoms aren't shown by all people.[61]

Several different treatments have been tried with hyperactive children. Stimulant drugs called amphetamines have been used for many years. Although amphetamines seem to speed up adults' behavior, they seem to slow down the behavior of children, including hyperactive children. Apparently, for both adults and children, amphetamines increase attention to cognitive tasks. Because sustaining attention on a cognitive task is particularly difficult for children, and because activity and attention are incompatible, hyperactive children administered amphetamines are less active.[62] Research has shown that, even when amphetamine treatment continues for as long as 15 months, children display fewer ADHD symptoms than if they have been given a placebo, and there are few negative side effects.[63] Various behavioral procedures have also been used as treatments. For example, there have been attempts to teach boys with ADHD to speak in a group only after raising their hands.[64] However, in general, using amphetamines is more effective in decreasing ADHD symptoms than is using behavioral treatments. Still more effective is using a combination of amphetamine and behavioral treatments.[65]

Now we should return to the reason that ADHD is included in this book—the possibility that some cases may be caused by eating certain things. Some research has shown that consumption of the toxins PCBs cause hyperactivity and impulsiveness in rats.[66] However, far more discussed is the possibility that ADHD is caused by sensitivities to food additives. Approximately 30 years ago, physician Ben F. Feingold proposed that hyperactivity in some children is due to their increased tendency to react to certain substances in their food. These substances include artificial flavors, artificial colors, the preservatives BHT and BHA, and salicylates, substances that occur naturally in foods such as almonds, apples, and tomatoes. Feingold reasoned that if all of these substances were removed from what's consumed, the hyperactive behavior should significantly decrease. Thus was born the Feingold diet for hyperactive children.[67]

Over the ensuing years, many experiments, conducted with people and other animals, have been conducted to find out whether the above substances are responsible for ADHD symptoms, but there is still no general agreement about what the results show. The National Institutes of Health have recently stated that there are no clear answers as to what causes ADHD, and they support only stimulant medication and behavioral treatments as methods for decreasing ADHD symptoms.[68] Some reviews of the research have concluded that sensitivities may be responsible for the symptoms of some ADHD children, while other reviews have come to the opposite conclusion.[69] The Center for Science in the Public Interest distributes information stating that a subset of ADHD children is affected by food additives and other specific substances in foods and drinks, and therefore parents should consider, as an initial treatment strategy, changing what their hyperactive children consume.[70] The reasoning behind this suggestion is that, in some studies, the behavior of a small number of children does improve when they follow something like the Feingold diet. The problem is that it can be very difficult to determine whether, in such a situation, this small number of children improve due to their being different from the other hyperactive children, or if this small number of children improve due to chance. On average with the passage of time, some children might, without any specific treatment, show improvements in their behavior. For these reasons, there's as yet no consensus on using approaches such as the Feingold diet. Further, it's important to remember that there are definite costs to using something like the Feingold diet. If this diet isn't effective at treating ADHD, the result can be loss of money, wasted effort, disappointment, and the possible avoidance of other more effective treatments.

Food for Thought: Conclusion

Scientists have made some dramatic discoveries in the past several decades about the effects of food consumption on our behavior. Although what we eat and drink may not influence hyperactivity in children to any great degree, it may influence how sleepy we are, how well we learn, how depressed we are, and whether we feel as if ants are crawling under our skin. To some degree, you are indeed what you eat and drink. The future will undoubtedly bring additional speculations and research that will test statements such as the following by Galileo who, in this interpretation by Bertolt Brecht, is a dedicated scientist who believes that plentiful supplies of food and drink are essential to his doing his research:

How can I work, with the tax collector on the doorstep? And my poor daughter will never acquire a husband unless she has a dowry, she's not too bright. And I like to buy books—all kinds of books. Why not? And what about my appetite? I don't think well unless I eat well. Can I help it if I get my best ideas over a good meal and a bottle of wine? They don't pay me as much as they pay the butcher's boy. If only I could have five years to do nothing but research! Come on. I am going to show you something else.[71]

CHAPTER 9

"Hunger Talks
a Most Persuasive Language"[1]

Anorexia and Bulimia

𝒞

Y ou are at an outdoor cafe on a pleasant summer evening. A young woman is sitting at a table with two other people. You look at her face. She has very prominent cheekbones and a sharp chin. She raises her right arm to reach for her water glass. You see that the arm is a mere stick with skin on it; her arm looks like a skeleton's with a flesh-colored covering. A waiter brings plates of food to the young woman and her companions. She uses her fork to push the food around her plate. Very occasionally she brings a small forkful of food to her mouth and chews and swallows the food. When the waiter takes her plate away, most of the food is still there.

This chapter and the next will discuss situations in which we eat inappropriate amounts of food—either too little or too much. The present chapter focuses on cases in which someone, such as the young woman just described, eats too little. Such behavior is described as *anorexia*, which literally means "lack of appetite." However, this definition is somewhat misleading because, as you'll learn, people with anorexia sometimes have a significant appetite; they just don't eat. This chapter is a very serious one, including discussion of life-threatening eating disorders. I hope that the information will be useful to you in understanding and dealing with these extremely difficult disorders.

When you read about the young woman at the start of this chapter, you may have immediately assumed that her anorexia was a symptom of anorexia nervosa, an eating disorder that will be discussed later in this chapter. However, the young woman's anorexia could actually have been due to many different factors. Anorexia is sometimes caused by infections, certain types of gastrointestinal diseases, decreases in taste and smell, Alzheimer's disease, and AIDS.[2] Some drugs, such as amphetamines, also decrease the amount eaten.[3] In addition, anorexia can be associated with mood, but the relationship is complex. For example, if someone is not a dieter and that person becomes depressed, then that person will tend to eat less than usual. On the other hand, if someone is a dieter and that person becomes depressed, then that person will tend to eat more than usual.[4] This chapter will review in detail one type of anorexia that has been investigated a great deal, the anorexia associated with cancer, as well as anorexia nervosa. Finally, because anorexia may occur as part of bulimia nervosa, an eating disorder characterized by intermittent periods of excess eating, the present chapter also includes information on bulimia.

But what about voluntarily not eating in order to improve your health? You have probably seen in newspapers and magazines some reports of research showing health benefits of severe calorie restriction. Experiments with rats and monkeys have shown that these animals may live longer and be less likely to become ill if, for many years, they eat a diet that is nutritionally balanced but contains about 60–70% of the calories that the animals would ordinarily eat.[5] However, not surprisingly, no comparable experiments have yet been done with people. Keep in mind that it's possible that the reduced-calorie diet must continue for years in order for there to be health benefits. Would you be able to eat 70% of your usual calories for years? The rats and monkeys had no choice, but you would constantly have to defy temptation. Also, it's very difficult to achieve a balanced diet with that kind of calorie intake. The scientists were able to do it for the rats and monkeys by carefully controlling what the experimental animals ate, but chances are you would not be as good at getting adequate nutrition given severe calorie restriction. Anemia (due to inadequate iron intake) or osteoporosis (due to inadequate calcium and vitamin D intake) are two likely results. Further, research suggests that a fluctuating weight has negative health consequences.[6] Therefore trying—and repeatedly failing—to restrict severely calorie intake could be worse than never trying to restrict calories at all. For all of these reasons, it seems unwise at this time for people to try to prolong their life spans by restricting their caloric intake.

When dealing with anorexia, as well as when dealing with overeating in the next chapter, it becomes critical to have good ways of measuring weight gain, loss, and the percentage of body fat. Over the years, many ways have been suggested and have gained and lost popularity. You're probably familiar with one or more of the many height-weight charts that state how much a woman or man should weigh given that person's height and body frame size. Other methods that have been used to estimate body size or fat include measuring waist circumference, measuring the thickness of various skinfolds such as the skin on the back of the upper arm, weighing the person under water, and using radiologic methods (such as x-rays).[7] Currently the most popular method is the body mass index, or BMI. Your BMI is equal to your weight (measured in kilograms) divided by the square of your height (measured in meters). A higher BMI means that someone has more body weight for a given height. In other words, if two people are the same height, the heavier one will have a larger BMI value. For example, someone who is 5 feet 4 inches tall (1.63 meters) and weighs 124 pounds (56 kilograms) will have a BMI of 21. You can easily calculate your own BMI by accessing the Web site, www.nhlbi.nih.gov/guidelines/obesity/ob_home.htm.

There has been a lot of controversy about what weights are and aren't healthy.[8] Many studies have been done to determine if, assuming everything else is held constant, people are more likely to become ill at certain weights than others. It does appear that, for example, being too thin can inhibit the immune system, and being too heavy can contribute to cancer, diabetes, heart disease, and stroke.[9] Currently, a popular method for assessing the health impact of different degrees of body weight combines use of both the BMI and of waist circumference. Table 9.1 shows how someone's risk of disease increases given a combination of a high BMI and a large waist circumference.

Cancer Anorexia

All too many of us have seen cancer patients who are terribly gaunt and who eat very little. Approximately 50% of cancer patients lose large amounts of weight, a process known as wasting. In fact, scientists believe that approximately 10–25% of all deaths from cancer are actually due to wasting.[10] Possible explanations of the anorexia and weight loss accompanying cancer

Table 9.1 Disease Risk Relative to Weight and Waist Circumference

Weight Category	BMI (kg/m^2)	Obesity Class	Waist Circumference Men ≤102 cm (≤40 in.) Women ≤88 cm (≤35 in.)	>102 cm (>40 in.) ≥88 cm (≥35 in.)
Underweight	<18.5		——	——
Normal	18.5–24.9		——	——
Overweight	25.0–29.9		Increased	High
Obesity	30.0–34.9	I	High	Very high
	35.0–39.9	II	Very high	Very high
Extreme Obesity	≥40	III	Extremely high	Extremely high

Source: Adapted from National Heart, Lung, and Blood Institute, *Clinical Guidelines on the Identification, Evaluation, and Treatment of Overweight and Obesity in Adults*, 1998. Available at: www.nhlbi.nih.gov/guidelines/obesity/ob_home.htm.

include changes in, for example, cancer patients' taste sensitivities, food preferences, and metabolisms. These changes may result from the cancer treatment or from the cancer itself.[11]

One approach that has been extremely helpful in understanding and treating some types of cancer anorexia makes use of the research on taste aversion learning, which was described in Chapter 6. Psychologists Ilene L. Bernstein and Mary M. Webster have conducted an imaginative and difficult series of experiments showing that children or adults given a novel-tasting ice cream prior to their chemotherapy acquired an aversion to that ice cream. Apparently illness resulting from the chemotherapy was paired with the taste of the ice cream, and taste aversions developed.[12]

Knowing that taste aversions can form during chemotherapy has helped clinicians figure out ways to minimize the adverse impact of such aversions, for example by development of the "scapegoat technique." It is used to prevent cancer patients from developing aversions to the foods that they usually eat. In one example of this technique, a patient is given a strong-tasting piece of candy prior to his or her chemotherapy session. The aversion then forms to the candy rather than to one of the last foods eating prior to the chemotherapy.[13]

Close to half of cancer patients may report nausea and even vomiting in anticipation of chemotherapy.[14] This apparently happens because, in the past, nausea caused by the chemotherapy treatment has been repeatedly associated with aspects of the patients' surroundings. Learning theory has been helpful in suggesting treatments for this type of anticipatory nausea and vomiting. One such treatment involves systematically exposing patients, while they are completely relaxed, to gradual approximations of the objects or aspects of their surroundings that are causing them problems. In the case of cancer chemotherapy nausea, patients are taught to relax while imagining the aspects of their surroundings that induce their nausea. This technique has been helpful in reducing patients' reports of nausea preceding chemotherapy. Therefore it should also be helpful in decreasing the learned taste aversions that contribute to cancer anorexia.[15]

"Enough Is as Good as a Feast":[16] Anorexia Nervosa

Hazel as a young teenager had enjoyed being popular and was quite flirtatious. She heard her father say, "Is she now going to be a teenager?" and this sounded to her as if he were disgusted and might reject her. Background for this anxiety was a much older half-sister who, according to the family saga, had been her father's declared darling but who had disappointed him.... [Hazel] wanted to deserve her father's love and admiration by excelling academically and in sports, and she restricted her food intake more and more. For her the issue became "mind over body," and she practiced it in the most literal sense. She expressed it: "When you are so unhappy and you don't know how to accomplish anything, then to have control over your body becomes a supreme accomplishment." You make out of your body your very own kingdom where you are the tyrant, the absolute dictator.[17]

Sarah was the only child of rather elderly parents who were both some-what obese. She had herself been plump from infancy and by the time she was sixteen she weighed [154 pounds]. She was used to being called "fatty" or "the lump" at school and was always embarrassed when she had to undress to change for games. She was a keen horsewoman and had some success in competition. Her occasional attempts at dieting became more determined after she came to the conclusion that her increasing weight was becoming a handicap to her riding. She dieted with the encourage-ment of her parents and set out to lose [30 pounds]. However, she passed this weight after less than three months, but continued to avoid fattening foods. After a further three months she weighed less than [98 pounds] and was unequivocally in a state of anorexia nervosa.[18]

[Grace] was the youngest of three girls, and the two older sisters had begun to menstruate at eleven. The sister next to her was very heavy and was con-tinuously criticized for not having the willpower to diet. Grace weighed [110 pounds] when her eleventh birthday approached; she was taller than most of her classmates and knew of no others who menstruated. She became alarmed when she noticed the first bloodstains, knowing that this was a harbinger of menstruation, and she felt unable to cope with the responsibilities involved, was fearful of being teased or having an odor or spotting her clothes. She wanted to postpone this event until she was four-teen or fifteen. Her determination to do something about it became even greater when a film about sexual development was shown in school. She dropped [27 pounds] within six weeks, and the signs of approaching puberty disappeared; she did not begin to menstruate until two years later.[19]

These case histories illustrate some of the many varieties of anorexia nervosa, a devastating eating disorder known all too well in the United States. The American Psychiatric Association defines someone as having anorexia nervosa if that person "refuses to maintain a minimally normal body weight, is intensely afraid of gaining weight, and exhibits a significant disturbance in the perception of the shape or size of his or her body."[20] Anorexics have body weights less than 85% of what is ideal and they tend to perceive their bodies as larger and heavier than they really are. Further, in order to be diagnosed with anorexia nervosa, a woman who has reached puberty must have become so thin that she does not menstruate.[21]

Officially, the American Psychiatric Association recognizes two subtypes of anorexia nervosa: the restricting subtype in which "weight loss is accomplished primarily through dieting, fasting, or excessive exercise," and the binge-eating/purging type, in which "the individual has regularly engaged in binge eating or purging (or both) during the current episode."[22] Purging consists of using self-induced vomiting or laxatives to remove the caloric consequences of eating. Keep in mind that the second subtype refers to someone who sometimes engages in binging and purging, but also engages in anorexic behaviors; someone whose eating disorder consists primarily of binging and purging would be diagnosed as having bulimia nervosa, a disorder discussed in more detail later in this chapter.

Anorexia nervosa is a disorder seen mostly in young women. More than 90% of anorexics are female. The average age at which anorexia nervosa starts is 17 years, although there's considerable variation around that age, with many cases first developing in the early teen years. About 1 in 200 women will develop anorexia nervosa over the course of their lifetimes. It's a very dangerous disorder. About 5% of women diagnosed with anorexia nervosa will die from it or will commit suicide in the 10-year period following when they were first diagnosed. Many anorexics remain too thin and abnormally concerned about their weights during their entire lives. Anorexia nervosa is much more common in industrialized countries where food is abundant.[23]

Even though a defining characteristic of anorexia nervosa is a lack of eating, and despite the literal meaning of anorexia (without appetite), anorexics are completely obsessed with food and food consumption. They carefully calculate just how many calories they can and do consume. They think and dream about food constantly, saying such things as: "Of course, I had breakfast; I ate my Cheerio," and "I won't even lick a postage stamp—one never knows about calories."[24]

When I was in college I was friendly with another student who I suspected was anorexic. She ate very little, was very thin, and was constantly referring to herself as being overweight. She knew that I was interested in psychology and eating and she knew about my suspicions that she was anorexic. However, she told me, she couldn't be anorexic because she thought about food all the time. This same woman mistakenly believed that someone would never have more fat cells than he or she had in the first 2 years of life. Therefore, when she had her first baby, she restricted his food. She proudly told me that his being thinner than other babies allowed him to stand up and walk earlier. She also told me that, when some friends were visiting, one exclaimed "What's wrong with that baby? Why is he so thin?" But the visitor's comment didn't seem to bother my friend. Unfortunately, her treatment of her baby isn't unique. Psychologist Kelly D. Brownell, one of the best known obesity researchers, reported in a 1991 paper that there have been a number of cases in which infants of affluent parents failed to grow and develop properly because their parents restricted the infants' food in the hope of preventing them from becoming overweight.[25]

In addition to eating abnormally small amounts of food, recent research suggests that anorexics may tend to eat certain kinds of foods more than others. For example, anorexics have been shown to have lower preference for high-fat foods than nonanorexics.[26] Further, in both girls and women, being a vegetarian and exhibiting eating disorder symptoms tend to go together.[27] Therefore, vegetarian girls and women should be scrutinized carefully for the presence of eating disorders. It may be that girls and women who are excessively concerned about their weight, the sort of people who develop eating disorders, tend to become vegetarians in the belief that this will help to keep their weight down.

Other aspects of anorexics' eating behaviors are also unusual. For example, anorexics' preference for food and how hungry they say they are decrease unusually quickly after eating.[28] In addition, anorexics who restrict food (as opposed to anorexics who occasionally binge and purge) take longer to eat their food and spend more time during a meal doing things such as pushing the food around on their plates.[29]

Origins

For several decades scientists have been investigating, sometimes in minute detail, characteristics of people with anorexia nervosa, as well as characteristics of people who might develop anorexia nervosa, to try to find out what causes this disorder. If what causes anorexia nervosa were known, then it might be possible to use that information to prevent this disorder or to improve its treatment. A huge number of different explanations for this disorder have been proposed, and many of these possible explanations have received some research confirmation. One hypothesized cause—sexual abuse—has not received support from the research, but many others have.[30] Anorexia nervosa probably doesn't have one single cause, which would help to explain why anorexics don't all appear to have exactly the same characteristics.

A prime suspect for one cause of anorexia nervosa is the culture in which we live. Have you heard the expression, "You can never be too rich or too thin"? Many authors have argued that the fashion image of thinness that has prevailed since the 1960s is a major contributing factor to the high incidence of anorexia nervosa.[31] This culture of thinness has been called the dominant appearance culture in the United States, and is far more prevalent among the many different ethnic groups in the United States than was previously realized.[32] Just look at the differences among three "perfect" figures from the 1950s, 1980s, and the present: Marilyn Monroe, Jamie Lee Curtis, and Calista Flockhart (see Figures 9.1a, b, and c). A quick comparison of past and current fashion magazines will demonstrate the same point. Fashionable women 50 years ago were heavier than fashionable women now. We see evidence of the culture of thinness all around us. Here are a few examples.

The 1990 film *Eating* chronicled a party celebrating the birthdays of three California women.[33] The party was attended by about 35 other women, almost all of whom held positions for which their appearance was extremely important (model, actress, wife of someone famous, etc.). Through the entire film the characters obsessed about gaining weight and eating food. Only one character, the mother of the woman whose 40th birthday was being celebrated, openly ate the birthday cake.

The cover story of a January 1993 issue of *People* magazine was about the eating habits of supermodels.[34] The story gave detailed information about the supposedly previous eating habits of Kim Alexis ("starved herself for days"), Beverly Johnson ("binged and purged"), and Carol Alt ("fainted from hunger"). In order to stay as thin as fashion dictated, they had to go to extreme measures. All reported being told by the modeling agencies, when they were first discovered, that they were too heavy and had to lose significant amounts of weight to work as models. When Kim Alexis was told this, she was 5 feet 10 inches tall and weighed 145 pounds, equivalent to a very healthy BMI of 21.

In the *People* article, the supermodels depicted all said that they have learned to eat in a much healthier way. But how healthy is that? Let's take Beverly Johnson. The article states that she runs and stretches every day and takes body sculpting classes several times every week. That's a lot of exercise. But when she describes what she eats in a typical day, including snacks it's only about 1,100 calories. More typical for a woman of her activity level would be about 2,000 calories. At Beverly Johnson's level of calorie intake, it's practically impossible for a woman to consume all of the nutrients that she needs, such as calcium and iron; osteoporosis and anemia could be the unfortunate result.

Our culture has not always demanded that women be so thin. Historian Joan Jacobs Brumberg's fascinating book, *The Body Project: An Intimate History of American Girls*, states that active attempts by girls to decrease their body weights didn't start until the 1920s. Prior to that time, one improved oneself by helping others and showing self-control. However, during the early 20th century, the calorie was discovered, and that discovery, plus greater freedom for women, resulted in women focusing more on their own appearances.[35]

My mother appears to have been one of the early dieters described by

Figure 9.1 (a) A "perfect" figure from the 1950s: Marilyn Monroe (with Cary Grant).(b) A "perfect" figure from the 1980s: Jamie Lee Curtis. (c) Today's "perfect" figure: Calista Flockhart. Copyright CORBIS.

Brumberg. In 1935, when she was 13 years old, my mother was with another girl and two boys. The boys invited the other girl to a dance but told my mother that they weren't inviting her because she was too fat. I've seen pictures of my mother at that time and she wasn't fat—perhaps slightly chubby, but definitely not fat. However, my mother immediately decided that she needed to lose weight. She had a vague notion that some foods were fattening and these she avoided. She remembers sometimes eating only lettuce. She also exercised. Her family had no scale at home so she used her small change to pay to weigh herself on scales in drugstores. During the next year she lost 20 pounds and grew 6 inches, turning into what she describes as a bean pole. She has proudly told me this story many, many times, ever since I was quite young.

Given the ever-present culture of thinness, it's not surprising that many women have an exaggerated view of their body size. This misperception is one of the defining characteristics, and possible causes, of anorexia nervosa. (See Conversation Making Fact #9.) Many methods have been developed to try to measure anorexics' precise perceptions of their body size. One

---

Conversation Making Fact #9

We would feel better about people dieting if we thought that the right people—that is, those who weigh too much—were primarily the ones doing it. Unfortunately, at least among young women, that may not be the case. Psychologist Caroline Davis and her colleagues made a disturbing discovery when they studied what physical characteristics of young women undergraduates were associated with dieting and body weight dissatisfaction. They found that whether a woman undergraduate dieted and was dissatisfied with her weight were best predicted by whether she had a large body frame. In contrast, knowing a woman's BMI or percentage of body fat did not result in as good a prediction of whether the woman dieted or was dissatisfied with her body weight. In other words, these results suggest that young women tend to be dissatisfied with their bodies and tend to diet, not because they're fat, but because of something that they can't change: their body frame size. These results are disturbing because they indicate that, even if the dieting is successful, these young women will still not be satisfied with their bodies. Further, given that they're dieting even when they're not overweight, these young women can gain no health benefit from the dieting, only possible health risks.[36]

example of such a technique is the Adjustable Light Beam Apparatus. This apparatus generates four beams of light that, projected on a screen or wall, form the outline of a human body. The width of one beam as it hits the wall represents the width of the cheeks, another beam the waist, another the hips, and the width of the fourth beam represents the width of the thighs. The apparatus can be adjusted so as to make the width of the beams as they hit the wall larger or smaller.[37] Thus a researcher or therapist can ask someone to adjust the beams to represent what that person thinks is the size of his or her own body, or of, for example, a mannequin's body. In this way it's possible to determine quite specifically which parts of which body someone does or does not perceive to be of accurate size.

Far more girls and young women are dissatisfied with the appearance of their bodies than are boys and young men, and this difference between females and males seems to be increasing.[38] Differences in body dissatisfaction between women and men are amply illustrated in a landmark study by psychologists April E. Fallon and Paul Rozin. This research involved 475 male and female undergraduate participants. The participants used sets of male and female figure drawings ranging from very thin to very heavy to indicate (a) the figure that looked most similar to their current shape, (b) the figure they most wanted to look like, (c) the figure they felt would be most attractive to the opposite sex, and (d) the figure of the opposite sex to which they felt they would be most attracted. The men chose very similar figures as representing their ideal figure, their current figure, and the figure that they thought would be most attractive to women; the women, however, chose a heavier figure as representing their current figure, and a thinner one as both their ideal and the one that they thought would be most attractive to men. In addition, although the male figure judged by the men to be most attractive to women was heavier than what the women actually preferred, the female figure judged by the women to be most attractive to men was thinner than what the men actually preferred. (See Figure 9.2.) Altogether, this study's findings show that most of the women, but not most of the men, were dissatisfied with their current figure in such a way that could encourage them to diet and to become anorexic.[39]

Differences in body size satisfaction also appear to be related to how people spend their time. For example, athletes such as distance runners, dancers, and gymnasts—athletes for whom being thin is thought to help performance and thus for whom appearance is extremely important—tend to have a higher prevalence of eating disorders than nonathletes.[40] In one sport, wrestling, athletes often attempt to gain an advantage by quickly decreasing their weights so as to qualify in lower weight classes. Wrestlers often use unhealthy methods to achieve these quick weight losses, such as extreme food deprivation, extreme sweating, and self-induced vomiting.

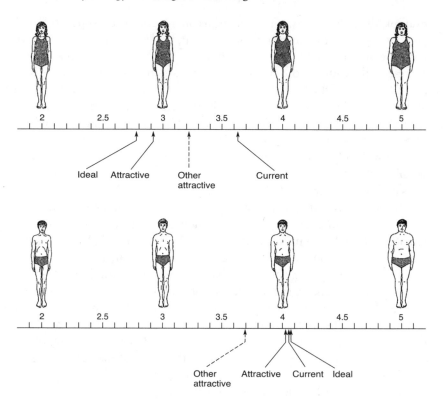

Figure 9.2 Average ratings of figures. Average ratings by women (top) and men (bottom) of current figure, ideal figure, and figure most attractive to the opposite gender; average ratings by men of the female figure that they find most attractive (top, labeled *other attractive*) and equivalent average ratings by women, on the bottom. (Adapted from A. E. Fallon and P. Rozin, "Sex Differences in Perceptions of Desirable Body Shape," *Journal of Abnormal Psychology* 94[1985]:102–105.)

Because of this dangerous behavior, in 1991 Wisconsin passed a rule stating that high school wrestlers could not wrestle in a weight class below a value set by their percentage body fat.[41] This prevented the wrestlers from using sudden weight loss strategies.

In another study almost 10% of women in the military were found to have serious eating disorders. This high frequency of eating disorders may be due to the involvement of these women in sports, as well as the ongoing fitness requirements for military women. Military women must meet specific weight standards two times per year, and if they don't meet those standards, their weights are checked more frequently. Ultimately, they can be forced to leave the military. At the same time, the food available to these women tends to be high calorie and high fat.[42] It's no wonder that many women develop eating disorders in such a situation.

On the plus side, some people believe that, due to the increasing involvement of women in athletics, there may be a new female body ideal arising. Up until now, there were two such ideals—how women wanted to appear (extremely thin) and how men wanted them to appear (with more curves). However, the new athleticism among women may be creating a third popular alternative: a sleek, muscular body, the sort of female body seen in fitness magazines,[43] similar to the body of Jamie Lee Curtis in Figure 9.1b. Unfortunately, even this ideal can be taken to extremes. Harrison G. Pope and his colleagues have recently asked that a new disorder be recognized: muscle dysmorphia. This is a disorder of body perception in which men and even some women are convinced that their bodies aren't muscular enough. People with this disorder engage in unhealthy behaviors such as steroid abuse and obsessive exercising.[44] It seems as if there's some sort of disorder custom fit for every situation.

Scientists have been studying families to try to figure out both which sorts of children might be likely to develop an eating disorder later on in life and what sorts of early experiences might be associated with the later development of an eating disorder. From this research we know, for example, that mothers who tend to restrict their own eating also tend to restrict the eating of their children;[45] that children as young as 5 years old can develop inhibited eating, secretive eating, and overeating-induced vomiting;[46] that, in a large sample of 431 children aged 7 to 10 years, 23% of the children (most of them girls) said that they had dieted or were dieting;[47] that 9- and 10-year-old children, particularly girls, are significantly influenced by their parents' (especially their mothers') comments about their weights;[48] and that girls' peers can also significantly influence the girls' likelihood of dieting, as has become abundantly apparent on the proeating disorders Web sites that have sprung up.[49] Thus it appears that abnormal eating behaviors can occur well before adolescence and that both mothers and peers can influence the development of those behaviors.

I remember vividly how, when I was about 12 and was at the pediatrician's office for my annual checkup, my mother suddenly started telling the pediatrician that she was concerned about my weight. She had made similar comments to me at home. She told the pediatrician that she was concerned that I was going to end up with a body similar to my overweight father's. The pictures of me around that time show a girl who was neither skinny nor small (my feet were size 8 1/2 by the time I was 11), but who was also definitely not fat or even chubby. Although I had some vague sense that I'd like to be thinner, the greatest impetus for me to lose weight was coming from my mother and, unlike some other girls of that age, I didn't value what she had to say too terribly much. Now that I look back on it, perhaps that was a good thing. Otherwise, with my large frame and a mother who took active steps to control both her weight and mine, I might have ended up with an eating disorder.

Several other explanations of the development of anorexia nervosa have focused on the interactions of girls with their surroundings. For example, anorexics have been seen as using anorexia as a way of gaining attention, as an attempt at individuality, as a denial of sexuality (in addition to not menstruating, girls who are severely underweight lack breasts and other secondary sexual characteristics), and as a way of dealing with problems caused by overdemanding parents.[50]

Let's consider more physiologically based possible explanations or causes of anorexia nervosa. To begin with, let's think about the fact that anorexics often exercise a great deal, supposedly to help remove the caloric consequences of what they eat. However, it's possible that the tendency of anorexics to exercise a great deal is an effect rather than a cause of low body weight. Hyperactivity, a behavior seen frequently in anorexics, has also been observed in people and other animals who have been deprived of food either in the laboratory or under natural conditions. The increase in activity level associated with food deprivation may help animals in nature to survive. If you haven't got much to eat, you may be more likely to find some food if you're active than if you're not.[51] Therefore, when hyperactivity is seen in anorexics, it's possible that it's occurring because of the anorexics' low body weights, and not the other way around.

Scientists have had similar discussions about the physiological abnormalities found in anorexia nervosa. Are these abnormalities a cause of the disorder or an effect of it? The physiological abnormalities include, in addition to menstrual and growth disturbances, low levels of some hormones, low thyroid activity, low insulin levels, low blood pressure, and increased activity of the neurotransmitter serotonin. The stomach also empties more slowly, which is thought to be responsible for the fact that anorexics claim to feel full so easily. Usually all of these abnormalities disappear when an anorexic gains weight, lending support to the argument that these abnormalities are effects, not causes, of anorexia nervosa. However, it's possible that some of these abnormalities, such as the increased serotonin activity, once put in motion by dieting, may have physiological consequences that contribute to the continuation of anorexia nervosa.[52]

Getting Better All the Time: Treatments

Given that anorexia nervosa is such a dangerous disorder, it's essential that we have effective treatments for it. The treatments for anorexia nervosa can be divided into two types: those designed to obtain an immediate weight gain, and those designed to maintain that weight gain.[53] The treatments designed to obtain an immediate weight gain are important for two reasons. First, some patients may be in danger of dying from starvation. In such cases, an immediate weight gain, which sometimes has to be achieved without the patient's consent, will help to ensure the patient's survival. The second reason that these sorts of treatments are important is based on the fact that, as you've just learned, some of the physiological effects of starvation may help to prolong anorexia nervosa. Therefore, it may not be possible to make any real progress in treating anorexia nervosa without first obtaining a weight gain.

The treatments used to help anorexics gain weight immediately include nurturance, behavior therapy, and drug therapy. Nurturance consists of one or more treatments that attempt to improve the patient's nutrition. A simple example of nurturance is a high-calorie diet combined with bed rest, which decreases the calories used by the patient. If a patient won't comply with this form of nurturance, force feeding may be used; food may be given to the patient through a tube down her throat or through a needle into one of her veins. Force feeding, unlike other treatments for anorexia nervosa, is usually given only in a hospital setting. Nurturance can be extremely successful in obtaining an immediate weight gain in patients.[54] In behavior therapy, anorexics aren't allowed to engage in pleasurable activities unless they eat. Behavior therapy is based on principles of learning established in the laboratory. Behavior therapy can be fairly successful in obtaining an initial weight gain, although probably not as successful as nurturance.[55] In drug therapy, any of a variety of medications may be given to anorexics to try to increase the amount that they eat. Most recently, based on the evidence of elevated levels of serotonin in patients with anorexia nervosa, physicians have been anxious to try to treat anorexia nervosa with medications known to affect serotonin levels. However, so far, no medication has been consistently and significantly shown to improve the treatment of anorexia nervosa.[56]

The sorts of treatments that are used to maintain a weight gain, or at least to prevent further weight loss, include individual, group, and family psychotherapy, as well as self-help groups. All of these treatments aim to maintain the health of a patient over a long period of time. In individual psychotherapy, the patient works with the therapist on a one-to-one basis. In group psychotherapy, a group of patients discusses their problems together with the therapist. In family psychotherapy, the therapist treats the whole family as a unit, rather than just treating the anorexic.[57] With each of these types of psychotherapy, a therapist may use one of many different styles of therapy, such as behavior therapy. Psychotherapy can also vary in length; each of these types of psychotherapy can last for as little as a few weeks or for as long as several years.

One type of psychotherapy that has recently become popular for treatment of anorexia nervosa is cognitive-behavior therapy. Cognitive-behavior therapy is similar to behavior therapy in that it's based on principles of learning established in the laboratory. However, instead of focusing on modifying the patient's eating behavior, the therapist works with the patient to modify the patient's reported thoughts and images. For example, the therapist may work with a patient to modify her reported perception of her body size, helping the anorexic to see herself as too thin, instead of too fat. So far there haven't been many controlled studies looking at the effectiveness of cognitive-behavior therapy in treating anorexia nervosa. However, the information available so far suggests that it can be helpful.[58]

Family therapy has been used with anorexia nervosa for many years. However, although family therapy is widely accepted as successful by clinical practitioners, there have again been few controlled studies investigating its effectiveness.[59]

Much more research, carefully conducted, is needed to determine the relative success of different forms of psychotherapy in treating anorexia nervosa. One difficulty in assessing the relative effectiveness of different types of therapies is that anorexics are often given more then one treatment at a time. For example, an anorexic might simultaneously participate in individual cognitive-behavior therapy as well as family therapy. Under these conditions, it can be very difficult to tell specifically what is or isn't helping the anorexic. Also, it's possible that some forms of treatment are more successful with some sorts of anorexics than others. Therefore research needs to determine what types of anorexics are best treated by what sort of therapy so that we can improve the chances of treating each and every patient with anorexia nervosa.

The last general category of treatments used to help maintain anorexics' weight is self-help groups. These groups serve many functions, including helping anorexics to find therapists, information, social support, and other types of assistance. Self-help groups are popular because they're relatively inexpensive and because they provide a number of services often not easily available through traditional mental health care institutions. With the proliferation of the World Wide Web, many self-help groups have gone online.[60] An advantage of these online self-help groups is that participants can use them at any time of the day or night; participants aren't limited to preset meeting times. For some examples of relevant Web sites and other types of self-help information, see the section on where to get help and information at the end of this chapter. Nevertheless, again, research needs to be done to determine the degree to which self-help groups, on the Web or otherwise, can assist in treating anorexia nervosa.[61]

Researchers are now beginning to study how anorexia nervosa and other eating disorders in young women can be prevented or caught early, presumably when they can be more easily treated. In one such attempt, Stanford University psychologist Traci Mann and her colleagues studied approximately 800 Stanford first-year college women. A recovered anorexic and a recovered bulimic spoke with some of the study's participants, presenting information on eating disorders and where to get help with any symptoms that the participants might have. No one spoke with the other young women. Approximately 1 month later, the women who heard the presentation on anorexia nervosa and bulimia nervosa reported slightly, but significantly, more eating disorder symptoms than the women in the other group. Possible explanations of this finding include that, by meeting people who spoke openly about their former eating disorders, the participants may have increased their engaging in such abnormal behaviors or may have felt less stigma in reporting these behaviors.[62] Another possibility is that the women who heard the presentation certainly might have been disabused of the possibility that eating disorders can result in death. After all, the presentation had been made by several women who had had eating disorders but who looked perfectly healthy. Given these possibilities, perhaps it would be better not to try to educate young women about dangerous eating disorders. However, this one study is insufficient to justify such a policy. We still need to distinguish between the reporting of more eating disorder symptoms and the actual exhibition of more disorder symptoms; the two don't necessarily go together. We also need to determine what specific kinds of educational programs will and won't work.

Does She or Doesn't She?: Bulimia Nervosa

Undoubtedly you've also heard of bulimia nervosa, another eating disorder. The American Psychiatric Association characterizes bulimia nervosa as consisting of "binge eating and inappropriate compensatory methods to prevent gain ... at least twice a week for 3 months.... A *binge* is defined as eating in a discrete period of time an amount of food that is definitely larger than most individuals would eat under similar circumstances."[63] There are two subtypes of bulimics: the purging subtype, in which the bulimic tries to prevent weight gain by self-induced vomiting (by far the most commonly used method of purging) or by inappropriate use of laxatives, diuretics, or enemas; and the nonpurging subtype, in which the bulimic tries to prevent weight gain primarily by fasting or excessive exercising. As you can see, there's some overlap in the definition of a nonpurging bulimic and the definition of a binge-eating/purging anorexic stated in the preceding section on anorexia nervosa. Also similar to anorexics, bulimics tend to be overly concerned with their body size and shape, and at least 90% of bulimics are female. However, unlike anorexics, bulimics are usually within normal weight range.[64]

Recent estimates are that approximately 1–3% of females develop bulimia nervosa, a higher frequency than anorexia nervosa. Further, the frequency of bulimia nervosa appears to be increasing.[65] It's possible that when groups of young women live together, such as in college dormitories, information spreads about binging and purging, which at first glance appears to be the perfect solution to dealing with both the wide availability of tempting food in college and the desire to be physically attractive according to prevailing standards. As one patient said, "I thought I had the problem licked; I couldn't understand why everyone didn't eat and then vomit."[66] Unfortunately, this brilliant dieting strategy doesn't work; adolescent girls who engage in bulimic behaviors are more likely to be overweight 4 years later than girls who ate normally.[67]

Bulimia even seems to have become an accepted, if sometimes ridiculed, part of our culture. I was flabbergasted when someone showed me a computer game called "Bulimic Blowdown at High Noon," produced a few years ago by www.zooass.com. In this game, characters with names such as Ally McBile, RegurgiKate Moss, and Latrine Dion compete to fill up their stomachs first, stick their fingers down their throats, and then spew vomit all over the opposing characters.

There are many negative physiological effects of binging and purging, and bulimics who persist with these behaviors are risking their health. For example, depending on the purging method used, bulimics may have abnormal body chemistry, fluid retention, and heart muscles.

Obviously, it's extremely important to detect bulimia nervosa and to get immediate professional help for anyone suffering from it. Unfortunately, it can be very difficult for a nonprofessional to detect that someone is suffering from bulimia nervosa. A bulimic can hide her binging and purging. In addition, as you've already learned, a bulimic's outward appearance is often similar to that of someone without an eating disorder. Nevertheless, there are two physiological changes in vomiting bulimics that can help a keen observer to detect the bulimia: those bulimics who induce vomiting by sticking their fingers in their throats develop a callus or scrape on the back of the hand that they use and, due to vomit's acidity, the tooth enamel on the back of the top teeth becomes eroded in most bulimics who have been vomiting for at least 4 years.[68] Thus dentists can play a critical role in detecting bulimia nervosa.

You might wonder, given the large amount of vomiting in which many bulimics engage, why it is that they don't develop taste aversions to the foods that they eat during binges. Why isn't the vomiting paired with the food eaten, so that an aversion develops to the food? Instead, bulimics continue to crave their binge foods. One possible explanation is that the vomiting is self-induced and isn't accompanied by nausea, a very different situation than what you find in experiments on taste aversion learning. Another possible explanation has to do with the fact that bulimics sometimes report that they're extremely used to vomiting; it's not aversive to them.[69] Experiments with rats show that nausea that's familiar is less likely to result in a taste aversion than nausea that's novel.[70]

Another very interesting physiological characteristic to examine in bulimics is metabolic rate. Better understanding of bulimics' metabolic rates could help identify ways for bulimics to control their weights other than severely restricting or purging the food that they eat. There have been reports of significantly lower, as well as significantly higher, metabolic rates in bulimics.[71] As you'll learn in the next chapter, metabolic rates are important because they help to determine how easy it is for someone to gain or lose weight. If two people, one with a high metabolic rate and one with a low metabolic rate, eat the same large meals for a week, the one with the low metabolic rate will gain more weight than will the one with the high metabolic rate. We don't yet understand why bulimics seem to have abnormal metabolic rates, and why some researchers have measured these rates as being abnormally high and others as being abnormally low. However, it's possible that these differing metabolic rates are due to the variation in how much bulimics eat. Metabolic rate rises when someone eats a lot and decreases when someone eats very little.[72] Therefore, if a bulimic has recently binged, you would expect her metabolic rate to be high, and if she has recently been restricting her intake, you would expect her metabolic rate to be low. Experiments need to be done in which bulimics' metabolic rates are tracked through several binge-purge and binge-restrict cycles.

As with anorexics, scientists have been carefully studying the eating behaviors of bulimics to look for clues as to why bulimics engage in abnormal eating behaviors. Different from anorexics, as bulimics eat, they generally don't report a sharp decrease in pleasure in the food they're eating. In fact, bulimics report less of a decrease in pleasure as they eat than people without an eating disorder. Similarly, bulimics, in comparison to nonbulimics, don't report as much of a decrease in hunger after having eaten food prior to a meal; and bulimics have a greater desire to continue to eat after a meal is over than do nonbulimics.[73] We don't yet know what causes these differences in hunger and satiety between bulimics and nonbulimics. Perhaps there is some predisposing difference in satiation between bulimics and nonbulimics that causes the binging and purging, or, similar to possibilities raised for anorexia nervosa, perhaps these differences in hunger and satiety are an effect of the binging and purging. As with anorexia nervosa, researchers believe that many of the physiological abnormalities found in bulimics may be an effect of the binging and purging, rather than their cause, and that these physiological abnormalities may help to maintain the binging and purging.[74]

Many of the possible explanations and causes that have been proposed for anorexia nervosa have also been proposed for bulimia nervosa. The weights reported as desirable by bulimics are far below healthy weights. Bulimics, similar to anorexics, seem to have a distorted view of their own weights. Further, bulimics, similar to anorexics, are obsessed with controlling their food intake. However, unlike an anorexic, who is successful at this control, a bulimic will regularly slip and consume huge amounts of food. Once the binge starts, it seems uncontrollable. Then the bulimic attempts to purge herself of the food.[75] Once the binging and purging are over, the bulimic attempts again to continue to restrict her food intake, but slips and binges again. It's a vicious cycle. For the bulimic, the continual struggle with binging and purging results in a preoccupation with food: how much to eat, when to eat, how to do it without the knowledge of others, and how to get enough food for a binge. Thus, bulimia has been seen by some researchers as an adverse consequence of dieting.[76]

Due to the vicious cycle in which bulimics can neither control their restricted eating nor their binging, bulimia has been seen as a problem of impulsiveness. Bulimics repeatedly engage in behaviors that offer them some current pleasure, or at least some decreased displeasure, but at the expense of their long-term health and happiness. With this in mind, some researchers have wondered if there might be some common underlying cause of bulimia nervosa and other impulsiveness disorders such as drug abuse and pathological gambling. Supporting this view is the fact that someone with one impulsiveness disorder is likely to have another, and someone whose family contains someone with an impulsiveness disorder is more likely to develop binge eating. There has been speculation that the common underlying cause of all impulsiveness disorders is a decreased level of the neurotransmitter serotonin.[77] Abnormal serotonin activity has been shown in the brains of recovered bulimics.[78]

The hypothesis that decreased levels of serotonin cause or contribute to bulimia nervosa gains further support from research on depression and bulimia. It has been repeatedly found that, on average, bulimics are more depressed than are nonbulimics, although there are certainly bulimics who aren't depressed.[79] It's also well known that depression is often associated with low levels of serotonin, as is food craving. In addition, several researchers have shown that bulimics tend to have low levels of insulin as well as serotonin.[80] You may remember that insulin is helpful in ensuring that tryptophan, the amino acid precursor of serotonin, enters the brain. Bulimics also salivate less in the presence of food than do nonbulimics.[81] Both salivation and insulin release are reflexes that occur when you come into contact with food. If you put all of this together, it suggests that for some reason bulimics have less physiological responses to food, and that this characteristic either causes, or contributes to, their having low levels of serotonin, which causes or contributes to their depression and feeding binges. However, although all of these findings seem to fit together, they still don't tell us what starts the cycle off—which is the chicken and which is the egg. It may be that there is no simple causal model in which A causes B, B causes C, and C causes D. We simply don't know yet what causes what. Given that bulimics tend to come from families with a history of mood disorders, and given that many mood disorders appear to be partly due to genetic influences, it has been suggested that there are genetic contributions to some or all of these relationships.[82] However, again, we simply don't know yet. Finally, we can't forget that, given that all bulimics aren't alike, it is unfortunately unlikely that one overarching cause will be found for all cases of bulimia nervosa.

These many investigations of the characteristics and possible causes of bulimia nervosa have resulted in a variety of suggestions for possible treatments. In many respects, the treatments parallel those used for anorexia nervosa. For example, various types of psychotherapy and drug therapy have been tried. The drug therapies have been based on the findings that bulimics tend to be depressed and have low serotonin levels. Therefore the medications used have primarily been ones that ameliorate depression and/or raise serotonin levels. There's substantial evidence that such medications are effective in treating bulimia nervosa. However, many patients don't improve with these medications, and many of those who do improve relapse after the medication is discontinued.[83]

The standard treatment for bulimia nervosa has become traditional cognitive-behavior therapy. This psychotherapeutic approach appears to be the best single method of treating bulimia nervosa, plus it doesn't have the side effects that can accompany drug therapy. Therefore, in many cases, it may be helpful for a bulimic to try first a course of cognitive-behavior therapy before considering the use of medication.[84]

Nevertheless, even with a combination of cognitive-behavior therapy and drug therapy, up to 50% of patients don't improve.[85] In addition, cognitive-behavior therapy can be expensive and not everyone lives near a qualified therapist. Therefore alternative methods of getting inexpensive care to bulimics are being developed. One method that has apparently proved quite successful involves use of a self-care manual with occasional sessions of cognitive-behavior therapy conducted by a therapist. This method has the further benefit of making the patient feel empowered with regard to her own care.[86] As described for anorexia nervosa, online support groups may also prove helpful,[87] although research is needed to confirm this. I've listed examples of Web sources of help following the conclusion to this chapter.

Enough Is Enough: Conclusion

This chapter has described anorexia and bulimia. Learning about these eating disorders can be scary; it seems as if as a group they're extremely common, difficult to cure, and dangerous. There is evidence that eating disorders are now becoming much more common in men.[88] Yet researchers have been making enormous progress in understanding and treating all of these disorders. We're no longer helpless when faced with an eating disorder diagnosis. And, although there has been much research on the possible physiological causes of eating disorders, much more is being discovered daily and will continue to be discovered. Combined with carefully conducted studies of the efficacy of different forms of psychotherapy, there's no question that even better treatments lie ahead. There's much to be hopeful about now in the treatment of eating disorders. Of course, a big help in preventing eating disorders would be for the fashion industry and the media to change their standards for attractive body weights. However, although such measures are being studied,[89] they appear unlikely to occur in the near future.

Where to Get Information and Help

Books

A great many books have been written for lay people about eating disorders. Here is a small selection of the recent helpful ones:

Am I Thin Enough Yet? The Cult of Thinness and the Commercialization of Identity by Sharlene Hesse-Biber (New York: Oxford University Press, 1996).

The Body Project: An Intimate History of American Girls by Joan Jacobs Brumberg (New York: Vintage, 1997).

Fat History: Bodies and Beauty in the Modern West by Peter N. Stearns (New York: New York University Press, 1997).

Real Gorgeous: The Truth About Body and Beauty by Kaz Cooke (New York: Norton, 1996).

When Dieting Becomes Dangerous: A Guide to Understanding and Treating Anorexia Bulimia by Deborah M. Michel and Susan G. Willard (New Haven: Yale University Press, 2003).

Organizations and Web Sites

National Eating Disorders Association, 603 Stewart Street, Suite 803, Seattle, WA 98101. Phone: (206) 382–3587. Provides eating disorder information, referrals, prevention programs, etc. Web site: www.nationaleatingdisorders.org

National Association of Anorexia Nervosa and Associated Disorders (ANAD), Box 7, Highland Park, IL 60036. Hotline counseling: (847) 831–3438. Provides support groups, referrals, information, etc. Web site: www.anad.org

The Renfrew Center: Provides resources for education and treatment of eating disorders. Web site: www.renfrew.org

CHAPTER 10

The Battle With the Bulge

Overeating and Obesity

℃

Here's the chapter that many of you have been waiting for: the chapter on overeating and obesity. Or perhaps you didn't wait. Perhaps you just went straight to this chapter without reading any of the preceding ones—despite their providing much information that would be helpful to you in understanding what's to come next! But prepared or not, here you are, and I'll do my best to explain to you what scientists know about food consumption so excessive that it's considered abnormal (overeating) and about body weight that's significantly greater than average (obesity).

Over 60% of men and almost 80% of women in the United States report monitoring what they eat in order to maintain their weight or lose weight.[1] Given this huge interest in preventing and treating obesity, including among those of you reading this chapter, I feel perhaps a particular responsibility about what I put in this chapter. Exacerbating this feeling is the fact that the published scientific literature on overeating and obesity is absolutely huge, so huge that it couldn't possibly be described by the content of many books, much less one chapter in one book. This means that I have to pick and choose very carefully the studies that I tell you about. And perhaps more importantly, I need to ensure that, when you've finished this chapter, you're an informed scientific consumer who knows the characteristics of a good study and how to interpret carefully the results from a study. In this way, when you encounter, as you certainly will, descriptions of research on overeating and obesity that aren't included in this chapter, you'll be able to decide for yourself what the results of that study may or may not mean.

You're probably going to find what this chapter has to say about overeating and obesity to be fairly depressing. There are, unfortunately, no easy solutions to the problem of weight control, at least not in surroundings such as ours in which there's much tasty food and people need to expend little physical energy. However, you and everyone else will have a far better chance of controlling your weight if you know something about the relevant research than if you ignore that research. Forewarned can be forearmed! To your credit, you've already come this far. So let's see what scientists know about overeating and obesity. I'll begin by telling you about the characteristics of obese people. Then I'll discuss the research concerning what causes overeating and obesity. And finally I'll discuss the research concerning how to decrease overeating and obesity.

Weighing in on Obesity

There have been a great many studies investigating the characteristics of people who are obese. In order to discuss these characteristics, we first need to define obesity based on measurements of body fat. Radiologic techniques are some of the most accurate ways for determining how much body fat someone has and where it's located. Examples include CT (computerized tomography) and MRI (magnetic resonance imaging) methods.[2] However, these methods are expensive and not easily accessible by most people. An alternative method uses the BMI (body mass index) described in the preceding chapter (see especially Table 9.1).[3] As you'll recall, BMI is equal to weight (measured in kilograms) squared and divided by height (measured in meters). Thus a higher BMI means that someone has more body weight for a given height. Researchers classify someone with a BMI between 25.0 and 29.9 as overweight, between 30.0 and 39.9 as obese, and someone with a BMI of 40.0 or more as extremely obese. BMIs are significantly correlated with the amount of body fat that someone has,[4] and using BMIs to estimate overweight and obesity is very popular among researchers. Anyone can calculate a BMI. But it's important to remember that sometimes two people have the same BMI even though one of them has a relatively high percentage of body fat and the other doesn't.

No matter which classification scheme you use, overweight and obesity are increasing in the United States and many other countries. In fact, many researchers and public health officials are now talking about an "obesity epidemic."[5] Here are some of the facts. Surveys show that just from around 1990 to 2000 the percentage of obese American adults (BMI $\geq$30.0) increased from approximately 23% to 31%. Almost 65% of adults in the United States are now classified as overweight (BMI $\geq$25.0).[6] The prevalence of obesity is particularly high in certain minority groups, including African Americans, Latinos and Latinas, the Pima Indians of the American Southwest, and Pacific Islanders in American Samoa. In the last two of these groups, the prevalence of obesity can exceed 80%.[7] Children are no exception to these trends. By 2000, the percentage of American girls, boys, and adolescents classified as obese was 15% (up from 11% in 1988–1994).[8] Even our pets are not immune—25% of cats and dogs in the Western world are now obese.[9]

These percentages become even scarier when you consider the health risks associated with being overweight and obese. Many studies have shown links between being overweight and obese and cardiovascular diseases, diabetes, and cancer.[10] Approximately 80% of obese adults have at least one of these diseases.[11] It has been estimated that even people with BMIs of just 26.0 or more will lose 1 to 10 years from their life spans.[12] In addition, abdominal fat is apparently associated with greater health risk than is fat elsewhere in the body (see Table 9.1). Once again, children are no exception to these trends. Approximately 60% of 5- to 10-year-old children who are overweight have at least one resulting health problem, such as increased levels of insulin.[13] Researchers estimate that obesity causes approximately 300,000 deaths per year.[14]

The total cost of the health problems associated with obesity is considerable and was estimated to be $99.2 billion in 1995. This amount includes the costs of visits to the doctor, hospitalizations, days lost from work, and so on and represents 5.7% of the 1995 United States national health expenditure.[15]

Thus we know that, at least in the United States, there's a huge number of people who are overweight or obese, that this number is increasing, and that people who have higher BMIs tend to have certain diseases. In addition to adverse health consequences, people who weigh more than average may be discriminated against socially and professionally, and they may be seen as unintelligent and lacking in self-control.[16] Clearly there are many reasons to prevent or remove excess weight. In order to understand how doing that may or may not be possible, we need to understand the causes of overeating and obesity.

Land of the Rising Fat

As you'll see, many different roads lead to overeating and obesity. It's important to understand these different causes because the success of different treatments may vary depending on the cause of a particular case of obesity. Some cases of obesity depend more on genetic or physiological causes, and some depend more on past experience or current surroundings. Unfortunately, virtually all of the studies that I'll report to you have been conducted with North Americans of European descent. It's simply not known if results obtained from such populations will also apply to other populations. This is a serious inadequacy in the scientific literature that needs to be addressed. It means that we have very limited information about the causes of the high obesity rates among certain minority groups such as African American women[17] and about the best ways to decrease those rates.

Body Not So Perfect: Genetic and Physiological Contributions

A major issue a couple of decades ago was whether genes had anything to do with how overweight someone is. Now that we've entered the 21st century, no one questions that genes have something to do with being overweight. Now the issue is what specific gene or genes contribute to someone's being overweight. There have been enormous advances in genetics that allow us to determine whether particular genes, or particular combinations of genes, contribute to obesity. However, as you read this material on the connections between genetics and obesity, keep in mind that, as clear as those connections may be, genes can't possibly explain everything to do with obesity. Obesity has drastically increased in the past several decades, but that's too short a time period for evolution or mutation to have affected the gene pool. In addition, there are significant correlations between the weights of adoptive children and their adoptive parents. Therefore people's surroundings, or how people interact with their surroundings, clearly have an impact on obesity.[18]

Now back to the genes. We've known for many decades that obese parents tend to have obese biological children; approximately 70% of children with two obese parents become obese.[19] However, parents and children share not only some genes, but their home surroundings—ranging from ones containing only low-fat/low-sugar foods to the exact opposite. Thus the tendency of obese parents to have obese biological children, by itself, doesn't prove that genes contribute to obesity, only that they may contribute. More convincing have been studies done with twins. Such studies have shown that the weights of identical twins, those who come from the same egg and sperm and thus have identical genes, are more similar than the weights of fraternal twins, who come from different eggs and sperm and who, similar to any siblings, on average share half of their genes.[20] Identical twins look exactly alike, and fraternal twins look no more alike than do any two siblings. Therefore, if how you look influences how someone treats you (and there is indeed good scientific evidence that this is the case), then identical twins may have more similar weights because people treat them more similarly, not because they have more similar genes. Still better evidence comes from studies of adopted children. The weights of these children tend to be more similar to those of their biological parents than to those of their adoptive parents.[21] It's difficult to conceive of an explanation for these results other than that genes have a strong influence on whether someone becomes obese.

Scientist Claude Bouchard and his colleagues published a 1990 twin study with an intriguing twist. These researchers overfed 12 pairs of identical twin men. None of the men had ever been obese and all were sedentary. For 120 consecutive days, the men were isolated and under 24-hour surveillance in a special section of a dormitory. Physical activity was limited. For 84 of these days, each man was fed 1,000 calories more per day than was needed to maintain his current weight. When the experiment was over, there were huge differences in how much weight different men had gained: between 10 and 29 pounds. On average, members of a twin pair were a great deal more similar in how much they had gained than were two unrelated men. The greater similarity among the members of the twin pairs applied not only to weight gain, but also to the amount of body fat and the distribution of body fat.[22] These results seem to suggest that there's a significant genetic component to weight gain and to where fat is gained. Unfortunately, the publication describing this experiment doesn't explain how the men were persuaded to participate. Participation in this experiment sounds like a truly miserable experience; I can't imagine what would have persuaded me.

Most recently, researchers have been able to identify in rodents specific genes that are responsible for certain types of overeating and obesity. Studies have also identified the specific genes responsible for certain rare conditions of extreme obesity that exist in people. For more common forms of obesity in people, the research seems to indicate that there are many genes involved. However, it's extremely important to remember that none of these genes cause obesity in any simple sense. Instead, they seem to make it likely that the people (or rats) who have them will become obese when exposed to certain conditions in their surroundings.[23] Even if you have lots of genes related to the deposit of excess abdominal fat, if your surroundings contain very little food and you exercise a lot, you'll have no calories to deposit as fat.

We need to think about not just whether someone's genetic background influences the degree to which that person is overweight, but how that influence might come about. What are the specific mechanisms by which the genes might exert their effects? Do genes change the body's chemistry so that more or less of the food that's eaten is stored as fat? Do they influence activity level, thus changing the number of calories burned? This is one of the reasons that it's important to study the various physiological aspects of obesity; such studies may possibly give us clues regarding how the genes exert their influence on obesity.

In considering the many different physiological bases of overeating and obesity, let's begin by considering adipose cells, the proper name for what you may have heard referred to as fat cells. These are the cells in your body that store fat. When they're full, you're less hungry; when they're not full, you're more hungry.[24] Thus, your adipose cells contribute to the regulation of your body's set point described in Chapter 2. Bouchard's study described in Chapter 2 is one of a number of pieces of evidence suggesting that heredity contributes to the number and distribution of adipose cells. In addition, we know that, although the number of adipose cells can increase when you gain weight, the number of adipose cells can never decrease.[25] When you lose weight, the fat cells become empty, but their numbers don't decrease. Therefore if you've been overweight at some time in your life, regardless of whether you're presently overweight, you'll have a relatively large number of adipose cells. Unless these many adipose cells are full of fat, you'll be hungry. In other words, if you've been overweight at any time in your life, you'll tend either to be overweight or hungry. This should help you to understand one of the reasons that it's so difficult for anyone to lose weight and then keep it off.

You'll recall from Chapter 2 that there are a number of possible indicators of the body's level of stored fat and that these indicators interact with other chemicals in the body to influence eating behavior. One of the indicators of stored fat, leptin, a hormone found in the blood and manufactured by the adipose cells, has been the recent focus of many obesity researchers. When there's little stored fat, there's less leptin; and when there's a great deal of stored fat, there's more leptin. Researchers originally hoped that the role of leptin in controlling weight would be so strong that manipulation of leptin level would lead to straightforward treatments for obesity, and great expectations were aroused. However, it now appears that leptin's role is more related to the physiological mechanisms involved in protecting the body against weight loss when fat stores shrink rather than vice versa.[26]

Now we come to what is, in my opinion, the most fascinating area of research concerning overeating and obesity—the effects of energy expenditure. The reason that I find this area the most fascinating will become apparent later in this chapter, when I explain how exercise is one of the very few successful methods that we have for losing and keeping off excess weight. As you know from the beginning of this chapter, the percentage of the population that is obese has been increasing, both in adults and in children. There are only three possible explanations for these increases: people are eating more, people are expending less energy, or people are doing both of these things. Many researchers have focused on the energy expenditure side of this equation. In the United States, when people travel outside their homes, approximately one fourth of those trips are less than 1 mile in length. Yet approximately three fourths of those short trips are by car.[27] We have become a nation accustomed to not only cars, but elevators, dishwashers, lawn mowers, food processors, washing machines, escalators, and moving walkways. And let's not forget the remote controls available for all kinds of electronic devices. I can now turn on and off my bedroom air conditioner without moving from my bed. Industrialization and technology have allowed us to expend far less energy in living our daily lives.

For a poignant example of the effects of these changes, consider the results of a study of two native Canadian populations: the Sandy Lake Oji-Cree and the Keewatin Inuit. The Oji-Cree currently live in small houses that have been completely winterized, and many own snowmobiles and cars. Although their food supply used to consist of wild animals and plants, now their primary food source is a company store. On average, members of this group are extremely sedentary. In contrast, the Inuit still live an active, fairly traditional lifestyle, including eating large amounts of fish. Not surprisingly, the average BMI of the Oji-Cree is 29.0, whereas that of the Inuit is 25.0. Also not surprisingly, there's significantly more heart disease and diabetes in the Oji-Cree than in the Inuit.[28]

Before discussing some of the experiments on energy expenditure in lean and obese people, and how different situations can affect that energy expenditure, it'll be helpful to understand a bit about the different types of energy that we all expend. Your total energy expenditure is composed of (a) your basal metabolic rate, which is the energy expended for basic metabolic functions such as respiration and circulation; (b) the extra energy your body uses as a result of voluntary and nonvoluntary physical activity such as walking and fidgeting; and (c) the extra energy your body uses following food consumption.[29] A low value for any of these three types of energy expenditure could increase your tendency to gain weight and to become obese. Let's review what scientists have to say about each of these three types of energy expenditure and their relationships with weight gain and obesity.

We'll begin with metabolic rate. It will probably not surprise you to know that even people who weigh exactly the same can have different metabolic rates. We all know people who seem to be able to eat a lot and not gain weight and vice versa. There are many different reasons for this. For example, fat supports a lower metabolic rate than muscle or bone.[30] Therefore if two people weigh the same but one person has a higher percentage of body fat than the other person, you would expect the first person to have a lower metabolic rate. An insidious factor contributing to low metabolic rates is decreased eating. When less food is eaten, metabolic rate goes down, and this lowered metabolic rate may continue for months after the level of food intake has returned to normal. This is why, when you're dieting, losing weight is much easier at the beginning and why, when you stop dieting, it's so easy to regain the lost weight. Such changes in metabolic rate were adaptive when people's food supplies were erratic and often inadequate; lowered metabolic rate as a result of food deprivation helped to prevent starvation. However, now, in the United States, low food intake is frequently due to people trying to lose weight. (See Figure 10.1.)[31]

ANDREW ARMSTRONG

"Around here, it's the survival of the fattest."

Figure 10.1 Drawing by Andrew Armstrong. (Reprinted by permission from *The Chronicle of Higher Education* [May 8, 1998]: B13.)

Lest you despair, there's a way to increase metabolic rate. It turns out that, in addition to exercise using energy in and of itself, under certain conditions exercise can increase metabolic rate. Even more importantly, that increase can last for hours beyond when the exercise has ceased, such as after a strenuous game of football.[32] However, we know very little about what type or duration of exercise will result in an increase in metabolic rate of a specific amount or duration. Further, there are individual differences in the degree to which exercise affects weight. Bouchard conducted an exercise study with twins that was similar in design to his overfeeding study with twins, and once again very challenging for the participants.[33] There were seven pairs of identical twin men in this study. Each man exercised 2 times per day for most of 93 days, using up about 1,000 calories per day. This is the equivalent of jogging about 45 minutes twice a day. During the 93 days, the amounts of nutrients and calories that the men ate were kept constant. The average amount of weight lost was 11 pounds. However, on average, the amounts of weight lost by members of a twin pair were more similar than for pairs of men who weren't related. You may also be interested to know that the lost weight was apparently due to the loss of fat, not due to loss of bone, muscle, and so forth.

One concern that people often have when considering the effects of exercise on metabolic rate is the possibility that exercising more can also make you eat more, thus countering any calorie-expending effects of exercise. The results on this issue have been mixed, with some studies finding that more food is eaten after intense exercise, and other studies finding that there is no change.[34]

One of the most disturbing areas of research on exercise and obesity concerns childhood obesity. Many studies have shown that the more that children watch TV, the heavier they tend to be.[35] The hypothesis is that children who watch TV use less energy and therefore weigh more. This reasoning isn't airtight, however. Rather than TV watching causing obesity, it's possible that the causation goes in the other direction, that obese children are more likely to watch TV. Nevertheless, the hypothesis that television watching causing obesity receives support from several related findings. For example, it has been shown that when preadolescent girls watch TV, their metabolic rates decrease.[36] To parents this should come as no surprise; children frequently seem to "zone out" in front of the TV; they recline, don't move, and don't respond when spoken to. In addition, it has been shown that children tend to snack while they watch TV and to prefer the very tasty, and unhealthy, salty and sweet foods and drinks that they see advertised on TV.[37] Together all of these results suggest that TV watching may be a major contributor to the huge problem of childhood obesity in the United States.

This brings us to the third component of total energy expenditure: the extra energy your body uses following food consumption. This energy is larger following a high-carbohydrate than a high-fat meal, but it is apparently similar regardless of whether the food eaten tastes good or not.[38] If food consumption is greater than usual, the energy used is also greater. Similar to the decrease in metabolic rate that accompanies food deprivation, this increase in energy used following increased food consumption helps animals to stay at a constant weight. However, if rats' weights are increased by continued free access to a high-fat diet, their adipose cells increase in number, and eventually the increased energy effect disappears; a new set point has been reached.[39]

Scientists James A. Levine, Norman L. Eberhardt, and Michael D. Jensen followed Claude Bouchard's lead by examining energy usage in 16 nonobese male and female volunteer participants who were fed extra food. Each of the 16 participants was fed 1,000 calories per day in excess of their energy requirements for 8 weeks. As in Bouchard and his colleagues' study, there was wide variation in how much weight each participant gained: between 3 and 16 pounds. On average, the participants' energy expenditure tended to increase, although again there was wide individual variation, with energy usage increasing more in people who gained less. By measuring or controlling each of the different aspects of energy expenditure, Levine and his colleagues were able to determine that the participants' energy usage probably increased due to increases in the participants' nonvoluntary activity, such as fidgeting and posture maintenance.[40] Therefore how much someone gains when overfed may be due to how much the person fidgets. However, several questions remain. First, why does overfeeding increase such activities as fidgeting in some people but not others, and which sorts of people are likely to show the fidgeting effect? Also, we know that fidgeting in response to overfeeding would help people stay at a certain weight, but why would that trait ever have helped anyone to survive? Why did we evolve to do this? Finally, what precise mechanism is responsible for the increase in fidgeting or similar activities following overeating?[41] Answers to these questions could be extremely useful in helping us to control weight gain.

Who's Counting? What's Eaten and How It's Eaten

We've talked about influences on obesity that focus primarily on what's going on inside of the body. But what about how people interact with their surroundings, particularly the food in their surroundings? How does what people eat and how they eat it contribute to overeating and obesity?

Let's begin by looking at the eating behavior of the obese. Do they eat more than other people? Do they eat more quickly or at different times than other people? There have been a great many experiments done on this subject with all kinds of results. However, overall there are no consistent differences in the eating behaviors of obese and nonobese people.[42] Nevertheless, anyone wishing to study or treat overeating or obesity must be very careful about relying on people's self-reports for how much they have eaten. Several recent studies have found that both obese and nonobese people who say that they eat very small amounts tend to eat more than they say they do.[43]

Now what about the types of food that are available to us? How might that contribute to obesity? First, remember from earlier chapters that we prefer the tastes of salt and sweet, as well as highly caloric, high-fat foods. These preferences helped us to survive when food was scarce and low in fat and energy content prior to the agricultural revolution and industrialization. Our food supply was simply very different back then. For example, in the Paleolithic period, people ate meat in the form of wild game, which had a fat content of about 4%, as compared to the approximately 30% in our meat today.[44] Currently in the United States, sweet, salty, and high-fat foods are widely and cheaply available. The combination of this availability and our preference for these foods results in our consuming them to excess, which contributes to obesity. Experiments with both rats and people have shown that when large amounts of good-tasting food are available, they'll overeat and become obese.[45]

Adding to the availability effect is a variety effect. Increasing the variety of foods available in a single meal can also increase the amount eaten.[46] This variety is another common characteristic of industrialized countries such as the United States. Although some diets may decrease eating by decreasing food variety, as soon as the diet is over a huge array of foods will again be available to most Americans.

In addition to there now being many more kinds of good-tasting food, the relatively low level of fiber in what we eat, as compared to prior to industrialization, may be contributing to our obesity. Some researchers believe that eating little fiber results in the secretion of more insulin, and that this increased insulin increases weight gain.[47]

Special attention must be paid to the role of our culture's frequent consumption of sweets in inducing overeating and obesity. It has been hypothesized that any sweet taste—artificial or not—may cause insulin to be released with resulting increased hunger through lowering the blood sugar level and with resulting increased storage of ingested food as fat.[48] Many experiments have been conducted on this topic.[49] In one experiment, when preschool children were offered highly caloric, chocolate milk versus plain milk at lunchtime, twice per week for 16 weeks, they drank much more of the chocolate milk than the plain milk but their intake of lunch foods was the same. Therefore the children consumed far more calories on the chocolate milk days than the plain milk days.[50] Children may have difficulties regulating the amounts of calories that they consume from extremely good-tasting sources.

Comparable hypotheses have been posed about the percentage of fat in our foods and overeating. Some people have claimed that we eat more total calories when foods are high in fat than when they're low in fat. Experimenters have investigated this hypothesis by secretly substituting a low-fat version of a food for a high-fat version and then determining how many total calories the experiment's participants ate. These experiments have found that, in such situations, the participants consume fewer total calories.[51] (See Conversation Making Fact #10.)

Conversation Making Fact #10

One food that has particularly interesting, though not completely understood, effects on how much we eat is soup. When people are given soup prior to a meal, they eat less of the meal. In fact, their total calorie consumption may decrease that day. It's possible that chunky soup is better at decreasing the amount eaten than is nonchunky soup, although nonchunky tomato soup also seems to be particularly effective at decreasing the amount of food subsequently eaten.[52] It may not surprise you to learn that soup is now usually my choice for a first course when I go out to eat at restaurants. I'm particularly happy when tomato soup is on the menu.

We have been discussing the circumstances under which most people eat more or less depending on the food available. However, not everyone reacts to the food around them in the same way. Some people are strongly affected by food cues in their surroundings—they're externally responsive—and other people aren't. People who are externally responsive generally demonstrate particular physiological responses to food cues. For example, their insulin levels increase. This, in turn, increases their hunger and the likelihood that any food that is eaten will be stored as fat.[53] In other words, externally responsive people are literally turned on by the sight of food. If you add to this the fact that some people are genetically predisposed to store fat in certain locations on their bodies, then the statement "I just look at chocolate cake and it goes to my hips" actually makes sense. There are many externally responsive people at every weight level.[54] Some people who are externally responsive find ways of restraining their eating so that they don't become obese. Unfortunately, we still know very little about what makes some people externally responsive and others not, or the degree to which external responsivity can be modified.

Stressful or stimulating surroundings can affect anyone's eating. Walk into any cocktail party and you'll see the guests eating a great many potato chips, pretzels, and hors d'oeuvres that they would not ordinarily eat. As the conversation flourishes, hands repeatedly dip into the bowls of peanuts and crackers. Laboratory research can help us to understand this behavior. Experiments with rats have shown that the stress of a mild tail pinch increases eating, to the point that the rats gain significant amounts of weight.[55] In addition, rats stressed in this way tend to prefer good-tasting food more than do nonstressed rats.[56] There are similar findings with people. When people work on a mildly stressful tracking task involving aiming a stylus at a rotating dot, they tend to consume snacks. When the task is made more difficult, they eat more snacks.[57] Further, experiments have shown that loud, fast music and loud noise, which can also be considered mild stressors, increase the rate at which people eat, as well as the amount they eat and their preference for sweet.[58] Restauranteurs who want high volume and fast turnover might be well advised to play loud, fast music in their restaurants.

External responsivity, eating less than you wish, and stress-induced eating may all be related to one another. One experiment with approximately 100 college women showed that, following exposure to a tempting food cue (the smell of a baking pizza), dieters were more likely to say they wanted to eat and to actually eat more in comparison to nondieters. These results suggest that dieters tend to be more externally responsive than are nondieters.[59] Psychologists Catharine G. Greeno and Rena R. Wing's review of the literature showed that women who are dieters are more likely to eat when under stress than women who aren't dieters.[60] Finally, a number of researchers believe that there may be common underlying causes of stress-induced eating and externally responsive eating.[61]

It's important to point out, however, that your past experiences also strongly influence whether you eat when it isn't necessary. People eat significantly more when they think that they're going to skip a meal, undoubtedly because they've learned through past experience that this will help them make it through the missed meal. This may explain why dieters who break their diets may then overeat. They're anticipating future food deprivation, that is, returning to their diets.[62] It has sometimes seemed to me that, when I'm thinking my weight is creeping up and I need to do something to decrease it, I actually eat more. Perhaps this is an example of eating more due to expected future food deprivation.

Whether other people are around can also affect how much someone eats. Several experiments have shown that people eat more when eating with other people than they do alone. However, the effect of other people on the amount that you eat may be more complex than that.[63] Psychologist Janet Polivy and her colleagues investigated whether the eating behavior of a woman (the model, whom we'll call Jane) affected the eating behavior of other women (whom we'll call the participants). (See Figure 10.2.) Jane was actually an accomplice of the experimenters, but the participants thought that she was another participant. Jane told half the participants that she was dieting and half the participants that she wasn't. The experimenter instructed Jane and the participants together to eat until they were full. Then Jane ate with each participant individually. Jane ate very little in the presence of half of the participants to whom she'd said that she was and wasn't dieting. She ate a lot in the presence of the other participants. This research design therefore resulted in four groups of participants. The participants to whom Jane had identified herself as dieting generally ate less than the participants to whom Jane had identified herself as not dieting. In addition, there was an overall tendency for all of the participants to eat more when Jane ate more and less when Jane ate less.[64] This effect persisted even when participants hadn't eaten for 24 hours.[65] So Polivy and her colleagues confirmed what you've undoubtedly seen yourself—one member of a group of women refusing dessert only to be followed by each of the other women saying the same thing.

Special Cases

There are several special types of overeating and obesity that are associated with particular behavioral characteristics. One such characteristic that has been extensively investigated is a person's mood. A number of studies have

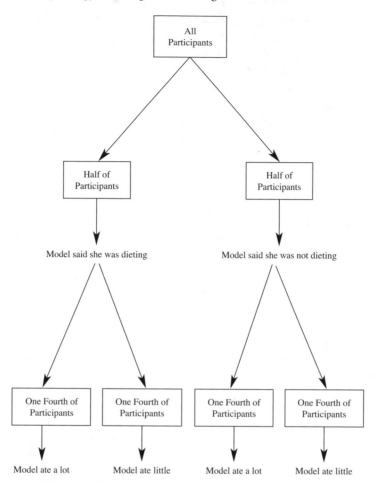

Figure 10.2 Design of Polivy, Herman, Younger, and Erskine's experiment. (Adapted from J. Polivy, C. P. Herman, J. C. Younger, and B. Erskine, "Effects of a Model on Eating Behavior: The Induction of a Restrained Eating Style," *Journal of Personality* 47[1979]:100–117.)

suggested that obese people are more likely to eat when they're experiencing aversive moods such as anxiety or depression than are people who aren't obese.[66] However, other more recent studies have suggested that whether someone is dieting is a better predictor than obesity as to whether that person will overeat when depressed. In fact, many researchers believe that dieting can lead to overeating, particularly binge eating, no matter what mood someone is in.[67]

In recent years binge eating, defined as "eating in a discrete period of time an amount of food that is definitely larger than most individuals would eat under similar circumstances,"[68] has come under close scrutiny by researchers and therapists. Approximately 20–30% of people who seek out obesity treatment appear to engage in problematic binge eating, and about 5–8% of all obese people do so.[69] In 1994 the American Psychiatric Association tentatively proposed a new diagnosis of binge eating disorder, defined as "recurrent episodes of binge eating associated with subjective and behavioral indicators of impaired control over, and significant distress about, the binge eating and the absence of the regular use of inappropriate compensatory behaviors (such as self-induced vomiting, misuse of laxatives and other medications, fasting, and excessive exercise) that are characteristic of Bulimia Nervosa."[70] People who engage in binge eating tend to be depressed and to come from families in which there are other impulsiveness disorders such as substance abuse.[71]

Possibly related to binge eating disorder is the eating engaged in by people with seasonal affective disorder (SAD). SAD tends to occur among susceptible people during the winter months, when they are exposed to less light. SAD is characterized by depression, a craving for carbohydrates, overeating, and weight gain. However, only a small proportion of obese people suffer from SAD.[72]

Another possibly related eating disorder is night eating syndrome (NES). This syndrome was first described by Albert Stunkard in 1955. However, only in the last few years has it received any attention in the research literature. The recent research has indicated that people with NES are obese and eat over half of their calories at night. They also, on average, eat 600 calories more in a 24-hour period than people who are obese but who don't have NES. People with NES also have great difficulty sleeping. They wake up an average of about 3.5 times per night, as compared with once every other night by people without NES. Further, people with NES eat during about half of their awakenings, but obese people without NES never do. Finally, people with NES tend to be more depressed than obese people without NES, and the mood of those with NES tends to worsen during the evening, something not seen in other obese people.[73]

Various physiological explanations have been proposed for these special cases of overeating and obesity. For example, it has been shown that people with NES don't show the usual rise in blood levels of leptin that is seen in other people. An increase in leptin may decrease appetite and enhance sleep. Therefore people who don't evidence this increase may eat excessively at night and have difficulty sleeping.[74]

The fact that obese people who eat excessively tend to be more depressed than other obese people and also tend to come from families with impulsiveness disorders, has led to another possible physiological explanation for overeating: the level of the neurotransmitter serotonin. A great many studies have shown that serotonin tends to be low in impulsive people, such as people who attempt suicide and in people who are depressed. In addition, high levels of serotonin are associated with decreased motivation to eat.[75] It has therefore been hypothesized that some cases of overeating, such as binging on carbohydrates and seasonal affective disorder, occur because the people with those disorders have low serotonin levels.[76] However, this hypothesis isn't yet firmly established. Another possibility is that dieting by itself causes people to be depressed and to binge.[77]

Get the Fat Out: Methods of Decreasing Overeating and Obesity

There are probably more how-to books on weight loss than on any other do-it-yourself subject. Many of these books are ignorant of the research on the origins of overeating and obesity and the methods for decreasing these phenomena. Fortunately, many people with research training have investigated weight-loss techniques. The rest of this chapter provides information about the scientific investigation of methods used to decrease overeating and obesity. Researchers want to determine which treatments work, in both the short run and the long run, and if some treatments are better for some types of obesity than others.

Shake That Body: Physiological Interventions

The most extreme type of physiological intervention consists of several kinds of surgery performed to restrict or bypass parts of the gastrointestinal tract, such as that undergone by Al Roker of the *Today Show*. These operations aim to decrease the amount that someone eats by making them feel full sooner after starting eating and by decreasing the absorption of food from the gastrointestinal tract. The operations are generally safe and very effective[78]; some studies have shown average weight losses of more than 100 pounds. However, this type of surgery isn't without risk. In addition to the slight risk from the operation itself, there can be side effects such as vomiting. However, in general, patients appear to be better adjusted and happier after surgery. They report that, as a result of losing weight, they're able to engage in physical activities that were previously impossible, they can wear a greater variety of attractive clothes, and they feel more sexually appealing. The benefits of these sorts of operations make them a viable choice for treating cases of severe obesity. Patients should be at least 100 pounds overweight and should have attempted (unsuccessfully) to lose weight using other, less drastic means. For other overweight people, those for whom obesity isn't life threatening, the potential dangers and side effects of surgery make it inadvisable.[79]

Humanity's ingenuity in devising surgical and mechanical interventions for overeating and obesity has known few bounds. In addition to the surgeries just described, jaw wiring and the long-term insertion of a balloon into the stomach have also been popular at various times. Jaw wiring, by allowing people to consume only liquids, definitely results in a short-term weight loss. However, when the jaw wiring is removed, the weight most often returns.[80] The balloon procedure involves first inserting a deflated balloon into the stomach. The balloon is then inflated and may be left thus in the stomach for many weeks.[81] Presumably this device was developed under the assumption that stomach distention will decrease food consumption. However, you should know from Chapter 2 that stomach distention is likely to affect appetite only if the distention is caused by something that has some nutrition to it, a condition that the balloon does not satisfy. It's perhaps not surprising, then, that in an elaborate study in which neither the participants nor the experimenters interacting with them knew who had really had a balloon inserted versus a pretend insertion, those with a real balloon insertion lost no more weight than those who only thought they had a balloon. Due to research results such as these, use of the stomach balloon is no longer recommended except for research purposes.[82]

Much better than surgery or a stomach balloon, much better than anything else that I can think of, would be a little pill that you could take to decrease overeating or facilitate weight loss. I'm not alone in these feelings; huge numbers of people would love to have drugs that prevent overeating and increase weight loss, and the pharmaceutical industry has spent untold amounts of money trying to get us what we want. By this point in the book, you've heard about all kinds of chemicals and physiological processes that occur when you see, smell, taste, eat, and digest food. Every one of those chemicals and physiological processes is a potential target for a drug that would decrease overeating or increase weight loss. As just one of many possible examples, you may remember from Chapter 2 that the chemical cholecystokinin (CCK) is produced during food digestion and may play a role in the termination of feeding. Therefore it's possible that artificially administering this chemical would make people eat less. Unfortunately, the CCK molecule is structured in such a way that it can't be given orally, but must be injected, which limits its attraction for most people.[83]

One drug that has been used as a weight-loss aid for many years is amphetamine. Although taking amphetamine does, without doubt, significantly decrease food consumption, there can be side effects such as increased blood pressure and the danger of addiction. Given these potentially very serious problems, and the fact that any weight loss achieved with amphetamine is temporary, amphetamine isn't recommended for weight loss purposes.[84]

Several new weight-loss drugs have recently been in the news. In 1999 the Food and Drug Administration (FDA) approved a drug, orlistat (also known by the trade name Xenical®), that blocks the body's absorption of about one third of consumed fat. Instead, the fat leaves the body in the feces. As a result, people taking orlistat lose more weight than people taking a placebo, but the difference isn't great. In addition, orlistat has some really great side effects such as blocking absorption of some vitamins, bloating, flatulence, oily feces, diarrhea, and, my favorite, fecal incontinence. Orlistat is also not cheap, costing about $4–$5 per day, and it isn't yet clear what happens to body weight after this drug is stopped. If orlistat is similar to other weight-loss drugs, any weight lost will be regained. But despite these possible problems, huge numbers of people are getting their doctors to prescribe orlistat, as well as another recently approved drug, Meridia® (also known as sibutramine), which suppresses appetite but can also raise blood pressure.[85]

You'd think that people would learn their lesson. It was only in 1997 that, in response to a request from the FDA, the manufacturers of fenfluramine and dexfenfluramine withdrew these weight-loss drugs from the market because of evidence suggesting that they cause heart valve problems. There had been good evidence that fenfluramine, administered over the long term, causes sustained weight loss. However, this drug can also apparently have serious side effects.[86] At least $3.75 billion in damages was ordered paid to the thousands of people who say that their heart valves were injured by taking the popular combination of fenfluramine and phentermine, a combination known to the public as fen-phen.[87] Another popular drug delivered as an herbal supplement, ephedrine, can be effective in weight reduction, but can also increase blood pressure leading to fatal heart attacks. [88] There simply is no magic drug that will solve your weight problems without causing any other problems.

There is, however, a subset of people who overeat or are obese that may be assisted by drug therapy. As you learned earlier in this chapter, there are some types of overeating and obesity that are associated with depression. These include people suffering from binge eating disorder, seasonal affective disorder, and night eating syndrome. Note that in at least some of these cases the overeating is associated with a craving for carbohydrates, and that, as you know from earlier material in this book, some researchers believe that eating carbohydrates can raise serotonin levels and that depression is associated with low serotonin levels. Therefore, some scientists have speculated that some cases of overeating and obesity—those associated with depression and/or carbohydrate craving—may be due to low levels of serotonin.[89] If this is correct, then giving such people drugs to raise their serotonin levels should decrease the overeating as well as alleviate the depression. There has been some success reported in alleviating carbohydrate craving and its associated depression by using drugs that raise serotonin levels.[90] However, this area of research remains quite controversial.

What about diets? Just about every women's magazine at the grocery store checkout counter contains advice about how to lose weight quickly and permanently by using the latest diet. There are low-calorie diets, low-carbohydrate diets, low-fat diets, total fasts, and many others. Why do you think that there are so many? Why are there always new ones? What do you think would happen if there were a diet that truly worked? A diet that allowed you to lose the weight you want without too much suffering, and the weight stayed off permanently?

Well, if there were such a diet, its fame would spread far and wide and there would be no need for any others. So guess what all of this marvelous variety of diets tells us? Diets don't work! Some weight may be lost, but it's almost always regained,[91] as seen so publicly in media stars such as Oprah. Even worse, some diets are extremely dangerous. Some can cause severe dehydration, excessive heart rate, or cardiac fibrillation, not to mention the fact that many diets are inadequate nutritionally.[92] More specifically, although the now-popular-again low-carbohydrate diets can induce weight loss, that weight loss tends to be regained and, over the long term, such diets may cause bone loss or kidney disease.[93] Finally, diets are not pleasant. In addition to the constant hunger many of them cause, people on diets show physiological symptoms of stress and have memory difficulties.[94]

So why don't diets result in permanent weight loss? It's important to keep in mind that there's no magic involved in losing weight. Calories from digested food don't disappear unless they're excreted, lost as heat, or used for metabolic or physical work. The only way to truly lose fat as a result of a diet is by eating fewer calories, by using more energy, or both.[95] In addition, as you learned about earlier in this chapter, for an unknown period of time, dieting can decrease metabolic rate, even after the diet has ceased, resulting in difficulty in losing weight and ease of regain once the diet is over. Weight loss may also not last because the person may have an increased appetite due to empty adipose cells, or because the person may simply resume the old food consumption and exercise behaviors that were responsible for the weight gain in the first place.

One method used by many dieters to decrease the number of calories consumed is the substitution of low-calorie foods and drinks for traditional ones. In my previous office, a popular break for my staff was a trip to the corner store to buy large amounts of Tasti D-Lite®. This sweet concoction looks like soft ice cream, but contains zero fat and relatively few calories. My staff believed that if they ate Tasti D-Lite instead of regular soft ice cream, they would at worst not gain the weight that they would by eating regular soft ice cream, and they might even lose weight. In these opinions they were not alone. It has been estimated that 80% of people in the United States are eating or drinking foods that are sugar- and fat-free, believing that this will help them with weight control.[96] But unfortunately, under many types of conditions, it appears that people eating low-calorie foods compensate to at least some degree by eating more total food.[97]

Independent of whether low-calorie foods decrease the total number of calories that you eat and drink, a major problem with these foods is that many don't taste good. People give the highest taste ratings to foods that are high in sugar and fat.[98] Further, in at least some studies, they expect low-fat foods not to taste good even before they try them, and they rate the taste of full-fat foods as less pleasant if they think they're low in fat.[99] Such judgments may be the result of long experience.[100] The fat in foods contributes significantly to their flavors and textures in the mouth.[101] It's therefore extremely difficult to manufacture low-fat foods that taste as good as high-fat foods. For this reason, many people have been excited about fat substitutes, especially olestra. Olestra is structurally similar to fat, and tastes like fat, but it can't be digested so it passes through the body without leaving behind any calories. Because olestra has structural similarities to fat, it can be used in baking and frying just as fat can.[102] Foods such as potato chips have been made with olestra so that, for example, 1 ounce of potato chips with olestra has 0 grams of fat and 60 calories, as compared to 10 grams of fat and 150 calories in regular potato chips.[103] This would all sound great except for a couple of problems. For one thing, olestra absorbs certain vitamins as it passes through the intestinal tract, so people need to take extra vitamins if they consume olestra. Worse, some people who eat olestra have resulting pain, diarrhea, and what's described as leakage (sounds great, doesn't it?).[104] An experiment showed that olestra infused directly into the first part of the small intestine doesn't make people feel full and doesn't cause the release of CCK, effects that are seen after infusion of digestible fat.[105] This doesn't bode well for the probability of olestra helping people to decrease the total number of calories that they consume.

Some researchers have argued that foods high in fiber and low in calorie density are more satiating than other types of foods.[106] However, there isn't yet firm agreement on this. Further, as stated previously, it's very difficult to get foods that are low in calories to taste good.[107]

One final aspect of the foods and drinks that you consume may be important in successful weight control. Experiments with rats and people have suggested that if you eat the same number of calories but divide it up into many small meals instead of eating those calories as one large meal you'll feel more full and will store less of what you eat as fat.[108] But there's a practical problem with this. These results were obtained in laboratories where the total numbers of calories eaten by the participants were strictly controlled. In the world outside of the laboratory, people eating many meals each day as opposed to one meal may eat more total calories, thus negating any beneficial effect of spreading the calories across many meals.

By now I'm sure you've confirmed my prediction and are pretty depressed. All I seem to be saying here is that no weight control techniques work without side effects. But you should know from the material presented at the beginning of this chapter that there's one technique that does work: exercise. For at least three reasons, exercise can be useful in decreasing obesity, preventing weight gain, and maintaining weight loss. First, exercise, even fidgeting, uses calories. Second, there's some evidence suggesting that, at least under some conditions, exercise can elevate the metabolic rate for several hours following exercise; more total calories are burned than would be burned by the exercise alone. Unfortunately, we as yet know very little about what kind of exercise has this lasting effect on metabolic rate. Third, exercising helps to maintain or build muscle and, pound for pound, muscle burns more calories than fat.[109] At least four other factors add to the attractiveness of exercise as a weight control technique. First, exercise can improve cardiovascular fitness and increase strength. Second, research suggests that exercise can help to improve mood, possibly through increasing serotonin levels.[110] Third, exercise can help to prevent osteoporosis (abnormally low bone mass).[111] Finally, exercise can increase people's relative amounts of HDL cholesterol, thus possibly decreasing cardiovascular risk.[112] It's no wonder that many researchers and therapists have promoted exercise as a useful component to any treatment for obesity. The main drawback to using exercise as a treatment for obesity or to prevent weight gain is the difficulty that many people have in adhering to an exercise program.[113]

How much exercise and what kind of exercise is needed to help you lose weight or prevent weight gain? There's been insufficient research on this issue to give a firm answer. However, we can get some ideas by looking at people who are and aren't successful in losing weight or maintaining weight loss and seeing how much they exercise. What such an examination shows is that people who are successful at losing weight or at maintaining weight loss tend to be more physically active than those who aren't. Many pieces of evidence suggest that what is needed is close to 1 hour of exercise per day (including brisk walking)—what is now recommended by the Institute of Medicine for health and weight maintenance.[114]

Data such as these have convinced me to try to exercise at least 1 hour per day, including walking. Living in New York City, even with a busy schedule, this isn't too difficult because I can walk efficiently as a good part of my work travel time. I often walk the 3 miles between my apartment building and the station where I get on the train to go to work. In addition, during my work day, I often go to buildings other than the one in which my office is located, and that also involves walking. However, at least 4 times per week, I go to a gym for about 1 1/4 hours where I do fairly intense aerobic and muscle-building exercises, as well as some stretching. Since I started this regime of at least 1 hour of exercise each day several years ago, it's been far easier to maintain my weight than it has been at any other time in my life. I still need to be careful about what I eat, but I gain much less easily. In addition, when I recently had my cardiac fitness level tested, I tested exceedingly well. So I've become a committed exerciser and I try to convince everyone else to exercise too. This can be extremely hard on those who work for me, because sometimes I "suggest" that they accompany me on my walks and they feel compelled to comply.

Your Body and Someone Else's: Interventions Involving Those Around You

You're probably aware that there have been, and continue to be, many attempts to use various forms of psychotherapy or related manipulations of the surroundings to help people lose weight. You can probably guess, from all that you've read so far, that these methods usually aren't too successful. People do often lose weight with the help of therapists and by manipulating aspects of their surroundings. However, that weight is usually regained. Nevertheless, given that these weight control methods are so prevalent, it's important for me to discuss them here.

One approach that has been used in decreasing obesity is to surround the obese person with a supportive group of people, some or all of whom are willing to help the obese person lose weight. These people need not be professionals; they may be trying to lose weight themselves. These are weight-loss community and self-help groups.

One type of weight-loss approach involving a community is weight-loss competitions among people at different work sites, such as workers at different banks. Attrition in this type of competition is very small, as is the number of dollars expended to run these programs. Average weight loss in one such set of competitions, each lasting from 12 to 15 weeks, was about 12 pounds.[115] However, no follow-up assessments were reported and, as you know, what counts is lost weight that stays lost.

More commonly used group methods for decreasing weight are self-help groups. These are groups consisting of people with a similar problem, in this case obesity. They meet to discuss common experiences, difficulties, and possible solutions. Some groups are entirely run by volunteers, and other groups, such as Weight Watchers, have much more structure. Weight Watchers was founded many decades ago and has had over 25 million members. Weight Watchers markets its own line of low-calorie foods as part of its weight-loss program.[116] All such organizations have high dropout rates, despite the fact that the people who join them are probably fairly motivated to lose weight. Even those who remain lose only moderate amounts of weight, with the exception of the Trevose Behavior Modification Program, a self-help program in which, after 5 years, the 23% of those still participating had lost an average of 18% of their body weight.[117] Self-help groups can provide emotional outlets and opportunities for socialization. In addition, participation in such groups usually has a low or moderate financial cost.[118]

In addition to community and self-help groups, many different kinds of psychotherapy are used to try to help people lose weight. One type that has frequently been used is psychodynamic therapy, which usually involves long-term individual psychotherapy. Many psychodynamic therapists believe that weight gain is due to emotional conflicts arising in early childhood. Therefore psychodynamic therapy seeks to treat these emotional conflicts rather than the obesity itself. Because psychodynamic therapists aren't usually researchers as well, there isn't a great deal of objective evidence available regarding the efficacy of psychodynamic therapy. Psychiatrists Colleen S. W. Rand and Albert J. Stunkard conducted a study to try to address this deficiency in the research literature. They mailed invitations to participate to all 572 members of the American Academy of Psychoanalysis. Approximately 104 of these psychodynamic therapists indicated a desire to participate and reported that they were currently treating at least 1 obese patient. A total of 70 completed more detailed questionnaires that were then sent to them (Questionnaire A), as well as another detailed questionnaire sent 18 months later (Questionnaire B). At the time of Questionnaire A, these therapists' obese patients had already been in treatment for an average of 31 months and had reportedly lost 10 pounds since entering treatment. By the time of Questionnaire B, this amount had reportedly risen to 21 pounds.[119]

A loss of 21 pounds would appear to be validation for the psychodynamic therapists' approach. However, there are some significant problems with this study. To begin with, psychodynamic therapy is extremely expensive, and therefore only the most motivated, as well as the wealthiest, patients would engage in it for years. Second, only a small proportion of the therapists completed questionnaires; therefore it's possible that only those therapists whose patients had been continuously losing weight for a long time chose to participate. Third, it's also possible that the therapists only reported data on the subset of their patients who were losing weight. Fourth, the weight measurements were simply what were reported on the questionnaires; it's impossible to assess their accuracy. Finally, this study assumed that underlying emotional problems are critical in causing obesity and that their treatment is important for long-term weight loss. This assumption is contrary to other information already presented in this book. For example, surgical interventions that result in severely obese patients losing weight are sufficient to improve the psychological well being of the patients. The information on metabolic and dietary determinants of obesity also seems to be contrary to the conception that an underlying emotional problem is usually the prime cause of obesity. Clearly, support for the psychodynamic treatment of obesity will have to await further research.

At the other end of the research spectrum are weight-loss methods using behavior therapy or cognitive-behavior therapy. Many behavior therapists see themselves as at least part-time researchers, therapists who are committed to a scientific approach to therapy. Therefore it's not surprising that by far the greatest amount of published research on psychotherapeutic treatments for obesity concerns behavior therapy. Well-known behavioral researchers acknowledge that even the best executed behavior therapy is unlikely to result in significant long-term weight loss.[120] Yet behavior therapists persist in trying to develop improved ways to help clients lose weight, and the techniques that have been a standard part of the behavioral weight-loss armamentarium are widely touted in the popular weight-loss literature.

For example, a common behavioral weight-loss technique is to make positive consequences such as money or engaging in pleasant activities contingent on appropriate weight-loss behavior. My husband employed this technique with me when we were about to graduate from college and get married in 1974. We decided I should lose about 10 pounds and he told me that he would pay me $5 for every pound that I lost. I was close to destitute at that time, and $50 seemed like a fortune. I lost the weight. However, it returned some years later and is still with me.

Behavior therapists also use techniques in which they teach clients to control the aspects of their surroundings that are likely to lead to overeating. These may include the precommitment devices discussed in Chapter 7, which involve patients learning to avoid situations in which they're likely to be tempted. For example, patients might learn to take limited money to the grocery store.

Behavior therapists further train their clients to engage in a variety of behaviors that are thought to be incompatible with overeating. These include combating anxiety by training people to relax their muscles and teaching people to eat slowly. However, this latter technique has been called into question by research showing no relationship between eating rate and obesity.[121]

An integral part of any behavior therapy weight-loss program is monitoring very carefully the patient's behavior and what's going on in the patient's surroundings. Every attempt is made to obtain reliable, objective data. Teaching self-monitoring of weight, calories consumed, time spent eating, and the like is often part of the process. Generally either the therapist or some trusted person other than the patient is responsible for monitoring, as well as delivering, any positive consequences.

Behavior therapy programs for decreasing obesity usually incorporate a variety of techniques, sometimes using drugs, exercise, and nutrition information, in addition to the behavioral techniques already described. This makes it difficult to assess the efficacy of any one particular aspect of treatment. Scientist Martha L. Skender and her colleagues conducted a careful experiment comparing three types of cognitive-behavioral treatment in 127 overweight men and women: treatment including a calorie-reduction diet but no exercise, exercise but no diet, and a combination of diet and exercise. To make sure that there were no differences among the participants before the treatments began, differences that might make it appear that one of the treatments was more or less successful than the others when it really wasn't, participants were assigned at random to one of the three treatments. Registered dieticians worked with the participants in each group every week for 3 months, then every other week for 1 1/2 more months, and then every month for 8 additional months.

At the end of 1 year, the combination group had lost the most weight, an average of 20 pounds, and the exercise only group the least, an average of 6 pounds. However, there was enough variation in weight loss among the members of the three groups that it was possible that these differences in average weight loss were due to chance; the differences among the three groups weren't what scientists call statistically significant. At the end of 2 years, however, there were statistically significant differences among the groups. All three groups had gained weight, such that the diet-only group now weighed 2 pounds more than when they had first started to diet. The exercise-only group and the combination exercise-diet group ended up 6 and 5 pounds below when they had started treatment, respectively. Skender and her colleagues concluded that people lose less weight by exercise than by dieting; however they regain less if they lose weight by exercising as opposed to dieting.[122]

People are apparently faced with a self-control problem: diet and get a quick, large loss that isn't good for you in the long run, or exercise and get an immediate small loss that will stick with you. No wonder it's hard for people to choose exercise rather than dieting for weight loss. One of the best future uses of behavior therapy may be to help people engage in more exercise and other healthy behaviors rather than lose weight per se.[123]

Particular instances of overeating and obesity may be best treated by particular interventions. For example, antidepressant medications may be useful in treating overeating that is associated with depression, which occurs in binge eating disorder.[124] A good technique for preventing obesity in children may be to decrease their sedentary activities such as television watching.[125] This has the added benefit of helping them to build strong bones,[126] and may even enhance school performance.[127] The increasing use of computers and hand-held electronic devices opens up new, though not necessarily improved, options for weight control. There are Web sites (for example, www.ediets.com) that will, in return for a fee, function as personal diet coaches. These sites also allow you to monitor your eating and dieting progress with all kinds of software on your electronic organizer.[128] I tried using the Web site, putting in my current weight and height and saying that I wanted to lose 25 pounds. My BMI, if you must know, is a healthy 22 (though, of course, I feel that I look too heavy). I wanted to see if the Web site would feed into the typical female American obsession of wanting to be too thin. The site would not let me set a goal weight below the healthy range. However, although the site agreed that I am at a healthy weight, it encouraged me to pay for services to lose at least 25 pounds.

The Bottom Line

Given all of this research, if you absolutely must lose weight, or if you have trouble preventing weight gain, what should you do? If you're extremely obese, you could qualify for surgical treatment. But what if you're not? Table 10.1 shows my best guess as to how to lose weight successfully and how to keep from gaining. Not all of my suggestions are definitively proven. However, all are at least consistent with the laboratory findings that we have so far. Weight control comes down to making what you eat and how you interact with your surroundings more similar to the conditions that existed when the human species was evolving. Not an easy task, but an achievable one.

Table 10.1 Research-Based Suggestions for Maintaining Current Weight or Losing Relatively Small Amounts of Weight

- Monitor calorie intake carefully.

- Cut back on calories very little, if at all.

- Eat low-fat, low-salt, low-sugar, high-fiber foods.

- Minimize the drinking of alcoholic beverages (see Chapter 11).

- To lose 1 pound in a week, maintain your current level of food intake while increasing your exercise so as to use an additional 3500 calories per week (for example, by jogging an additional 6 hours per week or by walking briskly an additional 10 hours per week).

- Exercise aerobically a minimum of 1 hour per day.

- Work out with weights so as to maintain or increase your muscle mass.

- Eliminate as many food cues in your surroundings as possible; this may involve obtaining the support of those with whom you live and work.

A Sense of Proportion: Conclusion

You've read in this chapter about the great many factors that contribute to our overeating and to our becoming, and staying, obese, as well as the small number of techniques—gastrointestinal surgery and exercise—that seem to result in lasting weight loss. This imbalance isn't really surprising. Our species evolved in surroundings that featured repeated periods of food scarcity.[129] As a result, our bodies are designed to ingest large amounts of calories and to retain those calories.[130] This is a particular problem in the United States, where the prevalence of many different types of very tasty, cheap, and highly advertised food and of labor-saving devices is perfect for facilitating obesity. As other countries "develop," their obesity rates also rise.[131]

Yet there's no consistent, healthy approach to the prevention and treatment of obesity. There have been insufficient efforts to curb the food industry's marketing of unhealthy eating.[132] In addition, it appears that physicians often don't advise obese people, who face real health problems, to lose weight or to increase their exercise levels.[133] At the same time, probably because of the current fashion image, many people, particularly women, who are slightly overweight or even of normal weight are continually trying to diet and lose weight. These efforts involve much time and money, may lead to eating disorders, and may facilitate future weight gain.[134] As pointed out so clearly by Yale psychologist Kelly D. Brownell and former University of Pennsylvania president Judith Rodin, even when someone's health improves by losing weight, that person is likely to regain the weight, and people whose weights cycle up and down seem to be more at risk for coronary heart disease and other health problems.[135]

For all of these reasons there has been much controversy over whether people should even attempt to lose weight. Many physicians and therapists now believe that people should try to lose weight only if their weight loss will result in significant health benefits.[136] An editorial in *The New England Journal of Medicine* in 1998 was even entitled "Losing Weight—An Ill-Fated New Year's Resolution."[137] But life can be hard on people who are overweight, even if they have no health problems. They may suffer from job discrimination and social rejection. They may be perceived as lazy or lacking will power, despite everything we know about the genetic and physiological determinants of obesity.[138]

So what do we do? Diet or not? Advise people to diet or not? Focus on increasing healthy behaviors no matter how overweight someone is? Pass more laws concerning the food industry? I don't think that complete answers to these questions are available yet. But in the meantime, for myself, I intend to exercise as much as is safe and possible and to try to structure my surroundings so that they contain limited amounts of high-fat, high-salt, high-sugar, and low-fiber foods.

CHAPTER 11

Drinking Your Life Away

Alcohol Use and Abuse

❧

Among U.S. Army troops stationed in Saudi Arabia in 1991 during the Gulf War, there were only about one third of the disciplinary problems as compared to troops stationed in other countries. In fact, in the first 6 months of the Gulf War, despite 300,000 troops being stationed in Saudi Arabia, there was a total of only 19 court-martials, fewer than 1 for every 15,000 soldiers.[1] The reason for this low rate of disciplinary problems? Saudi Arabian law, in accordance with the Muslim religion, does not allow any alcohol, and the U.S. Army followed this law while stationed in Saudi Arabia.

Far to the north, in a much different climate than Saudi Arabia— Moscow—in the early summer of 1999, 144 swimmers died in a span of 7 weeks, apparently almost all of them drunk. Russia has one of the highest rates of accidental death of any country, and vodka is usually involved.[2]

If people behave so much better when they're not under the influence of alcohol, why do so many people abuse the stuff? And if we want these people to stop drinking alcohol, what's the best method? This chapter will tell you what scientific research has found so far for the answers to these questions.

How Much Use and How Much Abuse?

People have made and drunk alcoholic beverages since the beginning of civilization. The archaeological evidence suggests that alcoholic beverages originated in the Near East and then spread to the West. There is evidence of the existence of wine at least 8,000 years ago and of beer at least 6,000 years ago.[3] For most of their existence, wine and beer have had fairly low alcohol contents and were two of the very few safe beverages; regular water supplies have often been contaminated. However, even after the water supply was made safe in most of the United States, and even after techniques were discovered that increased the concentration of alcohol in beverages, large amounts of alcoholic beverages have still been drunk by many people.[4]

Use of alcohol has waxed and waned in the United States. We are currently in one of the lower-use periods.[5] However, by no means is the amount of alcohol drunk by Americans small. Among all American adults, approximately 90% have drunk alcohol at some point in their lives.[6] As a specific example, in 1991, people living in Connecticut, New Jersey, and New York drank an average of 7 ounces of beer, 0.5 ounce of hard liquor, and 1 ounce of wine each day. Given that many people drink nothing, this average means that many people are drinking quite a lot.[7] As another example, although drinking has recently decreased among college students, they're still doing an enormous amount of it. A 1999 survey of freshmen just arriving on American campuses found that approximately 50% reported drinking beer frequently or occasionally in the past year.[8] Once students have some experience in college, the average amount of alcohol that they drink increases. An extensive 1997 survey of drinking in American colleges by the Harvard School of Public Health found that, although about 19% of those students abstained from drinking alcohol, 43% were binge drinkers, in which binge drinking was defined for men as consuming five or more drinks in a row during the 2 weeks prior to the survey (for women the amount was four drinks). The prevalence of binge drinking among students who reside in fraternities or sororities is terrifyingly high: approximately 81%.[9]

It's essential in your reading this chapter that you understand the enormous negative impact of all of this drinking. Although there's some evidence that moderate alcohol consumption can decrease coronary heart disease,[10] the cost of excess alcohol consumption—both to individuals and to society in general—is extremely high. Alcohol is one of the leading causes of preventable death in the United States; it's a factor in approximately 100,000 American deaths per year. These deaths occur not only because of the direct effects of alcohol, such as acute alcohol poisoning from the depressant effects of alcohol on the central nervous system, poor nutrition, and cirrhosis of the liver, but also from more indirect effects, such as an increased probability of all types of accidents including car accidents, aggravation of diseases such as bleeding peptic ulcer, a decreased probability of detecting when one is sick or injured, an increased probability of suicide and of being a victim of a homicide, and, in smokers, an increased frequency of smoking.[11] And that's just what can happen to the person who's doing the drinking. People who aren't drinking, but who happen to be near someone who is, are more likely to be the victims of car accidents, homicides, and domestic violence. In New York state alone there are about 60,000 arrests per year for driving while intoxicated.[12] On college campuses at which over half of the students are binge drinkers, almost 90% of nonbinging students report that they have had at least one problem due to binging students, such as being pushed, hit, or assaulted, or having experienced an unwanted sexual advance. This compares to around 30% who have experienced these problems at campuses at which no more than a third of the students are binge drinkers. Of college women who are diagnosed with a sexually transmitted disease, 60% were drunk at the time that they contracted the disease. It's no wonder that many college presidents report that the biggest problem on their campuses is alcohol abuse.[13]

But where is the dividing line between alcohol use and alcohol abuse? At what point should you start worrying about someone's alcohol consumption? What, specifically, am I talking about in this chapter when I talk about alcohol abuse and its treatment? The American Psychiatric Association defines alcohol abuse as alcohol consumption that results in drinkers not fulfilling their major responsibilities, risking physical harm, having legal problems, and/or exacerbating their social problems. Alcohol dependence is defined as tolerance exhibited to alcohol or symptoms of withdrawal from alcohol. Using these definitions, approximately 15% of American adults can be classified as having been alcohol abusers or alcohol dependent at some point in their lives. Alcohol abuse and dependence are much more common among men than women, and much less common among Asians than African Americans, Caucasians, and Hispanics.[14]

Given that almost half of Americans have had a family member with a serious alcohol problem,[15] the costs of alcohol abuse may seem all too familiar. Alcohol abuse is a terrible problem—for the abusers themselves and for those around them. In the meantime, alcohol manufacturers and bar owners do what they can to ensure that alcoholic beverages are consumed,[16] making the success of programs seeking to decrease or eliminate drinking all the more difficult. In order to better understand what's helping to maintain drinking, we'll start by taking a close look at the effects of drinking. Then, fortified with that information, we'll be better able to evaluate the myriad of treatments designed to treat alcohol abuse.

Expectations and Realities: The Effects of Drinking Alcohol

Folklore about the effects of drinking alcohol abounds. Consider, for example, the following American, German, and French proverbs:

> When drink enters, wisdom departs.[17]

> The drunken mouth reveals the heart's secrets.[18]

> There are more old drunkards than old doctors.[19]

202 · The Psychology of Eating and Drinking

And note this eloquent quotation from William Shakespeare's *Macbeth*:

> Drink, sir, is a great provoker of three things ... nose-painting, sleep, and urine. Lechery, sir, it provokes, and unprovokes; it provokes the desire, but it takes away the performance.[20]

How accurate are these beliefs? We'll consider both the research concerning the short-term, acute effects of drinking alcohol, and then the long-term effects. However, in order to evaluate this research, I must point out to you a difficulty in trying to figure out the effects of drinking alcohol. Someone's behavior may change after drinking either because of the direct effects of the alcohol or because of the person's expectations of the effects of alcohol. For example, if one person is told that drinking makes you act silly and another person is told that drinking makes you act serious, then, after drinking, the first person might act silly and the second person might act serious. Someone might even use drinking as an excuse to engage in socially unacceptable behavior.[21] Clearly we need to know what effects of alcohol are due to the drug itself and what are due to expectations; the former will be much harder to prevent or change than the latter.

Luckily scientists have figured out a way to tease apart the actual effects of alcohol and the effects of alcohol expectancies using something called the balanced-placebo design, developed by psychologist G. Alan Marlatt and his colleagues.[22] In experiments using this design, half of the participants drink alcohol and half don't, and of each of those two groups, half are led to believe that they've drunk alcohol and half aren't, for a total of four types of participants. In Figure 11.1, how type B participants behave after drinking shows the direct effects of alcohol uncontaminated by expectations, because type B participants drink alcohol but think that they haven't. How type C

PARTICIPANT EXPECTS TO RECEIVE

		Alcohol	No Alcohol
PARTICIPANT ACTUALLY RECEIVES	Alcohol	A	B
	No Alcohol	C	D

Figure 11.1 Balanced-placebo design. (Adapted from W. H. George and G. A. Marlatt, "Alcoholism: The Evolution of a Behavioral Perspective," in *Recent Developments in Alcoholism*, vol. 1, ed. M. Galanter, New York: Plenum, 1983.)

participants behave after drinking shows the effects of expectations uncontaminated by the direct effects of alcohol, because type C participants don't drink alcohol but think that they have. The experience of type A participants, who drink alcohol and think that they have, is similar to what happens in ordinary life outside of the laboratory. The behavior of type D participants, those who don't drink alcohol and think that they haven't, can be used as a comparison to the behavior of all of the other participant types. One example of what we've learned from experiments using the balanced-placebo design is that alcohol expectancies, and not the direct effects of alcohol, appear to be responsible for people becoming sexually aroused more easily after drinking.[23]

You're probably wondering how on earth people would think that they were drinking alcohol when they weren't and vice versa. You'll be happy to know that experimenters have become very good at such deceptions. Let's take a participant who's supposed to think that she drank alcohol but that wasn't the case. First the experimenter may ask the participant to rinse out her mouth with mouthwash to inhibit the participant's ability to taste what's to come. Then the experimenter will go to great pains to mix the participant's drink, with the participant watching, from two bottles clearly labeled vodka and tonic water. However, unbeknownst to the participant, all of the liquid in both bottles is tonic water. Finally, the edge of the participant's glass may be swabbed with alcohol to provide the participant with (misleading) odor and taste cues.

Acute Effects

Given the profound changes in the body's physiology after drinking, you'd expect alcohol to have at least some direct effects on behavior. When people drink, alcohol is metabolized in the liver first into acetaldehyde and eventually into carbon dioxide and water. Some of the acetaldehyde in the liver is absorbed into the bloodstream. Acetaldehyde affects most of the tissues in the body.[24] Approximately 50% of Chinese, Japanese, and Koreans lack an enzyme that rids them of small amounts of acetaldehyde. Such people tend not to drink very much, but when they do, they become flushed and can have severe heart palpitations.[25]

Alcohol has many direct physiological effects. In low doses it acts as a stimulant, but in high doses it acts as a depressant.[26] That's why you see people talking a lot at the beginning of a party, and then sitting in a stupor at the end. Relatively large amounts of alcohol and acetaldehyde can cause disruptions in breathing during sleep, a decrease in the amount of restful REM (rapid eye movement) sleep, headaches, and an inhibition of the synthesis of the male hormone testosterone.[27] (See Conversation Making Fact #11.)

Conversation Making Fact #11

Several different lines of research suggest that moderate drinkers tend to eat more and store more of what they eat as fat when they drink alcohol.[28] For example, scientists Margriet S. Westerterp-Plantenga and Christianne R. T. Verwegen conducted a fascinating experiment in which participants were repeatedly given an apéritif prior to eating as much as they wanted for lunch. On different days the apéritif consisted of wine, beer, fatty fruit juice, protein fruit juice, carbohydrate fruit juice, water, or nothing. All of the apéritifs (except the water) contained the same number of calories. When participants got a wine or beer apéritif, they ate more, faster, and longer, and got full later than when the apéritif didn't contain alcohol. Participants even ate more during the 24 hours following the apéritif if the apéritif contained alcohol.[29] These results strongly suggest that drinking increases the total number of calories you consume. However, because this experiment did not use a balanced-placebo design, it's difficult to know whether this increase in consumed calories was due to the direct effects of alcohol or due to people's expectations of the effects of drinking alcohol. In any case, data such as these suggest avoiding alcohol if you're trying to control your weight.

It has been firmly established that drinking increases aggression.[30] In recent years, psychologists have attempted to determine why that might be the case. One theory relates to the concept of self-control discussed in Chapter 7. You'll remember that self-control involves choosing something more delayed that is ultimately of more value over something that is less delayed but is of less value, with impulsiveness being the reverse. Some researchers believe that drinking somehow increases the discounting of delayed events—that it makes people more inclined to choose immediate rewards. Such behavior is called alcohol myopia.[31] If the delayed consequence of a choice is something negative, then alcohol could make someone act as if those negative consequences don't exist. So, for example, someone under the influence might impulsively hit someone, not thinking about the possibility of a jail term. Alcohol myopia might help to explain the greater tendency of intoxicated people to engage in risky behavior, including risky driving.[32]

One of the most investigated areas of alcohol's effects on psychological functioning is the acute effects of alcohol on memory. That alcohol should affect memory won't be a surprise to you. Everyone has heard of cases in which someone drank a lot one evening and then, although never losing consciousness, didn't remember much—or anything—about that evening, a so-called blackout. And it isn't a surprise to physiologists either. Alcohol inhibits the activity of the neurons in the hippocampus, a part of the brain that has been shown to be very important for memory.[33] But you may be surprised to know that, at least under some conditions, you don't have to drink a large amount of alcohol or have a blackout in order for alcohol to affect your memory. How much disruption of memory there is depends on how much you drink, what you're trying to remember, and what else is going on at the same time.[34] Even just thinking you drank can impair your memory.[35] How old you are also makes a difference; middle-aged people retain less information when they perform memory tasks after drinking than do younger people.[36]

In addition to disrupting memory, alcohol also disrupts other cognitive abilities. For example, it disrupts people's detection of behavioral errors, such as those that can occur when driving a car. The brains of people who have had alcohol react less when one of these errors occurs.[37]

There has also been substantial research on the question of how and under what conditions experienced drinkers show less effects of drinking alcohol. In other words, how and under what conditions does tolerance to alcohol develop? For example, people under the influence may drive better if they've had a lot of experience with driving drunk as opposed to never having attempted this risky behavior. Researchers have tried to figure out whether such changes with experience are due to a diminished physiological effect of the alcohol or to people learning in some way to compensate for alcohol's effects.[38] This is an important question because, to the degree that people enjoy feeling intoxicated, as tolerance develops they may feel compelled to drink larger amounts, resulting in more damage to their bodies. Information about the bases of tolerance may therefore be helpful in figuring out ways to help people cut down on their drinking.

There's substantial evidence indicating that learning is at least partly responsible for developing tolerance to alcohol's effects. Psychologist Bob Remington and his colleagues did an experiment in which some participants got a familiar drink (beer), and the others got an unfamiliar blue, peppermint drink. Both drinks contained exactly the same amount of alcohol, and the participants drank both at the same rate. After drinking, participants performed a hand-eye coordination task in which they searched for words within a grid of jumbled letters. Those participants who drank the unfamiliar blue, peppermint drink rated themselves as being more intoxicated and performed worse on the tasks than the participants who drank beer.[39] Somehow, people who drink a particular alcoholic beverage perform better not just when they have previous experience with any sort of alcohol, but when they have previous experience with that particular beverage.

One possible explanation of these findings is based on the concept of compensatory, opposite physiological reactions.[40] The idea is that any time a drug such as alcohol changes the body's physiology, there are opposite physiological reactions that return the body's state back to normal to maintain homeostasis; these opposite reactions help to keep the body in an optimal, stable state. Now assume that, with experience, these opposite physiological reactions get larger and that, through a learning process, they come to be generated by the aspects of the surroundings that are associated with the drug. Then, if someone repeatedly consumes a specific drug under the same conditions, the opposite physiological reactions will be large and will result in that person exhibiting tolerance to the drug. But if the surroundings or the appearance of the drug change, those opposite reactions won't be as strong and there will be less tolerance. This model has been used to explain why heroin addicts who take their usual doses of heroin in unfamiliar surroundings sometimes overdose. It's thought that in such cases the opposite reactions aren't as large and thus aren't strong enough to counteract the effects of the addicts' usual doses.[41]

Long-Term Effects

There's no question that, over the long term, the effects of several drinks each day can be extremely damaging to your body. For example, although moderate drinking (1–2 drinks per day), in comparison with abstention, can decrease cardiovascular risk, drinking larger amounts can result in increased cardiovascular risk and damage to the heart.[42] In addition, the acetaldehyde and excess hydrogen resulting from the metabolism of alcohol can eventually cause cirrhosis and hepatitis. I've already mentioned that repeatedly drinking alcohol can lead to tolerance and physical dependence on alcohol.[43] Physically dependent alcoholics can experience potentially dangerous withdrawal symptoms when they stop drinking.[44] Chapter 13 discusses at length how drinking by a pregnant woman can seriously harm the fetus that she's carrying.

Over time, drinking alcohol can also harm your nutrition. The acetaldehydes from the metabolism of alcohol decrease the effectiveness of vitamins. In addition, alcohol irritates the gastrointestinal tract. Finally, there's evidence that cirrhosis of the liver, which is often present in alcoholics, can cause disturbances in taste and smell, as well as cause decreased appetite. These factors can all combine to cause malnutrition in alcoholics.[45]

Despite what you read in the Conversation Making Fact #11 about moderate drinking contributing to weight gain, drinking very large amounts of alcohol over the long term does not necessarily result in weight gain.

When some people were given 2,200 calories of regular meals each day plus 2,000 calories of alcohol, they showed no consistent weight gain over a 4-week period. However, when other people were given 2,200 calories of regular meals each day plus 2,000 calories of chocolate, on average they gained about 6.5 pounds in 2 weeks. The lack of weight gain when large amounts of alcohol are drunk may be due to excess energy being released in the metabolism of alcohol.[46] Before you get too excited about the lack of any weight gain, however, keep in mind that drinking this amount of alcohol—equivalent to 19 1.5-ounce jiggers of water per day—is extremely damaging to the body in many ways.

Cognitive abilities are certainly not immune to the effects of long-term drinking. This would seem inevitable given that with repeated excess drinking, brain density decreases and other types of general brain damage occur.[47] Alcoholics tend to perform worse than nonalcoholics on many types of intellectual tasks, including tasks involving learning, perceptual-motor skills, abstraction, and problem solving. It isn't yet clear how much alcoholics' performance increases after a period of abstinence, if at all.[48] Memory is impaired in chronic alcoholics even when they're sober.[49] Damage to the liver may contribute to these memory deficits because such damage can cause toxins to build up in the blood, which then causes cognitive deficits.[50] Wernicke-Korsakoff syndrome, described in Chapter 8, is another example of how long-term excess alcohol consumption can adversely affect memory.

As yet there's no definitive evidence regarding how much drinking and for how long is necessary for cognitive deficits to occur. It's possible that even social drinkers who never consume large amounts of alcohol may have some deficits. More research is needed to settle this issue conclusively.[51] This is all a bit scary if you're a social drinker, as I am. It's hard to read all of the preceding paragraphs and not feel that everyone should be teetotalers. For the moment, I've decided to limit my drinking to a small amount each day.

Getting to the Bottom of the Bottle: Possible Causes of Drinking

With all of the terrible effects of alcohol, why does anyone drink, particularly large amounts? I'll now attempt to answer that question, beginning with information about the influences of the genes on drinking, and ending with information about the influences of our surroundings on drinking.

The Contributions of Our Genes

As with research on obesity, research on genetic influences on drinking began with investigations of whether genes are involved at all in how much someone drinks. Having answered that question in the affirmative, scientists are now attempting to identify the specific gene or genes that are involved.[52] A large variety of experiments has been conducted using rats, mice, and people.

One line of research has involved breeding strains of rats and mice that have specific reactions to alcohol. Researchers have hypothesized that if it proved possible to breed a nonhuman animal strain that behaved similarly to a human alcoholic, unusual aspects of that strain's physiology might provide clues about the physiological determinants of alcoholism.[53] A common strategy has been to test rats or mice for their preferences for alcohol, and then breed together those animals that show the least and the most preferences. In one experiment, the descendants of rats showing high preference for an alcohol/water mixture regularly reached blood alcohol concentrations equivalent to that of a 160-pound man who has drunk approximately 8 drinks in 1 hour.[54]

An experiment with mice used an increasingly popular approach to identifying the contributions of genes to alcohol use and abuse. In this approach the researchers don't look for a single gene that by itself is or isn't responsible for, say, the development of alcoholism. Instead they look for a group of genes, any one member of which is neither necessary nor sufficient for the development of alcoholism, but as a group seem to have some influence.[55] The idea is that a complex trait such as alcoholism won't develop unless a certain combination of genes is present. Using such an approach, researcher Kari Johnson Buck and her colleagues have found several genes that influence the severity of symptoms when mice go through alcohol withdrawal. These researchers believe that this information may help in future research on the identification of the genes that are involved in human alcoholism.[56]

Certainly these sorts of experiments are extremely useful in providing ideas about how genes might be involved in alcoholism. However, it's important to keep in mind that just because genes influence alcohol consumption in mice doesn't necessarily mean that comparable genes influence people. Let's turn to research on the effects of genes on alcohol use and abuse specifically in people.

One approach to determining whether genes influence human alcoholism been to examine people who do and don't have alcoholic relatives to see if there are any physiological traits or genes that tend to distinguish the two groups. Such studies have borne fruit. For example, scientists Marc A. Schuckit and Vidamantas Rayses selected two groups of young men who were similar in age, race, marital status, and drinking history. However, half of the young men had an alcoholic parent or sibling and the other half didn't. Then Schuckit and Rayses had each of the young men drink the equivalent of approximately 2 drinks over a 5-minute period and measured their blood acetaldehyde levels.[57] You'll recall that acetaldehyde is a chemical resulting from the metabolism of alcohol, a chemical that affects most of the body's tissues. As Figure 11.2 shows, the participants with alcoholic relatives had much higher levels of acetaldehyde than the participants with nonalcoholic relatives. Because both groups of participants had similar drinking histories, the differences

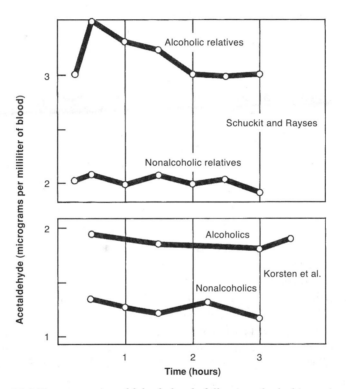

Figure 11.2 Top curve: Acetaldehyde levels following alcohol ingestion by non-alcoholic male participants with and without alcoholic relatives. (Adapted from M. A. Schuckit and V. Rayses, "Ethanol Ingestion: Differences in Blood Acetaldehyde Concentrations in Relatives of Alcoholics and Controls," *Science* 203 [1979]:54–55.) Bottom curve: Acetaldehyde levels following alcohol ingestion by nonalcoholics and alcoholics. (Adapted from M. A. Korsten, S. Matsuzaki, L. Feinman, and C. S. Lieber, "High Blood Acetaldehyde Levels after Ethanol Administration: Difference between Alcoholic and Nonalcoholic Subjects," *The New England Journal of Medicine* 292[8][1975]:386–389.) Note that the method of alcohol administration in the study by Schuckit and Rayses and the study by Korsten and his colleagues differed so that only the relative, and not the absolute, values obtained in the two studies can be compared.

between their acetaldehyde levels couldn't have been due to differences in experience with alcohol. Further, the results were comparable to results obtained by scientist Marc A. Korsten and his colleagues with alcoholics and nonalcoholics.[58] Thus it seems that there may be an inherited tendency for alcoholics and their relatives to metabolize alcohol differently than other people.

Schuckit has also studied hundreds of men who were similar except that only some were sons of alcoholics, from the time when these men were about 20 to when they were about 30. Although both groups of participants had similar drinking histories, Schuckit found that at age 20 the motor performance of the sons of alcoholics tended to be less affected by drinking alcohol. The sons of alcoholics also tended, on average, to report feeling less intoxicated after drinking than the sons of nonalcoholics. Further, 10 years later, those participants in both groups who had shown little reaction to alcohol at age 20 were much more likely to have become alcoholics than were participants who had shown more reaction to alcohol at age 20. Looking just at the sons of alcoholics, 56% of those who had shown little reaction to alcohol at age 20 had, by the age of 30, become alcoholics.[59] This research suggests, but does not prove, that in a society in which alcohol is easily available and frequently present, people who show little reaction to it may be likely to drink a great deal.

Another line of research comparing people who do and don't have alcoholic relatives has been conducted by scientists Henri Begleiter and others. This research has shown that, during some visual tasks, men and boys with alcoholic relatives show deficiencies in a particular brain wave called the P3 evoked potential, similar to deficiencies seen in abstinent adult alcoholics. These deficiencies aren't shown by men and boys who do not have alcoholic relatives.[60] Nevertheless, although we know that the size of the P3 evoked potential, which is important in cognitive tasks such as memory, is somehow related to the inheritance of alcoholism, we don't know the nature of that relationship. It's possible, for example, that some genes both directly decrease the size of the P3 evoked potential and make it more likely for someone to become an alcoholic.

Another approach to determining whether there are genetic contributions to alcoholism involves studying twins and adoptees. As explained in Chapters 5 and 10, if there are genetic contributions to alcoholism, then you would expect identical twins to be more similar in terms of alcoholism than fraternal twins, and you would expect adopted children to be more similar in terms of alcoholism to their biological parents than to their adoptive parents. Such studies have repeatedly shown that genes do contribute to whether someone becomes an alcoholic. However, even in identical twins, if one twin is alcoholic, there's only about a 50% chance that the other twin will be alcoholic. Further, most biological children of alcoholics don't themselves become alcoholics.[61] In other words, there's no question that, although genes influence whether someone becomes an alcoholic, other factors are involved.

Still another approach for assessing possible genetic contributions to alcoholism in people involves, as in mice, the search for a specific gene or genes that increase the probability of someone developing alcoholism. Since about 1990 attention has focused on a gene or genes that are related to the effectiveness of the neurotransmitter dopamine. Some researchers believe that problems with dopamine are involved in a large variety of addictive, impulsive, and compulsive behaviors.[62] However, whether a specific gene for the effectiveness of dopamine is related to alcoholism is presently quite controversial.[63]

There are more indirect ways that might provide hints as to whether heredity contributes to alcoholism. If certain personality types or physiological characteristics are associated with alcoholism, and if heredity seems to be involved in those personality types or physiological characteristics, then it's possible (though not certain) that heredity also contributes to alcoholism. Researchers have identified a number of personality traits and physiological characteristics that seem to be associated with alcoholism. The personality traits include sensation seeking (discussed in Chapter 5), impulsiveness (discussed in Chapter 7), anxiety (anxious alcoholics may drink to relieve anxiety), and antisocial personality disorder (defined as "a pervasive pattern of disregard for, and violation of, the rights of others that begins in childhood or early adolescence and continues into adulthood"[63]). There's evidence that each of these personality characteristics is to some degree influenced by heredity, or at least tends to occur in groups of family members.[65] With regard to physiological characteristics, you've already read how some Asians show more physiological effects of alcohol than others, and that people who are less affected by alcohol tend to drink more—both observations apparently involving the genes. You've also already read that certain types of brain activity are associated with alcoholism and are likely to have a genetic component. Finally, the level of the neurotransmitter serotonin appears to be related to how much alcohol is drunk. Both mice and people with low levels of serotonin tend to be impulsive and to drink more.[66] However, evidence from monkeys suggests that early childhood stress, more specifically separation from the mother, and not genes, is most important in determining serotonin levels in adult monkeys.[67] Consistent with these findings, people's exposure to traumatic events increases their probability of developing alcoholism.[68] However, there is as yet no evidence linking posttraumatic alcoholism to lowered serotonin levels.

The Contributions of Our Surroundings

Many aspects of people's surroundings also seem to affect whether they drink and how much they drink. To take a simple example, what time of day it is and whether other people are present can affect someone's drinking. More specifically, people tend to drink more later in the day and evening, on their days off, and, similar to how much you eat, people tend to drink more when they're with other people.[69] Expanding on that last finding a bit more, when they drink alone, people are more likely to perceive the effects of alcohol as negative, but when they drink with others, people are more likely to perceive the effects of alcohol as positive, reporting, for example, feelings of euphoria.[70]

However, simply being with someone else won't necessarily increase your drinking. It helps if that person drinks heavily. Scientists Donnie W. Watson and Mark B. Sobell conducted an experiment with 64 nonalcoholic men. The men were told that the experiment involved rating art objects and beers. The men were paired with an accomplice of the experimenters whom the men thought was another participant. All of the men rated the beers. In half of the cases, the accomplice also rated the beers and drank a lot. In the other half of the cases, the accomplice rated the art objects and did not drink. The men drank more while making their ratings if they were accompanied by a heavy-drinking accomplice.[71]

Watson and Sobell's experiment is one of many showing how people may drink amounts similar to what they see other people drinking, an effect called modeling. It's for this reason that researchers have thought that modeling could help treat excess drinking.[72] Certainly it appears to make a difference in adolescent excess drinking. Adolescents whose friends drink and who are involved in many social activities with their friends are much more likely to drink excessively than are other adolescents.[73]

Even when you're stuck in a plane, various aspects of your surroundings may affect how much you drink. John B. Reid happened to take a trip that combined three short flights 28, 18, and 35 minutes in length. During the first two legs of the journey, the flight attendants did not bring out the drink cart because they said there wasn't enough time to take it around between takeoffs and landings. However, the passengers were told that they were free to order drinks directly from the flight attendants. Nevertheless, during the first leg only 4 out of 103 passengers ordered a drink, and during the second leg only 1 out of 86. In contrast, during the third leg, when the flight attendants did bring out the cart, 42 out of 97 passengers ordered a drink.[74] Although it's not apparent which aspects of the situation affected drinking in this case (drink availability, opportunity to interact with flight attendants, modeling of other passengers' behavior, etc.), it's clear that the surroundings had a great deal to do with the amount of drinking that went on in this plane.

There are many other examples regarding how aspects of past or current surroundings can affect how much someone drinks. The interpretation of alcohol tolerance as a learned behavior, described previously in this chapter, is one such example. Another example involving learning comes from experiments with rats showing that they learn to prefer flavors associated with low concentrations of alcohol, even when the alcohol is infused directly into the stomach.[75] Scientists believe that this effect is due to the calories present in alcohol, that the rats associate the taste with the calories and therefore learn to prefer that taste. Similar to sugar, alcohol is an excellent source of energy.[76] This could help to explain why periods of alcohol deprivation appear to result in increased preference for alcohol in both rats and people; perhaps such effects are sometimes due not to alcohol dependence or withdrawal, but instead reflect an increased preference for a source of calories in a situation in which few calories have been forthcoming. Together these findings, and what you read earlier in this book, suggest that perhaps people initially don't like the taste of, say, bourbon, but come to like it after associating it with calories a number of times.

Another way in which researchers have thought that the effects of drinking might affect future drinking has been that some people drink to reduce tension, anxiety, or stress. According to this theory, because alcohol relieves these negative symptoms, people drink more. The only problem is that drinking often does not relieve these feelings, and then theories become very complex trying to explain the precise situations in which alcohol does or doesn't help someone feel better.[77] When I was about to enter the doctoral program in experimental psychology at Harvard, I tried to waive some first-year graduate courses by taking the exams normally given after the first year of graduate school. There were four 3-hour exams in 1 week, a very grueling schedule, and the last test was on my specialty: learning. Because I was worried about the other exams, I didn't study much for the learning exam. It was a lot tougher than I expected, and when I finished it I was convinced that I had done extremely poorly and that all of my efforts had been in vain; you had to pass every exam in order to waive any first-year course. On the phone from many miles away, my father strongly urged me to have a drink; that would make me feel better. So I had a few good belts, but instead of no longer being upset, now I felt drunk in addition to upset. That was my first experience with the inaccuracy of the popular belief that drinking can help you to escape your problems. (By the way, I passed all the exams.)

Our surroundings may also affect drinking by interacting with our motivations, as exemplified by the schedule-induced polydipsia (SIP) phenomenon described in Chapter 3. In demonstrations of SIP, rats drink huge amounts of freely available water when they're hungry and when food is delivered at regular intervals. Scientists think that the rats in this situation are motivated to eat, but can't eat whenever they want, and so they drink instead. A number of researchers have thought that SIP might be a good way to study alcohol abuse.[78] These researchers have hypothesized that some instances of excessive drinking may be due to people being unable to satisfy a variety of motivations or drives. Psychologist John L. Falk supported this hypothesis when, using rats, he substituted alcohol solutions for water in an SIP paradigm, and the rats drank enough alcohol to become physically dependent on it and to have continuously high blood alcohol levels.[79]

Another way in which motivation can affect drinking behavior has to do with the effects of money and economics on drinking, similar to the approaches to choice behavior discussed in Chapter 7. How much you drink depends on not only the inherent value of the alcohol, but on how difficult it is to get it and what alternatives are available. To begin with a well-known example, drinking decreased during Prohibition, when alcohol was less available and illegal.[80] Many laboratory experiments have been conducted to determine just what sorts of constraints and contingencies will result in less or more alcohol being drunk.[81] These experiments have shown that, as constraints such as the amount of effort needed to get alcohol increase, the amount of alcohol obtained and consumed decreases. In contrast, as the availability of rewards other than alcohol decreases, drinking of alcohol increases.[82] This last finding raises the possibility that some cases of alcohol abuse may be at least partially due to drinkers perceiving the effects of alcohol as the best part of their lives.

This section has described many possible contributors to the development of alcoholism, including factors mostly concerned with people's genes and physiology and factors that are mostly concerned with people's surroundings. It can be confusing trying to sort out what's really responsible for what. There are two basic conclusions that you can draw from all of this information. First, there may be different causes for different cases of alcoholism. This is an important conclusion because it's possible that different treatments may be more or less successful with different cases of alcoholism depending on the cause of a particular case. Second, each case of alcoholism is likely to be caused by more than one factor. Many scientists now ascribe to a theory of the origins of alcoholism in which there's an inherited tendency to develop it, but alcoholism only occurs if the surroundings that would promote it are also present.[83] In other words, it takes both certain genes and certain surroundings in order for alcoholism to occur.

Taking the Cure

Folklore also abounds about how to "cure" alcoholism, as in this Chinese proverb: "The best cure for drunkenness is while sober to see a drunken man."[84] But is this really the best way to cure alcoholism? Folklore does not always hold up to scientific scrutiny.

The Parameters of Successful Treatment

The first issue of importance to researchers trying to identify successful treatments of alcoholism is whether the treatment has long-lasting effects. Just as with weight control, alcoholism relapses are frequent. Therefore for a treatment to be successful it must have continued success over long follow-up periods.[85] This means that any study purporting to show that an alcoholism treatment works is suspect unless it reports data on the success of the treatment years after it has been completed.

A second issue concerns whether treatment should be on an inpatient or an outpatient basis. A large number of studies have been conducted on this issue. In particular, researchers have focused their attention on the benefits of treatment by for-profit, inpatient, private institutions, many of which are quite expensive, such as the Betty Ford Center. This research indicates that treatment is no more successful when it's inpatient, as opposed to outpatient, or when it's very, as opposed to less, intensive (except perhaps for seriously deteriorated alcoholics). What seems to make the most difference in terms of whether a treatment will be successful is the type of treatment used, not the setting within which the treatment is offered. Thus there seems to be little justification for expending the large number of dollars required for treatment by an expensive, inpatient, private institution, particularly when reimbursement by health care insurers is involved.[86]

Now we come to the most contentious area of all: abstinence versus controlled drinking. Some people, those who view alcoholism as a disease, see the only possible goal of alcoholism treatment as complete abstinence.[87] These people believe that a single sip will often result in a full-blown relapse for a recovered alcoholic. Other people, such as behavior therapists, who see alcoholism as due to a number of factors including aspects of the alcoholic's surroundings, feel that it's possible for some—not all—alcoholics to have as their treatment goal so-called controlled drinking: drinking moderate, safe amounts.[88] Complete abstinence has always been the approach adopted by the members of Alcoholics Anonymous (AA), as well as by the large majority of clinics and alcoholism treatment professionals.[89] This approach is supported by evidence that, for at least some alcoholics, abstinence is essential for full recovery.[90] Nevertheless, evidence has been accumulating over the past 25 years indicating that some alcoholics can successfully achieve controlled drinking, and that knowledge has split apart alcoholism treatment professionals.

The beginning of the controversy is marked by the 1978 publication of scientists Mark and Linda Sobell's book *Behavioral Treatment of Alcohol Problems*. In this book, the Sobells described their use of a variety of behavioral techniques to reduce alcohol consumption. They designed each patient's treatment individually, choosing for each patient a treatment goal of abstinence or social drinking, as well as choosing the particular behavioral techniques used. They stated that a goal of controlled drinking is easier for some patients to achieve than a goal of abstinence.[91]

Since the Sobells published their book, a large number of reviews of the alcoholism treatment literature have shown that some alcoholics can successfully learn, over the long term, to drink without problems.[92] Patients who show few symptoms of alcohol dependence and who believe that successful controlled drinking is a possibility have been the most likely to maintain long-term drinking without problems.[93] Indeed, several studies have shown that some alcoholics, without any treatment, will over time come to drink without problems,[94] although other research indicates that patients trying to achieve controlled drinking may be more likely to relapse than patients trying to achieve abstinence.[95]

In 1982, researchers Mary L. Pendery and Irving M. Maltzman began an attack against the controlled drinking approach. These researchers stated that controlled drinking does not work for most patients, and that it's dangerous to offer it as a treatment alternative. Pendery and Maltzman felt that the Sobells' patients' long-term outcomes had not been good, and they even accused the Sobells of having falsified their data to appear that the controlled-drinking approach was more successful that it actually had been.[96] For their part, the Sobells stated that Pendery and Maltzman had not compared the long-term outcomes of the controlled-drinking treated patients to patients who had been treated with a goal of abstinence, the best way to determine the effects of using controlled-drinking as the treatment goal.[97] The disagreements between the Sobells and Pendery and Maltzman received a great deal of media attention, even reaching the pages of *The New York Times*.[98] The Addiction Research Foundation appointed an outside committee to investigate the charges of fraud in the Sobells' work. This committee found no evidence of fraud.[99] An investigating group organized by the Alcohol, Drug Abuse and Mental Health Administration also found no evidence of fraud, although their investigation was hampered by a lack of full cooperation from parties on both sides of the controversy. This group felt that at times the Sobells could have been more careful in preparing their results for publication.[100]

One would have hoped that after all of this public debate, things might have quieted down, with the issues discussed only in scientific journals, but that was not to be. Although many researchers have felt and continue to feel that the evidence indicates the validity of using a goal of controlled drinking for some alcoholics, almost all treatment programs have persisted in using a goal of abstinence.[101] Under such conditions, it was probably inevitable that someone working in one of these programs who was aware of the research literature would try to change the usual treatment programs, and that controversy would result. This happened in the year 2,000, and again the controversy made the pages of *The New York Times* and *New York Magazine* and appeared on ABC television. The problem began when the television show *20/20* did a piece about how the Smithers Alcoholism and Treatment Center in New York City was using controlled drinking as a goal for some of its patients. Next, the Betty Ford Center wrote to ABC stating that the show was dangerous in that it promoted an unsafe treatment approach. A few weeks later, the Christopher D. Smithers Foundation (which had been previously but was no longer directly connected to the Smithers Center) ran large newspaper notices condemning the methods of the medical director of the Smithers Center, Alexander F. DeLuca. DeLuca had openly advocated controlled drinking for some alcoholics. One day later he was fired. Essentially simultaneously, the Smithers Foundation sued St. Luke's-Roosevelt Hospital Center, where the Smithers Center is located, stating that the hospital had changed the treatment philosophy of the Smithers Center's founder, R. Brinkley Smithers, who gave $10 million to open the center.[102]

On balance, the research appears to indicate that controlled drinking is a reasonable goal for some alcoholics. However, independent of the abstinence/controlled-drinking controversy, it seems exceedingly unfortunate that a major treatment center would be tied to using a certain treatment approach, regardless of what research might indicate was the best approach, due to constraints associated with the funds used to establish the center.

Which Treatments Work?

Dozens of different treatments have been proposed for alcoholism. These treatments vary tremendously and include behavior therapy, medication, and self-help group approaches, among others. For decades researchers have been trying to determine which of these treatments have at least some beneficial effect and which do not. Fortunately, in very recent years, many well-conducted studies have been done. Scientists can perform statistical tests of the results from groups of these studies to determine whether, as a whole, they indicate that the cessation of alcohol abuse was unlikely to occur by chance, but was instead likely due to the alcoholism treatment.

Psychologist William R. Miller and his colleagues conducted just such an analysis.[103] This analysis found that the most effective treatment is brief intervention. This technique consists of at most three treatment sessions. The content of these sessions may vary, possibly including such elements as assessment of the drinker's problems, advice, or counseling. The clients are usually given printed materials such as self-help manuals to supplement the treatment sessions. Often, the purpose of the sessions is described to the clients as education- rather than treatment-oriented. The sessions and the written materials often focus on using learning theory principles to modify drinking behavior through altering various aspects of the drinker's surroundings, including how other people's behaviors may be encouraging the drinking. Given this context, it's not surprising that the goal of brief interventions is usually to get clients to drink responsibly, rather than to get them to abstain from alcohol. For this reason, brief interventions are usually employed with people whose drinking problems aren't severe and who aren't physically dependent on alcohol. And herein lies the complication with Miller and his colleagues' finding that brief intervention is the most successful treatment. It's possible that brief intervention is the most successful because it's used only with problem drinkers who are in relatively good shape, not because it's the best treatment for alcoholics in general.[104]

Other treatments that Miller and his colleagues found very successful include social skills training (teaching patients how to cope with stressful situations),[105] motivational enhancement (methods of enhancing problem drinkers' motivations to change their drinking behaviors),[106] the community reinforcement approach (which restructures the contingencies in the surroundings so that "sober behavior is more rewarding than drinking behavior"),[107] and behavior contracting (having clients agree to contracts in which specific rewards are given for achieving approximations toward specific goals).[108] However, it's important to remember that, similar to brief intervention, it may be very difficult to use these treatments with seriously debilitated alcoholics. Alcohol abuse can severely limit the cognitive abilities of the abusers, both while they're drinking and when they're sober. These limitations may include problems with planning and with estimating quantities including the quantity of alcohol drunk, and so may inhibit the abilities of some alcoholics to participate in some types of treatments.[109] Over many years, the brain damage from alcohol that's responsible for these cognitive deficits may at least partially reverse.[110] However, treatment needs to be started long before that.

Miller and his colleagues' study also seemed to indicate that aversion therapy using nausea has some success. This type of therapy is based on the principles of taste aversion learning discussed in Chapter 6. The basic idea is to follow the taste of alcohol closely by nausea so that an aversion to the alcohol develops. A number of studies have shown this method to be extremely successful at decreasing drinking.[111] Laboratory research on taste aversion learning suggests a number of ways to ensure that nausea-based aversion therapy is as effective as possible. First, in order to obtain the strongest aversion, nausea should closely follow the taste of alcohol, and not precede the taste of alcohol.[112] Second, clinicians should anticipate that an alcoholic, after developing an aversion to one alcoholic beverage, may switch to another alcoholic beverage. In a study of 102 hospitalized alcoholics that I did with two psychology students, K. R. Logue (no relation) and Kerry E. Strauss, approximately 15% of the alcoholics reported taste aversions to alcoholic beverages, even though in many of these cases, prior to the aversions, the participants had had strong preferences for the beverages and had drunk them frequently. However, in very few of these cases did the aversions generalize to anything else, including to any other alcoholic beverages.[113] Thus, although the alcoholics sometimes naturally developed taste aversions to their highly preferred alcoholic beverages, they simply switched to drinking different alcoholic beverages. For aversion therapy to be successful with alcoholics it may be necessary to pair a number of different types of drinks with nausea. A final concern about how to conduct successful aversion therapy is how to induce nausea in a safe and effective manner. Using injected chemicals can be dangerous, and using mechanical methods such as a rotating chair can be messy.[114] A technique called covert sensitization avoids these problems, but is sometimes not as effective at inducing an aversion.[115] In covert sensitization the participants imagine that they feel ill. Unfortunately, with this method it's more difficult to ensure that sufficient illness has been generated.

Perhaps surprisingly, Miller and his colleagues' study shows that treating alcoholics with disulfiram (otherwise known as Antabuse®) appears to have very limited effectiveness. Antabuse blocks the normal metabolism of alcohol. If someone has recently taken Antabuse and then drinks alcohol, the acetaldehyde concentration is 5 to 10 times greater than if Antabuse had not been taken,[116] resulting in an extreme physical reaction including "nausea, vomiting, tachycardia, [and] marked drop in blood pressure."[117] This reaction lasts as long as there's alcohol in the blood and can occur even if Antabuse has been consumed as much as 14 days prior to drinking.[118] Thus alcoholics taking Antabuse are exposed to a taste aversion learning situation each time that they drink alcohol. Here the problems with effectiveness may lie with treatment compliance; there can be problems with getting clients to take Antabuse consistently. Scientist George Bigelow and his colleagues required their clients to first deposit a sum of money at a clinic. Each time a client failed to return to the clinic to receive disulfiram, a portion of his or her deposit was sent to charity. The remainder was returned to the client at the end of the study. Using this procedure, Bigelow and his colleagues found significant and consistent decreases in their clients' drinking.[119] Note that Bigelow and his colleagues' procedure is essentially a self-control precommitment technique, as discussed in Chapter 7.

Still another type of treatment approach for which Miller and his colleagues found some support is relapse prevention. This treatment uses a cognitive-behavior approach. Cognitive-behavior therapists have hypothesized that alcoholics relapse because they've previously learned that drinking alcohol is followed by various positive consequences, and that each time a relapse occurs it's an indication that they're not cured, which promotes further drinking. Therefore some cognitive-behavior therapists have actually advocated planned relapses for their clients. The client is encouraged to resume drinking briefly, and then the therapist helps the client to stop again, teaching the client how to cope with relapses in the future without the help of the therapist.[120]

Miller and his colleagues' study found that self-help manuals; behaviorally oriented marital and family therapy; and cognitive therapy, in which therapists attempt to get alcoholics to change inappropriate thoughts, have also evidenced small but positive effects. In contrast, behavioral self-control training, involving teaching alcoholics how to change their own drinking, has not shown any consistent positive effect. However, the findings from the individual self-control studies examined by Miller and his colleagues were quite mixed, and so behavioral self-control training may be useful under certain conditions.[121] You've already seen that some aspects of behavioral self-control training are integral to other, clearly successful treatments. A very recent experiment conducted by psychologists Reid K. Hester and Harold D. Delaney provided behavioral self-control training via a computer. The participants were nonalcoholic heavy drinkers and the goal of the treatment was moderate, nonproblematic drinking, not abstinence. Participants learned how to monitor their own behaviors, analyze their surroundings to see what might be facilitating drinking, set goals, set up rewards for reaching those goals, and the like. This experiment did find a lasting and positive effect of behavioral self-control training on drinking.[122]

In contrast, Miller and his colleagues' study showed that when controlled studies are conducted, hypnosis, confrontational counseling, and the opportunity to participate in AA have no positive effects whatsoever. The second of these, confrontational counseling, involves such therapist activities as videotaping problem drinkers while they are drunk and then showing the tapes to these people when they are sober.[123] AA is a self-help group that began in 1935 when two alcoholics decided to meet with other alcoholics to promote complete abstention from alcohol. Members are expected to go to meetings regularly and to be available to assist other members who are about to relapse. AA advocates a 12-step approach that begins with participants admitting that they're powerless over alcohol and ends with participants achieving a spiritual awakening. Membership in AA is anonymous and is extremely popular.[124] It's estimated that the total number of AA members in the United States alone is over 1 million.[125]

One recent experiment by researcher Barbara S. McCrady and her colleagues assessed the effectiveness of AA participation by comparing three types of treatment: behavioral couples therapy, behavioral couples therapy plus relapse prevention, and behavioral couples therapy plus participation in AA.[126] The participants were 90 men who abused or were dependent on alcohol, plus their female partners. The excessive drinking of approximately two thirds of the men significantly improved; however there was no evidence of greater improvement by the men assigned to the group involving AA participation. In fact, there was some evidence that, on average, the men in the group that involved AA participation did worse than the men in the other two groups. The findings did show that, of the men in the group that included AA participation, those men who regularly attended AA drank less than the other men in that group. However this could just mean that the participants who weren't doing well found ways to avoid the AA sessions; it doesn't mean that AA caused the men who attended to drink less. Despite all of these findings, similar to the self-help groups for obesity described in the previous chapter, AA may serve an important social and informational function, whether or not it decreases drinking.

An alternative approach to evaluating the success of different treatments has been taken by an ambitious study entitled Project MATCH (Matching Alcoholism Treatments to Client Heterogeneity). This experiment cost $27 million and was conducted with almost 2,000 clients around the country who had either current or previously severe problems with alcohol. The idea was to randomly assign these clients to one of three types of treatment so that the distribution of different types of people in each treatment group would be fairly similar. In addition, the characteristics of each client were to be carefully measured and then correlated with the treatment results. It was hoped that this experiment would show which types of client characteristics resulted in a good outcome with each of the types of treatment. The three types of treatment used were cognitive-behavioral coping skills therapy, motivational enhancement therapy, and 12-step facilitation therapy, modeled after the 12 steps in AA. Each treatment lasted for 12 weeks, and the clients' behaviors were monitored for 1 year after treatment. Contrary to what many people had expected, and contrary to the results of Miller and his colleagues' study, on average the clients in all three groups showed significant improvement, and there were no significant differences in the outcomes of the three types of treatment.[127]

How do we reconcile the results of Project MATCH with those of Miller and his colleagues? Apparently Project MATCH excluded anyone with a drug problem other than alcohol, the participants were all volunteers, and participants all had to have a permanent address and no problems with the law. In the world outside of the laboratory, people who need treatment for alcohol abuse frequently have concurrent problems with other drugs; are compelled to participate in alcohol treatment by the courts, their employers, or by social agencies; are transients; and have legal problems. In other words, the clients in Project MATCH weren't representative of most of the people who need treatment for alcohol abuse, a problem that plagues many studies of alcohol abuse treatment.[187] Further, the 12-step treatment used in Project MATCH wasn't identical to AA because it consisted of individual therapy, as opposed to group sessions. Group AA sessions can involve members being publicly confronted with their problems with alcohol. Some people find such a confrontational approach difficult to endure,[129] which could result in them avoiding participation in AA. However, such confrontations weren't a part of the 12-step facilitation therapy used in Project MATCH. This difference could explain why the 12-step treatment was successful in Project MATCH but not in the studies reviewed by Miller and his colleagues.

You may have noticed that all of the treatment approaches I've discussed are essentially psychological treatments that involve methods of changing drinkers' surroundings in order to change their drinking. With the exception of Antabuse, there's little in the way of effective drugs for alcohol abuse. There are drugs that help with the physical symptoms of withdrawal and drugs that can assist alcoholics who feel anxious or depressed,[130] but clearly drugs that block the positive feelings that people have after drinking would also be useful. If such feelings could be blocked, then drinking should decrease. In addition, researchers have hypothesized that, because alcohol abuse is associated with low serotonin levels, drugs that increase serotonin levels should help alcoholics to remain sober.[131] However, as yet, no drugs of these sorts have been shown to be effective.

Some populations have received special attention with regard to alcohol abuse, with treatments designed particularly for the special characteristics of those populations. One such population is poor Native Americans living on reservations. The effects of alcohol abuse on these people have been devastating. For example, in 1990, South Dakota Native Americans could expect to live approximately 15 years less than the average man or woman in the United States, with huge rates of alcoholism being largely responsible for their early deaths. As a result of such statistics, the sobriety movement is growing among Native Americans, and some treatment programs are incorporating elements of ancient Native American healing techniques such as sweat lodges.[132]

Another group that has received special attention with regard to treatment is college students, among whom, as you've already read, alcohol abuse is extremely high. Some campuses are instituting policies of zero tolerance, in which students caught engaging in problem drinking will be sent home or have their parents informed. Many are increasing the education about alcohol problems that they provide to students, including pointing out that many students don't binge drink. Alcohol-free events are being scheduled in an attempt to provide students with more alcohol-free entertainment. Colleges are even placing ads in major newspapers to alert parents to the possible problems that their children may have if they drink at college.[133] Further, brief intervention techniques are being modified specifically for college student populations, for example by developing cost-effective ways of giving students feedback on their drinking by mail.[134] In recognition of the depth of the college-student drinking problem, the National Institute on Alcohol Abuse and Alcoholism has set up the College Age Drinking Initiative to stimulate research on drinking among college students and how to prevent and decrease it.[135]

For someone who needs alcohol abuse treatment, the great many alternatives can be somewhat bewildering. I hope that this review of the literature has given you some idea of the range of alternatives as well as of which types of treatments are effective. For an alcoholic who isn't severely deteriorated, who has few symptoms of alcohol dependence, and who believes that controlled drinking is a realistic goal, brief outpatient treatment including assessment of the problem, advice about how to control drinking by modifying surroundings, and self-help manuals, with the aim of getting the alcoholic to drink responsibly, may be a sufficient and successful treatment. However, such a treatment approach will definitely not work for every alcoholic. Other alcoholics may require more extreme manipulations of their surroundings in order to decrease their drinking. For the present at least, psychologists—those who specialize in the origins of behavior and in the methods for changing behavior—have a major role to play in the effective treatment of alcohol abuse.[136]

Last Call: Conclusion

We know that despite the many problems associated with drinking alcohol, and the difficulties in treating it, people still drink. Obviously to some extent this is due to the positive feelings that many people experience when they drink, and people may have little else in their lives that provides them with positive feelings. If there are no good alternatives, alcohol will seem to have great value. Therefore, to decrease excessive drinking, our society will have to provide people who drink with other ways to obtain the rewards that they obtain by drinking. For example, good job opportunities must be provided in areas of the country where they're few and far between and where the associated alcoholism rates are high. Our society can also continue to take the strong steps of increasing the drinking age and enforcing drunk driving laws.[137] All of these steps are in addition to continuing the development of effective treatments for problem drinking.

However, the alcohol lobby is making it very difficult to decrease problem drinking. This is one of the wealthiest, most effective, and best connected lobbies. Its members frequently host fundraisers for political candidates, events that, of course, include alcohol. There are alcohol lobbyists in virtually every state capital. There are many other reasons why drinking and its associated problems continue. For example, alcohol ads frequently employ humor or animals that appeal to children under the legal drinking age. Alcoholic beverage manufacturers have also made sure that the possible beneficial effects of moderate drinking on heart disease are widely publicized. In addition, bars with cheap drinks proliferate near college campuses where binge drinking is common.[138] All of these make decreasing drinking a real challenge, despite alcohol abuse's huge economic and health costs. My hope is that books such as this one will be weapons in the fight against alcohol abuse.

CHAPTER 12

How Sweet It Is

Type 2 Diabetes

℃

D iabetes is a devastating disease in which either the pancreas produces insufficient insulin or the body does not react to the insulin that is produced. As you already know, insulin is a chemical involved in the metabolism of blood sugar, thus ensuring that sugar can be used by the body. With diabetes, blood sugar levels become abnormally high and excess sugar is excreted in the urine.

You're probably wondering why I chose to include a chapter on diabetes. Obviously the integral relationship between diabetes and insulin has something to do with my reasoning. In previous chapters you've learned about the important role that insulin plays in hunger, satiety, and fat storage. In this chapter you'll learn that the origins, effects, and treatment of diabetes are also linked to many other topics in this book, including the preference for sweet, the importance of exercise in obesity, weight maintenance, thirst, and the effects of food on cognition.

We need to use everything that we know about the psychology of eating and drinking to understand diabetes because of the terribly frequent harm that this disease is inflicting on people in industrialized countries, particularly the United States. The number and percentage of people in the United States with diabetes has been increasing astronomically. In 1958, there were only about 1.5 million Americans diagnosed with this disease, but in 1999 there were about 9 million diagnosed American diabetics.[1] Some authorities estimate that the total number of Americans with the disease is now about 16 million.[2] In 1998, 6.5% of all Americans were estimated to have diabetes, at a yearly cost of around $100 billion. Although diabetes was formerly seen primarily in older people, it's now becoming common at much younger ages; approximately 3.7% of Americans in their 30s are estimated to have it,[3] and at least 10% of Americans 50 or older.[4] So the chances are excellent that either you, or someone very close to you, will at some point suffer from diabetes.

There are striking differences in the frequency of diabetes among different racial and ethnic groups. For example, African Americans and Native Americans tend to have a much higher prevalence of diabetes than white European Americans. Approximately 25% of African American women over the age of 55 have the disease, and 12–13% of all African Americans, compared with 7% of white European Americans, have it.[5] A particularly disturbing example is Arizona's Pima Indians. Roughly one half of the adults in this group have been diagnosed with diabetes, and it is increasingly seen in Pima children.[6]

If left untreated, this very common disease has terrible effects on the body. To begin with, blood sugar levels that are too high can cause comas. In addition, over the long term diabetes can damage the walls of the small blood vessels, leading to a host of medical problems including blindness, nerve damage (including impotence in men), kidney disease, circulation problems that can result in amputation of the feet and legs, and cardiovascular diseases. In fact, it's thought that approximately 40% of all cardiovascular diseases in the United States may be due to diabetes.[7] Diabetes is also associated with high levels of harmful fat in the blood and with high blood pressure.[8] Given all of these terrible effects, it's no surprise that in 200 A.D., the Greek physician Aretaeus provided this description of the experience of those suffering with diabetes: "Life is short, disgusting, and painful."[9]

There are several different types of diabetes. Close to 95% of cases are what is called Type 2 diabetes, and it's on this type that the present chapter will focus. People are on the first rung of the ladder toward Type 2 diabetes when they demonstrate insulin resistance. With insulin resistance, the pancreas releases insulin, but the body's tissues don't react much to its presence. As a result, the pancreas may release increasing amounts of insulin, trying to maintain sugar metabolism. Blood sugar levels will be high—a condition known as impaired glucose tolerance—although not so high as to qualify for a diagnosis of diabetes. Eventually, the pancreas may be unable to keep up with the high blood sugar levels, or may even become unable to secrete much insulin. Then full-blown Type 2 diabetes is present.[10]

"So Sweet Was Ne'er So Fatal"[11]: The Causes of Type 2 Diabetes

As it turns out, Type 2 diabetes, by far the most common kind of diabetes, is intimately tied to eating behavior—both in terms of its origins and its effects. To understand the relationships between eating and diabetes, it will be helpful first to review a few basic facts from earlier chapters about the role of insulin in the eating behavior of the general population.

First recall that your pancreas releases insulin when you come into contact with food or with aspects of your surroundings that have previously been associated with food. For example, in many people, their pancreas releases insulin when they're about to eat a piece of chocolate cake. After it's released, insulin decreases blood sugar level and increases the probability that whatever is eaten will be stored as fat. Further, the insulin-caused decrease in blood sugar level that occurs when someone detects, but has not yet eaten, food may increase the probability that someone will eat. In other words, this change in blood sugar level may function as a hunger signal. Finally, research has suggested that you release more insulin when you eat foods that are sweet, taste good, or are low in fiber—all of which are consistent with other observations indicating that, when they eat those sorts of foods, people eat more and get fatter.

Now let's build on this information regarding what you eat and insulin levels to explain the origins of diabetes. In the past decade, researchers have begun to use a new food measurement to understand the relationships among types of foods, insulin levels, and Type 2 diabetes: the glycemic index. The glycemic index score for a given food has to do with your body's metabolic response to that food (see Table 12.1). More specifically, when you eat a certain number of calories of a particular type of food, the glycemic index measures how much total glucose is subsequently added to your blood during a specified period of time (see Figure 12.1).[12] If a particular food results in a lot of added blood sugar, then that food gets a high glycemic index score and vice versa. High glycemic scores are associated with hunger and low scores with satiety.[13] This is an explanation of satiety and blood sugar that takes into account how blood sugar changes over time (for another similar mechanism, see Chapter 2).

Table 12.1 Typical Glycemic Index Scores for Sample Foods

Food	Glycemic Index
Bread	100
Rice Bubbles cereal	116
Porridge oats	60
All-Bran cereal	43
Eggs and bacon	24

Source: S. Holt, J. Brand, C. Soveny, "Relationship of Satiety to Postprandial Glycaemic, Insulin, and Cholecystokinin Responses," *Appetite* 18[1992]:129–141.

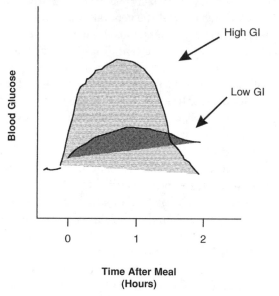

Figure 12.1 Effects of high and low glycemic index foods on blood glucose over time. (From S. B. Roberts and A. G. Pittas, "The Role of Glycemic Index in Type 2 Diabetes," *Nutrition in Clinical Care* 6[2003]:73–78. Reprinted with permission from International Life Sciences Institute.)

Many factors contribute to the glycemic index score. These factors include the chemical structure of a food, the amount of fiber in that food, and how the food has been processed. For example, oatmeal, which is high in fiber, has a lower glycemic index score than Rice Bubbles® cereal, which contains finely milled grains.[14]

In an intriguing experiment, scientists J. H. Lavin and N. W. Read gave 10 young men a radioactive, 300-calorie, orange-tasting, glucose drink and then measured the amounts of glucose and insulin in the men's blood for the next 3 hours, as well as the men's hunger ratings, fullness ratings, and amounts of radioactivity in the men's stomachs. Each man came to the laboratory twice; on one day he had the basic glucose drink, and on the other day he had that drink with the addition of guar gum. Guar gum is an inert substance that isn't digested. The results showed that after consuming the guar gum as compared to the regular drink, the participants' glycemic index scores, plasma insulin levels, and hunger were all lower. These results indicate that slowing the absorption of glucose, in this case by the use of guar gum, makes people feel more full. Lavin and Read also showed that there were no significant differences over time in the changes of the amounts of radioactivity in the stomach; there was no difference in how long the drink stayed in the stomach with and without the guar gum. Based on this evidence, the researchers believed that the guar gum drink was more satiating because it extended the contact between the molecules of glucose and the glucose receptor cells in the small intestine, the next location after the stomach on the drink's trip through the gastrointestinal tract.[15]

I do have one question about this experiment, however. Did the guar gum change the taste of the drink? We know that eating good-tasting foods results in the release of more insulin than eating not-so-good-tasting foods. Perhaps the guar gum drink resulted in a lower glycemic index score because the drink didn't taste as good with the guar gum. The authors don't discuss this possibility or report any data on the taste of the two drinks, so unfortunately, at present, there's no answer to my question.

In general, these sorts of experiments seem to indicate that the higher the glycemic index score, then the more insulin released, the less cholecystokin released in the small intestine (see Chapter 2), the lower the satiety, and the more food that's eaten. Further, people whose diets naturally contain high proportions of food with high glycemic scores are more likely to develop cardiovascular disease, to be obese, to be insulin resistant, and to develop Type 2 diabetes.[16] Thus there's much circumstantial, if not direct, evidence linking foods with high glycemic scores to the development of Type 2 diabetes.

Add to all of this the fact that the more fat on someone's body—particularly the upper abdomen—the more insulin is produced, and you've a vicious circle: the more insulin, the more fat, and the more fat, the more insulin. All of this is associated with insulin resistance, Type 2 diabetes, and cardiovascular disease. In fact, the relationship between body fat and Type 2 diabetes is so strong that most Type 2 diabetics are obese.[17] This relationship explains why Type 2 diabetes is on the rise among Americans; obesity is increasing and therefore so is diabetes.

Consistent with the research linking body fat to diabetes, much evidence suggests that activity levels are related to insulin levels and the presence of Type 2 diabetes. Studies have shown that men who are physically fit are much less likely to develop Type 2 diabetes later in life.[18] In addition, several studies with particular ethnic populations have shown that when one subset of the population exercises a lot and another subset exercises little, the latter group is much more likely to develop Type 2 diabetes.[19] In fact, decreased exercise, along with an increased percentage of body fat as opposed to muscle, may explain why elderly people tend to be more insulin resistant.[20] You may be getting quite tired by now of my repeated mentions of exercise as an important factor in maintaining lifelong health, but I can assure you that I write only what the data compel me to report!

There's also evidence that your genes play a role in whether you develop Type 2 diabetes. To begin with, it's possible to breed mice that lack a particular gene and, as a result, have increased insulin sensitivity and are less likely to be obese.[21] In people, if one identical twin has Type 2 diabetes, the other twin has a greater than 90% chance of developing it.[22] Further, many researchers believe that people with Native American genes are more likely to develop Type 2 diabetes than are people with Caucasian genes.[23] Of course, as you already know from the preceding paragraphs, genes by themselves are insufficient to cause Type 2 diabetes. People who exercise a lot, who are thin, and who eat predominantly low glycemic index foods are unlikely to develop diabetes no matter what their genetic makeup. However, unfortunately, Americans who live this way are rare indeed.

You may wonder why on earth it would be advantageous for people to have genes that inclined them toward diabetes in the first place. Why would we have evolved to have such genes? Why would people with such genes have been more likely to survive and reproduce than other people? One explanation is what's known as the thrifty gene hypothesis. According to a version of this theory, having a quick, large insulin response was very useful in surroundings in which food was often scarce. Insulin, as you'll recall, facilitates the storage of what you eat as fat. When food is scarce, having stored fat helps you to survive. It's thought, for example, that for centuries the Pima Indians experienced regular periods of famine, so that the only Pimas who survived were those who released much insulin and had high tendencies to store fat. However, when food is plentiful, as it is now for the Arizona Pimas, storing lots of fat isn't so good, and much insulin is produced, ultimately leading to insulin resistance and Type 2 diabetes.[24] In fact, among the Arizona Pimas, the frequency of Type 2 diabetes is the highest of any group in the world.[25] Once again, we see a mismatch between our bodies and our current surroundings, resulting in serious medical concerns.

Sweet and Low: How Type 2 Diabetes Affects Behavior

People and other animals with untreated diabetes behave differently than nondiabetics. Some of these characteristic behaviors are easily observable and can therefore be helpful in diagnosing diabetes. For example, diabetics tend to feel tired. They also drink and urinate frequently.[26] The high levels of blood sugar in diabetics result in unusually high levels of sugar in the urine. This, in turn, causes extra water to be drawn into the urine in order to dilute the unusually high sugar concentration in the urine. Thus there's more volume to the urine, more water is lost from the body, thirst increases, and the diabetic drinks excessively.[27]

Some aspects of diabetics' eating behaviors can help scientists to understand eating behaviors in the general population. Researchers reported some time ago that people eat more when insulin levels are high than when they're low.[28] Based on these results, you would expect diabetics, who have low insulin levels, to eat relatively little, even of the sugary foods on which many people gorge. However, people with diabetes can still eat very large amounts when sugary foods are available. Such observations lead scientists to believe that the eating of large amounts of sugary foods by the general population isn't due to high insulin levels.[29]

Nevertheless, there may indeed be some conditions under which diabetics eat less than nondiabetics. When diabetic and nondiabetic rats are given a fatty "appetizer" of corn oil, the diabetic rats subsequently eat less than the nondiabetic rats. This may be because the diabetic rats metabolize and make immediate use of more of the fat that they eat than do their nondiabetic counterparts, who are more likely to store the fat that they eat.[30] Unfortunately, comparable research hasn't yet been done in people. So we don't yet know if the bodies of diabetic people, similar to those of diabetic rats, would be able to use consumed fat as an energy source, while storing less of that fat. If this were indeed true, then high-fat diets might be healthier for diabetics than for nondiabetics. But we just don't know yet.

Not only amount eaten, but what's eaten, may be affected by diabetes. When a flavor is paired with glucose infused into rats' stomachs, diabetic rats subsequently develop less preference for the flavor than nondiabetic rats. This finding suggests that the release of insulin that normally occurs when glucose is eaten, but does not occur in diabetics, is necessary in order for this type of food preference to develop.[31] Once again, how such processes might or might not affect the food preferences of people with diabetes hasn't yet been investigated.

Another possible explanation for why diabetics and nondiabetics might show different food preferences concerns taste sensitivity. In general, diabetics are less sensitive to a variety of tastes, including the taste of glucose, than nondiabetics. The longer that someone has been diabetic, and the more medical complications that someone has had from diabetes, the more likely that person is to have taste deficits. These taste deficits may result from nerve damage due to long-term high blood sugar levels.[32] It's possible that the decreased sweet-taste sensitivity results in diabetics eating sweeter foods so that they'll still be able to taste sweet, but this thereby exacerbates their diabetes. Clearly we need research concerning how diabetics' taste deficits may affect the kinds of foods that they eat.

Given the many physiological effects of diabetes, it will probably not surprise you that diabetics' cognitive functions, such as their abilities to learn a list of symbol-number pairs, are also compromised by this disease. Similarly, declines in cognitive functioning are significantly more likely in elderly people with diabetes.[33] In fact, the high and irregular blood sugar levels associated with diabetes can themselves result in disturbances in cognition. Unfortunately, these cognitive problems can interfere with diabetics' abilities to participate in the diabetes treatments that I'll describe in the next section.[34]

The Sweet Smell of Success: Treatments

As you can see, diabetes is a truly devastating, and all too prevalent, disease. However, there's good news: There are many different, helpful treatments for Type 2 diabetes. (See Conversation Making Fact #12.) Some of these treatments are ones in which a diabetic can engage with minimal medical assistance, or none at all. Others require extensive medical monitoring and support.

Given that most patients with Type 2 diabetes are obese,[35] and given that obesity is thought to be a major cause of Type 2 diabetes, one of the first recommendations that any physician will give a Type 2 diabetic is to lose weight. There's no question that weight loss by itself will very frequently remove the symptoms of Type 2 diabetes. In fact, some researchers believe that a weight loss of as little as 10 pounds may reap significant benefits. But losing weight isn't easy, and keeping it off is even harder. Thus, by itself, weight loss is unlikely to serve very many Type 2 diabetics as an effective long-term treatment.[36]

Exercise can help us lose weight and then keep the lost weight off, whether we're diabetic or not.[37] However, exercise may have benefits with respect to diabetes that are independent of weight loss. An experiment with middle-aged men showed that 9 weeks of an aerobic exercise program, even with no accompanying weight loss, increased their insulin sensitivity.[38] Another

---

Conversation Making Fact #12

Diabetes, although sometimes difficult to manage, doesn't have to interfere with your life, even if you're very active. Gary Hall, Jr., a world-class swimmer, has Type 1 diabetes—similar to Type 2 in that there's insufficient insulin, but usually arising at younger ages largely due to genetic causes.[39] Yet despite his disease, Hall won two gold medals, one silver, and one bronze at the 2000 Sydney Olympics. He was diagnosed with diabetes midway between summer 1996 and summer 2000. After his diagnosis, three doctors told him that he could never again compete. However, he found another doctor who worked closely with him and, with the proper care, he was able to triumph.[40]

experiment with Type 2 diabetic men and women of varying ages showed that 3 months of a program of aerobic exercise, again even with no weight loss, decreased their need for insulin.[41] These effects may be related to changes in the amount of muscle in the experiments' participants. Although the participants' weights didn't change, their bodies may have gained muscle and lost fat. As you know, diabetes is more likely to occur the more body fat you have. Such factors may also be related to the greater tendency of Type 2 diabetes to develop in older people because they tend to have more fat and less muscle. Given this reasoning, it should be possible to help prevent diabetes in elderly people by ensuring that they participate in exercise throughout their lives.[42] Consistent with all of this research, sedentary people are more likely to develop diabetes, and men with Type 2 diabetes are more likely to die if they're physically inactive.[43]

Changing what you eat can also help treat diabetes. As you've already learned in this chapter, the probability of developing diabetes increases if someone eats many foods that have a high glycemic index score—foods that quickly increase blood sugar levels, for example soda, ice cream, and chocolate cake. Thus it shouldn't be surprising that eating in the opposite way, that is, eating foods that don't quickly increase blood sugar levels—high-fiber foods such as beans, whole-wheat bread, and oranges—may help normalize blood sugar levels and control diabetes.[44] Recent findings indicate that people who eat lots of fiber are less likely to have gained weight or to have abnormal insulin levels a decade later. So eating lots of fiber may help to prevent or control diabetes.[45] People who perceive themselves as generally able to accomplish their goals are relatively successful at controlling what they eat so as to live reasonably well with diabetes.[46]

When attempts to lose weight, exercise, and change what's eaten are insufficient to control someone's diabetes, the next alternative is drugs. Approximately one third of Type 2 diabetics use oral medication to help control their diabetes. Many drugs are available for this purpose, and the number and variety of drugs are constantly increasing. Some drugs cause the pancreas to release more insulin, some decrease blood sugar levels without affecting insulin levels, some decrease the rate of carbohydrate digestion, and some cause the body to react as if insulin were present.[47] As more is learned about the complex relationships among what's eaten, insulin levels, and diabetes, there are more opportunities for developing new drugs to treat diabetes, drugs that intervene at particular points in these relationships.[48] For example, consider the experiment with mice described earlier in which normal mice eating a lot of fat gained weight and showed insulin resistance. If a certain gene was disrupted in these mice, they didn't gain weight and remained sensitive to insulin. These findings suggest that it may be possible to treat Type 2 diabetes by blocking the effects of a particular gene.[49]

As a last resort, insulin injections are used to control Type 2 diabetes. Patients learn to monitor their blood sugar levels very carefully and to inject appropriate amounts of insulin. Approximately one third of Type 2 diabetics have to do this.[50] Yet even here there's some good news. There are improved ways to deliver insulin. Diabetics need not repeatedly test their blood and then stick insulin needles into their bodies each day. Small insulin pumps have been developed that are the size of a pager and can be worn on a waistband. A thin plastic tube carries insulin from the pump to where a needle is inserted into the diabetic's abdomen. This needle needs to be changed only once every few days. A diabetic can set the pump to deliver different amounts of insulin depending on what he or she eats, to release a certain amount of insulin each hour for baseline needs just as a normal pancreas would, and to release different amounts of insulin at different times of the day, according to the diabetic's different daily activities. A diabetic can also turn the pump off during intense exercise, which by itself will greatly lower blood sugar levels. Insulin pumps are becoming increasingly popular as diabetics and their physicians learn about them and how easy they are to wear.[51] A few years ago I saw a group of young women singers on the *Today Show* who started singing together because they all used insulin pumps, about which they sang enthusiastically and positively.

However, there's a sobering note in this story. Although there are many good treatments for diabetes, not everyone hears about them, and not everyone is given advice about what they should do to prevent Type 2 diabetes. These people tend to be poor and less educated. Such people see doctors less often, and even when they do, they are less likely to get the good medical advice that wealthier, more educated people receive.[52] People may not receive the same *quality* of medical care even when they receive the same *quantity* of medical care.

Parting Is Such Sweet Sorrow: Conclusion

Diabetes, particularly Type 2 diabetes, is a prevalent disease with extremely serious consequences. What you eat and how you maintain—or don't maintain—your weight have a lot to do with whether you develop Type 2 diabetes, as well as with whether you effectively treat it. Once more we can see that our current surroundings, as opposed to the surroundings in which we evolved, have done us in. In the surroundings in which we evolved, there were few high glycemic index foods, and our ancestors had to move around a fair amount in their daily lives, and Type 2 diabetes was extremely rare. Now the incidence of Type 2 diabetes has reached epidemic levels and is continuing to rise, including in countries other than the United States as they adopt eating and exercise patterns similar to those of Americans.[53] Yet we should take heart because there are ways to avoid or remove this disease. Medical professionals should work closely with susceptible populations not only to treat, but to prevent diabetes. We all have a responsibility to do what we can to ensure that those around us eat and exercise in ways that promote everyone's health.

CHAPTER 13

Strictly About Females

℃

The primary ways in which females reliably differ from males have to do with reproduction. In mammals the female produces an egg that is fertilized and nurtured within her body until the fetus is capable of surviving in the outside world. After birth, for periods ranging from weeks to years, young mammals continue to depend mainly on their mothers' milk for food. This chapter concerns the ways in which female mammalian reproduction affects what's eaten, as well as the ways in which what's eaten affects female mammalian reproduction. I'll focus on the female mammals of greatest concern to most of us: girls and women.

Just because this chapter focuses on females doesn't mean that there's no relationship between eating and male mammalian reproduction. It's possible, for example, that eating too little or the wrong things might affect sperm counts. However, research on such subjects appears to be essentially nonexistent. In contrast, research on the relationships between eating and female mammalian reproduction abounds.

It's not surprising that researchers have concentrated on how food and female mammalian reproduction affect each other. The female mammal is the ultimate provider of food to the young both during pregnancy and immediately after birth. This early nutritive relationship is critical to the survival of the offspring. For an infant to survive, the infant's mother must obtain adequate food for herself until the infant is old enough to be weaned.

Thus survival of the woman results in survival of her offspring as well. This means that conception shouldn't occur unless there's a high probability that there will be sufficient food to sustain the woman and her offspring throughout pregnancy and lactation. And this means that women's bodies should have evolved such that their reproductive functions and their eating and drinking behaviors are closely related. For example, given this reasoning you would predict that women should store more fat on their bodies than men, thus enabling women not only to survive but to reproduce during the frequent periods of food scarcity that occurred throughout our evolutionary history. Research supports this prediction: The average percentage of total body weight that consists of fat is 27% for young adult women but is 15% for young adult men.[1]

You'll encounter the evolutionary theme again and again throughout this chapter as we cover menstruation, pregnancy, and lactation. There are many ways in which eating and female reproduction evolved so as to ensure that as many offspring survive as possible.

Curses, Fed Again!

The menstrual cycle, fondly known to many women as "the curse," plays an essential role in human reproduction. There are a number of physical changes that occur during the menstrual cycle, including the release of an egg and the preparation of the uterine lining for the implantation and subsequent growth of an embryo and fetus. However, in addition to ovulation, the menstrual cycle can also involve changes in what and how a woman eats. There can be influence in the other direction as well: What a woman eats can affect her menstrual cycle.

Let's begin with how the menstrual cycle can influence what a woman eats. Many women experience cravings for particular foods, notably high-carbohydrate, high-fat, and chocolate foods, in the part of the menstrual cycle just prior to menstruation.[2] If these cravings are regularly accompanied by a number of other symptoms, such as depression, anxiety, irritability, and difficulty concentrating, the woman is said to suffer from premenstrual dysphoric disorder,[3] or, when the symptoms aren't severe, premenstrual syndrome (PMS). There has been much discussion about what causes these food cravings.

One possible explanation is based on the fact that basal metabolic rate is significantly higher during the luteal phase of the menstrual cycle,[4] the 2 weeks prior to menstruation. (Figure 13.1 gives a precise definition of the luteal phase.) You learned in previous chapters that people and other animals eat more when they're expending more calories. Therefore it shouldn't surprise you that women eat more calories during the luteal phase.[5] Remember also from previous chapters that people learn to prefer high-calorie foods when they're hungry. Therefore you would also expect that a woman would prefer high-calorie foods (such as chocolate) during the luteal phase.

However, there may be a problem with this explanation. There's evidence that the increased number of calories eaten by women during the luteal

DAY 1 2 3 4 5 6 7 8 9 10 11 12 13 14 15 16 17 18 19 20 21 22 23 24 25 26 27 28 1 2 3 4 5

Figure 13.1 A normal menstrual cycle. The first day of menstruation counts as day 1 of a cycle. During the follicular phase, in this example days 6–13, a follicle containing an egg develops in the ovary. At the time of ovulation, here occurring on day 14, the follicle ruptures, thus releasing the mature egg and allowing conception to occur. During the subsequent luteal phase (days 15–28 in this figure), the follicle, which has remained in the ovary, becomes the corpus luteum and secretes several hormones that prepare the uterine lining for implantation of the fertilized egg (should conception occur). If conception does not occur, as in the present example, menstruation and a new cycle begin. (Adapted from M. P. Warren, "Reproductive Endocrinology," in *Handbook of Behavioral Medicine for Women*, eds. E. A. Blechman and K. D. Brownell, New York: Pergamon, 1988.)

phase can be greater than the increased calories that they burn up at that time: Energy expenditure has been found to be 8–20% higher in the luteal phase than prior to ovulation, but energy intake (i.e., calories eaten) has been found to be 10–30% higher during the luteal phase than prior to ovulation.[6] Therefore, compensating for extra energy expenditure can't be the sole explanation of premenstrual food cravings. Nevertheless, if you think about this situation in the context of our evolving in surroundings with inadequate food supplies, consuming extra calories in the luteal phase might not be such a bad idea. These extra calories would be stored in the woman's body as fat. Then, if conception should occur, there would be an increased chance that the woman and her offspring would survive.

Another explanation of premenstrual food cravings is related to the carbohydrate craving seen in people with seasonal affective disorder (SAD) and in obese carbohydrate cravers, both discussed in Chapter 10. Similar to people with SAD (whose symptoms tend to be worst in the winter) and obese carbohydrate cravers (whose symptoms tend to be worst at certain times of the day), women with PMS experience cyclical symptoms. In addition, people with each of these disorders crave carbohydrates, and these cravings can be suppressed by drugs that increase the level of the neurotransmitter serotonin in the brain. For these reasons psychologists Richard J. Wurtman and Judith J. Wurtman have hypothesized that PMS, as well as SAD and obesity due to carbohydrate craving, are caused or aggravated by insufficient levels of serotonin in the brain. Serotonin levels are affected by the earth's light-dark cycle, thus explaining the periodicity of all three disorders. According to the Wurtmans, when people with these disorders eat carbohydrates, their serotonin levels increase, as do their feelings of well-being.[7] Not all scientists avidly adopt this theory, however. More research is needed showing that low serotonin levels are specifically responsible for premenstrual food cravings.

A final approach to explaining premenstrual food cravings involves looking to see if there are any changes in taste or smell sensitivity across the menstrual cycle. Such changes, if they exist, might explain why women's eating behaviors change across the menstrual cycle. There hasn't been a great deal of research in this area. One study found no changes in sweet preference as a function of menstrual cycle phase.[8] In contrast, it has been fairly well established that sensitivity to smells increases around the time of ovulation. This may be a side effect of a mechanism designed to increase the probability of conception. Around the time of ovulation, mucus secretions in a woman's body, including those around the cervix and the olfactory epithelium (the tissue up inside your nose that detects odors), become thinner. This may make it easier for the sperm to reach the egg, and it also makes it easier for the woman to detect odors.[9] Perhaps this increased odor sensitivity makes the woman more likely to eat her favorite foods. Again, more research is needed to be sure.

Now let's consider the flip side of the coin: How might what you eat affect your menstrual cycle? All of the information on this topic flows from the fact that a woman needs approximately 50,000 to 80,000 calories in order to produce a full-term baby.[10] Anything less is likely to result in an underweight, or perhaps even nonviable, baby. From an evolutionary standpoint, producing a substandard offspring would be a waste of the woman's energy, and therefore should be avoided if at all possible. If the woman can't get enough food to produce a healthy infant, then she shouldn't even conceive. Given this reasoning, it's not surprising that inadequate food will disrupt the menstrual cycle and inhibit ovulation.[11] Even simply eating with restraint—eating less than you want—has been associated with menstrual irregularity.[12] This fact was noted in Chapter 9, where I pointed out that anorexics don't menstruate. (Hence the title of the present section: "Curses, Fed Again!") Consistent with these findings, excessive feeding may hasten puberty. Young girls seem to be initiating breast development at earlier ages—an average of 9–10 years, and the explanation may be the increased weight of girls in this age group.[13]

There have been two competing hypotheses as to the mechanism that causes food deprivation to disrupt ovulation.[14] Scientist Rose E. Frisch has proposed that what's critical is the woman's percentage of body fat.[15] Women's bodies can't make female hormones such as estrogen and progesterone without fat.[16] Humanity's first artistic expressions seemed to recognize this link between fatness and fertility with such pieces of art as the 22,000-year-old figurine of a very heavy female known as the Venus of Willendorf.[17]

Psychologists Jill E. Schneider and George N. Wade have proposed an alternative hypothesis. They believe that what's important for ovulation to occur is the general availability of fuel. Fatty acids metabolized from stored fat are only one component of this available fuel. Also important is the glucose obtained from what's eaten.[18] This hypothesis can help to explain why nonovulating women who have had inadequate food for a long period of time will resume ovulating if given adequate food for a relatively short period.[19]

An interesting question that doesn't yet have a clear answer is how the effects of exercise on menstruation fit into this controversy. Exercise can apparently contribute to menstrual irregularity. Women who exercise a great deal sometimes have lower hormone levels, or even stop menstruating, as well as have fewer premenstrual symptoms.[20] However, we don't know whether exercise is exerting its effect by inducing an energy deficit and decreasing the percentage of body fat, or if exercise is exerting an effect that is independent of the effects of amount of food eaten and percentage of body fat.[21] It's possible that all three factors—amount of food eaten, amount of stored fat, and exercise level—play a role in menstrual regularity.

Even if we assume that all three factors are involved in menstrual regularity, we still don't know what level of any of these three factors is needed before fertility is impaired. Obviously, if a woman eats so little, exercises so much, or becomes so thin that she has no menstrual cycle, reproduction cannot occur. But isn't it possible that eating a bit more, exercising a bit less, or having a bit more body fat might be enough for menstruation to continue, but not enough for ovulation to occur properly? There's laboratory evidence supporting this possibility in hamsters. One experiment gave six hamsters 50% of their usual food intake for 4 days, the length of one estrous cycle (now you know why hamsters can multiply their numbers so quickly). Despite the fact that the hamsters were only partially deprived of food and that this partial deprivation lasted for only 4 days, one of the hamsters didn't ovulate at all and the number of eggs released by each of the other hamsters decreased from an average of 11 to an average of 9.[22]

If it's indeed the case that partial food deprivation inhibits fertility in women, this raises a host of concerns. Some women are chronic dieters, and so may have chronically low metabolic rates, forcing them to eat small amounts even when not dieting in order not to gain weight. Other women will eat very little at breakfast and lunch in order to eat a large dinner at a restaurant in the evening. In addition, some 60% of American women try at least one weight-reduction diet each year, and approximately one third of American women between the ages of 19 and 39—the prime reproductive years—diet at least once per month.[23] Perhaps all such women are at risk for impaired fertility. Some studies suggest that relatively brief, partial limitations in food at the time of conception can lead to premature birth.[24] And impaired fertility, including menstrual irregularity, isn't the only negative consequence of this behavior. When women diet it's very hard for them to obtain sufficient amounts of essential nutrients such as iron. If it wasn't already abundantly clear from earlier chapters, now you should truly understand that cutting back on calories can have many deleterious effects.

Some additional thoughts before we leave the curse, or rather, after we leave it. How do all of these relationships among eating, hormones, and metabolic rate change after women reach menopause? Let's focus first on metabolic rate. It has only been in the last 15 years that scientists have realized that metabolic rate is higher during the luteal phase of the menstrual cycle. I remember this vividly because I'd suspected for a long time that this was the case; I'd found it easier to lose or maintain my weight in the luteal phase, and wondered if hormonal effects at that time might help to counteract the decreased metabolic rate that often accompanies dieting. I can't tell you how brilliant I felt when researchers confirmed my hypothesis. Now that I've reached that certain age among women, along with many other baby boomers, I'm wondering about menopause. As far as I'm aware, no investigations have yet been done on the metabolic rates of women after menopause. It's possible that, lacking any luteal phases, post-menopausal women may have very low metabolic rates and thus be more likely to gain weight. But can regular exercise prevent this from happening? And what does hormonal replacement therapy have to do with metabolic rate, if anything? We just don't know yet. Perhaps, though, by continuing to observe myself I can again obtain information that anticipates the research findings!

Finally, the subject of eating can even help to explain why menopause exists at all. For many years scientists wondered what possible evolutionary advantage there could be to women living long after they could reproduce, what advantage there could be to the many postmenopausal years. Now there's evidence from groups of people living without the trappings of modern civilization indicating that reproductive women who have post-menopausal women (that is, grandmothers) assisting them in obtaining food are more likely to have many healthy children.[25] Having a grandmother can definitely be an advantage.

Eating and Drinking for Two: Pregnancy

A variety of changes take place in a woman's body once conception has occurred. Once again, many of these changes are directed at survival of the fetus: The fetus must get adequate nutrition—either from what the woman eats or from what's stored in her body, or both. However, although what a woman eats or drinks during pregnancy usually has positive effects on the embryo and fetus, some things, when eaten or drunk, can do severe damage. In this section I'll first consider how a woman's food preferences and food aversions may change during pregnancy. Then I'll focus on the relationships between pregnancy and weight gain. Finally, I'll look at how food and drink consumed by the mother may adversely impact her fetus.

Cravings and Aversions

Who hasn't heard about the food cravings that pregnant women reputedly evidence? Ice cream, pickles, you name it. Surveys show that these cravings aren't just rumor; some women do indeed develop food cravings during pregnancy. The cravings may be for high-calorie foods such as ice cream. However, some food cravings are for low-calorie foods such as fruit or vinegar. Pregnant women may even crave eating such items as clay and earth.[26]

Various explanations have been proposed for all of these sorts of food cravings. When the cravings are for high-calorie foods such as ice cream, it's possible to invoke the energy deficit explanation used to account for the high-calorie food cravings sometimes seen during the luteal phase of the menstrual cycle. As in the luteal phase, metabolic rate is relatively high during pregnancy.[27] The fetus imposes additional caloric requirements on pregnant women. Therefore you would expect pregnant women to show an increased preference for high-calorie foods. Other explanations for the food cravings in pregnancy include changes in pregnant women's sensitivity to sour tastes, the detoxifying properties of clay that may make its consumption advantageous to pregnant women, and the increased release of special, natural, narcotic-like chemicals in pregnant women's bodies.[28]

Other changes in women's bodies during pregnancy may also affect what they do and don't want to eat. During pregnancy there are changes in the digestive tract. For example, increased amounts of the small intestine chemical cholecystokinin (CCK), important in digestion, are released, particularly during the first trimester. The increased CCK contributes to the sleepiness felt by women at this time and, because the increased CCK slows the passage of food through the intestinal tract, it also contributes to the nausea and vomiting experienced by over 25% of women during the first trimester,[29] so-called morning sickness. This may explain why some women find high-fat foods aversive at this time. High-fat foods pass more slowly through the digestive tract than low-fat ones.[30] Increased sensitivity to odors has also been hypothesized to contribute to morning sickness.[31]

You might think that morning sickness would be bad for the fetus because the pregnant woman eats less and often vomits. However, some scientists believe that the opposite is actually the case. For example, scientist Margie

Profet has hypothesized that morning sickness, with its associated increased odor and food sensitivities and food aversions, increases the survival of the fetus. She believes that these reactions decrease the amounts that the pregnant woman eats of bitter foods and foods with pungent odors, foods that may be toxic for the fetus even in small amounts. In support of this hypothesis, Profet points to the fact that women who vomit during early pregnancy or who feel severely nauseated are less likely to miscarry.[32] However, it's important to remember that such hypotheses, as intriguing and appealing as they may be, are based only on suggestive evidence. There is as yet no evidence showing a causal link between morning sickness and miscarriage.

I hope that this discussion of morning sickness reminds you of what you read about one of the most powerful forms of learning, taste aversion learning, in Chapter 6. You should recall that, with this form of learning, people and other animals can acquire long-lasting aversions to foods whose consumption has been followed only once by nausea. Furthermore, these aversions can form whether the illness was actually caused by the food or not. What if the nausea and vomiting of morning sickness become accidentally paired with specific foods so that taste aversions occur? Women do retrospectively report a significant correlation between when they felt sick during pregnancy and when they developed food aversions. Taste aversion learning may help to explain some of the food aversions of pregnant women. However, we need detailed study of women during their pregnancies in order to confirm or refute this hypothesis.[33]

You may be very surprised to discover that morning sickness can affect the food preferences of not only the pregnant woman, but also her resulting offspring. Women who experience a great deal of vomiting during their pregnancies are more likely to have offspring who, both as babies and as adults, prefer salt more than the offspring of mothers who experienced little vomiting during their pregnancies. One possible explanation is that the increased salt preference is somehow related to the mothers becoming dehydrated as a result of their vomiting.[34]

Causes and Effects of Weight Gain

Despite their food aversions and relatively high metabolic rates, pregnant women do manage to gain weight. Even in the first trimester women's fat stores increase. This increase can't be due to a greater amount of food eaten during that period. Instead, it's probably another effect of the increased CCK release during the first trimester.[35] Clearly, during human evolution, a tendency for pregnant women to store consumed food as fat, particularly at a time when eating is sometimes inhibited by nausea, would have increased the probability of survival of the mother and her infant. The stored fat is there to help sustain the mother and her fetus if food supplies are inadequate or if the mother becomes ill.

Nevertheless, weight gain is a major concern of many pregnant women. They fear that too much weight will be gained and that not all of that weight will be lost once the baby is born. On average, women gain 33 pounds during pregnancy, of which about 9 pounds consists of stored fat.[36] The Institute of Medicine recommends that a woman gain different amounts during pregnancy depending on how heavy she is for her height—a weight gain of 25–35 pounds for a woman whose weight for her height is average, but more if she's pregnant with twins.[37] Women frequently name pregnancy as contributing to weight gain over their lifetimes.[38] In fact, the greatest risk of obesity among women (and men) occurs in the age range of 25–44 years— the childbearing years.[39] However, by themselves, these data don't prove that pregnancy causes permanent weight gain. Most people gain weight as they age, whether or not they've been pregnant.[40] One study did find persistent weight gains after pregnancy, but only for first pregnancies and only 4 to 7 pounds. Nevertheless, such a study doesn't eliminate the possibility that there's a subgroup of women who gain large, permanent amounts when they're pregnant. Some evidence suggests that such subpopulations may be particularly prevalent among African American women even though, on average, African American women tend to gain less during pregnancy.[41]

Now let's consider how what pregnant women eat and weigh can affect their babies. First, what happens if the woman doesn't eat very much and doesn't gain very much weight? One effect is simply that the resulting infant will weigh too little, which puts such an infant at risk.[42] One study found that teenagers who didn't gain enough during their pregnancies ate about 1,878 calories per day while pregnant, while those who did gain enough weight ate about 2,232 calories per day; and teenagers who didn't gain enough weight were more likely to have low birth weight babies.[43] I've already noted that African American women, on average, gain less weight during their pregnancies. Consistent with this fact, African American women are also more likely to deliver babies whose weights are below clinical standards.[44]

A fascinating study conducted by epidemiologist Jie Mi and her colleagues in Beijing, China, demonstrates one of the deleterious effects of low birth weight on offspring. This study of men and women averaging 45 years of age found that those whose weights were low when they were born were more likely to show insulin resistance as adults, a characteristic that can lead to Type 2 diabetes and all of its adverse effects (see Chapter 12). The authors point out that a society can accomplish much long-term good for its citizens by ensuring that all pregnant women are adequately nourished.[45]

There can be additional adverse effects on their offspring when pregnant women gain insufficient amounts of weight. A historical study of

300,000 males who either had been conceived but not yet born or had just been born at the time of the Dutch famine of 1944–1945 showed that extreme food deprivation during the first half of pregnancy was associated with high obesity rates in these men. The authors hypothesize that the increased obesity may have been due to the early pregnancy-related food deprivation interfering with the development of the hypothalamus, a part of the brain that is, as you know, very important in hunger and satiety. On the other hand, extreme food deprivation during the last trimester of pregnancy and the first few months of life tended to result in low obesity rates, an effect that the authors hypothesize may have been due to interference with adipose cell development.[46]

What if a woman is very heavy during pregnancy or gains large amounts of weight? If she does not already have Type 2 diabetes, such a woman is more likely to develop gestational diabetes, a problem in approximately 3–5% of all pregnancies. Gestational diabetes is similar to Type 2 diabetes and is due to placental hormones interfering with the function of a pregnant woman's insulin. Babies born to women with diabetes tend to be very large at birth, so large that their delivery can be difficult or even dangerous for their mothers unless delivery is by caesarean section. In addition, such babies may be born with malformations of the spinal cord or the brain.[47] In fact, such defects are more likely to occur in offspring of overweight pregnant women, even if they don't have diabetes.[48] Clearly it's extremely important for a pregnant woman's blood sugar level, in addition to her weight, to be monitored closely and kept as close to normal limits as possible for the duration of her pregnancy. Nevertheless this does not mean that overweight pregnant women should diet. Dieting may not be advisable during pregnancy because if a woman's preexisting fat stores are metabolized, toxins contained in that fat, such as pesticides, can be released into her bloodstream and thus passed to the fetus.[49]

When Eating or Drinking Is Harmful

Probably the best known, and certainly one of the most devastating, effects on a fetus of what the mother eats or drinks is fetal alcohol syndrome (FAS). This syndrome consists of a number of specific physiological and behavioral changes that can occur in the offspring of women who drink alcohol while pregnant. First, the facial appearance of a child born with FAS is different from that of a normal child. The head circumference and nose are smaller, the nasal bridge is lower, and the upper lip is thinner than those of a non-FAS infant. The FAS infant also has folds of skin at the inside corners of the eyes that are absent in normal infants. These external physical characteristics remain as the child ages, but may be less prominent. (See Figure 13.2.) The brains of FAS infants and adults are smaller than the brains of non-FAS infants and adults. As FAS infants age, it becomes apparent that their intelligence is significantly below average. FAS infants and adults also tend to be hyperactive, depressed, distractible, irritable, and impulsive and to show poor coordination, memory, spatial ability, and arithmetic ability.[50]

We don't yet know precisely why maternal drinking during pregnancy has such terrible effects on the offspring, though we do have some clues. The arteries and veins in isolated human umbilical cords have been shown to contract and spasm when exposed to a concentration of alcohol equivalent to that in the blood of a pregnant woman 30 minutes after ingesting 1 to 1.5 drinks of 100-proof whiskey. Such an effect deprives a fetus of essential oxygenated blood.[51] Experiments with fetal rats near term and with very young rat pups have shown that exposure to alcohol can kill millions of brain cells in particular parts of the brain.[52]

So far, most of what I've said about alcohol and pregnancy isn't very controversial. What's controversial is just how much alcohol a pregnant woman has to drink, and when, in order for FAS to occur. How much is safe? It's now believed that social drinking causes deleterious effects on the fetus. The more alcohol that is drunk, the worse the effects on the fetus.[53] One study consistently found deleterious effects of alcohol on the offspring of women who drank an average of about 1.5 drinks per day before they found out they were pregnant, and an average of about 1 drink every 2 days after.[54] Further, it appears that even alcohol drunk in the very earliest part of

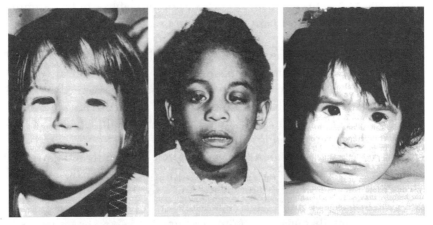

Figure 13.2 Physical appearance of three children with FAS. Copyright 1980 American Association for the Advancement of Science. (Reprinted with permission from A. P. Streissguth, S. Landesman-Dwyer, J. C. Martin, and D. W. Smith, "Teratogenic Effects of Alcohol in Humans and Laboratory Animals," *Science* 209[1980]:353–361.)

pregnancy, in the month before the woman realizes she is pregnant, can be harmful to the fetus.[55]

Therefore it now appears that the surgeon general's and the National Institute on Alcohol Abuse and Alcoholism's recommendations in the 1980s that pregnant women should drink no alcohol, which was controversial at the time, were very likely wise recommendations.[56] It's important to keep in mind that, due to differences between men's and women's bodies, the same amount of alcohol may result in a higher blood alcohol level and more brain damage in a woman than a man, even though the man and the woman are the same height and weight.[57] We have progressed from FAS not even being known in 1970 to, beginning in 1989, the government requiring warnings to pregnant women on all alcoholic beverage labels.[58]

This is very serious stuff. Millions of American women have alcohol-related problems, and many, many more don't have problems but don't abstain. After learning that they're pregnant, 20% of women drinkers don't stop drinking. Many more drink until they find out that they're pregnant. Even with all of the current warnings, in the United States each year there are about 12,000 children born with full-blown FAS, and many more with less obvious deleterious effects of alcohol.[59]

In addition to alcohol, many other substances can harm a growing fetus when they are consumed by the mother. For example, studies using women as well as females of other species have shown that caffeine consumption can result in various reproductive disorders, such as miscarriages and stillbirths. There's also evidence that caffeine consumption can sometimes be linked to birth defects.[60] Thus pregnant women should probably avoid consuming caffeine. As still another example, mental retardation can result in a fetus if the mother consumes fish contaminated with the toxic chemical methylmercury.[61] Pregnant women should eat and drink with caution. Medical consultation and nutritional counseling early in pregnancy are clearly extremely important. If all of the pregnant women in the United States ate and drank properly, the benefits to our society and economy in terms of healthier, better functioning children who became healthier, better functioning adults would be enormous.[62]

Before we leave the inside of the womb, I'd be remiss if I didn't mention what goes on with the fetus's own eating and drinking behaviors. That's right, I'm talking about ingestion by the fetus. You already know that right after a fetus ceases being a fetus, right after she or he is born and is classified as an infant, that infant can taste sweet and shows a preference for it. It turns out that the taste cells of the fetus acquire their final structure at about fourteenth week of pregnancy. Furthermore, beginning at about the twelfth week of pregnancy, a fetus swallows amniotic fluid. By the end of pregnancy, a fetus may be swallowing over 3 cups per day. Such behavior may actually be important in keeping the amount of amniotic fluid within a reasonable range. But in addition to the possible effects on the amniotic fluid volume, a fetus may taste chemicals present in the amniotic fluid. Amniotic fluid contains a wide range of chemicals including sugars, fats, and proteins. The relative amounts of these different chemicals can change significantly during the course of a pregnancy, including right after a fetus urinates. Now you didn't think that the first time a baby ever urinated was right after it was born, did you? A fetus swallows liquids while in the womb and so it also urinates there. What we don't know is to what degree what a fetus tastes during pregnancy influences its later food preferences.[63]

The Essence of Mammalhood: Breast Feeding

Women who choose to breast feed are well aware of the importance of this task for the survival of their infants. As psychologist Peter Wright has stated, "The overriding concern of all mothers, once they have established that their newborn baby is alive and well, is the establishment of a successful feeding relationship."[64] However, breast-feeding mothers may not realize the complexity of the relationship into which they have entered with their infants. There are multiple effects of breast feeding on both the mother and her infant. We'll start by looking at how breast feeding affects the infant, and then look at how it affects the mother.

Breast milk is specifically designed to meet the needs of growing infants. Although it can be contaminated with potential toxins, such as caffeine and other drugs,[65] breast milk, unlike formula, is never mixed at the wrong concentration with unsanitary water. In addition, breast milk contains antibodies, formed in the mother's body, that can help protect the infant from infection.[66] There can be times when the nutrition of breast-fed infants is inadequate due to inadequate amounts of breast milk or the infant not feeding properly, with resultant damage to the infant including low IQ scores later in life. In general, however, breast feeding is an excellent way to feed an infant.

Breast feeding, and suckling milk in general, have still other positive effects on infants. Drinking milk may help to calm infants by releasing special, natural, narcotic-like substances in the infants' bodies. The result is that the infants make less noise, move around less, and are more tolerant of discomfort. In addition to these effects being appreciated by the mother, they may also be good for the baby, because these behavioral changes help the baby to conserve energy.[67] Remember that one of the overriding themes of the mother-infant relationship, indeed of this whole book, is that we have evolved to behave in ways that would help us to survive in surroundings in which lots of readily available good food isn't present.

Suckling may, in and of itself, have effects similar to infants ingesting milk. The physical act of suckling, whether or not any milk is ingested, triggers the release of chemicals in the infant's intestinal tract that improve digestion and the use of ingested fuel, but it also induces sleepiness, again helping to conserve the infant's energy. These positive effects explain why the use of a pacifier can be advisable, unless parents intend for a child to breast or bottle feed continuously—unlikely in the American culture.[68]

Another effect of breast feeding that has been explored is the connection between breast- versus bottle-fed infants and adulthood obesity. As you can imagine, it's difficult to conduct controlled experiments on relationships of this type. Doing an experiment in which you randomly assign infants to be breast or bottle fed, and then checking to see whether they are obese 30 or 40 years later would be extremely challenging. However, it does appear that infants who are breast fed are less likely to become obese, and that the longer the breast feeding goes on, the less likely the infants are to become obese as adults. This raises the possibility that infants who are breast fed will also be less likely as adults to develop diseases, such as cardiovascular diseases, that are associated with obesity.[69] One explanation for the relationship between breast feeding and later obesity may be that, with a bottle, caregivers are more likely to try to persuade the infant to consume a certain number of ounces of formula even though the infant isn't that hungry.[70] Nevertheless, keep in mind that we don't really know that breast feeding by itself decreases the probability of later obesity. It's possible that mothers who choose to breast feed also tend to have less of other food available for children, are more likely to feed their children healthy food, or exercise more. Further, even if we assume that adult obesity may be influenced by whether an infant is breast fed, it's important to remember that there are many other influences as well, influences that you read about in earlier chapters, such as individual differences in metabolic rate and whether someone's biological parents are obese.[71]

Now we come to what I think is the most interesting aspect of how breast feeding can influence infants: the effects on infants of the tastes and odors present during breast feeding. Over 10 years ago, when I wrote the second edition of my book *The Psychology of Eating and Drinking*, I stated

> It is possible that substances present in breast milk as a result of particular foods and drinks consumed by breast-feeding women influence infants' food preferences. Recall that this is one of the mechanisms by which rat pups learn to eat the safe, nutritious food that adult rats have learned to prefer. Advantages should accrue to children were such a mechanism inherent in the breast-feeding relationship (or disadvantages, depending on what were the resulting food preferences). However, there have been no detailed studies of this possibility.[72]

Now, at the beginning of the 21st century, I'm happy to report that the past decade has finally seen many experiments conducted on this subject. To begin with, we now know that infants live in a much richer gustatory and olfactory world than many people originally supposed. Newborn infants can detect a variety of tastes and smells. Further, in the first few days of life, infants, whether breast fed or not, prefer the odors of lactating breasts. With time, breast feeding infants learn to prefer the odors of their particular mothers' breasts and armpits over those of other breast feeding women.[73] It has even been shown that 4-day-old bottle-fed infants prefer the odors of amniotic fluid to the odors of formula or distilled water, suggesting that familiarity with amniotic fluid results in a long-lasting preference for it.[74] All of these preferences would help to keep an infant near his or her own mother, which, particularly in the sort of surroundings in which we evolved, would increase the likelihood of an infant's survival.

Taking this a step further, experiments have now shown that what a lactating mother eats can affect tastes and odors in her breast milk, and thereby can affect the food preferences of her infant. The majority of this research has been conducted by psychologists Julie A. Mennella and Gary K. Beauchamp of the Monell Chemical Senses Center in Philadelphia.[75] In one such experiment women drank either water or carrot juice while they either were in the last trimester of pregnancy or were lactating. The babies of the carrot-juice-drinking mothers later showed more preference for cereal made with carrot juice (as opposed to water) than the babies of the other women.[76] We also know that infants accidentally fed on a formula deficient in the chemical chloride have an increased preference for salty foods (sodium chloride) when they grow up.[77] Further, infants show a preference for alcohol in breast milk and may learn to like aspects of their surroundings associated with such breast milk.[78] Thus we now have a number of indicators that what a mother eats or drinks can subsequently affect the eating and drinking of her child.

Also yet to be determined are both the short-term and the long-term effects of cigarette smoking on the breast-fed infant. Mennella and Beauchamp have shown that adults can tell which samples of breast milk come from cigarette smoking women and which do not, and that adults' abilities to identify milk from lactating women who smoke correlates with the concentration of nicotine in the milk. Therefore, in addition to the obvious risks of nicotine in breast milk from smoking mothers, it's possible that infants can detect tastes and odors in breast milk associated with cigarette smoking, and that this experience influences their tendencies to smoke later in life.[79] Once again, we simply don't know the answer to this question; more research is needed. (See Conversation Making Fact #13.)

Conversation Making Fact #13

It's widely believed in many cultures, including in the United States, that drinking alcohol will improve both the quantity and quality of breast milk. Toward this end, some women, although not drinking much when they're pregnant, will drink once they're lactating. Unfortunately, this appears to be one case in which folklore is contrary to actual fact. Infants actually consume less breast milk when their mothers have drunk alcohol. One possible explanation of this effect might be that infants don't prefer breast milk that has tastes and odors added from the mother's drinking, but this doesn't appear to be what's going on. In fact, the reverse appears to be true—infants whose breast feeding mothers drink frequently seem to show the most preference for breast milk to which experimenters have added alcohol. Instead, the explanation for why infants get less breast milk when their mothers drink seems to be that drinking mothers don't produce as much milk.[80] However, once again, more research is needed, especially investigating infants feeding on their mothers' milk when their mothers have and haven't recently been drinking. Perhaps infants whose breast feeding mothers drank frequently grow up to have a greater preference for alcohol than would have otherwise been the case.

Not only are infants affected by what occurs during or prior to breast feeding, but breast feeding also affects lactating women. How lactating women are affected can be understood best by remembering that they need even more calories and nutrients than pregnant women, approximately 765 to 980 calories more per day than before they became pregnant.[81] Therefore lactating women should, and do, consume more calories than nonpregnant women.[82] In addition, it's possible that the levels of bodily chemicals important in digestion, such as CCK, change during lactation in order to ensure that lactating women eat more and metabolize well what they eat.[83] You'll recall that metabolic rate is higher in pregnant than nonpregnant women. In lactating women, it's only relatively high after these women eat; at other times, the metabolic rate of lactating women is similar to that of women who have given birth but aren't lactating;[84] this helps lactating women to avoid being depleted by the caloric demands of lactation.

Many women see the lactation period as a time to lose the extra fat accumulated during pregnancy. Overweight breast-feeding women who diet and exercise to lose, on average, 1 pound per week have infants who grow normally;[85] thus losing weight while lactating doesn't appear to be harmful to the baby. And, indeed, lactating women are better able to lose weight from their hips and abdomen, where weight is deposited during pregnancy and places from which it's traditionally difficult to lose weight. However, suckling an infant seems to decrease the heat generated by the muscles and to increase energy storage in certain parts of the lactating woman's body. It also makes the woman sleepy. This sleepiness, and the consequently decreased activity level, may be useful for the survival of the infant in that these effects tend to keep the mother nearby.[86] Shakespeare, the consummate observer of our behavior, alluded to such effects when he had Cleopatra say: "Does thou not see my baby at my breast, that sucks the nurse asleep?"[87] All of these suckling effects decrease the woman's energy usage, thus lessening the effects of the caloric drain of the production of milk. This could help to explain the fact that most women who have given birth—at least for the first time— don't lose sufficient weight to return to their prepregnancy weight.

"A Woman Is a Dish for the Gods"[88]: Conclusion

Eating, drinking, and female reproduction are inextricably intertwined. Many aspects of eating behavior help to ensure that healthy children are produced and that their mothers are healthy enough to continue to produce. This chapter demonstrates clearly, perhaps more than any other chapter, how the psychology of eating and drinking is tied to our bodies' and our genes' survival. We can't survive, and we can't reproduce, unless we eat and drink properly. Therefore natural selection has resulted in a variety of mechanisms to ensure that appropriate eating and drinking behaviors will meet the unusual nutritional requirements of conception, pregnancy, and lactation. However, natural selection has not provided for every modern-day adverse contingency. We did not evolve in surroundings in which toxins such as caffeine or alcohol were common. Further, some of the adaptations that are present, such as the tendency of pregnant and lactating women to store fat, although useful in the surroundings in which we evolved, aren't as necessary now, and can even cause weight problems in a society in which having sufficient food isn't a problem for most people. As research continues, the resulting information will make it even easier for parents and their physicians to ensure the health of mothers and their offspring.

CHAPTER 14

When and Why Smoking Affects Your Weight

❦

Approximately 72% of the people in the United States smoke cigarettes at some point in their lives. This huge percentage is tragic because smoking is responsible for more disease and death than any other preventable behavior. Approximately 400,000 deaths per year in the United States are attributed to smoking. Smoking increases the risk of heart diseases, respiratory diseases, stroke, and cancer, to name a few. In addition, cigarette smoking is responsible for millions of dollars being spent on cigarettes that could be spent on something else, for days lost from work, and for increases in health care insurance costs. Most people who quit smoking take three to four attempts before they're finally able to quit, and as many as 90% of those who attempt to quit experience physical withdrawal from their addiction to nicotine. The withdrawal symptoms include depression, insomnia, irritability, anxiety, and difficulty concentrating.[1]

Given all of these horrible consequences, why do people start smoking, and if they do smoke, why do they not all quit? There are many good answers that can be given to this question, most of which are beyond the scope of this book. However, there's one answer that is within the scope of this book: body weight.

Several different studies have shown that a great many people believe that smoking helps control weight. For example, in one study, approximately 10% of male smokers and 5% of female smokers started smoking because they thought that it would help them to lose weight. In another study, 47% of men and 59% of women continued to smoke because they feared that they would gain weight if they stopped. In fact, some of the study's participants—most often women—after stopping smoking had restarted because they feared that stopping caused them to gain weight. A 1997 survey of men by *Psychology Today* found that 30% stated that they smoke to control their weight. In another recent study, among children 9 to 14 years of age, those who reported that they were thinking of starting to smoke were also those who tended to be worried about their weight.[2] Finally, one reason that scientists have proposed for the increase in adult obesity in the United States has been the fact that an increased number of people have been trying to give up smoking.[3]

There certainly are a lot of people who believe that cigarette smoking helps you lose or maintain your weight, and that stopping smoking makes you gain weight. How accurate are these beliefs? If smoking does affect weight, by what mechanisms do such effects occur? Once we know the facts concerning smoking and body weight, we can develop strategies for ensuring that, when someone is deciding whether or not to smoke, that person won't be thinking about his or her weight.[4]

As has been the case in prior chapters, answering questions about eating behavior in this chapter will frequently require consideration of results from experiments conducted with rats. Conducting experiments with rats allows researchers to control various aspects of the experiments to a degree that would not be possible if the experiments were conducted with people. I'll first present the research about weight and starting or continuing smoking, and then about weight and stopping smoking. All comments in this chapter refer only to the smoking of tobacco cigarettes. (For information about smoking marijuana see Conversation Making Fact #14.)

You're *Smoking*, But How About Your Metabolic Rate?

Let's begin at the beginning. What happens to body weight when people start or continue smoking, and why does it happen? People who begin smoking cigarettes do, on average, lose weight; in addition, on average, smokers weigh less than nonsmokers. (See Figure 14.1.) An exception to this generalization appears to be black women, among whom obesity rates are relatively high whether or not they're smokers.[5]

Rats exposed to nicotine show effects similar to those shown by people. Psychologist Neil E. Grunberg and his colleagues Kathryn A. Popp and Suzan E. Winders gave rats regular ground laboratory chow plus ground Oreo® cookies, ground potato chips, and water—a food selection guaranteed to get the rats to pig out, so to speak. Sometimes the rats were infused with nicotine, and other times they were infused with saline (salty water that has no physiological effects). When the rats were receiving infusions of nicotine, they ate fewer Oreo cookies and weighed less than when they were receiving saline infusions.[6]

Conversation Making Fact #14

Smoking marijuana cigarettes has vastly different effects on appetite and eating than smoking tobacco cigarettes. People who say that smoking marijuana gives them the munchies are basically correct. Scientists Richard W. Foltin, Marian W. Fischman, and Maryanne F. Byrne investigated these effects in an extremely difficult experiment in which six men (in two groups of three men each) lived in a residential laboratory for 13 days. The participants had no direct contact with anyone else, and their eating behaviors were continuously monitored. Each day of the experiment, the participants smoked either four marijuana cigarettes or four placebo cigarettes. The amounts of food eaten at meals did not differ significantly on marijuana and placebo days. However, on marijuana days, the participants greatly increased the amounts of certain types of food that they ate (sweet solid snacks such as candy bars) so that in total on these days the participants' caloric intakes increased by a whopping 40%. Not surprisingly, participants gained significant amounts of weight on the marijuana days.[7] So, in addition to many other reasons, if you want to control your weight, don't smoke marijuana!

All of these results show that smoking tobacco or exposure to nicotine by themselves constrain body weight. The question then becomes: What's responsible for this constraint on weight? Therefore, next I'll consider the evidence for and against three explanations: the possible effects of smoking on the total number of calories eaten, on the amount of sweet foods eaten, and on energy expenditure.

The first possible explanation for the lower body weights associated with smoking is that smoking decreases the total number of calories eaten. In people this decrease in calories eaten could, in turn, be due to a decrease in appetite, changes in the ways we use our hands (picking up a cigarette instead of food), changes in the ways we use our mouths (putting a cigarette in the mouth instead of food), and so on.[8] You might think that the fact that rats, just like people, eat less and weigh less when infused with nicotine indicates that changes in hand or oral activity can't explain the effects of smoking on people's eating and weight. Rats are usually exposed to nicotine by means of a needle, not a cigarette, so it's not possible to explain any nicotine-related decreases in rats' eating as due to changes in hand activity or oral activity. However, keep in mind that, in rats as well as in people, more than one

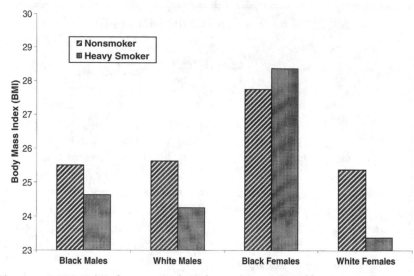

Figure 14.1 BMI (Body Mass Index) for male and female, white and black, nonsmokers and heavy smokers. (Adapted from R. C. Klesges, M. DeBon, and A. Meyers, "Obesity in African American Women: Epidemiology, Determinants, and Treatment Issues," in *Body Image, Eating Disorders, and Obesity: An Integrative Guide for Assessment and Treatment*, ed. J. K. Thompson, Washington, DC: American Psychological Association, 1996.)

mechanism could be responsible for any decrease in eating resulting from smoking or nicotine exposure. Therefore, even though changes in hand or oral activity can't explain the effects seen in rats, such mechanisms could still be at work in people.

Unfortunately, research concerning any decrease due to smoking in the total amount eaten is very limited, and concerns only the amount of calories eaten and reported hunger. Some studies have looked at the amount that someone eats as a function of the amount that the person smokes. The theory examined by these studies is that if smoking decreases the total number of calories eaten, then the more someone smokes, the less that person should eat. One such study, conducted by psychologist Joan B. Beckwith using 766 women age 20–30 years, found that the degree to which these women felt compelled to eat wasn't significantly correlated with their levels of smoking.[9] Consistent with this finding, an experiment conducted by scientist Kenneth A. Perkins and his colleagues found no differences in hunger or amount eaten among men and women smokers who, after abstaining from smoking overnight, had been exposed to different amounts of nicotine. Some participants had been given an unlit cigarette, some had smoked only a very low nicotine cigarette, and some had smoked their usual cigarette.[10] These data all seem to show that, at least in people, a decrease in appetite and the amount of calories eaten does not appear to explain the lower weights among smokers.

In contrast, evidence collected with rats suggests that the lower weights associated with smoking are indeed due to a decrease in the total amount of food eaten. Rats given injections of nicotine, as well as rats given long-term exposure to smoke, decrease the amount of food that they eat to the point of having a suppressed growth rate. In addition, exposure to smoke or nicotine raises these rats' blood sugar levels, thus, perhaps, making them less hungry and less likely to eat.[11] It's not clear if the differences between the results obtained with people and rats are due to actual species differences or to the many procedural differences in the experiments with people and rats.

Let's consider a second explanation for the lower body weights of smokers. Perhaps smoking and exposure to nicotine decrease the amount of sweet foods that someone eats.[12] According to this explanation, when someone starts smoking, the total number of calories eaten doesn't change, but the proportion of calories that comes from sweet foods decreases. You should remember from Chapter 10 that some researchers believe that eating good-tasting foods, such as sweet foods, can lead to obesity; the taste of sweet may lead to increased storage of what's eaten as fat.

Psychologist Neal E. Grunberg and his colleague David E. Morse investigated this hypothesis by using a rather large sample: the behavior of all the people in the United States. These researchers examined the average number of cigarettes smoked per person as a function of the average amount each person ate of 41 different foods over the years 1964–1977. There were substantial differences in the numbers of cigarettes smoked per person in some of these years. As it turned out, in years when the number of cigarettes per person was relatively high, the number of pounds of sugar eaten was relatively low and vice versa.[13] However, it's important to note that Grunberg and Morse's data, although very suggestive, consist entirely of correlations between the numbers of cigarettes smoked and the pounds of sugar eaten. (See Figure 14.2.) This means that variation in one of these variables might not necessarily cause the variation in the other variable; instead, some third variable—say, for example, the amount of alcohol drunk—could cause the variation in both the number of cigarettes smoked and the pounds of sugar eaten.

Looking at the behavior of individuals, we find data that more directly support the hypothesis that smoking decreases the eating of sweet foods. Results from laboratory experiments including the experiment by Grunberg, Popp, and Winders described earlier in this chapter, show that when people or rats smoke or are exposed to nicotine they eat fewer sweet foods while not changing how much they eat of other foods.[14]

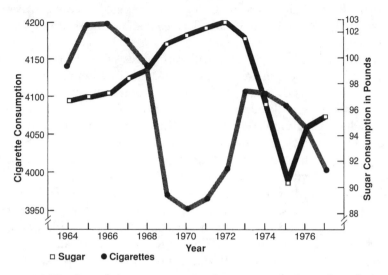

Figure 14.2 Number of cigarettes consumed per person and number of pounds of sugar consumed per person during the years 1964–1977. (Adapted from N. E. Grunberg and D. E. Morse, "Cigarette Smoking and Food Consumption in the United States," *Journal of Applied Social Psychology* 14[1984]: 310–317.)

One possible explanation for the decrease in the amount of sweet foods eaten by smokers is a decreased preference for the taste of sweet. We know that people are less sensitive to some odors when they smoke,[15] so perhaps they're also less sensitive to some tastes and thus prefer those tastes less. In fact, women smokers perceive high concentrations of sugar water to be less sweet than do women nonsmokers.[16] This could result in these smokers consuming fewer very sweet foods than nonsmokers.

Another possible explanation for the decrease in the amounts of sweet foods eaten by smokers comes from work on preferences for different brands of cigarettes. A smoker's rated pleasantness of a particular brand or rated satisfaction provided by a particular brand is highly correlated with the smoker's reported perception of the sweetness of that brand.[17] Perhaps smokers eat fewer sweet foods because their desire for the taste of sweet is satisfied by the cigarettes themselves. It's beyond me how cigarettes could seem sweet, but I'm not a smoker. In any case, as far as I'm aware, there has been no research investigating the possibility that cigarettes help to satisfy smokers' desire for the taste of sweet.

At last we come to the third, and most likely, explanation of the lower weights among smokers: Perhaps smoking increases the number of calories expended by increasing metabolic rate.[18] If this were so, and if smokers ate the same total amount as nonsmokers—something that we have already established—then smokers would weigh less than nonsmokers.

There is indeed evidence supporting this hypothesis.[19] For example, one experiment found that smokers' metabolic rates were 10% higher during a 24-hour period when they smoked than during a 24-hour period when they abstained from smoking.[20] However, there's a difficulty in interpreting these results. Because chronic smokers were used, we don't know if the metabolic rates observed in the smokers when they were smoking, which were greater than when they weren't smoking, were also greater than before they started smoking. It's possible that starting smoking doesn't change metabolic rate, but that stopping smoking decreases it.

In summary, there doesn't appear to be firm evidence supporting the hypothesis that the decreased weight in smokers is due to a decrease in the total number of calories eaten. On the other hand, there's at least some evidence supporting both the hypothesis that smoking results in a decrease in the total amount of sweet foods eaten and in an increased metabolic rate. However, all of these hypotheses deserve additional research.

The Enlarging Effects of Quitting

Many people who stop smoking gain weight. One study measured the weights of over 5,000 African American and European American men and women when they quit smoking. On average, those of European descent gained 9.3 pounds, and those of African descent gained 14.6 pounds.[21] People who manage to remain abstinent for a long period of time are more likely to gain weight than people who remain abstinent for only a short period of time.[22] Thus successful quitting often comes with an unwelcome consequence: noticeable weight gain.

However, this picture may not be as bad as it seems. For one thing, it's possible that the weight gained by quitting is no more than the weight that wasn't gained or that was lost because the person smoked in the first place. In addition, there are individual differences in whether someone gains weight after quitting; some people don't gain any weight at all. By examining what types of people do and don't gain weight when they stop smoking, and under what conditions there's a weight gain, it may be possible to obtain clues as to what causes these weight gains to occur. Even more importantly, it may be possible to develop strategies for preventing a weight gain when someone quits smoking. Researchers have examined the possible effects of a number of factors on quitting-related weight gain.

Some of these factors are closely related to ones that I discussed in the previous section of this chapter as possibly responsible for the lower weights associated with starting or continuing smoking. Such factors include the amount eaten (hypothesized to increase when someone quits), the percentage of sweet foods eaten (also hypothesized to increase when someone quits), and metabolic rate (hypothesized to decrease when someone quits). There are data to support each of these hypotheses, and so researchers have looked even deeper, trying to determine exactly why each of these factors might increase weight after quitting. For example, researchers have examined the possibility that the amount eaten after quitting increases because people are coping with stress, because pleasant odors (such as those of food) help to decrease the urge to smoke, because nicotine withdrawal disrupts insulin levels, or because of the need to continue to satisfy a high oral drive.[23] When my father, a long-time three-pack-a-day smoker, quit he took to sucking constantly on hard candies, a significant problem for his teeth for the short period that he continued to have any teeth. In the case of the increased preference for sweet following quitting, perhaps quitters try to substitute for the sweetness provided by their now-absent cigarettes.[24] The lower metabolic rate that occurs when people quit smoking may be due to the effects of nicotine on certain parts of the nervous system,[25] thus helping to explain the lower weight gain of ex-smokers who use nicotine gum, and the fact that ex-smokers who engage in relatively more aerobic exercise are less likely to gain weight.[26] As you learned earlier in Chapter 10, exercise can raise metabolic rate. Exercise appears to be a useful strategy for weight control, even in ex-smokers.

There's been additional work investigating the relationship between removal of the chemical nicotine and the weight gain seen in ex-smokers. Heavier smokers are more likely to gain weight when they quit than are moderate or light smokers.[27] In addition, when people quit, the more they chew nicotine gum, or the greater the concentration of nicotine in their gum, the less likely they are to gain weight.[28] Finally, when rats used to receiving nicotine injections instead receive saline injections, they eat significantly greater amounts of Oreos and gain significantly more weight than other rats.[29] Thus, there's indeed a clear relationship between removal of nicotine and weight gain. However, these experiments by themselves don't tell us why nicotine removal tends to cause weight gain. It may be that nicotine removal affects metabolic rate as suggested in the previous paragraph. But nicotine removal may also affect appetite, food preferences, and activity level. One study speaks to some of these possibilities. Scientists Janet Gross, Maxine L. Stitzer, and Janelle Maldonado found that ex-smokers who chewed nicotine gum reported smaller increases in hunger and amounts of food eaten following quitting than ex-smokers who chewed placebo gum (gum that the participants thought contained nicotine but didn't).[30] Unfortunately, data on the possible ways that nicotine removal may affect weight gain are very limited. It would be particularly interesting to find out if the effects of nicotine skin patches are similar to those of nicotine gum, or if the act of chewing the gum, and not just the nicotine in the gum, is somehow important in the appetite decreases seen in nicotine gum chewers.

A final factor hypothesized to be responsible for the weight gain following quitting smoking is an ex-smoker's personality. There are suggestions in the research literature that some personality traits may be correlated with how much weight smokers gain after quitting. It has been shown that women with histories of serious depression are more likely to gain weight after quitting than women who don't have histories of serious depression. The reverse appears to be true for men; men who with histories of depression gain less after quitting.[31] In addition, the sorts of people who tend to continue to eat excessively once they know that they have broken their diet, people whose eating can become what's called disinhibited, also tend to gain relatively more weight after quitting smoking.[32] These studies are intriguing, but much remains to be done to tie down just what sorts of personality traits are consistently associated with weight gain after quitting smoking.

In summary, some people gain weight when they stop smoking, and in some cases this may be due to their eating more food, particularly more sweet food. However, a decrease in metabolic rate that occurs following quitting probably also causes weight gain in some people. It's not yet clear precisely what role nicotine plays in the weight gain that can occur following quitting. Table 14.1 puts together the research-based suggestions for minimizing weight gain after quitting that have been discussed in this section. Future research will undoubtedly continue to pursue all of these issues.

Table 14.1 Research-Based Suggestions for Minimizing Weight Gain After Quitting Smoking

---

■ Chew nicotine gum; nicotine skin patches may also be helpful.

■ If you're a woman and you've a history of depression, it would probably be helpful to ensure that the depression is well under control when quitting smoking, possibly by the combined use of cognitive behavior therapy and antidepressant medication.[33]

■ It may be helpful not to quit during a stressful period.

■ Engage in regular aerobic exercise.

■ Consider following some or all of the suggestions listed in Table 10.1.

The Butt Stops Here: Conclusion

The widespread opinion that smokers weigh less than nonsmokers and that ex-smokers risk weight gain is an accurate one. These unfortunate consequences may encourage people to begin this dangerous habit and, once they have started, contribute to making it difficult to quit. This is particularly the case because the weight changes occur fairly close in time to the smoking. In contrast, the negative health consequences of smoking are often very delayed. Therefore, similar to some of the other choices that we analyzed earlier in this book, even though the negative health consequences of the weight gained from stopping smoking aren't as severe as the ultimate negative health consequences of continuing to smoke,[34] some people have difficulty seeing the greater advantage of quitting than of continuing to smoke. Medication that helps to delay the weight gain associated with quitting may help keep quitters from relapsing.[35] People probably also believe—incorrectly—that every person who stops smoking will gain large numbers of pounds. Not only are there individual differences in weight gain that seem to be related to people's specific characteristics, but particular actions such as the use of nicotine gum and aerobic exercise can help to prevent a weight gain—assuming such a gain isn't desired. Researchers are beginning to understand the many complex factors responsible for these findings, such as types of foods eaten, metabolic rate, and stress. Ultimately, these research results can be used to help free smokers from feeling that they must keep smoking, or resume smoking, in order not to gain excess weight.

CHAPTER 15

We Do Not Live by Bread Alone

Cuisine, Beer, and Wine

℃

> I believe that how you eat and how you choose your food is an act
> that combines the political—your place in the world of other
> people—with the most intensely personal—the way you use your
> mind and your senses, together, for the gratification of your soul.
>
> Alice Waters (1994)[1]

Thus wrote Alice Waters, founder in 1971 of Berkeley's famed Chez Panisse restaurant which, along with master chef Julia Child's early 1960s television show, helped to inspire an American cuisine that went beyond the postwar period's canned vegetables, pot roast, fruit cocktail, and TV dinners.[2] If you're over the age of 40 you probably remember those days when adventuresome eating was an occasional pizza or Chinese food, and salad often contained Jell-O®. Now there are many thousands of outstanding American chefs and home cooks creating new flavor and texture combinations using traditional American foods such as tomatoes, corn, and chocolate. Many restaurants feature American-grown ingredients, as well as American wines and locally made beers.

But what makes American cuisine *American*? In fact, what makes any cuisine a *cuisine*? What factors are responsible for the particular characteristics of a given cuisine? This chapter will provide you with answers to these questions, as well as with some information about beer and wine tasting. Research described in previous chapters concerning how and why people choose certain foods and drinks comes together in this chapter to help you understand how people end up consuming certain combinations or patterns of specific foods and drinks. Here you'll gain a sense of how scientific investigations—with rats as well as people—can give you both a better understanding of and better enjoyment of the food and drink that you consume. You'll see how your genes, your experiences, and evolutionary processes all contribute to what you do when you actually sit down to dinner. This chapter is about love and war and their interactions with the pleasures of the palate. As Julia Child would say, "Bon appétit!"

Cooking With Gas: Cuisine

More than anyone else, Elisabeth Rozin, cookbook writer and culinary historian, has enabled us to understand the nature of cuisine. When I was in graduate school, one of the Harvard faculty told me about Rozin's first cookbook, *Ethnic Cuisine: The Flavor-Principle Cookbook*, first published in 1973 by Hawthorn Books but now out of print and never widely circulated. This book held what amounted to cult status among psychologists. It quickly became my favorite cookbook because not only did it contain fascinating, easy-to-make recipes from many different cuisines, but it explained some of the psychological principles behind cuisine, principles that I'd never previously contemplated and found absolutely absorbing. For example, from this cookbook I learned that it was possible, in principle, to create a Chinese hamburger. For a budding experimental psychologist who loved to eat but who had a raft of food aversions, this was a safe way into the food world using scientific analysis.

In her fascinating writings Rozin has elucidated for all of us the primary elements of cuisine. These elements consist of the foods used, the techniques employed to modify those foods, the flavorings added to those foods, and cultural constraints that restrict what types of food may be eaten or how the foods may be prepared.[3] Put all of this together and, voilà, you have a cuisine. (See Figure 15.1.) Although the behaviors of animals other than people may demonstrate certain elements of cuisine, such as the salting of sweet potatoes by monkeys described in Chapter 1, true cuisine with all of its characteristics appears to be a uniquely human enterprise. In this section you'll be treated first to a thorough description of the elements of cuisine, then to examples of various cuisines and information about two of the most famous, and most desired, flavor principles—chile pepper and chocolate— and finally to two examples of cultural constraints—the sacred cow and cannibalism.

The Building Blocks of Cuisine

The elements of cuisine begin with the foods around you. Particular foods can be a part of your cuisine only if they're present in your surroundings. However, those foods, and thus the nature of a given cuisine, can change as people move to new locations and bring their old foods with them or bring

Figure 15.1 The result of scientific study of cuisine. (From *The Chronicle of Higher Education* [December 1, 1993]:B3. Reprinted with permission from E. Stein.)

foods back from other locations. Although many people dispute whether Columbus's first visit to the Americas was of positive historical significance, no one can dispute the resulting enormous changes in many of the world's cuisines. You may not realize that tomatoes, chile peppers, and chocolate are all native to the Americas and thus weren't part of non-American cuisines until well after 1492.[4] Just try to imagine Italian cuisine without tomatoes, Szechuan cooking without chile peppers, and Swiss dessert without chocolate. But the fact is that those foods have only been a part of those cuisines for the last several hundred years.

Nevertheless, not all of the foods that are available will become part of a given cuisine. Among the most powerful factors determining whether they do is whether the foods are inherently pleasurable to the senses of sight, smell, and taste. As you've learned in previous chapters, people find certain tastes more pleasurable than others. Among the highly preferred tastes are those that are sweet or salty, or that have been associated with lots of calories. Thus, for example, people learn to like foods that are very high in fat. (See Conversation Making Fact #15.) When psychologist Luna Abdallah and her colleagues asked 102 normal-weight men to rate 39 biscuits and cakes that differed in terms of their fat and sugar contents, the ones that were rated the most pleasant had (big surprise) the highest sugar and fat contents.[5]

> ### Conversation Making Fact #15
>
> *Given what you know about food preferences, it shouldn't surprise you to learn that some well-known chefs have (anonymously) reported that their secret ingredient is, you guessed it, fat. When restaurant patrons wonder why food in a restaurant tastes so much better than at home, it may be because the restaurant uses far more fat than any home cook ever would. One famous New York restaurant's menu has included a poached halibut with Swiss chard, which sounds low in calories. But the restaurant poached the halibut by immersing it in a quart of hot goose fat for 13 minutes.[6] So all of you fish eaters out there who feel so virtuous when you order poached fish, beware! You may be taking in more fat than I am when I eat my nice lean beef fillet.*

There are also cases in which people learn to like foods that are inherently aversive—such as chile peppers and coffee—and those foods become part of a cuisine. I'll discuss how this happens with chile peppers in a later section. Earlier you learned how associating coffee with sugar, milk, or caffeine might result in people coming to like this initially aversive beverage.

Whether an available food becomes part of a cuisine may also depend on the ability of people to digest or metabolize that food. For example, when we discussed genetic contributions to food preferences, you learned that many adults are lactose intolerant. If most of the people in a cultural group are lactose intolerant, then milk isn't likely to be a part of that group's cuisine. As another example, although fava beans are toxic for some people, they may increase resistance to malaria. Therefore, in populations in which resistance to malaria is more useful than the toxicity of fava beans is damaging—which occurs in various Mediterranean populations—fava beans should be, and are, a part of that population's cuisine.[7]

The technology available to a particular group of people is also an important determinant of that group's cuisine. Until fermentation was discovered, no cuisine could contain alcoholic beverages. I wonder, then, what will be the implications for cuisine of what's happening now to food technology? In their efforts to create new and exciting dishes, chefs are broaching new frontiers, such as the alliance forged between the chef of a well-known English restaurant and a physicist at the University of Bristol. Together these two professionals have been developing new ways of cooking food and combining flavors. For example, they have developed a new way of cooking lamb slowly that does not have the usual effects on the lamb's muscle fibers and thus results in a more tender final product.[8]

Another important factor in determining the constituents of any cuisine is the nutrition provided by the cuisine. The only cultures that will survive are obviously those that obtain and consume foods that are nutritionally balanced. There are many different ways of doing this. One way is by combining the foods eaten. In the northeastern United States a typical, nutritionally complete meal might consist of a piece of chicken, salad, and a baked potato. But in Mexico, a nutritionally complete meal might consist of corn tortillas, beans, and tomatoes. Another way to ensure a nutritionally complete cuisine is by treating particular foods. Native Americans developed a method of treating corn with an alkali solution that significantly enhances the nutritional value of the corn.[9]

Another factor influencing which foods are part of a cuisine has to do with cost. By this I don't just mean how much money a food costs, but also the amount of energy required to prepare a food. If a group of 10 people living at subsistence level must walk 50 miles through a desert in order to obtain grain and then spend several days working to make a single loaf of bread from that grain, bread won't be a part of that group's cuisine.

Other people's food preferences and practices—what we might call food cultural beliefs—can also affect a cuisine, as you learned when we discussed the contributions of our surroundings to food preferences. This can involve such relatively simple matters as what people like to eat for breakfast and dinner; North Americans prefer "breakfast" foods such as scrambled eggs and "dinner" foods such as green beans at the meals that they have learned are appropriate for these foods.[10] Cultural beliefs can also involve what kinds of substances are even considered food. Among some Africans, Southeast Asians, and Latin Americans, eating insects is considered perfectly acceptable, but among other groups of people it isn't. Of course, sometimes your neighbors will surprise you. Consider the members of the New York Entomological Society.[11] For their 100th anniversary dinner they asked a caterer to prepare a special feast that included "crunchy mealworms [think peanuts] ... live honeypot ants, their abdomens swollen with peach nectar; roasted kurrajong grubs, each the size of a small finger ... and for dessert, a rich chocolate cricket torte."[12]

As another example, the laws of *kashrut*, which determine the kosher food practices of Jews, are passed from generation to generation. The cultural traditions of *kashrut* are so strong that they can affect the consumption of foods that appear not to be kosher, but actually are. You've already learned that people have trouble eating things that aren't forbidden foods but look like them.[13] In 1985 my sister married the son of an Orthodox rabbi. There wasn't much money for this event, so she and I made all of the food. Jews who observe *kashrut*, such as my sister's future father-in-law, won't eat both meat and dairy products as part of the same meal, so meals have to contain either meat and no dairy or vice versa. We chose to make a dairy meal for the wedding, which included a mushroom pâté. It looked just like a regular meat pâté, but it was made entirely of vegetable and dairy products. I'll never forget how my sister's future father-in-law looked at it. "What's that?" he asked suspiciously. "Mushroom pâté," we replied. After much persuasion, he finally ate it, but he didn't look happy about it.

Cultural beliefs about which foods are appropriate to eat may or may not help to ensure that people eat foods that are good for them. In Kenya, among the Mbeere people, pregnant women were traditionally not allowed to consume bitter substances such as certain medicinal juices, a practice that, as described in Chapter 13, may have helped to protect these women's fetuses. However, in western Kenya, women in some ethnic groups have traditionally not been allowed to eat eggs, even when there were a great many eggs available.[14] Perhaps originally there was some health benefit to this prohibition, but any such benefit isn't clear now. Similarly, the practice of keeping kosher, in which Jews eat only certain foods or combinations of foods, results in food consumption that may have ensured health in ancient times but may not be relevant now. [15]

Perhaps one of the best examples of how food cultural beliefs affect a cuisine occurs when a person moves from one culture to another. People, particularly young people, tend to acquire food preference patterns of their new cultures.[16] By looking at how cuisines spread or die out, one may see which cultures are dominating others. As noted by Anthelme Brillat-Savarin, a famous French gastronome who lived at the turn of the 19th century, "Tell me what you eat and I will tell you who you are."[17]

The final factor influencing cuisines that I'll discuss is neophobia—the fear of new foods—which you learned about when we discussed the contributions of our experiences to food preference. This fear of new foods is probably responsible for the fact that most cuisines revolve around a number of flavor principles, or characteristic flavorings. The flavor principles identify dishes as belonging to a particular tradition.[18] They make the food seem familiar and safe. People add these flavorings to many of the dishes in a given cuisine. Thus you can take hamburger, a food not present in Asian cuisines, add soy sauce, rice wine, and ginger root to it, and end up with a hamburger that tastes "Chinese." Someone who usually eats Chinese food would be much more likely to try hamburger when it's imbued with these characteristic Chinese flavorings than otherwise.[19] This same preference for familiar foods results in cuisines often containing foods from people's childhoods and causes people far from home to miss their usual foods. As a Philadelphia native now living in New York City, I find the Web site www.tasteofphiladelphia.com to be very appealing. This site makes available for purchase and delivery some of my childhood favorites such as soft pretzels and Tastykakes®.

The craving for familiar foods hit me personally when I spent 3 weeks in Japan in the early 1990s. Remember that I'm very low on the trait of sensation seeking and I eat no fish. Japanese food often uses ingredients or cooking techniques unfamiliar to Americans and often contains fish or fish sauce. The result was that in Japan I simply couldn't find satisfying food. Everything seemed strange or impossible to eat, and I could never get full. Even a dessert such as chocolate cake in what was billed as a Western-style restaurant seemed too light and airy, not at all satisfying (it was probably just low in fat). In desperation, one dinnertime I persuaded my husband to go to Denny's, someplace we would never go in the United States. I ordered what was billed on the menu as a hamburger, but what I got was a ground meat patty that tasted very different from American hamburger meat, no bun, and the patty was drowning in gravy. Even with this disappointment, I thought I'd have no problem when I ordered vanilla ice cream for dessert. But it came sprinkled with ground-up frosted corn flakes cereal. I ate it, but it was very strange. Now truly desperate, I took my 5-year-old son on a lengthy trip on public transportation to Tokyo Disneyland. Surely there we would find familiar, satisfying food. While walking around we saw a sign for pizza. In ecstasy I approached the restaurant selling it only to find that they had just two kinds of pizza—with pineapple or shrimp topping. The shrimp was definitely out and at that time I'd never heard of putting fruit on pizza, so we left the restaurant without getting any food. My trip to Japan was the only trip I've ever been on during which I lost weight. When I came back I couldn't stop stuffing myself with typical high-fat, high-sugar American food and I quickly gained back all of the weight that I'd lost.

Eating by Example: Some Cuisines and Flavor Principles

Elisabeth Rozin has provided extensive listings of the flavor principles of different cuisines in her cookbooks.[20] Table 15.1 shows examples of the flavor principles that Rozin believes are the most important factors in identifying any ethnic cuisine. Note that cultures that are in close geographical proximity tend to have overlapping flavor principles. For instance, soy sauce is common to Japanese, Chinese, and Korean cuisines, and olive oil is common to many Mediterranean cuisines. Cuisines can be influenced by immigrant groups as well. South African Cape Malay cuisine shows the influence of South African Dutch, French, Indian, and Indonesian immigrants, as well as of the indigenous cuisine; and Vietnamese cuisine blends the flavors of China, France, India, Thailand, Laos, and Cambodia.[21]

For a detailed example of the influences that shape a particular cuisine, I'd like to tell you about Cajun cuisine, a cuisine that I find particularly fascinating. The Cajuns are a group of people who live in an area of Louisiana

Table 15.1 Flavor Principles in Different Cuisines

Cuisine	Flavor Principles
China	Soy sauce, rice wine, and ginger root:
Peking	+ miso and/or garlic and/or sesame
Szechuan	+ sweet-sour-hot
Canton	+ black bean-garlic
Japan	Soy sauce, sake, and sugar
Korea	Soy sauce, brown sugar, sesame, and chile
India	Curry:
Northern India	cumin, ginger, garlic + variations
Southern India	mustard seed, coconut, tamarind, chile + variations
Central Asia	Cinnamon, fruit, nut
Middle East	Lemon, parsley
West Africa	Tomato, peanut, chile
Northeastern Africa	Garlic, cumin, mint
Morocco	Cumin, coriander, cinnamon, ginger + onion and/or tomato and/or fruit
Greece	Olive oil, lemon, oregano
Southern Italy and Southern France	Olive oil, garlic, parsley, and/or anchovy
Italy, France	Olive oil, garlic, basil
Provence	Olive oil, thyme, rosemary, marjoram, sage
Spain	Olive oil, onion, pepper, tomato
Northern and Eastern Europe	Sour cream, dill or paprika or allspice or caraway
Normandy	Apple, cider, calvados
Northern Italy	Wine vinegar, garlic
Mexico	Tomato, chile

Source: Adapted from E. Rozin, *Ethnic Cuisine: The Flavor-Principle Cookbook*, Brattleboro, VT: The Stephen Greene Press, 1983.

close to New Orleans. The word *Cajun* comes from the word *Acadian*; Cajuns were originally from Nova Scotia (Acadia) in French Canada. They were transported involuntarily to Louisiana by British soldiers in the 18th century.[22] The area where they arrived has also been inhabited by, among others, the French, Native Americans, and Africans brought there as slaves.

The Cajuns's new location, the bayou, was near the Gulf of Mexico and filled with swamps, lakes, and islands. Seafood was plentiful, particularly oysters, crawfish (a larger variety of the crayfish), and crab. Chile peppers also grew well in the area. Okra was also a popular food among the Africans, and a popular seasoning among the Native Americans was a powder made from sassafras leaves.

The various groups of people in the area had their own unique cooking techniques. Both the Cajuns and the French were familiar with *roux*, a sauce base that's made by combining melted butter and flour. The Africans used a slow-tempered cooking fire along with a heavy iron pot.

The combination of all of these ingredients and techniques resulted in the now-famous Cajun dish called gumbo. This particular dish, more than any other, is identified with Cajun cooking because it represents the unique mixture of cultures that is Cajun cooking. Cajun cuisine is quite different from Creole cuisine in nearby New Orleans; Creole cuisine is almost identical to French except that local ingredients are used instead of traditional French ingredients.[23]

One of the most perplexing and intriguing flavor principles is chile pepper. Most people initially find eating chile pepper unpleasant. The physical effects of chile pepper in the mouth are similar to the effects of being burned; there's a sensation of pain, and the skin is irritated.[24] As a result, chile pepper has been sold as a powder for hikers and skiers to apply to their feet to keep them warm in cold weather. It's been used on fences to keep elephants away from crops, as a spray to deter attackers of both the human and the grizzly bear variety, and as an ingredient in early 20th century wallpaper paste in Appalachia to keep rats from eating wallpaper.[25] Yet, amazingly, this New World plant is now grown and eaten around the globe. Chile peppers are an integral part of cuisines as diverse as Mexican, Szechuan, and Hungarian.[26] There's even a Chile Pepper Institute at New Mexico State University that disseminates and preserves information about chile peppers. The institute's Web site, www.chilepepperinstitute.org, can tell you the best way to decrease mouth burn after eating chile peppers (eat or drink dairy products) and the hotness of different kinds of chile peppers (habaneros are far hotter than jalapenos). Because chile pepper seems such an unlikely popular food, by examining how people come to like it, we can perhaps elucidate some of the many ways in which flavors come to be frequently used flavor principles.

Let's start by looking at who does and doesn't like to eat chile pepper. Rats exposed to chile pepper won't eat it, but they can learn to prefer it if they're exposed to other rats that have eaten it.[27] Similarly, chimpanzees exposed to chile peppers through contact with people can acquire a preference for it.[28] Nevertheless, we're the only omnivores that regularly eat chile pepper; preference for chile pepper is one of the few differences between the real-world food preferences of people and other animals. But it's important to keep in mind that there are significant individual differences in how much different people like chile pepper. Some people prefer large amounts, and some people don't like it at all.

Now let's consider some of the reasons that some people may come to prefer chile pepper while others don't. First, there may be genetic differences in how much pain someone feels upon eating chile pepper, with people who feel less pain preferring chile pepper more. Scientists have been able to construct transgenic mice that lack the receptor cells that detect the burn of chile pepper.[29] These mice—as well as perhaps some people—may prefer large amounts of chile pepper because, for genetic reasons, they don't detect the chile pepper burn. In contrast, PTC/PROP (phenylthiocarbamide and 6-N-propylthiouracil) supertasters, whose unusually sensitive taste trait is genetically based, as described in Chapter 4, tend to perceive more burn from chile pepper, probably because they tend to have more cells in their mouths that are specialized for pain detection.[30] Given the greater burn that they feel, PTC/PROP supertasters may prefer chile pepper less than other people.

But even granted that there may be genetic factors responsible for some of the differences in chile pepper preference among people, it's still very unusual for a child to prefer chile pepper the first time that the child eats it. Only after a number of exposures to chile pepper does preference for it increase, with a great many adults coming to prefer it.[31] Therefore our experiences, and not just our genes, contribute to our liking chile pepper.

Initially, people may sample chile pepper because of social pressure. Later, they may come to like it because of the large amounts of vitamins A and C that it contains; the increase in salivation and gastric movement that it engenders, which assists in the digestion of starchy foods; or the zest that it adds to a meal. Other possible explanations are that it masks the odors and tastes of spoiled food and that it causes sweating and thus body cooling, which is useful in hot climates. However, as of yet we have little or no direct evidence supporting any of these possible explanations. Another possibility is that the pain that accompanies eating chile pepper is enjoyed because it seems dangerous but is actually safe—a manifestation of the sensation-seeking trait.[32] There's also evidence that, although repeated bites of chile pepper in the same meal greatly increase the burn, repeated meals of chile pepper over periods of days greatly decrease the burn, thus suggesting another way in which experience could increase the preference for chile pepper.[33] However, it's been argued that the decrease in chile pepper burn (the pain) that comes from daily exposure to chile pepper is too small to explain the accompanying increase in chile preference.[34] Still another possible explanation is that the negative physiological reaction on first tasting chile pepper—that is, the pain—may, with experience, come to be counteracted or even overwhelmed by an opposite, positive, physiological reaction.[35] This hypothesis has received some support in experiments with another widely consumed but initially aversive substance, coffee.[36]

Recent evidence has confirmed what has been suspected for some time, that chile pepper kills food bacteria and therefore may be particularly useful in warm climates where food can spoil more quickly. Scientist Paul W. Sherman and his colleagues have shown that chile pepper can inhibit a whopping 80% of bacterial growth in food, and that cookbooks from warm climates are more likely to contain recipes that use chile pepper.[37] Yet as intriguing as these results may be, they can't explain why people in cold climates also often like chile pepper. It's possible that there are many ways by which different people may come to prefer chile pepper.

The other flavor principle that I'd like to cover is chocolate. Chocolate is every bit as, if not more, fascinating than chile pepper. Similar to chile pepper, chocolate is popular all over the world. However, again like chile pepper, it originated in the New World and has only been available to most of the world for the past several hundred years. In fact, it was only after chocolate was brought to Europe that it was manufactured with sugar and milk into the form of chocolate with which we are most familiar today: milk chocolate. Prior to that time, for more than a thousand years, the Maya and Aztecs used chocolate for religious and ceremonial purposes.[38] Today, similar to chile pepper, chocolate is big business. The Mars family, manufacturers of Mars chocolate, is one of the richest in the world, and the profits from the Hershey Foods Corporation support one of the wealthiest orphanages in the world.[39]

But here is where the similarities between chile pepper and chocolate stop. Chocolate isn't aversive the first time someone tastes it. Even though some people get migraine headaches about 24 hours after eating chocolate,[40] most people love it the first time, and every time, they eat it. Studies have found that chocolate is one of the most frequently craved foods. For example, close to 50% of American women crave it.[41] One sample of self-described chocoholics, 92% of whom were women, reported eating, on average, 12 2-ounce bars of chocolate per week.[42] The Miramax film *Chocolat*, released in 2001 and based on Joanne Harris's book by the same name, caused a sensation. There are chocolate clubs and chocolate guides.[43] When I was traveling in

Germany a few years ago I stumbled upon the Imhoff Stollwerk Museum for the History of Chocolate in Köln. This modern museum covers everything you would ever want to know about chocolate, from how the cacao tree's seeds are processed to make chocolate, to images of chocolate in art—and, oh yes, there are plenty of free samples. My favorite was the sugar wafers that had been dipped in a huge fountain of liquid chocolate. I wasn't alone in loving this museum; it was extremely crowded with people of all ages and types. Chocolate obsession even frequents the Internet. Table 15.2 lists chocolate "rules" that I received in an e-mail from Sarah Wahlert, whose father, John Wahlert, is a biology professor who worked with me and who will do (almost) anything as long as you give him chocolate.

What factor or factors are responsible for this incredible liking for chocolate? Although we now know that chocolate contains substantial amounts of chemicals that are extremely helpful in preventing cardiovascular and other diseases,[44] these effects have only been recently discovered and probably occurred too long after eating chocolate for our ancestors to have eaten chocolate in order to obtain those medicinal benefits. But there are several factors that undoubtedly contribute to our eating so much chocolate. One

---

Table 15.2 Chocolate Rules

1. Put "eat chocolate" at the top of your list of things to do today. That way, at least you'll get one thing done.

2. If you've got melted chocolate all over your hands, you're eating it too slowly.

3. Chocolate covered raisins, cherries, orange slices, and strawberries all count as fruit, so eat as many as you want!

4. The problem: How to get 2 pounds of chocolate home from the store in a hot car. The solution: Eat it in the parking lot.

5. Diet tip: Eat a chocolate bar before each meal. It'll take the edge off your appetite and you'll eat less.

6. Chocolate has many preservatives. Preservatives make you look younger.

7. **Q:** Why is there no such organization as Chocoholics Anonymous?
   A: Because no one wants to quit.

8. A nice box of chocolates can provide your total daily intake of calories in one place . . . isn't that handy?

9. If you can't eat all your chocolate, it will keep in the freezer. But if you can't eat all your chocolate, what's wrong with you?

---

is that the chocolate that we eat is usually mixed with sugar, thus tapping into our largely innate preference for sweet tastes and arousing strong sensual and pleasurable sensations.[45] Another reason is that chocolate is high in fat. You'll remember from our discussion of the contributions of our experiences to food preferences that we learn to prefer foods that are high in calories, and that fat contains more calories per ounce than carbohydrates or protein. One ounce of milk chocolate contains about 150 calories, as well as significant amounts of calcium, potassium, magnesium, vitamin A, and vitamin B$_3$, all essential nutrients.[46] Chocolate also contains caffeine, which has an unusual flavor by itself. One ounce of bittersweet chocolate contains about one third the amount of caffeine as a cup of tea. Chapter 8 discussed the fact that caffeine is a stimulant. So it's possible that some people who eat very large amounts of chocolate find its stimulating effects to be rewarding, as do rats.[47] Chocolate also has a smooth, pleasant texture and melts at body temperature, thus adding to its appeal.

This brings us to love (remember I promised that this chapter would cover love, as well as war; the war part is later). Soon after it was brought to Europe, chocolate was touted as an aphrodisiac.[48] Both the film and the originating book *Chocolat* link chocolate with love. And of course you're all familiar with the strong association of chocolate with Valentine's Day. Doesn't this all seem to be a bit too much of a coincidence? Why is it that chocolate, throughout its history, has been continually associated with love and sex? One reason may have to do with chocolate's chemistry. However, so far, there's been no scientific proof of this scintillating possibility.

Chocolate may have other chemical effects on the body that people find pleasurable or rewarding. For example, it's been shown that there are chemicals in chocolate that may have effects on the brain similar to marijuana.[49] In addition, there's discussion by scientists that people who crave chocolate tend, on average, to be more depressed than are noncravers, and that such people claim that eating chocolate makes them less depressed. In support of these claims, there's evidence that a particular kind of antidepressant medication also eliminates chocolate craving.[50]

Researchers' fascination with chocolate is beginning to mirror that of consumers'. There are many different possible factors responsible for our huge preference for chocolate, each of which can be richly mined by scientists. You may remember from earlier chapters the Cuisine Group to which I used to belong. This was a small informal group of psychologists, historians, anthropologists, and the like who were all interested in food and cuisine. We met once a month to discuss various topics concerning food. Each meeting had a theme. I'll never forget the day we did chocolate. It was right before Easter and Barbara Kirshenblatt-Gimblett, the New York University professor in whose New York City loft we met, had bought us huge chocolate bunnies and other chocolate items made by hand in a candy store in Queens. We had chocolate for lunch, listened to lectures about chocolate in the afternoon, and went to a restaurant that served a dessert entitled "Death by Chocolate" in the evening. We discussed such matters as which part of the chocolate bunny you eat first and why, how difficult it is to manufacture artificial chocolate flavor, and the possible connections of chocolate with sexual behavior. Total heaven.

Thou Shalt Not Eat: Two Examples of Forbidden Eating, The Sacred Cow and Cannibalism

In this section I'll discuss two examples of cultural constraints on cuisine that have received particular attention: the sacred cow in India and cannibalism. Both examples concern situations in which a readily available food could be part of a cuisine but, for cultural reasons, is not. In both cases, research evidence discussed in earlier chapters can be brought to bear to understand why these cultural constraints may or may not exist.

In India, Hindus have a prohibition against eating cows, which are considered sacred. Hindu pilgrims will even touch their foreheads to a cow's tail for purification purposes. Given that so many people in India don't have enough food, and that the cows in India may be causing harm to the environment by overgrazing, treating cows as sacred seems counterproductive. However, using the sorts of food choice analyses described earlier in this book, scientist Marvin Harris and others have contended that treating cows in India as sacred is actually greatly beneficial to India's economy.

According to Harris, oxen (castrated male cattle) are essential to the Indian agricultural system, providing the power necessary to till the soil. It's difficult for farmers to share oxen because, as a result of the monsoon rains, all of the crops tend to become ready for harvesting at the same time. Therefore most farmers need to have their own oxen. Oxen also provide transportation. And in order to get oxen, cows are necessary. During droughts, cows may become infertile. However, if they're not kept alive, there won't be any cows to produce oxen.

At times when there's little food to give the farm animals, for example in the spring when it's hot and dry in India, cattle are allowed to wander along the roads. Although it may appear that the cattle are permitted to wander freely because they're "sacred," they're actually eating the grass along the road so that their owners don't have to feed them. When wandering cows end up in downtown, religiously conservative New Delhi, where they may cause traffic accidents and die from eating plastic bags, municipal cow catchers gently capture the cows and take them to a suburban location where they can comfortably live for the rest of their lives.

If a farmer has to make a choice between feeding his cows or his oxen, the oxen are usually fed, thus protecting the farmer's immediate survival, though perhaps sacrificing future survival. Further, in general, the food that's given to cattle consists mostly of the parts of plants that people can't eat.

Cattle also provide dung, which is very important in India both as cooking fuel and as fertilizer. In some parts of India virtually 100% of the dung is used for these purposes.

Finally, statistics on the relative number of cows versus oxen show that there are far more oxen than cows, perhaps because of differential amounts of neglect. In any case, when a cow does die, it can be touched only by a member of the lowest Indian caste, the Untouchables. A member of this caste will take the carcass, eat the meat, and use the hide for leather. This provides a sort of welfare system for some of India's poorest people.

For all of these reasons Harris and others believe that the treatment of cows in India as sacred is actually beneficial to the Indian economy. Through the centuries, those Indians who treated cows as sacred may have been more likely to survive than people who didn't. Thus a cultural trait concerning food choice that appears to be based in religion may actually be a result of a complex array of economic, ecological, and political factors.[51] Given that people evolved in surroundings in which the food supplies were often inadequate, it's not surprising that cuisines, as well as other aspects of culture, often reflect optimal solutions for maximizing survival.[52]

The prohibition against eating the flesh of your own species seems less difficult to figure out. After all, if we regularly ate other people then the human species would be less likely to survive. In this respect we are similar to rats which, as you learned about in Chapter 6, are also unlikely to eat members of their own species. Eating each other has fueled our imaginations on Broadway in the show *Sweeney Todd: The Demon Barber of Fleet Street* and at the movie theaters in the films *Hannibal* and *Silence of the Lambs*, not to mention our continuing fascination with the Donner Party. However cannibalism has rarely been a part of our species' reality, except when people were facing situations of absolute starvation, situations that have been perceived as regrettable acts or antisocial behavior, rather than as accepted practice.[53] Such a situation was described in Chapter 6 in relation to the book *Alive*.

But are we so sure that cannibalism has never been a regular practice? Or is that just what we'd like to believe? After all, as discussed in Chapter 1, one of our closest relatives, chimpanzees, will hunt and kill some of their closest relatives, monkeys. For decades researchers have argued over whether there have been human societies in which cannibalism was a regular occurrence. Some researchers have felt that, prior to 1900, there may have been societies that engaged in regular cannibalism, but accurate, complete records from that time have been difficult to obtain.[54] Research in Spain has found human bones dating back approximately 750,000 years that were arrayed in a way consistent with butchering processes. Remains of Neanderthals in France from approximately 100,000 years ago provide similar evidence. Other researchers have claimed that there's much evidence for cannibalism around 1000 A.D. by the Anasazi Indians in the American Southwest.[55] Yet there have always been ways to explain away what was found. For example, the sorts of remains found could have been due to ritual executions.[56]

However, dramatic recent findings establish firmly that cannibalism did take place, at least on one occasion, among the Anasazi Indians. This research takes advantage of the relatively new field of biogeochemistry, which permits scientists to analyze the body parts of living and dead animals to determine what foods they ate, allowing scientists to put a new twist on an old slogan, "You are what you eat."[57]

A few years ago pathologist Richard A. Marlar and his colleagues published a ground-breaking article in *Nature* firmly demonstrating an instance of Anasazi cannibalism. These scientists investigated an archaeological site near the Four Corners area of the American Southwest. This particular site contained several pit houses that were suddenly abandoned around 1150 A.D. Two of the pit houses contained the remains of seven people—males and females of varying ages. The bodies had been taken apart, defleshed, and burned in a manner consistent with butchering and cooking. Butchering tools with blood residue were found near the bodies, as was a cooking pot containing a type of human protein. However, these items can be explained as something other than cannibalism; by itself, none of this evidence proves definitively that the seven people were killed on purpose or that they were eaten. The key evidence was in the third pit house. In that dwelling were the remains of a hearth, and in that hearth was a human coprolite (fossil fecal remains) that wasn't burned and so had been deposited after the last fire there. Analyses showed that the coprolite had resulted from a meal that consisted of almost entirely meat, and that it contained protein found only in nonintestinal human cells. Thus, this coprolite resulted from a human eating human flesh.

Apparently this happened at a time of severe drought in the Four Corners area, resulting in great stress among the tribes there. Scientists believe that one group of Anasazi attacked another, killed them, ate them, and defecated in their hearth as a parting gesture of contempt. (This is the part of the chapter on war that I promised you.) We don't know if that exact scenario is true, but cannibalism definitely took place at this site. This information wasn't welcomed by the descendants of the Anasazi, members of the Hopi and Zuni tribes. However, it's important to point out that many scientists believe that, during times of inadequate food supply, cannibalism has been frequent in human history throughout the world, and thus is just part of what it means to be human.[58]

The prohibition against eating members of your own species can extend to species closely associated with your own. You'll remember in Chapter 6 I described how a rat is unlikely to eat mice if the rat has been raised with a mouse. People generally don't eat the members of other species with which they live and which they consider to possess human traits. In the United States and other Western countries, such species include cats and dogs.

Before we leave the fascinating topic of eating members of our own or related species, I'd like to make a few final comments about vegetarianism. Vegetarianism and its variants—avoiding all flesh foods, avoiding all flesh foods except fish, and avoiding all flesh foods except fish and fowl—is fairly common in Western countries. You learned in Chapter 9 that vegetarianism in teenage girls is often associated with eating disorders. People also avoid meat for reasons of health—the additives or fat that meat contains. However, another reason that people avoid meat is because of their concerns about the ethics of how animals are raised for food or because of their disgust at eating meat.[59] Given these findings and the material in the preceding paragraphs, one wonders if some of these cases of meat avoidance are generalizations or expansions of the prohibition against eating human meat. The flesh foods that are generally the most acceptable—fish and fowl—are also those that are most dissimilar to human meat. Consistent with such a hypothesis, to try to convince us that eating or killing other animals is wrong, animal rights activists engage in advertising campaigns in which nonhuman animals appear to possess human traits, such as the talking cows in the 2001 Super Bowl TV commercial. The communication system of cows, including what they communicate, is quite limited and is qualitatively different from that of people. But if we think that Bessie is feeling just as we are, then we'll be less likely to eat her.

Pleasures of the Palate With a Kick: Beer and Wine Tasting

When my husband and I were in graduate school, and when we came to New York for our first jobs, money was scarce. But we wanted to have interesting parties so, on several occasions, we had beer-tasting parties (they're a lot cheaper than wine-tasting parties). At these parties we distributed the beer in small, clear plastic cups without any identifying information and asked everyone attending to rate their preferences for the different beers. We awarded prizes to those people who gave the highest rankings to the most expensive beers and to those people who gave the highest rankings to the cheapest beers. Interestingly, partygoers who really liked beer tended to give high rankings to the more expensive beers, and those who didn't like beer (such as me) tended to give high rankings to the less expensive beers. This apparently happened because the more expensive beers also tended to be the strongest tasting. Many years later, we now know that PTC/PROP super-tasters (such as me), discussed in detail in Chapters 4 and 5, tend to perceive beer, among other items, as more bitter than nontasters. So if you don't like beer, the next time someone makes fun of you for turning up your nose at some expensive microbrewed ale, you can explain that it's because you possess a taste sensitivity that the ale lover does not, and it's the ale lover who's really obtuse.

Much more common than beer tasting is wine tasting, a great vehicle for demonstrating how the varied scientific approaches that underlie the psychology of eating and drinking can come together to help us understand particular eating and drinking behaviors. An examination of the wine-tasting process can help us understand not only how wines are evaluated, but how any food or drink is evaluated, as well as the factors that affect those evaluations.

Given that many of you have probably never engaged in formal wine tasting, it will be helpful if I begin by briefly describing the wine-tasting procedure. The first step is simply to look at the wine. Then it's swirled in the glass to increase its aroma and bouquet, which are smelled in the next step. Finally the wine is tasted in small sips. It's rolled over the tongue and bits of bread or cheese may be taken between sips. Some wine tasters spit out the sips of wine without swallowing them. This prevents the possible adverse effects of alcohol on sensory sensitivity.[60]

Each of these steps is performed separately, quietly, and with as little distraction as possible. This separation and isolation in the wine-tasting process permit more attention to be focused on each of the steps. People are more likely to report detecting low levels of specific tastes or odors under these conditions. Another way to help increase people's reported sensitivity to tastes and odors during wine tasting is to offer rewards for accurate judgments or to set up a competition among the wine tasters. A factor that affects everyone's odor sensitivity no matter how motivated they are is the temperature of the wine. When wine is very cold it's harder to smell. Most people who taste wine without distractions, and when the wine is at the appropriate temperature, can become skilled at discriminating among various types of wine.[61]

To judge the odor of a wine, wine tasters pay attention to both the wine's aroma, which consists of the odors arising from the type of grape used in making the wine, and the wine's bouquet, which consists of the odors derived from fermentation, processing, or aging. Calling the various odors by specific names may help in their identification. For example, many people describe the aroma of the Sauvignon Blanc grape as spicy. In judging the taste of the wine, the wine is rolled around on the tongue so that all of the taste receptors are stimulated.[62]

In addition to smell and taste, the senses of vision and touch are critical to wine tasting. The visual judgment of a wine includes judging both the wine's color and its appearance, for example, whether it's cloudy.[63] If the color of a wine is unusual for its type, this may affect the wine taster's judgment of other aspects of the wine, such as the wine's taste. Certain tastes are associated with certain colors, and it's harder to detect a taste if its usually associated color isn't present.[64] If the wine is cloudy, a taster may be more likely to judge the wine's taste as below par. This probably happens because, in the past, that taster has encountered cloudy wine and it did not taste good. However, given that appearance and taste aren't always correlated, it's important to try to prevent such interactive effects. One solution is to drink the wine out of a glass painted black, so that it's impossible to see the wine. Then the merits of the wine's taste can be judged by themselves.[65]

To assess the touch of the wine, a wine taster notes any astringency on the tongue, as well as whether the wine feels full or thin. The wine feels thin when there's a low alcohol content and full when there's a high alcohol content.[66] Beer has also been studied with regard to touch. How thirst quenching a beer is turns out to depend on the degree to which it's carbonated and the density of bubbles in the beer—the more bubbles, the more thirst quenching.[67]

There are several psychological processes that you have to watch out for when wine tasting because they can interfere with your making good judgments. One of these is that when sensory cells, such as those for taste and smell, are repeatedly stimulated during a wine-tasting session, they tire out and are less likely to respond than at the beginning of the wine tasting. This is why wine tasters may take bites of bread between sips and why they taste slowly. They're trying to keep their sensory cells at maximum sensitivity.

Another problem has to do with the words used to describe what's seen, smelled, tasted, and felt. Terms such as *fruity, pale yellow,* and *woody* are used frequently. However, there's no guarantee that the same word used by two different people has the same meaning for both of them. In addition, over time the use of certain words may change.[68]

Memory is also very important in wine tasting. A taster needs to compare wines to absolute standards developed from previous tastings. In addition, if too large a series of wines is tasted during one session, those tasted in the middle are likely to suffer in terms of the taster's memory of them. People tend to remember the beginning and end of a long series of items better than they do the middle.[69] A rating form can help a taster to remember what has been tasted.[70]

There's no question that wine tasting is a complex, fascinating subject that draws on the knowledge of several different scientific areas. Given all of this scientific discussion, you now probably believe that people who follow the tasting guidelines above will use their accumulated knowledge of specific wines to buy highly rated wines. However, it's possible that other factors influence which wines we buy. Scientist Adrian C. North and his colleagues showed that when a British supermarket played German Bierkeller music, customers were more likely to buy German wine, and when the supermarket played French accordion music, customers were more likely to buy French wine.[71] Next time you're going to the store to buy wine, it just might be a good idea to wear earplugs.

Parting Is So Sweet and Sour

This chapter's coverage of cuisine and beer and wine tasting provides excellent examples of the advantages of taking an interdisciplinary, scientific approach to the psychology of eating and drinking. Our enjoyment of food and drink will continue to be enhanced by this type of approach, which takes into account all of our senses, past experiences, genes, and current surroundings, including our companions.

I'd like to end this final chapter with two quotations that illustrate the eternal value of food and drink.

> Kissing don't last: cookery do!
> George Meredith, 19th century
> English novelist and poet[72]

> We may live without poetry, music and art;
> We may live without conscience, and live without heart;
> We may live without friends; we may live without books;
> But civilized man cannot live without cooks.
> He may live without books,—what is knowledge but grieving?
> He may live without hope,—what is hope but deceiving?
> He may live without love,—what is passion but pining?
> But where is the man that can live without dining?
> Edward Robert Bulwer Lytton,
> 19th century English statesman and poet[73]

References

Chapter 1: Introductions

1. W. Shakespeare, *Twelfth Night* in *The Complete Works of William Shakespeare*, ed. W. A. Wright, Garden City, NY: Garden City Books, 1623/1936, p. 707.
2. H. Gleitman, *Psychology*, New York: W. W. Norton, 1981, p.1.
3. W. J. Davis, "Motivation and Learning: Neurophysiological Mechanisms in a 'Model' System," *Learning and Motivation* 15(1984):377–393.
4. E. M. Blass and M. H. Teicher, "Suckling," *Science* 210(1980):15–22.
5. C. Thorne, "Feeding Behavior of Domestic Dogs and the Role of Experience," in *The Domestic Dog: Its Evolution, Behaviour, and Interactions with People,* ed. J. Serpell, New York: Cambridge University Press, 1995.
6. R. J. Herrnstein and E. G. Boring, *A Source Book in the History of Behavior,* Cambridge, MA: Harvard University Press, 1965.
7. C. Boesch and H. Boesch-Achermann, "Dim Forest, Bright Chimps," *Natural History* (September 1991):50–57.
8. H. Van Lawick-Goodall, *In the Shadow of Man*, New York: Dell, 1971.
9. M. Kawai, "Newly-Acquired Pre-Cultural Behavior of the Natural Troop of Japanese Monkeys on Koshima Islet," *Primates* 6(1965):1–30.
10. C. B. Stanford, "Chimpanzee Hunting Behavior and Human Evolution," *American Scientist* (May/June 1995):256–261.
    Van Lawick-Goodall, *In the Shadow of Man.*
11. C. B. Stanford, "To Catch a Colobus," *Natural History* (January 1995):48–55.
12. S. A. Barnett, *The Rat: A Study in Behavior*, Chicago: Aldine, 1963.
13. J. J. Wurtman and R. J. Wurtman, "Sucrose Consumption Early in Life Fails to Modify the Appetite of Adult Rats for Sweet Foods," *Science* 205(1979):321–322.
14. Barnett, *The Rat.*
15. H. R. Kissileff, J. L. Guss, and L. J. Nolan, "What Animal Research Tells Us about Human Eating," in *Food Choice, Acceptance and Consumption*, eds. H. L. Meiselman and H. J. H. MacFie, New York: Blackie Academic & Professional, 1996.

Chapter 2: Down the Hatch

1. J. Z. Young, "Influence of the Mouth on the Evolution of the Brain," in *Biology of the Brain*, ed. P. Person, Washington, DC: American Association for the Advancement of Science, 1968, p. 21.

2. M. P. Longnecker, J. M. Harper, and S. Kim, "Eating Frequency in the Nationwide Food Consumption Survey (U.S.A.), 1987–1988," *Appetite* 29(1997):55–59.

3. W. B. Cannon, "Organization for Physiological Homeostasis," *Physiological Reviews* 9(1929):399–431.

4. J. M. De Castro, "Methodology, Correlational Analysis, and Interpretation of Diet Diary Records of the Food and Fluid Intake of Free-Living Humans," *Appetite* 23(1994):179–192.

   A. Drewnowski and C. Hann, "Food Preferences and Reported Frequencies of Food Consumption as Predictors of Current Diet in Young Women," *American Journal of Clinical Nutrition* 70(1999):28–36.

   R. Mattes, "Hunger Ratings Are Not a Valid Proxy Measure of Reported Food Intake in Humans," *Appetite* 15(1990):103–113.

   M. Porrini, R. Crovetti, G. Testolin, and S. Silva, "Evaluation of Satiety Sensations and Food Intake after Different Preloads," *Appetite* 25(1995):17–30.

5. W. B. Cannon and A. L. Washburn, "An Explanation of Hunger," *The American Journal of Physiology* 29(1912):441–454.

6. W. B. Cannon, "Hunger and Thirst," in *The Foundations of Experimental Psychology*, ed. C. Murchison, Worcester, MA: Clark University Press, 1929.

7. E. Stellar, "The Physiology of Motivation," *Psychological Review* 61(1954):5–22.

   A. J. Stunkard and S. Fox, "The Relationship of Gastric Motility and Hunger: A Summary of the Evidence," *Psychosomatic Medicine* 33(1971):123–134.

8. Ibid.

9. J. Le Magnen, *Neurobiology of Feeding and Nutrition*, New York: Academic Press, 1992.

   T. L. Powley, "The Ventromedial Hypothalamic Syndrome, Satiety, and a Cephalic Phase Hypothesis," *Psychological Review* 84(1977):89–126.

10. G. M. Finch, J. E. L. Day, Razak, D. A. Welch, and P. J. Rogers, "Appetite Changes under Free-Living Conditions during Ramadan Fasting," *Appetite* 31(1998):159–170.

11. J. R. Brobeck, "Food Intake as a Mechanism of Temperature Regulation," *Journal of Biology and Medicine* 20(1948):545–552.

12. E. S. Kraly and E. M. Blass, "Increased Feeding in Rats in a Low Ambient Temperature," in *Hunger: Basic Mechanisms and Clinical Implications*, eds. D. Novin, W. Wyrwicka, and G. A. Bray, New York: Raven Press, 1976.

    Le Magnen, *Neurobiology of Feeding and Nutrition*.

13. H. D. Janowitz and M. I. Grossman, "Some Factors Affecting the Food Intake of Normal Dogs and Dogs with Esophagostomy and Gastric Fistula," *American Journal of Physiology* 159(1949):143–148.

14. G. P. Smith, "Pregastric and Gastric Satiety," in *Satiation: From Gut to Brain*, ed. G. P. Smith, New York: Oxford University Press, 1998.

15. P. J. Rogers and H. G. Schutz, "Influence of Palatability on Subsequent Hunger and Food Intake: A Retrospective Replication," *Appetite* 19(1992):155–156.

    M. G. Tordoff and M. I. Friedman, "Drinking Saccharin Increases Food Intake and Preference–IV. Cephalic Phase and Metabolic Factors," *Appetite* 12(1989):37–56.

    "Saccharin Consumption Increases Food Consumption in Rats," *Nutrition Reviews* 48(1990):163–165.

16. D. G. Mook and M. C. Votaw, "How Important Is Hedonism? Reasons Given by College Students for Ending a Meal," *Appetite* 18(1992):69–75.

17. Janowitz and Grossman, "Some Factors Affecting the Food Intake of Normal Dogs and Dogs with Esophagostomy and Gastric Fistula."

    H. D. Janowitz and F. Hollander, "Effect of Prolonged Intragastric Feeding on Oral Ingestion," *Federation Proceedings* 12(1953):72.

    I. Share and E. Martyniuk, "Effect of Prolonged Intragastric Feeding on Oral Food Intake in Dogs," *American Journal of Physiology* 169(1952):229–235.

18. S. J. French, "Intestinal Factors in Fat-Induced Satiety in Animals and Humans," *Appetite* 25(1995):298.

    M. Yao and S. B. Roberts, "Dietary Energy Density and Weight Regulation," *Nutrition Reviews* 59(2001):247–258.

19. B. J. Rolls, E. A. Bell, and M. L. Thorwart, "Water Incorporated into a Food but Not Served with a Food Decreases Energy Intake in Lean Women," *American Journal of Clinical Nutrition* 70(1999):448–455.

   B. J. Rolls, V. H. Castellanos, J. C. Halford, A. Kilara, D. Panyam, C. L. Pelkman, G. P. Smith, and M. L. Thorwart, "Volume of Food Consumed Affects Satiety in Men," *American Journal of Clinical Nutrition* 67(1998):1170–1177.

20. D. Greenberg, "Intestinal Satiety," in *Satiation: From Gut to Brain*, ed. G. P. Smith, New York: Oxford University Press, 1998.

   Smith, "Pregastric and Gastric Satiety."

21. J. Mayer, "The Glucostatic Theory of Regulation of Food Intake and the Problem of Obesity," *Bulletin of the New England Medical Center* 14(1952):43–49.

22. Ibid.

23. G. C. Kennedy, "The Role of Depot Fat in the Hypothalamic Control of Food Intake in the Rat," *Proceedings of the Royal Society of London*, 140B(1953):578–592.

   Mayer, "The Glucostatic Theory of Regulation of Food, Intake and the Problem of Obesity."

   J. Mayer, "Regulation of Energy Intake and the Body Weight: The Glucostatic Theory and the Lipostatic Hypothesis," *Annals New York Academy of Sciences* 63(1955):15–43.

24. J. M. Friedman, "The Function of Leptin in Nutrition, Weight, and Physiology," *Nutrition Reviews* 60(2002):S1–S14.

   T. Gura, "Obesity Sheds Its Secrets," *Science* 275(1997):751–753.

   J. Le Magnen, "Interactions of Glucostatic and Lipostatic Mechanisms in the Regulatory Control of Feeding," in *Hunger: Basic Mechanisms and Clinical Implications*, eds. D. Novin, W. Wyrwicka, and G. A. Bray, New York: Raven Press, 1976.

25. S. Ritter, "Glucoprivation and the Glucoprivic Control of Food Intake," in *Feeding Behavior: Neural and Humoral Controls*, eds. R. C. Ritter, S. Ritter, and C. D. Barnes, New York: Academic Press, 1986.

26. J. P. Flatt, "The Difference in the Storage Capacities for Carbohydrate and for Fat, and Its Implications in the Regulation of Body Weight," in *Human Obesity*, eds. R. J. Wurtman and J. J. Wurtman, New York: New York Academy of Sciences, 1987.

27. M. G. Tordoff and M. I. Friedman, "Hepatic Control of Feeding: Effect of Glucose, Fructose, and Mannitol Infusion," *American Journal of Physiology* 254 (Regulatory Integrative Comparative Physiology 23)(1988):R969–R976.

28. L. A. Campfield, "Metabolic and Hormonal Controls of Food Intake: Highlights of the Last 25 Years," *Appetite* 29(1997):135–152.

   L. A. Campfield and F. J. Smith, "Systemic Factors in the Control of Food Intake: Evidence for Patterns as Signals," in *Handbook of Behavioral Neurobiology: Vol. 10. Neurobiology of Food and Fluid Intake*, ed. E. M. Stricker, New York: Plenum, 1990.

29. D. A. Vanderweele, "Insulin as a Satiating Signal," in *Satiation: From Gut to Brain*, ed. G. P. Smith, New York: Oxford University Press, 1998.

30. G. P. Smith and J. Gibbs, "The Satiating Effects of Cholecystokinin and Bombesin-Like Peptides," in *Satiation: From Gut to Brain*, ed. G. P. Smith, New York: Oxford University Press, 1998.

31. A. Weller, G. P. Smith, and J. Gibbs, "Endogenous Cholecystokinin Reduces Feeding in Young Rats," *Science* 247(1990):1589–1591.

32. N. Geary, "Glucagon and the Control of Meal Size," in *Satiation: From Gut to Brain*, ed. G. P. Smith, New York: Oxford University Press, 1998.

33. C. De Graaf and T. Hulshof, "Effects of Weight and Energy Content of Preloads on Subsequent Appetite and Food Intake," *Appetite* 26(1996):139–151.

34. S. D. Poppitt and A. M. Prentice, "Energy Density and Its Role in the Control of Food Intake: Evidence from Metabolic and Community Studies," *Appetite* 26(1996):153–174.

35. J. D. Latner and M. Schwartz, "The Effects of a High-Carbohydrate, High-Protein or Balanced Lunch upon Later Food Intake and Hunger Ratings" *Appetite* 33(1999):119–128.

   Porrini, Crovetti, Testolin, and Silva, "Evaluation of Satiety Sensations and Food Intake after Different Preloads."

B. J. Rolls, I. C. Fedoroff, J. F. Guthrie, and L. J. Laster, "Foods with Different Satiating Effects in Humans," *Appetite* 15(1990):115–126.

A. Tournier and J. Louis-Sylvestre, "Effect of the Physical State of a Food on Subsequent Intake in Human Subjects," *Appetite* (1991):17–24.

36. Smith, "Pregastric and Gastric Satiety."

37. H. Bruch, "The Frölich Syndrome: Report of the Original Case," *American Journal of Diseases of Children* 58(1939):1282, 1283, 1285.

38. A. W. Hetherington and S. W. Ranson, "Hypothalamic Lesions and Adiposity in the Rat," *Anatomical Record* 78(1940):149–172.

39. B. G. Hoebel and P. Teitelbaum, "Hypothalamic Control of Feeding and Self-Stimulation," *Science* 135(1962):375–377.

40. J. Mayer and N. B. Marshall, "Specificity of Gold Thioglucose for Ventromedial Hypothalamic Lesions and Hyperphagia," *Nature* 178(1956):1399–1400.

41. B. K. Anand and J. R. Brobeck, "Localization of a 'Feeding Center' in the Hypothalamus of the Rat," *Proceedings of the Society for Experimental Biology and Medicine* 77(1951):323–324.

42. Hoebel and Teitelbaum, "Hypothalamic Control of Feeding and Self-Stimulation."

43. Stellar, "The Physiology of Motivation."

44. W. Wyrwicka, *Brain and Feeding Behavior*, Springfield, IL: Charles C. Thomas, 1988.

45. J. R. Stellar and E. Stellar, *The Neurobiology of Motivation and Reward*, New York: Springer-Verlag, 1985.

46. H. J. Grill and J. M. Kaplan, "Caudal Brainstem Participates in the Distributed Neural Control of Feeding," in *Handbook of Behavioral Neurobiology: Vol. 10. Neurobiology of Food and Fluid Intake*, ed. E. M. Stricker, New York: Plenum, 1990.

A. J. W. Scheurink, "Neuroscience of Energy Substrate Homeostasis," in *Food Intake and Energy Expenditure*, eds. M. S. Westerterp-Plantenga, E. W. H. M. Fredrix, and A. B. Steffens, Boca Raton, FL: CRC Press, 1994.

P. Winn, "The Lateral Hypothalamus and Motivated Behavior: An Old Syndrome Reassessed and a New Perspective Gained," *Current Directions in Psychological Science* 4(1995):182–187.

47. Winn, "The Lateral Hypothalamus and Motivated Behavior."

48. R. D. Myers and M. L. McCaleb, "Feeding: Satiety Signal from Intestine Triggers Brain's Noradrenergic Mechanism," *Science* 209(1980):1035–1037.

49. Stellar and Stellar, *The Neurobiology of Motivation and Reward*.

50. S. E. Leibowitz, "Hypothalamic Neurotransmitters in Relation to Normal and Disturbed Eating Patterns," in *Human Obesity*, eds. R. J. Wurtman and J. J. Wurtman, New York: New York Academy of Sciences, 1987.

K. J. Simansky, "Serotonin and the Structure of Satiation," in *Satiation: From Gut to Brain*, ed. G. P. Smith, New York: Oxford University Press, 1998.

51. M. M. Leguid, A. Laviano, and F. Rossi-Fanelli, "Food Intake Equals Meal Size Times Mean Number," *Appetite* 31(1998):404.

52. B. G. Stanley and E. R. Gillard, "Hypothalamic Neuropeptide Y and the Regulation of Eating Behavior and Body Weight," *Psychological Science* 3(1994):9–15.

53. M. Cabanac and D. Richard, "The Nature of the Ponderostat: Hervey's Hypothesis Revived," *Appetite* 26(1996):45–54.

54. A. H. Merrill, Jr., "Apo A-IV: A New Satiety Signal," *Nutrition Reviews* 51(1993):273–275.

55. L. A. Campfield, "Metabolic and Hormonal Controls of Food Intake: Highlights of the Last 25 Years."

S. C. Woods, "The Insulin Story: A 25-Year Perspective," *Appetite* 28(1997):281–282.

56. Gura, "Obesity Sheds Its Secrets."

S. C. Woods, R. J. Seeley, D. Porte, and M. W. Schwartz, "Signals that Regulate Food Intake and Energy Homeostasis," *Science* 280(1998):1378–1383.

57. Campfield, "Metabolic and Hormonal Controls of Food Intake."

T. H. Moran and E. E. Ladenheim, "Identification of Receptor Populations Mediating the Satiating Actions of Brain and Gut Peptides," in *Satiation: From Gut to Brain*, ed. G. P. Smith, New York: Oxford University Press, 1998.

58. J. A. Hogan, "Homeostasis and Behaviour," in *Analysis of Motivational Processes*, eds. E. M. Toates and T. R. Halliday, London: Academic Press, 1980.

59. S. Higgs, "Memory for Recent Eating and Its Influences on Subsequent Food Intake," *Appetite* 39(2002):159–166.

60. P. Rozin, S. Dow, M. Moscovitch, and S. Rajaram, "What Causes Humans to Begin and End a Meal? A Role for Memory for What Has Been Eaten, as Evidenced by a Study of Multiple Meal Eating in Amnesic Patients," *Psychological Science* 9(1998):392–396.

61. D. S. Ramsay, R. J. Seeley, R. C. Bolles, and S. C. Woods, "Ingestive Homeostasis: The Primacy of Learning," in *Why We Eat What We Eat: The Psychology of Eating*, ed. E. D. Capaldi, Washington, DC: American Psychological Association, 1996.

62. E. L. Gibson and D. D. Booth, "Food-Conditioned Odour Rejection in the Late Stages of the Meal, Mediating Learnt Control of Meal Volume by Aftereffects of Food Comsumption," *Appetite,* 34(2000):295–303.

63. L. L. Birch, L. McPhee, S. Sullivan, and S. Johnson, "Conditioned Meal Initiation in Young Children," *Appetite* 13(1989):105–113.

64. H. Bruch, *Eating Disorders*, New York: Basic Books, 1973.

65. Ibid.

66. G. Collier and D. F. Johnson, "Who Is in Charge? Animal vs. Experimenter Control," *Appetite* 29(1997):159–180.

    G. A. Lucas and W. Timberlake, "Interpellet Delay and Meal Patterns in the Rat," *Physiology and Behavior* 43(1988):259–264.

    J. E. R. Staddon, "Obesity and the Operant Regulation of Feeding," in *Analysis of Motivational Processes*, eds. E. M. Toates and T. R. Halliday, London: Academic Press, 1980.

67. D. A. Booth, "The Behavioral and Neural Sciences of Ingestion," in *Handbook of Behavioral Neurobiology: Vol. 10. Neurobiology of Food and Fluid Intake*, ed. E. M. Stricker, New York: Plenum, 1990.

    H. R. Kissileff, J. L. Guss, and L. J. Nolan, "What Animal Research Tells Us about Human Eating," in *Food Choice, Acceptance and Consumption*, eds. H. L. Meiselman and H. J. H. MacFie, New York: Blackie Academic & Professional, 1996.

    E. Stellar, "Brain and Behavior," in *Handbook of Behavioral Neurobiology: Vol. 10. Neurobiology of Food and Fluid Intake*, ed. E. M. Stricker, New York: Plenum, 1990.

    E. M. Stricker, "Homeostatic Origins of Ingestive Behavior," in *Handbook of Behavioral Neurobiology: Vol. 10. Neurobiology of Food and Fluid Intake*, ed. E. M. Stricker, New York: Plenum, 1990.

Chapter 3: *"You Never Miss the Water Till the Well Runs Dry"*

1. P. Rosenzweig, *The Book of Proverbs*, New York: Philosophical Library, 1965, p. 3.

2. F. Herbert, *Dune*, New York: Ace Books, 1965, p. 36.

3. H. A. Guthrie, *Introductory Nutrition*, Saint Louis: Mosby, 1975.

4. J. T. Fitzsimons, "Thirst and Sodium Appetite," in *Handbook of Behavioral Neurobiology: Vol. 10. Neurobiology of Food and Fluid Intake*, ed. E. M. Stricker, New York, Plenum, 1990.

5. E. F. Adolph, "Water Metabolism," *Annual Review of Physiology* 9(1947):381–408.

    N. Kleitman, "The Effect of Starvation on the Daily Consumption of Water by the Dog," *American Journal of Physiology* 81(1927):336–340.

6. D. Engell, "Interdependency of Food and Water Intake in Humans," *Appetite* 10(1988):133–141.

    S. Lepkovsky, R. Lyman, D. Fleming, M. Nagumo, and M. M. Dimick, "Gastrointestinal Regulation of Water and Its Effect on Food Intake and Rate of Digestion," *American Journal of Physiology* 188(1957):327–331.

7. Lepkovsky et al., "Gastrointestinal Regulation of Water and Its Effect on Food Intake and Rate of Digestion."

8. E. M. Stricker and J. G. Verbalis, "Hormones and Behavior: The Biology of Thirst and Sodium Appetite," *American Scientist* 76(3)(1988):261–267.

J. G. Verbalis, "Clinical Aspects of Body Fluid Homeostasis in Humans," in *Handbook of Behavioral Neurobiology: Vol. 10. Neurobiology of Food and Fluid Intake*, ed. E. M. Stricker, New York, Plenum, 1990.

9. B. J. Rolls and E. T. Rolls, *Thirst*, Cambridge, NY: Cambridge University Press, 1982.
10. Fitzsimons, "Thirst and Sodium Appetite."
11. Rolls and Rolls, *Thirst*.
12. Fitzsimons, "Thirst and Sodium Appetite."
E. M. Stricker, "Homeostatic Origins of Ingestive Behavior," in *Handbook of Behavioral Neurobiology: Vol. 10. Neurobiology of Food and Fluid Intake*, ed. E. M. Stricker, New York, Plenum, 1990.
13. Rolls and Rolls, *Thirst*.
14. J. E. Brody, *Jane Brody's The New York Times Guide to Personal Health,* New York: Avon Books, 1982.
15. K. Oatley, "Dissociation of the Circadian Drinking Pattern from Eating," *Nature* 229(1971):494–496
16. Engell, "Interdependency of Food and Water Intake in Humans."
17. Rolls and Rolls, *Thirst*.
18. Rosenzweig, *The Book of Proverbs*, p. 73.
19. R. S. Weisinger, "Conditioned and Pseudoconditioned Thirst and Sodium Appetite," in *Control Mechanisms of Drinking*, eds. G. Peters, J. T. Fitzsimons, and L. Peters-Haefeli, Berlin: Springer-Verlag, 1975.
20. J. L. Falk, "The Nature and Determinants of Adjunctive Behavior," *Physiology and Behavior* 6(1971):577–588.
21. T. F. Doyle and H. H. Samson, "Schedule-Induced Drinking in Humans: A Potential Factor in Excessive Alcohol Use," *Drug and Alcohol Dependence* 16(1985):117–132.
22. W. B. Cannon, "The Physiological Basis of Thirst," *Proceedings of the Royal Society*, London 90(1917–1918):283–301.
W. B. Cannon, "Hunger and Thirst," in *The Foundations of Experimental Psychology*, ed. C. Murchison, Worcester, MA: Clark University Press, 1929.
23. E. F. Adolph, *Physiology of Man in the Desert*, New York: Hafner, 1969.
24. Rolls and Rolls, *Thirst*.
25. N. E. Miller, R. I. Sampliner, and P. Woodrow, "Thirst-Reducing Effects of Water by Stomach Fistula vs. Water by Mouth Measured by Both a Consummatory and an Instrumental Response," *Journal of Comparative and Physiological Psychology* 50(1957):1–5.
26. K. Schmidt-Nielsen, "How Are Control Systems Controlled?" *American Scientist* 82(1994): 38–44.
27. Rolls and Rolls, *Thirst*.
28. R. T. Bellows, "Time Factors in Water Drinking in Dogs," *American Journal of Physiology* 125(1939):87–97.
29. M. F. Montgomery, "The Role of the Salivary Glands in the Thirst Mechanism," *American Journal of Physiology* 96(1931):221–227.
F. R. Steggerda, "Observations on the Water Intake in an Adult Man with Dysfunctioning Salivary Glands," *American Journal of Physiology* 132(1941):517–521.
30. S. C. Wooley and O. W. Wooley, "Salivation to the Sight and Thought of Food: A New Measure of Appetite," *Psychosomatic Medicine* 35(1973):136–142.
31. J. M. Brunstrom and A. W. Macrae, "Effects of Temperature and Volume on Measures of Mouth Dryness, Thirst and Stomach Fullness in Males and Females," *Appetite* 29(1997):21–42.
32. Fitzsimons, "Thirst and Sodium Appetite."
Rolls and Rolls, *Thirst*.
33. B. Andersson, "Polydipsia Caused by Intrahypothalamic Injections of Hypertonic NaCl-Solutions," *Experientia* 8(1952):157–158.
34. B. Andersson and S. M. McCann, "Drinking, Antidiuresis and Milk Ejection from Electrical Stimulation within the Hypothalamus of the Goat," *Acta Physiologica Scandinavica* 35(1955):191–201.

35. P. Teitelbaum, "Disturbances in Feeding and Drinking Behavior after Hypothalamic Lesions," in *Nebraska Symposium on Motivation*, ed. M. R. Jones, Lincoln: University of Nebraska Press, 1961.

   P. Teitelbaum and A. N. Epstein, "The Lateral Hypothalamic Syndrome: Recovery of Feeding and Drinking after Lateral Hypothalamic Lesions," *Psychological Review* 69(1962):74–90.

36. Rolls and Rolls, *Thirst.*

37. Fitzsimons, "Thirst and Sodium Appetite."

38. A. C. Guyton, "Blood Pressure Control—Special Role of the Kidneys and Body Fluids," *Science* 252(1991):1813–1816.

39. B. G. Hoebel, "Neuroscience and Appetitive Behavior Research: 25 Years," *Appetite* 29(1997): 119–133.

40. Rolls and Rolls, *Thirst.*

   P. J. Russell, A. E. Abdelaal, and G. J. Mogenson, "Graded Levels of Hemorrhage: Thirst and Angiotensin II in the Rat," *Physiology and Behavior* 15(1975):117–1179.

41. Fitzsimons, "Thirst and Sodium Appetite."

   Rolls and Rolls, *Thirst.*

42. I. Kupfermann, "Hypothalamus and Limbic System II: Motivation," in *Principles of Neural Science*, 2nd ed., eds. E. R. Kandel and J. H. Schwartz, New York: Elsevier, 1985.

43. Stricker and Verbalis, "Hormones and Behavior."

44. Falk, "The Nature and Determinants of Adjunctive Behavior."

45. E. S. Kraly, "Physiology of Drinking Elicited by Eating," *Psychological Review* 91(1984):478–490.

   E. S. Kraly, "Histamine: A Role in Normal Drinking," *Appetite* 6(1985):153–158.

46. M. Jijande, P. Lopez-Sela, J. I. Brime, R. Bernardo, F. Diaz, M. Costales, and B. Marin, "Insulin Stimulation of Water Intake in Humans," *Appetite* 15(1990):81–87.

47. Weisinger, "Conditioned and Pseudoconditioned Thirst and Sodium Appetite."

48. F. M. Toates, "Homeostasis and Drinking," *The Behavioural and Brain Sciences* 2(1979):95–139.

49. B. J. Rolls and P. A. Phillips, "Aging and Disturbances of Thirst and Fluid Balance," *Nutrition Reviews* 48(1990):137–144.

   A. J. Triana, V. Apanius, C. Richmond, and V. H. Castellanos, "Restricting Fluid Intake during a Single Meal Did Not Affect Food Intake in Older Adults," *Appetite* 41(2003):79–86.

50. R. Chernoff, "Thirst and Fluid Requirements," *Nutrition Reviews* 52(1994):S3–S5.

51. Rolls and Phillips, "Aging and Disturbances of Thirst and Fluid Balance."

52. R. S. Cooper, C. N. Rotimi, and R. Ward, "The Puzzle of Hypertension in African-Americans," *Scientific American* 280(2)(1999):56–63.

Chapter 4: The Nose Knows (and So Does the Tongue)

1. L. Bartoshuk, "Separate Worlds of Taste," *Psychology Today* 14(1980):48–49, 51, 54–56, 63.

2. The Fragrance Foundation, *New York* (November 13, 1995):133.

3. F. A. Geldard, *The Human Senses*, 2nd ed., New York: Wiley, 1972.

4. T. Engen, *The Perception of Odors*, New York: Academic Press, 1982.

5. V. B. Duffy and L. M. Bartoshuk, "Sensory Factors in Feeding," in *Why We Eat What We Eat: The Psychology of Eating*, ed. E. D. Capaldi, Washington, DC: American Psychological Association, 1996.

6. J. M. Auel, *The Clan of the Cave Bear*, Toronto: Bantam, 1980, p. 37.

7. J. Garcia, E. R. Ervin, and R. A. Koelling, "Learning with Prolonged Delay of Reinforcement," *Psychonomic Science* 5(1966):121–122.

8. C. Pfaffmann, M. Frank, and R. Norgren, "Neural Mechanisms and Behavioral Aspects of Taste," *Annual Review of Psychology* 3(1979):283–325.

9. M. I. Friedman and R. D. Mattes, "Chemical Senses and Nutrition," in *Smell and Taste in Health and Disease*, eds. T. V. Getchell, L. M. Bartoshuk, R. L. Doty, and J. B. Snow, New York: Raven Press, 1991.

10. J. E. Steiner, "Facial Expressions of the Neonate Infant Indicating the Hedonics of Food-Related Chemical Stimuli," in *Taste and Development*, ed. J. M. Weiffenbach, Bethesda, MD: U.S. Department of Health, Education, and Welfare, 1977.

11. L. M. Bartoshuk, "Taste," in *Stevens' Handbook of Experimental Psychology*, 2nd ed., vol.1, eds. R. C. Atkinson, R. J. Herrnstein, G. Lindzey, and R. D. Luce, New York: Wiley, 1988.
    Geldard, *The Human Senses*.

12. Ibid.

13. Bartoshuk, "Separate Worlds of Taste."

14. C. Pfaffmann, "Gustatory Nerve Impulses in Rat, Cat and Rabbit," *Journal of Neurophysiology* 18(1955):429–440.

15. K. Arvidson and U. Friberg, "Human Taste: Response and Taste Bud Number in Fungiform Papillae," *Science* 209(1980):807–808.

16. I. J. Miller and L. M. Bartoshuk, "Taste Perception, Taste Bud Distribution, and Spatial Relationships," in *Smell and Taste in Health and Disease*, eds. T. V. Getchell, L. M. Bartoshuk, R. L. Doty, and J. B. Snow, New York: Raven Press, 1991.

17. Pfaffmann, et al., "Neural Mechanisms and Behavioral Aspects of Taste."

18. S. McLaughlin and R. F. Margolskee, "The Sense of Taste," *American Scientist* 82(1994):538–545.

19. T. R. Scott and C. R. Plata-Salaman, "Coding of Taste Quality," in *Smell and Taste in Health and Disease*, eds. T. V. Getchell, L. M. Bartoshuk, R. L. Doty, and J. B. Snow, New York: Raven Press, 1991.

20. Pfaffmann, et al., "Neural Mechanisms and Behavioral Aspects of Taste."
    T. R. Scott, B. K. Giza, and J. Yan, "Electrophysiological Responses to Bitter Stimuli in Primate Cortex," in *Olfaction and Taste XII: An International Symposium*, ed. C. Murphy, New York: New York Academy of Sciences, 1998.
    Scott and Plata-Salaman, "Coding of Taste Quality."

21. Scott et al., "Electrophysiological Responses to Bitter Stimuli in Primate Cortex."

22. Bartoshuk, "Separate Worlds of Taste."
    L. M. Bartoshuk, G. P. Dateo, D. J. Vandenbelt, R. L. Buttrick, and L. Long, "Effects of Gymnema Sylvestre and Synsepalum Dulcificum on Taste in Man," in *Olfaction and Taste: Proceedings of the Third International Symposium*, ed. C. Pfaffman, New York: Rockefeller University Press, 1969.
    K. Kurihara, Y. Kurihara, and L. M. Beidler, "Isolation and Mechanism of Taste Modifiers: Taste-Modifying Protein and Gymnemic Acids," in *Olfaction and Taste: Proceedings of the Third International Symposium*, ed. C. Pfaffman, New York: Rockefeller University Press, 1969.

23. G. Borg, H. Diamant, B. Oakley, L. Strom, and Y. Zotterman, "A Comparative Study of Neural and Psychophysical Responses to Gustatory Stimuli," in *Olfaction and Taste II*, ed. T. Hayashi, Oxford, UK: Pergamon, 1963.

24. Bartoshuk, "Separate Worlds of Taste."
    Bartoshuk et al., "Effects of Gymnema Sylvestre and Synsepalum Dulcificum."
    G. J. Henning, J. N. Brouwer, H. van der Well, and A. Francke, "Miracle, the Sweetness-Inducing Principle from Miracle Fruit," in *Olfaction and Taste: Proceedings of the Third International Symposium*, ed. C. Pfaffman, New York: Rockefeller University Press, 1969.
    Kurihara et al., "Isolation and Mechanism of Taste Modifiers."

25. Bartoshuk, "Taste."

26. A. Caicedo and S. D. Roper, "Taste Receptor Cells that Discriminate between Bitter Stimuli," *Science* 291(2001):1557–1560.
    J. Chandrashekar, K. L. Mueller, M. A. Hoon, E. Adler, L. Feng, W. Guo, and C. S. Zuker, "T2Rs Function as Bitter Taste Receptors," *Cell* 100(2000):703–711.

27. D. V. Smith and R. F. Margolskee, "Making Sense of Taste," *Scientific American* (March 2001):32–39.

28. T. A. Gilbertson, D. Liu, D. A. York, and G. A. Bray, "Dietary Fat Preferences Are Inversely Corelated with Peripheral Gustatory Fatty Acid Sensitivity," in *Olfaction and Taste XII: An International Symposium*, ed. C. Murphy, New York: New York Academy of Sciences, 1998.

S. S. Schiffman, B. G. Graham, E. A. Sattely-Miller, and Z. S. Warwick, "Orosensory Perception of Dietary Fat," *Current Directions in Psychological Science* 7(1998):137–143.

29. J. E. Amoore, "Specific Anosmias," in *Smell and Taste in Health and Disease*, eds. T. V. Getchell, L. M. Bartoshuk, R. L. Doty, and J. B. Snow, New York: Raven Press, 1991.

30. M. Barinaga, "How the Nose Knows: Olfactory Receptor Cloned," *Science* 252(1991):209–210.

H. Zhao, L. Ivic, J. Otaki, M. Hashimoto, K. Mikoshiba, and S. Firestein, "Functional Expression of a Mammalian Odorant Receptor," *Science* 279(1998):237–242.

31. R. Axel, "The Molecular Logic of Smell," *Scientific American* (October 1995):154–159.

32. W. S. Cain, "Olfaction," in *Stevens' Handbook of Experimental Psychology*, 2nd ed., vol. 1, eds. R. C. Atkinson, R. J. Herrnstein, G. Lindzey, and R. D. Luce, New York: Wiley, 1988.

33. Axel, "The Molecular Logic of Smell."

B. D. Rubin and L. C. Katz, "Optical Imaging of Odorant Representations in the Mammalian Olfactory Bulb," *Neuron* 23(1999):499–511.

34. B. J. Doleman, E. J. Severin, and N. S. Lewis, "Trends in Odor Intensity for Human and Electronic Noses: Relative Roles of Odorant Vapor Pressure vs. Molecularly Specific Odorant Binding," *Proceedings of the National Academy of Sciences* 95(1998):5442–5447.

M. S. Freund and N. S. Lewis, "A Chemically Diverse Conducting Polymer-Based 'Electronic Nose,' " *Proceedings of the National Academy of Sciences* 92(1995):2652–2656.

35. G. K. Beauchamp and J. R. Mason, "Comparative Hedonics of Taste," in *The Hedonics of Taste*, ed. R. C. Bolles, Hillsdale, NJ: Lawrence Erlbaum Associates, 1991.

36. G. Nevitt, "Foraging by Seabirds in an Olfactory Landscape," *American Scientist* 87(1999):46–53.

37. C. J. Wysocki, J. D. Pierce, and A. N. Gilbert, "Geographic, Cross-Cultural, and Individual Variation in Human Olfaction," in *Smell and Taste in Health and Disease*, eds. T. V. Getchell, L. M. Bartoshuk, R. L. Doty, and J. B. Snow, New York: Raven Press, 1991.

38. L. M. Bartoshuk, "Bitter Taste of Saccharin Related to the Genetic Ability to Taste the Bitter Substance 6-N-Propylthiouracil," *Science* 205(1979):934–935

Bartoshuk, "Taste."

A. Drewnowski, S. A. Henderson, and A. B. Shore, "Taste Responses to Naringin, a Flavonoid, and the Acceptance of Grapefruit Juice Are Related to Genetic Sensitivity to 6-N-Propylthiouracil," *American Journal of Clinical Nutrition* 66(1997):391–397.

A. Drewnowski, S. A. Henderson, A. B. Shore, and A. Barratt-Fornell, "Sensory Responses to 6-N-Propylthiouracil (PROP), or Sucrose Solutions and Food Preferences in Young Women," in *Olfaction and Taste XII: An International Symposium*, ed. C. Murphy, New York: New York Academy of Sciences, 1998.

H. Kalmus, "Inherited Sense Defects," *Scientific American* 186(5)(1952):64–70.

K. L. Keller, L. Steinmann, R. J. Nurse, and B. J. Tepper, "Genetic Taste Sensitivity to 6-N-Propylthiouracil Influences Food Preference and Reported Intake in Preschool Children," *Appetite* 38(2002):3–12.

39. L. M. Bartoshuk and V. B. Duffy, "Supertasting and Earaches: Genetics and Pathology Alter Our Taste Worlds," *Appetite* 23(1994):292–293.

U. Kim, E. Jorgenson, H. Coon, M. Leppert, N. Risch, and D. Drayna, "Positional Cloning of the Human Quantitative Trait Locus Underlying Taste Sensitivity to Phenylthiocarbamide," *Science* 299(2003):1221–1225.

40. Kalmus, "Inherited Sense Defects."

41. S.-W. Guo, F.-M. Shen, Y.-D. Wang, and C.-J. Zheng, "Threshold Distributions of Phenylthiocarbamide (PTC) in the Chinese Population," in *Olfaction and Taste XII: An International Symposium*, ed. C. Murphy, New York: New York Academy of Sciences, 1998.

42. Bartoshuk and Duffy, "Supertasting and Earaches."

43. M. Proust, *Swann's Way*, New York: Vintage Books, 1970, p. 36.

44. W. S. Cain, "To Know with the Nose: Keys to Odor Identification," *Science* 203(1979):467–470.

M. D. Rabin and W. S. Cain, "Odor Recognition: Familiarity, Identifiability, and Encoding Consistency," *Journal of Experimental Psychology: Learning, Memory, and Cognition* 10(1984):316–325.

45. R. S. Herz and T. Engen, "Odor Memory: Review and Analysis," *Psychonomic Bulletin & Review* 3(1996):300–313.

46. R. S. Herz, "Emotion Experienced during Encoding Enhances Odor Retrieval Cue Effectiveness," *American Journal of Psychology* 110(1997):489–505.

47. P. Pliner and C. Steverango, "Effect of Induced Mood on Memory for Flavors," *Appetite* 22(1994):135–148.

48. R. L. Doty, L. M. Bartoshuk, and J. B. Snow, "Causes of Olfactory and Gustatory Disorders," in *Smell and Taste in Health and Disease*, eds. T. V. Getchell, L. M. Bartoshuk, R. L. Doty, and J. B. Snow, New York: Raven Press, 1991.

49. J. C. Stevens, W. S. Cain, A. Demarque, and A. M. Ruthruff, "On the Discrimination of Missing Ingredients: Aging and Salt Flavor," *Appetite* 16(1991):129–140.

50. M. L. Pelchat, "You Can Teach an Old Dog New Tricks: Olfaction and Responses to Novel Foods by the Elderly," *Appetite* 35(2000):153–160.

51. J. M. Weiffenbach, "Chemical Senses in Aging," in *Smell and Taste in Health and Disease*, eds. T. V. Getchell, L. M. Bartoshuk, R. L. Doty, and J. B. Snow, New York: Raven Press, 1991.

52. T. Engen, *Odor Sensation and Memory*, New York: Praeger, 1991.
   H. J. Hoffman, E. K. Ishii, and R. H. Macturk, "Age-Related Changes in the Prevalence of Smell-Taste Problems among the United States Adult Population," in *Olfaction and Taste XII: An International Symposium*, ed. C. Murphy, New York: New York Academy of Sciences, 1998.
   Weiffenbach, "Chemical Senses in Aging."

53. Weiffenbach, "Chemical Senses in Aging."

54. M. E. Briley, "Food Preferences of the Elderly," *Nutrition Reviews* 52(1994):S21–S23.
   Friedman and Mattes, "Chemical Senses and Nutrition."

55. R. L. Doty, P. Shaman, S. L. Applebaum, R. Giberson, L. Siksorski, and L. Rosenberg, "Smell Identification Ability: Changes with Age" *Science* 226(1984):1441–1443.

56. Stevens et al., "On the Discrimination of Missing Ingredients."

57. T. Hummel, C. Rothbauer, S. Barz, K. Grosser, E. Pauli, and G. Kobal, "Olfactory Function in Acute Rhinitis," in *Olfaction and Taste XII: An International Symposium*, ed. C. Murphy, New York: New York Academy of Sciences, 1998.

58. R. D. Fowler, "A Matter of Taste," *APA Monitor* (May 1997):3.

59. T. R. Scott, "The Role of Taste in Feeding," *Appetite* 37(2001):111–113.

Chapter 5: Genes Rule—Or Do They?

1. U.S. Department of Agriculture and U.S. Department of Health and Human Services, *Nutrition and Your Health: Dietary Guidelines for Americans*, 4th ed., 1995. Available at: http://www.nalusda.gov/fnic/dga/dga95.html.

2. J. Money and A. A. Ehrhardt, *Man and Woman, Boy and Girl*, Baltimore, MD: Johns Hopkins University Press, 1972.

3. C. Pfaffmann, "Biological and Behavioral Substrates of the Sweet Tooth," in *Taste and Development*, ed. J. M. Weiffenbach, Bethesda, MD: U.S. Department of Health, Education, and Welfare, 1977.

4. J. Brody, *Jane Brody's Nutrition Book*, New York: Norton, 1981.
   K. K. Kiple and K. C. Omelas, eds., *The Cambridge World History of Food*, Cambridge, UK: Cambridge University Press, 2000.
   Pfaffmann, "Biological and Behavioral Substrates of the Sweet Tooth."

5. P. Rozin, "Human Food Selection: The Interaction of Biology, Culture and Individual Experience," in *The Psychobiology of Human Food Selection*, ed. L. M. Barker, Westport, CT: AVI Publishing, 1982.

6. J. E. Brody, "Drunk on Liquid Candy, U.S. Overdoses on Sugar," *The New York Times* (November 24, 1998):F7.

7. H. A. Guthrie, *Introductory Nutrition*, St. Louis: Mosby, 1975.

8. T. R. Maone, R. D. Mattes, J. C. Bernbaum, and G. K. Beauchamp, "A New Method for Delivering a Taste without Fluids to Preterm and Term Infants," *Developmental Psychobiology* 23(1990):179–191.

9. J. E. Steiner, "Facial Expressions of the Neonate Infant Indicating the Hedonics of Food-Related Chemical Stimuli," in *Taste and Development*, ed. J. M. Weiffenbach, Bethesda, MD: U.S. Department of Health, Education, and Welfare, 1977, pp. 174–175.

10. H. J. Grill and R. Norgren, "Chronically Decerebrate Rats Demonstrate Satiation but Not Bait Shyness," *Science* 201(1978):267–269.

11. N. W. Jerome, "Taste Experience and the Development of a Dietary Preference for Sweet in Humans: Ethnic and Cultural Variations in Early Taste Experience," in *Taste and Development*, ed. J. M. Weiffenbach, Bethesda, MD: U.S. Department of Health, Education, and Welfare, 1977.

12. R. R. Bell, H. H. Draper, and J. G. Bergan, "Sucrose, Lactose, and Glucose Tolerance in Northern Alaskan Eskimos," *The American Journal of Clinical Nutrition* 26(1973):1185–1190.

13. Jerome, "Taste Experience and the Development of a Dietary Preference for Sweet in Humans."

14. G. K. Beauchamp and M. Moran, "Dietary Experience and Sweet Taste Preference in Human Infants," *Appetite* 3(1982):139–152.

15. J. J. Wurtman and R. J. Wurtman, "Sucrose Consumption Early in Life Fails to Modify the Appetite of Adult Rats for Sweet Foods," *Science* 205(1979):321–322.

16. J. A. Desor and G. K. Beauchamp, "Longitudinal Changes in Sweet Preferences in Humans," *Physiology and Behavior* 39(1987):639–641.

    J. A. Desor, L. S. Greene, and O. Maller, "Preferences for Sweet and Salty in 9- to 15-Year Old and Adult Humans," *Science* 190(1975):686–687.

    A. W. Logue and M. E. Smith, "Predictors of Food Preferences in Humans," *Appetite* 7(1986):109–125.

    Wurtman and Wurtman, "Sucrose Consumption Early in Life Fails to Modify the Appetite of Adult Rats for Sweet Foods."

17. Desor et al., "Preferences for Sweet and Salty in 9- to 15-Year Old and Adult Humans."

18. M. T. Conner and D. A. Booth, "Preferred Sweetness of a Lime Drink and Preference for Sweet over Non-Sweet Foods, Related to Sex and Reported Age and Body Weight," *Appetite* 10(1988):25–35.

    Logue and Smith, "Predictors of Food Preferences in Humans."

    S. Parker, N. Kamel, and D. Zellner, "Food Craving Patterns in Egypt: Comparisons with North America and Spain," *Appetite* 40(2003):193–195.

    H. Tuorila-Ollikainen and S. Mahlamaki-Kultanen, "The Relationship of Attitudes and Experiences of Finnish Youths to Their Hedonic Responses to Sweetness in Soft Drinks," *Appetite* 6(1985):115–124.

19. S. Damak, M. Rong, K. Yasumatsu, Z. Kokrashvili, V. Varadarajan, S. Zou, P. Jiang, Y. Ninomiya, and R. F. Margolskee, "Detection of Sweet and Umami Taste in the Absence of Taste Receptor T1r3," *Science* 301(2003):850–853.

    M. Frank, "The Distinctiveness of Responses to Sweet in the Chorda Tympani Nerve," in *Taste and Development*, ed. J. M. Weiffenbach, Bethesda, MD: U.S. Department of Health, Education, and Welfare, 1977.

20. R. Coopersmith and M. Leon, "Enhanced Neural Response to Familiar Olfactory Cues," *Science* 225(1984):849–851.

21. Bell et al., "Sucrose, Lactose, and Glucose Tolerance in Northern Alaskan Eskimos."

    R. H. Larson, "Sugar Ingestion and Caries," in *Taste and Development*, ed. J. M. Weiffenbach, Bethesda, MD: U.S. Department of Health, Education, and Welfare, 1977.

22. L. L. Birch, "Children's Food Preferences: Developmental Patterns and Environmental Influences," in *Annals of Child Development*, vol. 4, ed. R. Vasta, Greenwich, CT: JAI Press, 1987.

    B. G. Galef, "Mechanisms for the Transmission of Acquired Patterns of Feeding from Adult to Weanling Rats," in *Taste and Development*, ed. J. M. Weiffenbach, Bethesda, MD: U.S. Department of Health, Education, and Welfare, 1977.

B. G. Galef, "Communication of Information Concerning Distant Diets in a Social, Central -Place Foraging Species: *Rattus Norvegicus*," in *Social Learning: Psychological and Biological Perspectives*, eds. T. R. Zentall and B. G. Galef, Hillsdale, NJ: Lawrence Erlbaum Associates, 1988.

23. J. Yudkin, "Patterns and Trends in Carbohydrate Consumption and Their Relation to Disease," *Nutrition Society Proceedings* 23(1964):149–162.

24. G. K. Beauchamp and B. J. Cowart, "Congenital and Experiential Factors in the Development of Human Flavor Preferences," *Appetite* 6(1985):357–372.

25. E. M. Blass, "The Ontogeny of Motivation: Opioid Bases of Energy Conservation and Lasting Affective Change in Rat and Human Infants," *Current Directions in Psychological Science* 1(1992):116–120.

26. M. Nachman, "The Inheritance of Saccharin Preference," *Journal of Comparative and Physiological Psychology* 52(1959):451–457.

27. L. S. Greene, J. A. Desor, and O. Maller, "Heredity and Experience: Their Relative Importance in the Development of Taste Preference in Man," *Journal of Comparative and Physiological Psychology* 89(1975):279–284.

    M. Krondl, P. Coleman, J. Wade, and J. Milner, "A Twin Study Examining the Genetic Influence on Food Selection," *Human Nutrition: Applied Nutrition* 37A(1983):189–198.

28. Greene et al., "Heredity and Experience."

29. D. Denton, *The Hunger for Salt*, New York: Springer-Verlag, 1982.

    J. Schulkin, *Sodium Hunger: The Search for a Salty Taste*, New York: Cambridge University Press, 1991.

30. L. M. Bartoshuk and G. K. Beauchamp, "Chemical Senses," *Annual Review of Psychology* 45(1994):419–449.

31. M. R. Bloch, "The Social Influence of Salt," in *Human Nutrition*, San Francisco: W. H. Freeman, 1978.

    Denton, *The Hunger for Salt.*

32. Bloch, "The Social Influence of Salt."

33. Denton, *The Hunger for Salt.*

34. A. N. Epstein, "Prospectus: Thirst and Salt Appetite," in *Handbook of Behavioral Neurobiology: Vol. 10. Neurobiology of Food and Fluid Intake*, ed. E. M. Stricker, New York: Plenum, 1990.

    N. E. Rowland, "Sodium Appetite," in *Taste, Experience, and Feeding*, eds. E. D. Capaldi and T. L. Powley, Washington, DC: American Psychological Association, 1990.

35. A. N. Epstein, "Hormonal Synergy as the Cause of Salt Appetite," in *The Physiology of Thirst and Sodium Appetite*, eds. G. de Caro, A. N. Epstein, and M. Massi, New York: Plenum, 1986.

    M. Massi and A. N. Epstein, "Angiotensin/Aldosterone Synergy Governs the Salt Appetite of the Pigeon," *Appetite* 14(1990):181–192.

36. U. Roze, "How to Select, Climb, and Eat a Tree," *Natural History* (May 1985):63–69.

37. R. J. Contreras and M. Frank, "Sodium Deprivation Alters Neural Responses to Gustatory Stimuli," *The Journal of General Physiology* 73(1979):569–594.

38. T. R. Scott and B. K. Giza, "Coding Channels in the Taste System of the Rat," *Science* 249(1990):1585–1587.

39. B. G. Galef, "Social Interaction Modifies Learned Aversions, Sodium Appetite, and Both Palatability and Handling-Time Induced Dietary Preference in Rats (*Rattus Norvegicus*)," *Journal of Comparative Psychology* 100(1986):432–439.

40. L. Wilkins and C. P. Richter, "A Great Craving for Salt by a Child with Cortico-Adrenal Insufficiency," *Journal of the American Medical Association* 114(1940):866–868.

41. Desor et al., "Preferences for Sweet and Salty, in 9- to 15-Year Old and Adult Humans."

42. Y. Dejima, S. W. Kim, H. Kashiwazaki, and T. Suzuki, "A Spontaneous Increase of Salt Intake and Changes of Colonic Temperature in Mice Exposed to Cold," *Appetite* 16(1991):169–191.

43. M. Leshem, A. Abutbul, and R. Eilon, "Exercise Increases the Preference for Salt in Humans," *Appetite* 32(1999):251–260.

44. Epstein, "Prospectus."

45. J. P. Midgley, A. G. Matthew, C. M. T. Greenwood, and A. G. Logan, "Effect of Reduced Dietary Sodium on Blood Pressure: A Meta-Analysis of Randomized Controlled Trials," *Journal of the American Medical Association* 25(1996):1590–1597.

U.S. Department of Agriculture and U.S. Department of Health and Human Services, *Nutrition and Your Health.*

46. P. Elliott, J. Stamler, R. Nichols, A. R. Dyer, R. Stamler, H. Kesteloot, and M. Marmot, "Intersalt Revisited: Further Analyses of 24 Hour Sodium Excretion and Blood Pressure within and across Populations," *British Medical Journal* 312(1996):1249–1253.

Midgley et al., "Effect of Reduced Dietary Sodium on Blood Pressure."

G. Taubes, "The (Political) Science of Salt," *Science* 281(1998):898–901, 903–907.

47. G.K. Beauchamp, "The Human Preference for Excess Salt," *American Scientist* 75(1)(1987): 27–33.

48. R. L. Huggins, R. Di Nicolantonio, and T. O. Morgan, "Preferred Salt Levels and Salt Taste Acuity in Human Subjects after Ingestion of Untasted Salt," *Appetite* 18(1992):111–119.

49. N. Ayya and G. K. Beauchamp, "Short-Term Effects of Diet on Salt Taste Preference," *Appetite* 18(1992):77–82.

50. N. Kretchmer, "Lactose and Lactase," in *Human Nutrition*, San Francisco: W. H. Freeman, 1978.

51. Ibid.

52. Ibid.

F. J. Simoons, "Geography and Genetics as Factors in the Psychobiology of Human Food Selection," in *The Psychobiology of Human Food Selection*, ed. L. M. Barker, Westport, CT: AVI Publishing, 1982.

53. Kretchmer, "Lactose and Lactase."

54. Ibid.

55. "Season, Latitude, and Ability of Sunlight to Promote Synthesis of Vitamin D3 in Skin," *Nutrition Reviews* 47(1989):252–253.

56. Simoons, "Geography and Genetics as Factors in the Psychobiology of Human Food Selection."

57. U.S. Department of Agriculture and U.S. Department of Health and Human Services, *Nutrition and Your Health.*

58. D. France, "Groups Debate Role of Milk in Building a Better Pyramid," *The New York Times* (June 19, 1999):F7.

59. J. A. Anliker, L. Bartoshuk, A. M. Ferris, and L. D. Hooks, "Children's Food Preferences and Genetic Sensitivity to the Bitter Taste of 6-*N*-Propylthiouracil (PROP)," *American Journal of Clinical Nutrition* 54(1991):316–320.

60. R. Wrangham, "The Taste of Birds: *Pitohui!*" *Science* 258(1992):1867.

61. Steiner, "Facial Expressions of the Neonate Infant Indicating the Hedonics of Food-Related Chemical Stimuli," p.175.

62. Ibid.

63. Grill and Norgren, "Chronically Decerebrate Rats Demonstrate Satiation but Not Bait Shyness."

64. F. A. Geldard, *The Human Senses*, 2nd ed, New York: Wiley, 1972.

E. V. Glanville and A. R. Kaplan, "Food Preference and Sensitivity of Taste for Bitter Compounds," *Nature* 205(1965):851–853.

Rozin, "Human Food Selection."

65. D. I. Lozano, S. L. Crites, and S. N. Aikman, "Changes in Food Attitudes as a Function of Hunger," *Appetite* 32(1999):207–218.

G. D. Mower, R. G. Mair, and T. Engen, "Influence of Internal Factors on the Perceived Intensity and Pleasantness of Gustatory and Olfactory Stimuli," in *The Chemical Senses and Nutrition*, eds. M. R. Kare and O. Maller, New York: Academic Press, 1977.

66. J. J. Wurtman, "Neurotransmitter Regulation of Protein and Carbohydrate Consumption," in *Nutrition and Behavior*, ed. S. A. Miller, Philadelphia: Franklin Institute, 1981.

R. J. Wurtman and J. J. Wurtman, "Nutrients, Neurotransmitter Synthesis, and the Control of Food Intake," in *Eating and Its Disorders*, eds. A. J. Stunkard and E. Stellar, New York: Raven Press, 1984.

R. J. Wurtman and J. J. Wurtman, "Do Carbohydrates Affect Food Intake via Neurotransmitter Activity?" *Appetite* 11(Supplement)(1988):42–47.

67. J. D. Fernstrom, "Food-Induced Changes in Brain Serotonin Synthesis: Is There a Relationship to Appetite for Specific Macronutrients?" *Appetite* 8(1987):163–182.

S. F. Leibowitz and G. Shor-Posner, "Brain Serotonin and Eating Behavior," *Appetite* 7(Supplement)(1986):1–14.

68. M. Zuckerman, *Sensation Seeking: Beyond the Optimal Level of Arousal*, Hillsdale, NJ: Lawrence Erlbaum Associates, 1979.

69. Logue and Smith, "Predictors of Food Preferences in Humans."

70. M. Zuckerman, ed., *Biological Bases of Sensation Seeking, Impulsivity, and Anxiety*, Hillsdale, NJ: Lawrence Erlbaum Associates, 1983.

Chapter 6: One Person's Meat Is Another Person's Poison

1. S. W. Mintz, *Tasting Food, Tasting Freedom: Excursions into Eating, Culture, and the Past*, Boston: Beacon Press, 1996, p. 8.

2. M. R. Berenbaum, *Bugs in the System: Insects and Their Impact on Human Affairs*, Reading, MA: Addison-Wesley, 1995.

3. P. D. Balsam, J. D. Deich, and R. Hirose, "The Roles of Experience in the Transition from Dependent to Independent Feeding in Ring Doves," in *Developmental Psychobiology*, ed. G. Turkewitz, New York: New York Academy of Sciences, 1992.

    B. G. Galef, "Weaning from Mother's Milk to Solid Foods: The Developmental Psychobiology of Self-Selection of Foods by Rats," in *Developmental Psychobiology*, ed. G. Turkewitz, New York: New York Academy of Sciences, 1992.

    J. A. Mennella and G. K. Beauchamp, "Early Flavor Experiences: Research Update," *Nutrition Reviews* 56(1998):205–211.

4. P. Rozin, "The Selection of Foods by Rats, Humans, and Other Animals," in *Advances in the Study of Behavior*, vol. 6, eds. J. S. Rosenblatt, R. A. Hinde, E. Shaw, and C. Beer, New York: Academic Press, 1976.

5. K. Schmidt-Nielsen, "How Are Control Systems Controlled?" *American Scientist* 82(1994): 38–44.

6. C. P. Richter, "Total Self Regulatory Functions in Animals and Human Beings," *The Harvey Lecturers* 38(1942–1943):63–103.

7. C. M. Davis, "Self Selection of Diet by Newly Weaned Infants," *American Journal of Disease of Children* 36(1928):651–679.

    C. M. Davis, "Can Babies Choose Their Food?" *The Parents' Magazine* (January 1930):22, 23, 42, 43.

    C. M. Davis, "Results of the Self-Selection of Diets by Young Children," *The Canadian Medical Association Journal* (September 1939):257–261.

8. W. F. Hill, "Effects of Mere Exposure on Preferences in Nonhuman Animals," *Psychological Bulletin* 85(1978):1177–1198.

9. Hill, "Effects of Mere Exposure on Preferences in Nonhuman Animals."

    R. B. Zajonc, "Attitudinal Effects of Mere Exposure," *Journal of Personality and Social Psychology* (Monograph Supplement 9) (No. 2, Part 2)(1968):1–27.

10. A. Arvola, L. Lähteenmäki, and H. Tuorila, "Predicting the Intent to Purchase Unfamiliar and Familiar Cheeses: The Effects of Attitudes, Expected Liking and Food Neophobia," *Appetite* 32(1999):113–126.

    B. Raudenbush and R. A. Frank, "Assessing Food Neophobia: The Role of Stimulus Familiarity," *Appetite* 32(1999):261–271.

11. P. Pliner, "The Effects of Mere Exposure on Liking for Edible Substances," *Appetite* 2(1982):283–290.

12. L. L. Birch, L. McPhee, B. C. Shoba, E. Pirok, and L. Steinberg, "What Kind of Exposure Reduces Children's Food Neophobia," *Appetite* 9(1987):171–178.

13. L. L. Birch and M. Deysher, "Caloric Compensation and Sensory Specific Satiety: Evidence for Self Regulation of Food Intake by Young Children," *Appetite* 7(1986):323–331.

    Hill, "Effects of Mere Exposure on Preferences in Nonhuman Animals."

    E. H. Zandstra, C. De Graaf, and H. C. M. Van Trijp, "Effects of Variety and Repeated In-Home Consumption on Product Acceptance," *Appetite* 35(2000):113–119

14. D. J. Stang, "When Familiarity Breeds Contempt, Absence Makes the Heart Grow Fonder: Effects of Exposure and Delay on Taste Pleasantness Ratings," *Bulletin of the Psychonomic Society* 6(1975):273–275.

15. B. J. Rolls, E. T. Rolls, and E. A. Rowe, "The Influence of Variety on Human Food Selection and Intake," in *The Psychobiology of Human Food Selection*, ed. L. M. Barker, Westport, CT: AVI Publishing, 1982.

16. B. J. Rolls, "Experimental Analyses of the Effects of Variety in a Meal on Human Feeding," *The American Journal of Clinical Nutrition* 42(1985):932–939.

17. P. Rozin, "Specific Aversions as a Component of Specific Hungers," in *Biological Boundaries of Learning*, eds. M. E. P. Seligman and J. L. Hager, New York: Appleton-Century-Crofts, 1972.

18. American Psychiatric Association, *Diagnostic and Statistical Manual of Mental Disorders* (Rev. ed.), 4th ed., Washington, DC: APA, 2000.

    M. Cooper, *Pica*, Springfield, IL: Charles C. Thomas, 1957.

    Rozin, "The Selection of Foods by Rats, Humans, and Other Animals"

19. Rozin, "The Selection of Foods by Rats, Humans, and Other Animals."

20. Rozin, "Specific Aversions as a Component of Specific Hungers."

21. E. D. Capaldi, "Conditioned Food Preferences," in *Why We Eat What We Eat: The Psychology of Eating*, ed. E. D. Capaldi, Washington, DC: American Psychological Association, 1996.

    A. Sclafani, "Learned Controls of Ingestive Behaviour," *Appetite* 29(1997):153–158.

22. Rozin, "The Selection of Foods by Rats, Humans, and Other Animals."

23. E. L. Gibson and J. Wardle, "Energy Density Predicts Preferences for Fruit and Vegetables in 4-Year-Old Children," *Appetite* 41(2003):97–98.

24. D. A. Booth, P. Mather, and J. Fuller, "Starch Content of Ordinary Foods Associatively Conditions Human Appetite and Satiation, Indexed by Intake and Eating Pleasantness of Starch-Paired Flavours," *Appetite* 3(1982):163–184.

25. L. L. Birch and M. Deysher, "Conditioned and Unconditioned Caloric Compensation: Evidence for Self Regulation of Food Intake in Young Children," *Learning and Motivation* 16(1985): 341–355.

26. U.S. Department of Agriculture and U.S. Department of Health and Human Services. *Nutrition and Your Health: Dietary Guidelines for Americans*, 1995. Available at: http://www.nalusda.gov/fnic/dga/dga95.html.

27. A. W. Logue, I. Ophir, and K. E. Strauss, "The Acquisition of Taste Aversions in Humans," *Behaviour Research and Therapy* 19(1981):319–333.

28. A. W. Logue, "Taste Aversion and the Generality of the Laws of Learning," *Psychological Bulletin* 86(1979):276–296.

    M. L. Pelchat and P. Rozin, "The Special Role of Nausea in the Acquisition of Food Dislikes by Humans," *Appetite* 3(1982):341–351.

    Rozin, "The Selection of Foods by Rats, Humans, and Other Animals."

29. S. A. Barnett, *The Rat: A Study in Behavior*, Chicago: Aldine, 1963.

30. M. E. P. Seligman and J. L. Hager, eds., *Biological Boundaries of Learning*, New York: Appleton-Century-Crofts, 1972.

31. J. Garcia, D. J. Kimeldorf, and R. A. Koelling, "Conditioned Aversion to Saccharin Resulting from Exposure to Gamma Radiation," *Science* 122(1955):157–158.

32. M. Nachman and J. H. Ashe, "Learned Taste Aversions in Rats as a Function of Dosage, Concentration, and Route of Administration of LiCl," *Physiology and Behavior* 10(1973):73–78.

33. C. S. Mellor and H. P. White, "Taste Aversions to Alcoholic Beverages Conditioned by Motion Sickness," *American Journal of Psychology* 135(1978):125–126.

34. S. Lamon, G. T. Wilson, and R. C. Leaf, "Human Classical Aversion Conditioning: Nausea versus Electric Shock in the Reduction of Target Beverage Consumption," *Behaviour Research and Therapy* 15(1977):313–320.

35. J. Garcia and R. A. Koelling, "Relation of Cue to Consequence in Avoidance Learning," *Psychonomic Science* 4(1966):123–124.

36. B. M. Slotnick, F. Westbrook, and F. M. C. Darling, "What the Rat's Nose Tells the Rat's Mouth: Long Delay Aversion Conditioning with Aqueous Odors and Potentiation of Taste by Odors," *Animal Learning and Behavior* 25(1997):357–369.

37. F. Etscorn and R. Stephens, "Establishment of Conditioned Taste Aversions with a 24-Hour CS-US Interval," *Physiological Psychology* 1(1973):251–253.

38. J. Garcia, B. K. McGowan, and K. F. Green, "Biological Constraints on Conditioning," in *Biological Boundaries of Learning*, eds. M. E. P. Seligman and J. L. Hager, New York: Appleton-Century-Crofts, 1972.

   H. Hoffmann, P. Hunt, and N. E. Spear, "Ontogenetic Differences in CS Palatability Following Conditioned Taste Aversion Training," *Learning and Motivation* 22(1991):329–352.

39. J. Garcia and A. R. Gustavson, "Carl R. Gustavson (1946–1996) Pioneering Wildlife Psychologist," *APS Observer* (January 1997):34–35.

   C. R. Gustavson, "Comparative and Field Aspects of Learned Food Aversions," in *Learning Mechanisms in Food Selection*, eds. L. M. Barker, M. R. Best, and M. Domjan, Waco, TX: Baylor University Press, 1977.

   C. R. Gustavson, L. P. Brett, J. Garcia, and D. J. Kelly, "A Working Model and Experimental Solutions to the Control of Predatory Behavior," in *Behavior of Captive Wild Animals*, eds. H. Markowitz and V. J. Stevens, Chicago: Nelson-Hall, 1978.

40. F. Baeyens, P. Eelen, O. Van den Bergh, and G. Crombez, "Flavor-Flavor and Color-Flavor Conditioning in Humans," *Learning and Motivation* 21(1990):434–455.

   M. S. Fanselow and J. Birk, "Flavor-Flavor Associations Induce Hedonic Shifts in Taste Preference," *Animal Learning and Behavior* 10(1982):223–228.

41. D. A. Zellner, P. Rozin, M. Aron, and C. Kulish, "Conditioned Enhancement of Human's Liking for Flavor by Pairing with Sweetness," *Learning and Motivation* 14(1983):338–350.

42. K. Ackroff and A. Sclafani, "Flavor Preferences Conditioned by Sugars: Rats Learn to Prefer Glucose Over Fructose," *Physiology & Behavior* 50(1991):815–824.

43. L. L. Birch, D. Birch, D. W. Marlin, and L. Kramer, "Effects of Instrumental Consumption on Children's Food Preference," *Appetite* 3(1982):125–134.

44. L. L. Birch, S. I. Zimmerman, and H. Hind, "The Influence of Social-Affective Context on the Formation of Children's Food Preferences," *Child Development* 51(1980):856–861.

45. J. O. Fisher and L. L. Birch, "Restricting Access to Palatable Foods Affects Children's Behavioral Response, Food Selection, and Intake," *American Journal of Clinical Nutrition* 69(1999):1264–1272.

46. S. K. Escalona, "Feeding Disturbances in Very Young Children," *American Journal of Orthopsychiatry* 15(1945):76–80.

47. Ibid., p. 78.

48. J. E. Steiner, "Facial Expressions of the Neonate Infant Indicating the Hedonics of Food-Related Chemical Stimuli," in *Taste and Development*, ed. J. M. Weiffenbach, Bethesda, MD: U.S. Department of Health, Education, and Welfare, 1977.

49. T. M. Field, R. Woodson, R. Greenberg, and D. Cohen, "Discrimination and Imitation of Facial Expressions by Neonates," *Science* 218(1982):179–181.

50. F. Baeyens, D. Vansteenwegen, J. De Houwer, and G. Crombez, "Observational Conditioning of Food Valence in Humans," *Appetite* 27(1996):235–250.

51. L. L. Birch, "Generalization of a Modified Food Preference," *Child Development* 52(1981):755–758.

   L. L. Birch, "Children's Food Preferences: Developmental Patterns and Environmental Influences," in *Annals of Child Development*, vol. 4, ed. R. Vasta, Greenwich, CT: JAI Press, 1987.

52. L. L. Birch, "Effects of Peer Models' Food Choices and Eating Behaviors on Preschoolers' Food Preferences," *Child Development* 51(1980):489–496.

53. L. V. Harper and K. M. Sanders, "The Effect of Adults' Eating on Young Children's Acceptance of Unfamiliar Foods," *Journal of Experimental Child Psychology* 20(1975):206–214.

54. K. Hobden and P. Pliner, "Effects of a Model on Food Neophobia in Humans," *Appetite* 25(1995):101–114.

55. B. G. Galef, "Mechanisms for the Social Transmission of Acquired Food Preferences from Adult to Weanling Rats," in *Learning Mechanisms in Food Selection*, eds. L. M. Barker, M. R. Best, and M. Domjan, Waco, TX: Baylor University Press, 1977.

56. K. Hikami, Y. Hasegawa, and T. Matsuzawa, "Social Transmission of Food Preferences in Japanese Monkeys (*Macaca fuscata*) after Mere Exposure or Aversion Training," *Journal of Comparative Psychology* 104(1990):233–237.

   M. D. Suboski and C. Bartashunas, "Mechanisms for Social Transmission of Pecking Preferences to Neonatal Chicks," *Journal of Experimental Psychology* 10(1984):182–194.

   W. Wyrwicka, *The Development of Food Preferences*, Springfield, IL: Charles C. Thomas, 1981.

57. B. G. Galef and E. E. Whiskin, "Socially Transmitted Food Preferences Can Be Used to Study Long-Term Memory in Rats," *Animal Learning and Behavior* 31(2003):160–164.

58. B. G. Galef and M. Stein, "Demonstrator Influence on Observer Diet Preference: Analyses of Critical Social Interactions and Olfactory Signals," *Animal Learning and Behavior* 13(1985):31–38.

59. B. G. Galef, J. R. Mason, G. Preti, N. J. Bean, "Carbon Disulfide: A Semiochemical Mediating Socially-Induced Diet Choice in Rats," *Physiology and Behavior* 42(1988):119–124.

60. M. J. Lavin, B. Freise, and S. Coombes, "Transferred Flavor Aversions in Adult Rats," *Behavioral and Neural Biology* 28(1980):15–33.

   S. Revusky, S. Coombes, and R. W. Pohl, "US Preexposure: Effects on Flavor Aversions Produced by Pairing a Poisoned Partner with Ingestion," *Animal Learning and Behavior* 10(1980):83–90.

61. W. J. Carr, S. Y. Choi, E. Arnholt, and M. H. Sterling, "The Ontogeny of a Natural Food Aversion in Domestic Rats (*Rattus norvegius*) and House Mice (*Mus musculus*)," *Journal of Comparative and Physiological Psychology* 97(1983):260–268.

   W. J. Carr, J. T. Hirsch, B. E. Campellone, and E. Marasco, "Some Determinants of a Natural Food Aversion in Norway Rats," *Journal of Comparative and Physiological Psychology* 93(1979):899–906.

   W. J. Carr, M. R. Landauer, R. E. Wiese, and D. H. Thor, "A Natural Food Aversion in Rats," *Journal of Comparative and Physiological Psychology* 93(1979):574–584.

62. P. P. Read, *Alive*, New York: Avon Books, 1974.

63. A. C. Huston, B. A. Watkins, and D. Kunkel, "Public Policy and Children's Television," *American Psychologist* 44(1989):424–433.

64. H. L. Taras and M. Gage, "Advertised Foods on Children's Television," *Archives of Pediatrics and Adolescent Medicine* 149(1995):649–652.

65. J. P. Galst and M. A. White, "The Unhealthy Persuader: The Reinforcing Value of Television and Children's Purchase-Influencing Attempts at the Supermarket," *Child Development* 47(1976):1089–1096.

   M. E. Goldberg, G. J. Gorn, and W. Gibson, "TV Messages for Snack and Breakfast Foods: Do They Influence Children's Preferences?" *Journal of Consumer Research* 5(1978):73–81.

66. D. B. Jeffrey, D. Bolin, N. B. Lemnitzer, J. S. Hickey, M. J. Hess, and J. M. Stroud, "The Impact of Television Advertising on Children's Eating Behaviour: An Integrative Review," *Catalog of Selected Documents in Psychology* 10(1980):11 (MS. No. 2011).

   D. B. Jeffrey, R. W. McLellarn, and D. T. Fox, "The Development of Children's Eating Habits: The Role of Television Commercials," *Health Education Quarterly* 9(1982):174–189.

   D. B. Jeffrey, R. W. McLellarn, J. S. Hickey, N. B. Lemnitzer, M. J. Hess, and J. M. Stroud, "Television Food Commercials and Children's Eating Behavior: Some Empirical Evidence," *Journal of the University Film Association* 32(1980):41–43.

67. F. M. Kramer, K. Rock, and D. Engell, "Effects of Time of Day and Appropriateness on Food Intake and Hedonic Ratings at Morning and Midday," *Appetite* 18(1992):1–13.

   R. I. Stein and C. J. Nemeroff, "Moral Overtones of Food: Judgments of Others Based on What They Eat," *Personality and Social Psychology Bulletin* 21(1995):480–490.

   H. Tuorila, "Selection of Milks with Varying Fat Contents and Related Overall Liking, Attitudes, Norms and Intentions," *Appetite* 8(1987):1–14.

   D. A. Zellner, W. F. Stewart, P. Rozin, and J. M. Brown, "Effect of Temperature and Expectations on Liking for Beverages," *Physiology and Behavior* 44(1988):61–68.

68. J. Brody, *Jane Brody's Nutrition Book*, New York: Norton, 1981.

69. L. Rappoport, G. R. Peters, R. Downey, T. McCann, and L. Huff-Corzine, "Gender and Age Differences in Food Cognition," *Appetite* 20(1993):33–52.

A. Stafleu, W. A. Van Staveren, J. B. De Graaf, and J. G. A. J. Hautvast, "Family Resemblance in Beliefs, Attitudes, and Intentions towards Consumption of 20 Foods: A Study among Three Generations of Women," *Appetite* 25(1995):201–216.

70. L. Dubé and I. Cantin, "Promoting Health or Promoting Pleasure? A Contingency Approach to the Effect of Informational and Emotional Appeals on Food Liking and Consumption," *Appetite* 35(2000):251–262.

71. P. Rozin and A. Fallon, "The Psychological Categorization of Foods and Non-Foods: A Preliminary Taxonomy of Food Rejections," *Appetite* 1(1980):193–201.

72. Rozin and Fallon, "The Psychological Categorization of Foods and Non-Food."

73. P. Rozin and A. E. Fallon, "A Perspective on Disgust," *Psychological Review* 94(1987):23–41.

74. S. Drucker, "Who Is the Best Restaurateur in America?" *The New York Times Magazine* (March 10, 1996):45–47, 104.

75. "No Seconds," *Time* (May 23, 1994):14.

Chapter 7: This or That

1. S. R. X. Dall, I. C. Cuthill, N. Cook, and M. Morphet, "Learning about Food: Starlings, Skinner Boxes, and Earthworms," *Journal of the Experimental Analysis of Behavior* 67(1997):181–192.

   F. D. Provenza and R. P. Cincotta, "Foraging as a Self-Organizational Learning Process: Accepting Adaptability at the Expense of Predictability," in *Diet Selection: An Interdisciplinary Approach to Foraging Behaviour*, ed. R. N. Hughes, Oxford: Blackwell Scientific, 1993.

2. M. L. Platt, E. M. Brannon, T. L. Briese, and J. A. French, "Differences in Feeding Ecology Predict Differences in Performance between Golden Lion Tamarins (*Leontopithecus rosalia*) and Wied's Marmosets (*Callithrix kuhli*) on Spatial and Visual Memory Tasks," *Animal Learning and Behavior* 24(1996):384–393.

3. K. Milton, "Diet and Primate Evolution," *Scientific American* (August 1993):86.

4. Milton, "Diet and Primate Evolution," pp. 86–93.

5. B. Heinrich and J. Marzluff, "Why Ravens Share," *American Scientist* 83(1995):342–349.

6. G. S. Wilkinson, "Food Sharing in Vampire Bats," *Scientific American* (February 1990):76–82.

7. W. M. Baum, "On Two Types of Deviation from the Matching Law: Bias and Undermatching," *Journal of the Experimental Analysis of Behavior* 22(1974):231–242.

   R. J. Herrnstein, "On the Law of Effect," *Journal or the Experimental Analysis of Behavior* 13(1970):243–266.

8. P. de Villiers, "Choice in Concurrent Schedules and a Quantitative Formulation of the Law of Effect," in *Handbook of Operant Behavior*, eds. W. K. Honig and J. E. R. Staddon, Englewood Cliffs, NJ: Prentice Hall, 1977.

   T. M. Foster, W. Temple, B. Robertson, V. Nair, and A. Poling, "Concurrent-Schedule Performance in Dairy Cows: Persistent Undermatching," *Journal of the Experimental Analysis of Behavior* 65(1996):57–80.

9. W. M. Baum, "Choice in Free-Ranging Wild Pigeons," *Science* 185(1974):78–79.

10. G. W. Ainslie, "Impulse Control in Pigeons," *Journal of the Experimental Analysis of Behavior* 21(1974):485–489.

    A. W. Logue, *Self-Control: Waiting until Tomorrow for What You Want Today*, Englewood Cliffs, NJ: Prentice Hall, 1995.

    H. Rachlin and L. Green, "Commitment, Choice and Self Control," *Journal of the Experimental Analysis of Behavior* 17(1972):15–22.

11. B. F. Skinner, *Notebooks*, Englewood Cliffs, NJ: Prentice Hall, 1980, p. 59.

12. Logue, *Self-Control*.

13. M. A. Wogar, C. M. Bradshaw, and E. Szabadi, "Effect of Lesions of the Ascending 5-Hydroxy-tryptaminergic Pathways on Choice between Delayed Reinforcers," *Psychopharmacology* 111(1993):239–243.

14. A. R. Damasio, "On Some Functions of the Human Prefrontal Cortex," in *Structure and Functions of the Human Prefrontal Cortex*, eds. J. Grafman, K. J. Holyoak, and F. Boller, New York: New York Academy of Sciences, 1995.

15. F. S. Arana, J. A. Parkinson, E. Hinton, A. J. Holland, A. M. Owen, and A. C. Roberts, "Dissociable Contributions of the Human Amygdala and Orbitofrontal Cortex to Incentive Motivation and Goal Selection," *The Journal of Neuroscience* 23(2003):9632–9638.

16. G. W. Ainslie, "Specious Reward: A Behavioral Theory of Impulsiveness and Impulse Control," *Psychological Bulletin* 82(1975):463–496.

    H. Rachlin, "Self-Control," *Behaviorism* 2(1974):94–107.

17. J. E. Mazur and A. W. Logue, "Choice in a Self Control Paradigm: Effects of a Fading Procedure," *Journal of the Experimental Analysis of Behavior* 30(1978):11–17.

    J. B. Schweitzer and B. Sulzer-Azaroff, "Self-Control: Teaching Tolerance for Delay in Impulsive Children," *Journal of the Experimental Analysis of Behavior* 50(1988):173–186.

18. W. Mischel, Y. Shoda, and M. L. Rodriguez, "Delay of Gratification in Children," *Science* 244(1989):933–938.

19. Mischel et al., "Delay of Gratification in Children."

20. J. Grosch and A. Neuringer, "Self-Control in Pigeons under the Mischel Paradigm," *Journal of the Experimental Analysis of Behavior* 35(1981):3–21.

    A. W. Logue and T. E. Peña-Correal, "Responding during Reinforcement Delay in a Self-Control Paradigm," *Journal of the Experimental Analysis of Behavior* 41(1984):267–277.

21. A. W. Logue and J. E. Mazur, "Maintenance of Self-Control Acquired through a Fading Procedure: Follow-Up on Mazur and Logue (1978)," *Behavior Analysis Letters* 1(1981):131–137.

22. L. B. Forzano and R. J. Corry, "Self-Control and Impulsiveness in Adult Human Females," *Learning and Motivation* 29(1998):184–199.

    Grosch and Neuringer, "Self-Control in Pigeons under the Mischel Paradigm."

23. B. F. Skinner, *Walden Two*, New York: Macmillan, 1948, pp. 107–108.

24. L. B. Forzano and A. W. Logue, "Self-Control in Adult Humans: Comparison of Qualitatively Different Reinforcers," *Learning and Motivation* 25(1994):65–82.

    K. Jackson and T. D. Hackenberg, "Token Reinforcement, Choice, and Self-Control in Pigeons," *Journal of the Experimental Analysis of Behavior* 66(1996):29–49.

25. Logue, *Self-Control.*

    A. W. Logue, M. L. Rodriguez, T. E. Peña-Correal, and B. C. Mauro, "Choice in a Self-Control Paradigm: Quantification of Experience-Based Differences," *Journal of the Experimental Analysis of Behavior* 41(1984):53–67.

26. E. W. Menzel and E. J. Wyers, "Cognitive Aspects of Foraging Behavior," in *Foraging Behavior: Ecological, Ethological, and Psychological Approaches*, eds. A. C. Kamil and T. D. Sargent, New York: Garland, 1981, p. 355.

27. Menzel and Wyers, "Cognitive Aspects of Foraging Behavior."

28. A. C. Kamil and T. D. Sargent, "Introduction," in *Foraging Behavior: Ecological, Ethological, and Psychological Approaches*, eds. A. C. Kamil and T. D. Sargent, New York: Garland, 1981.

29. J. Allison, "Economics and Operant Conditioning," in *Predictability, Correlation, and Contiguity*, eds. P. Harzem and M. D. Zeiler, New York: Wiley, 1981.

    S. R. Hursh, "Economic Concepts for the Analysis of Behavior," *Journal of the Experimental Analysis of Behavior* 34(1980):219–238.

    S. E. G. Lea, "The Psychology and Economics of Demand," *Psychological Bulletin* 85(1978): 441–466.

    H. Rachlin, "Economics and Behavioral Psychology," in *Limits to Action*, ed. J. E. R. Staddon, New York: Academic Press, 1980.

30. J. E. R. Staddon, *Adaptive Behavior and Learning*, New York: Cambridge University Press, 1983.

31. G. H. Pyke, "Honeyeater Foraging: A Test of Optimal Foraging Theory," *Animal Behaviour* 29(1981):878–888.

    G. H. Pyke, "Optimal Foraging in Hummingbirds: Rule of Movement between Inflorescences," *Animal Behaviour* 29(1981):889–896.

G. H. Pyke, "Why Hummingbirds Hover and Honeyeaters Perch," *Animal Behaviour* 29(1981):861–867.

32. S. H. Mitchell and J. Brener, "Energetic and Motor Responses to Increasing Force Requirements," *Journal of Experimental Psychology: Animal Behavior Processes* 17(1991):174–185.

33. H. L. Meiselman, D. Hedderley, S. L. Staddon, B. J. Pierson, and C. R. Symonds, "Effect of Effort on Meal Selection and Meal Acceptability in a Student Cafeteria," *Appetite* 23(1994):43–55.

34. S. E. G. Lea, "The Analysis of Need," in *Animal Cognition and Behavior*, ed. R. L. Mellgren, New York: North-Holland, 1983.

J. G. Goode, K. Curtis, and J. Theophano, "Group Shared Food Patterns as a Unit of Analysis," in *Nutrition and Behavior*, ed. S. A. Miller, Philadelphia: Franklin Institute, 1981.

35. S. M. Cantor and M. B. Cantor, "Socioeconomic Factors in Fat and Sugar Consumption," in *The Chemical Senses and Nutrition*, eds. M. R. Kare and O. Maller, New York: Academic Press, 1977.

M. Krondl and D. Lau, "Social Determinants in Human Food Selection," in *The Psychobiology of Human Food Selection*, ed. L. M. Barker, Westport, CT: AVI Publishing, 1982.

N. S. Scrimshaw and L. Taylor, "Food," *Scientific American* (September 1980):78–88.

J. Yudkin, "Patterns and Trends in Carbohydrate Consumption and Their Relation to Disease," *Nutrition Society Proceedings* 23(1964):149–162.

36. E. A. Smith, "Optimization Theory in Anthropology: Applications and Critiques," in *The Latest on the Best: Essays on Evolution and Optimality*, ed J. Dupre, Cambridge, MA: MIT Press, 1987.

B. Winterhalder, "The Analysis of Hunter-Gatherer Diets: Stalking an Optimal Foraging Model," in *Food and Evolution: Toward a Theory of Human Food Habits*, eds. M. Harris and E. B. Ross, Philadelphia: Temple University Press, 1987.

37. K. Hill and A. M. Hurtado, "Hunter-Gatherers of the New World," *American Scientist* (September/October 1989):436–443.

38. M. R. Berenbaum, *Bugs in the System: Insects and Their Impact on Human Affairs*, Reading, MA: Addison-Wesley, 1995.

39. E. Fantino, "The Future Is Uncertain: Eat Dessert First," *Behavioral and Brain Sciences* 18(1995):125–126.

40. L. B. Forzano and A. W. Logue, "Predictors of Adult Humans' Self-Control and Impulsiveness for Food Reinforcers," *Appetite* 19(1992):33–47.

J. M. Kirk and A. W. Logue, "Effects of Deprivation Level on Humans' Self-Control for Food Reinforcers," *Appetite* 28(1997):215–226.

41. *Annie* (October 20, 1981). Manuscript in the Theatre Collection in the New York Public Library for the Performing Arts, New York, NY.

42. A. W. Logue, M. E. Smith, and H. Rachlin, "Sensitivity of Pigeons to Prereinforcer and Postreinforcer Delay," *Animal Learning and Behavior* 13(1985):181–186.

W. Timberlake, D. J. Gawley, and G. A. Lucas, "Time Horizons in Rats Foraging for Food in Temporally Separated Patches," *Journal of Experimental Psychology: Animal Behavior Processes* 13(1987):302–309.

43. A. W. Logue, G. R. King, A. Chavarro, and J. S. Volpe, "Matching and Maximizing in a Self-Control Paradigm Using Human Subjects," *Learning and Motivation* 21(1990):340–368.

44. A. I. Houston and J. M. McNamara, "Imperfectly Optimal Animals," *Behavioral Ecology and Sociobiology* 15(1984):61–64.

A. C. Janetos and B. J. Cole, "Imperfectly Optimal Animals," *Behavioral Ecology and Sociobiology* 9(1981):203–209.

45. W. M. Baum, "Optimization and the Matching Law as Accounts of Instrumental Behavior," *Journal of the Experimental Analysis of Behavior* 36(1981):387–403.

A. I. Houston, "Optimality Theory and Matching," *Behaviour Analysis Letters* 3(1983):1–15.

J. E. R. Staddon and J. M. Hinson, "Optimization: A Result or a Mechanism?" *Science* 221 (1983):976–977.

M. D. Zeiler, "On Optimal Choice Strategies," *Journal of Experimental Psychology: Animal Behavior Processes* 13(1987):31–39.

Chapter 8: You Are What You Eat and Drink

1. W. Shakespeare, *Julius Caesar* in *The Complete Works of William Shakespeare*, ed. W. A. Wright, Garden City, NY: Garden City Books, 1599/1936, p. 634.
2. L. Carroll, *The Annotated Alice*, United States: Bramhall House, 1960, p. 57.
3. C. M. Hasler, "Functional Foods: The Western Perspective," *Nutrition Reviews* 53(1996):S6–S10.
   A. R. P. Walker, "Dietary Advice: From Folklore to Present Beliefs," *Nutrition Reviews* 53(1995):8–10.
   W. Weng and J. Chen, "The Eastern Perspective on Functional Foods Based on Traditional Chinese Medicine," *Nutrition Reviews* 54(1996):S11–S16.
4. A. R. Lecours, M. Mandujano, and G. Romero, "Ontogeny of Brain and Cognition: Relevance to Nutrition Research," *Nutrition Reviews* 59(2001):S7–S12.
   E. Pollitt, "Timing and Vulnerability in Research on Malnutrition and Cognition," *Nutrition Reviews*, 54(1996):S49–S55.
   M. Sigman, "Nutrition and Child Development: More Food for Thought," *Directions in Psychological Science* 4(1995):52–55.
5. J. L. Brown and E. Pollitt, "Malnutrition, Poverty and Intellectual Development," *Scientific American* (February 1996):38–43.
6. H. N. Ricciuti, "Nutrition and Mental Development," *Psychological Science* 2(1993):43–46.
7. J. Blumberg, "Nutrient Requirements of the Healthy Elderly—Should There Be Specific RDAs?" *Nutrition Reviews* 52(1994):S15–S18.
   J. E. Morley, "Nutritional Modulation of Behavior and Immunocompetence," *Nutrition Reviews* 52(1994):S6–S8.
8. D. Benton and P. Y. Parker, "Breakfast, Blood Glucose, and Cognition," *American Journal of Clinical Nutrition* 67(1998):772S–778S.
   E. Pollitt, E. Jacoby, and S. Cueto, "School Breakfast and Cognition among Nutritionally At-Risk Children in the Peruvian Andes," *Nutrition Reviews* 54(1996):S22–S26.
9. R. B. Kanarek and D. Swinney, "Effects of Food Snacks on Cognitive Performance in Male College Students," *Appetite* 14(1990):15–27.
10. A. Smith, A. Ralph, and G. McNeill, "Influences of Meal Size on Post-Lunch Changes in Performance Efficiency, Mood, and Cardiovascular Function," *Appetite* 16(1991):85–91.
11. N. Bleichrodt, R. M. Shrestha, C. E. West, J. G. A. J. Hautvast, F. J. R. Van de Vijver, and M. Ph. Born, "The Benefits of Adequate Iodine Intake," *Nutrition Reviews* 54(1996):S72–S78.
    N. F. Sheard, "Iron Deficiency and Infant Development," *Nutrition Reviews* 52(1994):137–140.
    M. H. Malloy, B. Graubard, H. Moss, M. McCarthy, S. Gwyn, P. Vietze, A. Willoughby, G. G. Rhoads, and H. Berendes, "Hypochloremic Metabolic Alkalosis from Ingestion of a Chloride-Deficient Infant Formula: Outcome 9 and 10 Years Later," *Pediatrics* 87(1991):811–822.
12. J. E. Alpert and M. Fava, "Nutrition and Depression: The Role of Folate," *Nutrition Reviews* 55(1997):145–149.
13. B. A. Golomb, "Cholesterol and Violence: Is There a Connection?" *Annals of Internal Medicine* 128(1998):478–487.
    J. R. Kaplan, M. F. Muldoon, S. B. Manuck, and J. J. Mann, "Assessing the Observed Relationship between Low Cholesterol and Violence-Related Mortality: Implications for Suicide Risk." *Annals of the New York Academy of Sciences* 836(1997):57–80.
14. L. Pauling, "Orthomolecular Psychiatry," *Science* 160(1968):265–271.
15. American Psychiatric Association, *Diagnostic and Statistical Manual of Mental Disorders* (Rev. ed.), 3rd ed. Washington, DC: APA, 1987.
    S. C. Bowden, "Separating Cognitive Impairment in Neurologically Asymptomatic Alcoholism from Wernicke-Korsakoff Syndrome: Is the Neurological Distinction Justified?" *Psychological Bulletin* 107(1990):355–366.
    P. M. Dreyfus, "The Nutritional Management of Neurological Disease," in *Nutrition and Behavior*, ed. S. A. Miller, Philadelphia: Franklin Institute, 1981.
16. T. A. Ban, "Megavitamin Therapy in Schizophrenia," in *Nutrition and Behavior*, ed. S. A. Miller, Philadelphia: Franklin Institute, 1981.

M. Barinaga, "Vitamin C Gets a Little Respect," *Science* 254(1991):374–376.

Pauling, "Orthomolecular Psychiatry."

17. K. Leutwyler, "Suicide Prevention," *Scientific American* (March 1997):18, 20.

P. I. Markowitz and E. F. Coccaro, "Biological Studies of Impulsivity, Aggression, and Suicidal Behavior," in *Impulsivity and Aggression*, eds. E. Hollander and D. J. Stein, New York: Wiley, 1995.

J. B. Richards and H. de Wit, "Effects of Serotonin Depletion in Rats on Three Models of Impulsive Behavior," *Pharmacology, Biochemistry and Behavior* 57(1997):620.

18. Golomb, "Cholesterol and Violence."

19. B. Spring, "Effects of Foods and Nutrients on the Behavior of Normal Individuals," in *Nutrition and the Brain*, vol. 7, eds. R. J. Wurtman and J. J. Wurtman, New York: Raven Press, 1986.

H. M. van Praag and C. Lemus, "Monoamine Precursors in the Treatment of Psychiatric Disorders," in *Nutrition and the Brain*, vol. 7, eds. R. J. Wurtman and J. J. Wurtman, New York: Raven Press, 1986.

20. J. D. Fernstrom, "Nutrition, Brain Function and Behavior," in *Nutrition and Behavior*, ed. S. A. Miller, Philadelphia: Franklin Institute, 1981.

R. J. Wurtman and J. J. Wurtman, "Nutrients, Neurotransmitter Synthesis, and the Control of Food Intake," in *Eating and Its Disorders*, eds. A. J. Stunkard and E. Stellar, New York: Raven Press, 1984.

21. S. N. Young, "The Clinical Psychopharmacology of Tryptophan," in *Nutrition and the Brain*, vol. 7, eds. R. J. Wurtman and J. J. Wurtman, New York: Raven Press, 1986.

22. C. R. Markus, G. Panhuysen, A. Tuiten, H. Koppeschaar, D. Fekkes, and M. L. Peters, "Does Carbohydrate-Rich, Protein-Poor Food Prevent a Deterioration of Mood and Cognitive Performance of Stress-Prone Subjects When Subjected to a Stressful Task?" *Appetite* 31(1998):49–65.

23. Carroll, *The Annotated Alice*, p. 73.

24. R. M. Church, H. A. Broadbent, and J. Gibbon, "Biological and Psychological Description of an Internal Clock," in *Learning and Memory: The Behavioral and Biological Substrates*, eds. I. Gormezano and E. A. Wasserman, Hillsdale, NJ: Lawrence Associates, 1992.

H. M. Lloyd, P. J. Rogers, D. I. Hedderley, and A. F. Walker, "Acute Effects on Mood and Cognitive Performance of Breakfasts Differing in Fat and Carbohydrate Content," *Appetite* 27(1996):151–164.

W. H. Meck and R. M. Church, "Nutrients That Modify the Speed of Internal Clock and Memory Storage Processes," *Behavioral Neuroscience* 101(1987):467–475.

P. J. Rogers, A. Kainth, and H. J. Smit, "A Drink of Water Can Improve or Impair Mental Performance Depending on Small Differences in Thirst," *Appetite* 36(2001):57–58.

Spring, "Effects of Foods and Nutrients on the Behavior of Normal Individuals."

25. B. Spring, J. Chiodo, M. Harden, M. J. Bourgeois, J. D. Mason, and L. Lutherer, "Psychobiological Effects of Carbohydrates," *Journal of Clinical Psychiatry* 50(Supplement)(1980):27–33.

26. E. Hartman, "Effects of L-Tryptophan on Sleepiness and on Sleep," *Journal of Psychiatric Research* 17(1982/83):107–113.

P. D. Leathwood and P. Pollet, "Diet-Induced Mood Changes in Normal Populations," *Journal of Psychiatric Research* 17(1982/83):147–154.

B. Spring, J. Chiodo, and D. J. Bowen, "Carbohydrates, Tryptophan, and Behavior: A Methodological Review," *Psychological Bulletin* 102(1987):234–256.

M. W. Yogman, S. H. Zeisel, and C. Roberts, "Assessing Effects of Serotonin Precursors on Newborn Behavior," *Journal of Psychiatric Research* 17(1982/83):123–133.

27. B. Spring, O. Maller, J. Wurtman, L. Digman, and L. Cozolino, "Effects of Protein and Carbohydrate Meals on Mood and Performance: Interactions with Sex and Age," *Journal of Psychiatric Research* 17(1982/83):155–167.

28. M. L. Wolraich, D. B. Wilson, and J. W. White, "The Effect of Sugar on Behavior or Cognition in Children: A Meta-Analysis," *Journal of the American Medical Association* 274(1995): 1617–1621.

29. R. A. Baron and M. I. Bronfen, "A Whiff of Reality: Empirical Evidence Concerning the Effects of Pleasant Fragrances on Work-Related Behavior," *Journal of Applied Social Psychology* 24(1994):1179–1203.

30. L. M. Bartoshuk, "Taste," in *Stevens' Handbook of Experimental Psychology*, 2nd ed., vol. 1, eds. R. C. Atkinson, R. J. Herrnstein, G. Lindzey, and R. D. Luce, New York: Wiley, 1988.

31. G. O. Kermode, "Food Additives," in *Human Nutrition*, San Francisco: W. H. Freeman, 1978.

　　C. B. Nemeroff, "Monosodium Glutamate-Induced Neurotoxicity: Review of the Literature and Call for Further Research," in *Nutrition and Behavior*, ed. S. A. Miller, Philadelphia: Franklin Institute, 1981.

32. M. Barinaga, "Amino Acids: How Much Excitement Is Too Much?" *Science* 247(1990):20–22.

33. Nemeroff, "Monosodium Glutamate-Induced Neurotoxicity."

34. Barinaga, "Amino Acids."

　　M. Barinaga, "MSG: A 20-Year Debate Continues," *Science* 247(1990):21.

35. D. Benton and S. Nabb, "Carbohydrate, Memory, and Mood," *Nutrition Reviews* 61(2003): S61–S67.

　　P. E. Gold, L. Cahill, and G. L. Wenk, "The Lowdown on Ginkgo Biloba," *Scientific American* (April 2003):87–91.

36. L. D. Dickey, *Clinical Ecology*, Springfield, IL: Charles C. Thomas, 1976.

　　M. Barinaga, "Better Data Needed on Sensitivity Syndrome," *Science* 251(1991):1558.

37. G. Guroff, "Inborn Errors of Amino Acid Metabolism in Relation to Diet," in *Nutrition and Behavior*, ed. S. A. Miller, Philadelphia: Franklin Institute, 1981.

38. "The Maternal Phenylketonuria Collaborative Study: A Status Report," *Nutrition Reviews* 52(1994):390–393.

39. D. S. King, "Food and Chemical Sensibilities Can Produce Cognitive-Emotional Symptoms," in *Nutrition and Behavior*, ed. S. A. Miller, Philadelphia: Franklin Institute, 1981.

40. American Psychiatric Association, *Diagnostic and Statistical Manual of Mental Disorders* (Rev. ed.), 4th ed., Washington, DC: APA, 2000.

41. L. R. Caporael, "Ergotism: The Satan Loosed in Salem," *Science* 192(1976):21–26.

　　M. K. Matossian, "Ergot and the Salem Witchcraft Affair," *American Scientist* 70(July/August 1982):355–357.

42. W. N. Arnold, "Absinthe," *Scientific American* 260(June 1989):112–117.

43. J. A. French, C. J. Wainwright, and D. A. Booth, "Caffeine and Mood: Individual Differences in Low-Dose Caffeine Sensitivity," *Appetite* 22(1994):277–279.

　　G. K. Mumford, S. M. Evans, B. J. Kaminski, K. L. Preston, C. A. Sannerud, K. Silverman, and R. R. Griffiths, "Discriminative Stimulus and Subjective Effects of Theobromine and Caffeine in Humans," *Psychopharmacology* 115(1994):1–8.

　　L. Ryan, C. Hatfield, and M. Hofstetter, "Caffeine Reduces Time-of-Day Effects on Memory Performance in Older Adults," *Psychological Science* 13(2002):68–71.

　　A. Smith, A. Kendrick, A. Maben, and J. Salmon, "Effects of Breakfast and Caffeine on Cognitive Performance, Mood and Cardiovascular Functioning," *Appetite* 22(1994):39–55.

　　A. Smith, A. Maben, and P. Brockman, "Effects of Evening Meals and Caffeine on Cognitive Performance, Mood and Cardiovascular Functioning," *Appetite* 22(1994):57–65.

44. S. H. Mitchell, H. de Wit, and J. P. Zacny, "Caffeine Withdrawal Symptoms and Self-Administration Following Caffeine Deprivation," *Pharmacology Biochemistry and Behavior* 51(1995):941–945.

45. N. J. Richardson, P. J. Rogers, and N. A. Elliman, "Conditioned Flavour Preferences Reinforced by Caffeine Consumed after Lunch," *Physiology and Behavior* 60(1996):257–263.

46. S. D. Comer, M. Haney, R. W. Foltin, and M. W. Fischman, "Effects of Caffeine Withdrawal on Humans Living in a Residential Laboratory," *Experimental and Clinical Psychopharmacology* 5(1997):399–402.

　　A. Nehlig, "Are We Dependent upon Coffee and Caffeine? A Review on Human and Animal Data," *Neuroscience and Biobehavioral Reviews* 23(1999):563–576.

　　E. C. Strain, G. K. Mumford, K. Silverman, and R. R. Griffiths, "Caffeine Dependence Syndrome: Evidence from Case Histories and Experimental Evaluations," *Journal of the American Medical Association* 272(1994):1043–1048.

47. J. E. Brody, "Breaking, or at Least Taming, the Caffeine Habit," *The New York Times* (September 13, 1995):C9.

48. A. Astrup, S. Toubro, S. Cannon, P. Hein, L. Breum, and J. Madsen, "Caffeine: A Double-Blind, Placebo-Controlled Study of Its Thermogenic, Metabolic, and Cardiovascular Effects in Healthy Volunteers," *American Journal of Clinical Nutrition* 51(1990):759–767.

   J. E. Brody, "The Latest on Coffee? Don't Worry. Drink Up," *The New York Times* (September 13, 1995):C1, C6.

49. American Psychiatric Association, *Diagnostic and Statistical Manual of Mental Disorders* (Rev. ed.), 4th ed, p. 232.

50. B. J. Brockel and D. A. Cory-Slechta, "Lead-Induced Decrements in Waiting Behavior: Involvement of D_2-Like Dopamine Receptors," *Pharmacology, Biochemistry and Behavior* 63(1999): 423–434.

51. H. L. Needleman, S. K. Geiger, and R. Frank, "Lead and IQ Scores: A Reanalysis," *Science* 227(1985):701–702, 704.

52. H. L. Needleman, J. A. Riess, M. J. Tobin, G. E. Biesecker, and J. B. Greenhouse, "Bone Lead Levels and Delinquent Behavior," *Journal of the American Medical Association* 275(1996): 363–369.

53. J. Eisinger, "Sweet Poison," *Natural History* (July 1996):48–53.

54. "Was the Ill-Fated Franklin Expedition a Victim of Lead Poisoning," *Nutrition Reviews* 47(1989):322–323.

55. S. Waldman, "Lead and Your Kids," *Newsweek* (July 15, 1991):42–48.

56. H. W. Mielke, "Lead in the Inner Cities," *American Scientist* 87(1999):62–73.

57. Eisinger, "Sweet Poison."

58. H. L. Needleman and C. A. Gatsonis, "Low-Level Lead Exposure and the IQ of Children," *Journal of the American Medical Association* 263(1990):672–678.

59. P. J. Hilts, "Lower Lead Limits Are Made Official," *The New York Times* (October 8, 1991):C3.

60. J. Palca., "Panel Clears Needleman of Misconduct," *Science* 256(1992):1389.

   J. Palca, "Lead Researcher Confronts Accusers in Public Hearing," *Science* 254(1992): 437–438.

61. American Psychiatric Association, *Diagnostic and Statistical Manual of Mental Disorders*, (Rev. ed.), 4th ed.

62. J. L. Rapoport, M. S. Buchsbaum, T. P. Zahn, H. Weingartner, C. Ludlow, and E. J. Mikkelsen, "Dextroamphetamine: Cognitive and Behavioral Effects in Normal Prepubertal Boys," *Science* 199(1978):560–563.

   M. A. Stewart, "Hyperactive Children," *Scientific American* 222(April 1970):94–99.

63. C. Gillberg, H. Melander, A.-L. Von Knorring, L.-O. Janols, G. Thernlund, B. Hagglof, L. Eidevall-Wallin, P. Gustafsson, and S. Kopp, "Long-Term Stimulant Treatment of Children with Attention-Deficit Hyperactivity Disorder Symptoms," *Archives of General Psychiatry* 54(1997):857–864.

64. H. D. Posavac, S. M. Sheridan, and S. S. Posavac, "A Cueing Procedure to Control Impulsivity in Children with Attention Deficit Hyperactivity Disorder," *Behavior Modification* 23(1999): 234–253.

65. E. Taylor, "Development of Clinical Services for Attention-Deficit/Hyperactivity Disorder," *Archives of General Psychiatry* 56(1999):1097–1099.

   The MTA Cooperative Group, "A 14-Month Randomized Clinical Trial of Treatment Strategies for Attention-Deficit/Hyperactivity Disorder," *Archives of General Psychiatry* 56(1999): 1073–1086.

   The MTA Cooperative Group, "Moderators and Mediators of Treatment Response for Children with Attention-Deficit/Hyperactivity Disorder," *Archives of General Psychiatry* 56(1999): 1088–1096.

66. D. F. Berger, J. P. Lombardo, P. M. Jeffers, A. E. Hunt, B. Bush, A. Casey, and F. Quimby, "Hyperactivity and Impulsiveness in Rats Fed Diets Supplemented with Either Aroclor 1248 or PCB-Contaminated St. Lawrence River Fish," *Behavioural Brain Research* 126(2001):1–11.

67. B. E. Feingold, "Dietary Management of Behavior and Learning Disabilities," in *Nutrition and Behavior*, ed. S. A. Miller, Philadelphia: Franklin Institute, 1981.

68. National Institutes of Health, *NIH Consensus Statements: 110. Diagnosis and Treatment of Attention Deficit Hyperactivity Disorder*, (November 16–18, 1998). Available at: http://odp.od. nih. gov/consensus/cons/110/110_statement.htm.

69. P. Marshall, "Attention Deficit Disorder and Allergy: A Neurochemical Model of the Relation between the Illnesses," *Psychological Bulletin* 106(1989):434–446.

C. A. Perry, J. Dwyer, J. A. Gelfand, R. R. Couris, and W. W. McCloskey, "Health Effects of Salicylates in Foods and Drugs," *Nutrition Reviews* 54(1996):225–240.

70. Center for Science in the Public Interest, *Diet, ADHD & Behavior: A Quarter-Century Review*, (1999). Available at: http://www.cspinet.org/new/adhd_resch_bk02.pdf.

71. B. Brecht, *Galileo*, trans. C. Laughton, New York: Grove, 1966, p. 61.

Chapter 9: "Hunger Talks a Most Persuasive Language"

1. P. Rosenzweig, *The Book of Proverbs*, New York: Philosophical Library, 1965, p. 89.

2. M. S. Exton, "Infection-Induced Anorexia: Active Host Defence Strategy," *Appetite* 29(1997): 369–383.

L. M. Hecker and D. P. Kotler, "Malnutrition in Patients with AIDS," *Nutrition Reviews* 48(1990):393–401.

S. Rivière, S. Gillette-Guyonnet, F. Nourhashemi, and B. Vellas, "Nutrition and Alzheimer's Disease," *Nutrition Reviews* 57(1999):565–567.

S. B. Roberts, "Energy Regulation and Aging: Recent Findings and Their Implications," *Nutrition Reviews* 58(2000):91–97.

H. P. Weingarten, "Mechanisms of Food Intake Suppression Induced by Inflammation of the Intestines," Paper presented at the Columbia University Seminar on Appetitive Behavior, New York, May 14, 1992.

3. J. E. Blundell, "Psychopharmacology of Centrally Acting Anorectic Agents," in *Psychopharmacology and Food*, eds. M. Sandler and T. Silverstone, New York: Oxford University Press, 1985.

4. D. H. Baucom and P. A. Aiken, "Effect of Depressed Mood on Eating among Obese and Nonobese Dieting and Nondieting Persons," *Journal of Personality and Social Psychology* 41(1981):577–585.

J. Polivy and C. P. Herman, "Clinical Depression and Weight Change: A Complex Relation," *Journal of Abnormal Psychology* 85(1976):338–340.

5. G. S. Roth, M. A. Lane, D. K. Ingram, J. A. Mattison, D. Elahi, J. D. Tobin, D. Muller, and E. J. Metter, "Biomarkers of Caloric Restriction May Predict Longevity in Humans," *Science* 297(2002):811–812.

R. S. Sohal and R. Weindruch, "Oxidative Stress, Caloric Restriction, and Aging," *Science* 273(1996):59–63.

R. B. Verdery, D. K. Ingram, G. S. Roth, and M. A. Lane, "Caloric Restriction Increases HDL_2 Levels in Rhesus Monkeys (*Macaca mulatta*)," *American Journal of Physiology* 273(1997): E714–E719.

6. R. F. Kushner, "Body Weight and Mortality," *Nutrition Reviews* 51(1993):127–136.

L. Lissner, P. M. Odell, R. B. D'Agostino, J. Stokes, B. E. Kreger, A. J. Belanger, and K. D. Brownell, "Variability of Body Weight and Health Outcomes in the Framingham Population," *The New England Journal of Medicine* 324(1991):1839–1844.

7. "Estimating Body Fat in Lean and Obese Women," *Nutrition Reviews* 50(1992):80–81.

G. Plourde, "The Role of Radiologic Methods in Assessing Body Composition and Related Metabolic Parameters," *Nutrition Reviews* 55(1997):289–296.

T. B. Vanltallie, "Waist Circumference: A Useful Index in Clinical Care and Health Promotion," *Nutrition Reviews* 56(1998):300–302.

8. G. D. Foster, "Reasonable Weights: Determinants, Definitions and Directions," in *Obesity Treatment: Establishing Goals, Improving Outcomes, and Reviewing the Research Agenda*, eds. D. B. Allison and F. X. Pi-Sunyer, New York: Plenum, 1995.

J. E. Manson, W. C. Willett, M. J. Stampfer, G. A. Colditz, D. J. Hunter, S. E. Hankinson, C. H. Hennekens, and F. E. Speizer, "Body Weight and Mortality among Women," *The New England Journal of Medicine* 333(1995):677–685.

310 · References to Chapter 9

9. Exton, "Infection-Induced Anorexia.

   National Heart, Lung, and Blood Institute, *Clinical Guidelines on the Identification, Evaluation, and Treatment of Overweight and Obesity in Adults*, (1998). Available at: http://www.nhlbi.nih.gov/guidelines/obesity/ob_home.htm.

10. D. Grady, "Unusual Molecule Could Be Key to Cancer Patients' Weight Loss," *The New York Times* (March 12, 1996):C3.

    B. E. Meyerowitz, T. G. Burish, and S. M. Levy, *Cancer, Nutrition, and Eating Behavior: Introduction and Overview*, in *Cancer, Nutrition, and Eating Behavior*, eds. T. G. Burish, S. M. Levy, and B. E. Meyerowitz, Hillsdale, NJ: Lawrence Erlbaum Associates, 1985.

11. I. L. Bernstein and C. M. Treneer, "Learned Food Aversions and Tumor Anorexia," in *Cancer, Nutrition, and Eating Behavior*, eds. T. G. Burish, S. M. Levy, and B. E. Meyerowitz, Hillsdale, NJ: Lawrence Erlbaum Associates, 1985.

    N. E. Grunberg, "Specific Taste Preferences: An Alternative Explanation for Eating Changes in Cancer Patients," in *Cancer, Nutrition, and Eating Behavior*, eds. T. G. Burish, S. M. Levy, and B. E. Meyerowitz, Hillsdale, NJ: Lawrence Erlbaum Associates, 1985.

    P. Todorov, P. Cariuk, T. McDevitt, B. Coles, K. Fearon, and M. Tisdale, "Characterization of a Cancer Cachectic Factor," *Nature* 379(1996):739–742.

12. I. L. Bernstein and M. M. Webster, "Learned Food Aversions: A Consequence of Cancer Chemotherapy," in *Cancer, Nutrition, and Eating Behavior*, eds. T. G. Burish, S. M. Levy, and B. E. Meyerowitz, Hillsdale, NJ: Lawrence Erlbaum Associates, 1985.

13. D. J. Broberg and I. L. Bernstein, "Candy as a Scapegoat in the Prevention of Food Aversions in Children Receiving Chemotherapy," *Cancer* 60(1987):2344–2347.

14. R. A. Boakes, N. Tarrier, B. W. Barnes, and M. H. N. Tattersall, "Prevalence of Anticipatory Nausea and Other Side-Effects in Cancer Patients Recieving Chemotherapy," *European Journal of Cancer* 29A(1993):866–870.

15. G. R. Morrow and P. L. Dobkin, "Anticipatory Nausea and Vomiting in Cancer Patients Undergoing Chemotherapy Treatment: Prevalence, Etiology, and Behavioral Interventions," *Clinical Psychology Review* 8(1988):517–556.

16. Rosenzweig, *The Book of Proverbs*, p. 18.

17. H. Bruch, *The Golden Cage*, Cambridge, MA: Harvard University Press, 1978, p. 62.

18. R. L. Palmer, *Anorexia Nervosa*, New York: Penguin, 1980, p. 20.

19. Bruch, *The Golden Cage*, p. 61.

20. American Psychiatric Association, *Diagnostic and Statistical Manual of Mental Disorders* (Rev. ed.), 4th ed., Washington, DC: APA, 2000, p. 583.

21. Ibid.

22. Ibid., p. 585.

23. Ibid.

    B. T. Walsh and M. J. Devlin, "Eating Disorders: Progress and Problems," *Science* 280(1998): 1387–1390.

24. Bruch, *The Golden Cage*, p. 3.

25. K. D. Brownell, "Dieting and the Search for the Perfect Body: Where Physiology and Culture Collide," *Behavior Therapy* 22(1991):1–12.

26. Y. Simon, F. Bellisle, M.-O. Monneuse, B. Samuel-Lajeunesse, and A. Drewnowski, "Taste Responsiveness in Anorexia Nervosa," *British Journal of Psychiatry* 162(1993):244–246.

27. J. A. McLean and S. I. Barr, "Cognitive Dietary Restraint Is Associated with Eating Behaviors, Lifestyle Practices, Personality Characteristics and Menstrual Irregularity in College Women," *Appetite* 40(2003):185–192.

    D. Neumark-Szfainer, M. Story, M. D. Resnick, and R. W. Blum, "Adolescent Vegetarians: A Behavioral Profile of a School-Based Population in Minnesota," *Archives of Pediatric Adolescent Medicine* 151(1997):833–838.

28. K. A. Halmi and S. R. Sunday, "Temporal Patterns of Hunger and Fullness Ratings and Related Cognitions in Anorexia and Bulimia," *Appetite* 16(1991):219–237.

    B. J. Rolls, "The Role of Sensory-Specific Satiety in Food Intake and Food Selection," in *Taste, Experience, and Feeding*, eds. E. D. Capaldi and T. L. Powley, Washington, DC: American Psychological Association, 1990.

29. Halmi and Sunday, "Temporal Patterns of Hunger and Fullness Ratings and Related Cognitions in Anorexia and Bulimia."

S. R. Sunday and K. A. Halmi, "Micro- and Macroanalyses of Patterns within a Meal in Anorexia and Bulimia Nervosa," *Appetite* 26(1996):21–36.

K. A. Tappe, S. E. Gerberg, D. J. Shide, B. J. Rolls, and A. E. Anderson, "Videotape Assessment of Changes in Aberrant Meal-Time Behaviors in Anorexia Nervosa After Treatment," *Appetite* 30(1998):171–184.

30. E. Stice, "Risk and Maintenance Factors for Eating Pathology: A Meta-Analytic Review," *Psychological Bulletin* 128(2002):825–848.

31. Brownell, "Dieting and the Search for the Perfect Body."

H. Bruch, *Eating Disorders*, New York: Basic Books, 1973, p. 4.

P. E. Garfinkel and D. M. Garner, *Anorexia Nervosa*, New York: Brunner/Mazel, 1982.

Walsh and Devlin, "Eating Disorders."

32. M. N. Altabe, "Issues in the Assessment and Treatment of Body Image Disturbance in Culturally Diverse Populations," in *Body Image, Eating Disorders, and Obesity: An Integrative Guide for Assessment and Treatment*, ed. J. K. Thompson, Washington, DC: American Psychological Association, 1996.

S. Kumanyika, "Cultural Factors in Desirable Body Shapes and Their Impact on Weight Loss and Maintenance," in *Obesity Treatment: Establishing Goals, Improving Outcomes, and Reviewing the Research Agenda*, eds. D. B. Allison and F. X. Pi-Sunyer, New York: Plenum, 1995.

33. International Rainbow Pictures (producer) and H. Jaglom (director), *Eating* (film), 1990.

34. "Famous Models, Dangerous Diets," *People* (January 11, 1993):3, 80–86.

35. J. J. Brumberg, *The Body Project: An Intimate History of American Girls*, New York: Vintage, 1997.

36. C. Davis, J. V. G. A. Durnin, M. Gurevich, A. Le Maire, and M. Dionne, "Body Composition Correlates of Weight Dissatisfaction and Dietary Restraint in Young Women," *Appetite* 20(1993):197–207.

37. J. K. Thompson, "Assessing Body Image Disturbance: Measures, Methodology, and Implementation," in *Body Image, Eating Disorders, and Obesity: An Integrative Guide for Assessment and Treatment*, ed. J. K. Thompson, Washington, DC: American Psychological Association, 1996.

38. A. Feingold and R. Mazzella, "Gender Differences in Body Image Are Increasing," *Psychological Science* 9(1998):190–195.

39. A. E. Fallon and P. Rozin, "Sex Differences in Perceptions of Desirable Body Shape," *Journal of Abnormal Psychology* 94(1985):102–105.

40. K. D. Brownell, "Eating Disorders in Athletes," in *Eating Disorders and Obesity: A Comprehensive Handbook*, eds. K. D. Brownell and C. G. Fairburn, New York: The Guilford Press, 1995.

J. Polivy and L. Thomsen, "Dieting and Other Eating Disorders," in *Handbook of Behavioral Medicine for Women*, eds. E. A. Blechman and K. D. Brownell, New York: Pergamon, 1988.

41. "Weight Loss Rule Passes," *The New York Times* (September 19, 1991):B8.

42. T. D. Lauder, M. V. Williams, C. S. Campbell, G. D. Davis, and R. A. Sherman, "Abnormal Eating Behaviors in Military Women," *Medicine and Science in Sports and Exercise* 31(1999):1265–1271.

E. Ruggero, *Duty First: A Year in the Life of West Point and the Making of American Leaders*, New York: Perennial, 2001.

43. H. Brubach, "The Athletic Esthetic," *The New York Times Magazine* (June 23, 1996):48–51.

44. J. A. O'Dea and S. Abraham, "Eating and Exercise Disorders in Young College Men," *Journal of American College Health* 50(2002):273–278.

H. G. Pope, A. J. Gruber, P. Choi, R. Olivardia, and K. A. Phillips, "Muscle Dysmorphia: An Unrecognized Form of Body Dysmorphic Disorder," *Psychosomatics* 38(1997):548–557.

45. J. O. Fisher and L. L. Birch, "Restricting Access to Foods and Children's Eating," *Appetite* 32(1999):405–419.

M. Tiggemann and J. Lowes, "Predictors of Maternal Control over Children's Eating Behaviour," *Appetite* 39(2002):1–7.

46. E. Stice, W. S. Agras, and L. D. Hammer, "Risk Factors for the Emergence of Childhood Eating Disturbances: A Five-Year Prospective Study," *International Journal of Eating Disorders* 25(1999):375–387.

47. M. Kostanski and E. Gullone, "Dieting and Body Image in the Child's World: Conceptualization and Behavior," *Journal of Genetic Psychology* 160(1999):488–496.

48. L. Smolak, M. P. Levine, and F. Schermer, "Parental Input and Weight Concerns among Elementary School Children," *International Journal of Eating Disorders* 25(1999):263–271.

49. P. J. Lattimore and M. Butterworth, "A Test of the Structural Model of Initiation of Dieting among Adolescent Girls," *Journal of Psychosomatic Research* 46(1999):295–299.

    M. Udovitch, "A Secret Society of the Starving," *The New York Times Magazine* (September 8, 2002):18, 20, 22, 66–67.

50. Bruch, *Eating Disorders.*

51. J. A. Dinsmoor, "The Effect of Hunger on Discriminated Responding," *Journal of Abnormal and Social Psychology* 47(1952):67–72.

    W. D. Pierce and W. F. Epling, "Activity Anorexia: An Interplay between Basic and Applied Behavior Analysis," *The Behavior Analyst* 17(1994):7–23.

    J. L. Weed, M. A. Lane, G. S. Roth, D. L. Speer, and D. K. Ingram, "Activity Measures in Rhesus Monkeys on Long-Term Calorie Restriction," *Physiology and Behavior* 62(1997):97–103.

52. C. G. Fairburn, "Physiology of Anorexia Nervosa," in *Eating Disorders and Obesity: A Comprehensive Handbook*, eds. K. D. Brownell and C. G. Fairburn, New York: The Guilford Press, 1995.

    D. S. Goldbloom and S. H. Kennedy, "Medical Complications of Anorexia Nervosa," in *Eating Disorders and Obesity: A Comprehensive Handbook*, eds. K. D. Brownell and C. G. Fairburn, New York: The Guilford Press, 1995.

    W. H. Kaye, "Neurotransmitters and Anorexia Nervosa," in *Eating Disorders and Obesity: A Comprehensive Handbook*, eds. K. D. Brownell and C. G. Fairburn, New York: The Guilford Press, 1995.

53. S. S. Van Buskirk, "A Two-Phase Perspective on the Treatment of Anorexia Nervosa," *Psychological Bulletin* 84(1977):529–538.

54. W. S. Agras and H. C. Kraemer, "The Treatment of Anorexia Nervosa: Do Different Treatments Have Different Outcomes?" in *Eating and Its Disorders*, eds. A. J. Stunkard and E. Stellar, New York: Raven Press, 1984.

    Garfinkel and Garner, *Anorexia Nervosa.*

55. Agras and Kraemer, "The Treatment of Anorexia Nervosa."

    G. R. Leon, *Treating Eating Disorders*, Brattleboro, VT: Lewis Publishing, 1983.

    Van Buskirk, "A Two-Phase Perspective on the Treatment of Anorexia Nervosa."

56. W. H. Kaye, "Neurotransmitters and Anorexia Nevosa."

    B. T. Walsh, "Pharmacotherapy of Eating Disorders," in *Eating Disorders and Obesity: A Comprehensive Handbook*, eds. K. D. Brownell and C. G. Fairburn, New York: The Guilford Press, 1995.

57. Garfinkel and Garner, *Anorexia Nervosa.*

58. K. M. Pike, K. Loeb, and K. Vitousek, "Cognitive-Behavioral Therapy for Anorexia Nervosa and Bulimia Nervosa," in *Body Image, Eating Disorders, and Obesity: An Integrative Guide for Assessment and Treatment*, ed. J. K. Thompson, Washington, DC: American Psychological Association, 1996.

    J. K. Thompson, L. J. Heinberg, and A. J. Clarke, "Treatment of Body Image Disturbance in Eating Disorders," in *Body Image, Eating Disorders, and Obesity: An Integrative Guide for Assessment and Treatment*, ed. J. K. Thompson, Washington, DC: American Psychological Association, 1996.

59. C. Dare and I. Eisler, "Family Therapy and Eating Disorders," in *Eating Disorders and Obesity: A Comprehensive Handbook*, eds. K. D. Brownell and C. G. Fairburn, New York: The Guilford Press, 1995.

60. A. Winzelberg, "The Analysis of an Electronic Support Group for Individuals with Eating Disorders," *Computers in Human Behavior* 13(1997):393–407.

61. M. K. Jacobs and G. Goodman, "Psychology and Self Help Groups," *American Psychologist* 44(1989):536–545.

62. T. Mann, S. Nolen-Hocksema, D. Burgard, A. Wright, and K. Hanson, "Are Two Interventions Worse than None? Joint Primary and Secondary Prevention of Eating Disorders in College Females," *Health Psychology* 16(1997):215–225.
63. American Psychiatric Association, *Diagnostic and Statistical Manual of Mental Disorders*, p. 589.
64. Ibid.
65. Ibid.
    Walsh and Devlin, "Eating Disorders."
66. Garfinkel and Garner, *Anorexia Nervosa*, p. 5.
67. E. Stice, R. P. Cameron, J. D. Killen, C. Hayward, and C. B. Taylor, "Naturalistic Weight-Reduction Efforts Prospectively Predict Growth in Relative Weight and Onset of Obesity among Female Adolescents," *Journal of Consulting and Clinical Psychology* 67(1999):967–974.
68. J. E. Mitchell, "Medical Complications of Bulimia Nervosa," in *Eating Disorders and Obesity: A Comprehensive Handbook*, eds. K. D. Brownell and C. G. Fairburn, New York: The Guilford Press, 1995.
69. G. Russell, "Bulimia Nervosa: An Ominous Variant of Anorexia Nervosa," *Psychological Medicine* 9(1979):429–448.
70. A. W. Logue, "Taste Aversion and the Generality of the Laws of Learning." *Psychological Bulletin* 86(1979):276–296.
    A. W. Logue, K. R. Logue, and K. E. Strauss, "The Acquisition of Taste Aversions in Humans with Eating and Drinking Disorders," *Behaviour Research and Therapy* 21(1983):275–289.
71. "Energy Expenditure and the Control of Body Weight," *Nutrition Reviews* 47(1989):249–252.
    H. E. Gwirtsman, W. H. Kaye, E. Obarzanek, D. T. George, D. C. Jimerson, and M. H. Ebert, "Decreased Caloric Intake in Normal-Weight Patients with Bulimia: Comparison with Female Volunteers," *American Journal of Clinical Nutrition* 49(1989):86–92.
    T. Léonard, C. Foulon, and B. Samuel-Lajeunesse, "High Resting Energy Expenditure in Normal-Weight Bulimics and Its Normalization with Control of Eating Behavior," *Appetite* 27(1996):223–233.
72. "Influence of Altered Body Weight on Energy Expenditure," *Nutrition Reviews* 53(1995): 265–268.
73. C. M. Hadigan, B. T. Walsh, M. J. Devlin, J. L. LaChaussée, and H. R. Kissileff, "Behavioral Assessment of Satiety in Bulimia Nervosa," *Appetite* 18(1992):233–241.
    Rolls, "The Role of Sensory-Specific Satiety in Food Intake and Food Selection."
    Sunday and Halmi, "Micro- and Macroanalyses of Patterns within a Meal in Anorexia and Bulimia Nervosa."
74. K. A. Halmi, "Eating Disorder Research in the Past Decade," in *Women and Mental Health*, eds. J. A. Sechzer, S. M. Pfafflin, F. L. Denmark, A. Griffin, and S. J. Blumenthal, New York: New York Academy of Sciences, 1996.
    Walsh and Devlin, "Eating Disorders."
75. Leon, *Treating Eating Disorders*.
    Russell, "Bulimia Nervosa."
76. A. J. Stunkard and T. A. Wadden, "Restrained Eating and Human Obesity," *Nutrition Reviews* 48(1990):78–86.
    R. J. Tuschl, "From Dietary Restraint to Binge Eating: Some Theoretical Considerations," *Appetite* 14(1990):105–109.
77. M. R. Lowe and K. L. Eldredge, "The Role of Impulsiveness in Normal and Disordered Eating," in *The Impulsive Client*, eds. W. G. McCown, J. L. Johnson, and M. B. Shure, Washington, DC: American Psychological Association, 1993.
    S. L. McElroy, H. G. J. Pope, P. E. J. Keck, and J. I. Hudson, "Disorders of Impulse Control," in *Impulsivity and Aggression*, eds. E. Hollander and D. J. Stein, New York: Wiley, 1995.
78. W. H. Kaye, G. K. Frank, C. C. Meltzer, J. P. Price, C. W. McConaha, P. J. Crossan, K. L. Klump, and L. Rhodes, "Altered Serotonin 2A Receptor Activity in Women Who Have Recovered from Bulimia Nervosa," *The American Journal of Psychiatry* 158(2001):1152–1155.
79. E. Stice and W. S. Agras, "Subtyping Bulimic Women along Dietary Restraint and Negative Affect Dimensions," *Journal of Consulting and Clinical Psychology* 67(1999):460–469.
    Walsh and Devlin, "Eating Disorders."

80. K. M. Pirke, "Physiology of Bulimia Nervosa," in *Eating Disorders and Obesity: A Comprehensive Handbook*, eds. K. D. Brownell and C. G. Fairburn, New York: The Guilford Press, 1995.

　　T. E. Weltzin, M. H. Fernstrom, and W. H. Kaye, "Serotonin and Bulimia Nervosa," *Nutrition Reviews* 52(1994):399–408.

81. C. M. Bulik, R. H. Larson, and F. A. Carter, "Salivary Reactivity in Restrained and Unrestrained Eaters and Women with Bulimia," *Appetite* 27(1996):15–24.

82. J. I. Hudson, P. S. Laffer, and H. G. Pope, "Bulimia Related to Affective Disorder by Family History and Response to the Dexamethasone Suppression Test," *American Journal of Psychiatry* 139(1982):685–687.

　　H. G. Pope and J. I. Hudson, *New Hope for Binge Eaters*, New York: Harper & Row, 1984.

　　M. Strober, B. Salkin, J. Burroughs, and W. Morrell, "Validity of the Bulimia-Restricter Distinction in Anorexia Nervosa: Parental Personality Characteristics and Family Psychiatric Morbidity," *The Journal of Nervous and Mental Disease* 170(1982):345–351.

83. R. W. Foltin, M. Haney, S. D. Comer, and M. W. Fischman, "Effect of Fluoxetine on Food Intake of Humans Living in a Residential Laboratory," *Appetite* 27(1996):165–181.

　　Walsh, "Pharmacotherapy of Eating Disorders."

　　Walsh and Devlin, "Eating Disorders."

84. Walsh, "Pharmacotherapy of Eating Disorders."

　　M. L. Whittal, W. S. Agras, and R. A. Gould, "Bulimia Nervosa: A Meta-Analysis of Psychosocial and Pharmacological Treatments," *Behavior Therapy* 30(1999):117–135.

85. Walsh and Devlin, "Eating Disorders."

86. C. G. Fairburn, "Short-Term Psychological Treatments for Bulimia Nervosa," in *Eating Disorders and Obesity: A Comprehensive Handbook*, eds. K. D. Brownell and C. G. Fairburn, New York: The Guilford Press, 1995.

　　C. Thiels, U. Schmidt, J. Treasure, R. Garthe, and N. Troop, "Guided Self-Change for Bulimia Nervosa Incorporating Use of a Self-Care Manual," *American Journal of Psychiatry* 155(1998):947–953.

87. Winzelberg, "The Analysis of an Electronic Support Group for Individuals with Eating Disorders."

88. H. G. Pope, K. A. Phillips, and R. Olivardia, *The Adonis Complex: The Secret Crisis of Male Body Obsession*, New York: The Free Press, 2000.

89. A. Frean and R. Watson, "TV Curb on Thin Women to Help Anorexics," *The Times* (June 22, 2000):1, 9.

Chapter 10: The Battle With the Bulge

1. G. Kolata, "Days off Are Not Allowed, Experts Argue," *The New York Times* (October 18, 2000):A1, A20.

2. G. Plourde, "The Role of Radiologic Methods in Assessing Body Composition and Related Metabolic Parameters," *Nutrition Reviews* 55(1997):289–296.

3. National Heart, Lung, and Blood Institute, *Clinical Guidelines on the Identification, Evaluation, and Treatment of Overweight and Obesity in Adults*, 1998. Available at: http://www.nhlbi.nih.gov/guidelines/obesity/ob_home.htm.

4. Ibid.

5. G. Taubes, "As Obesity Rates Rise, Experts Struggle to Explain Why," *Science* 280(1998):1367–1368.

　　I. Wickelgren, "Obesity: How Big A Problem?" *Science* 280(1998):1364–1367.

6. J. O. Hill, H. R. Wyatt, G. W. Reed, and J. C. Peters, "Obesity and the Environment: Where Do We Go from Here?" *Science* 299(2003):853–855.

7. A. Drewnowski, "As Obesity Rates Rise, Experts Struggle to Explain Why," *Science* 280(1998):1367–1368.

　　J. P. Koplan and W. H. Dietz, "Caloric Imbalance and Public Health Policy," *JAMA* 282(1999):1579–1581.

8. Hill et al., "Obesity and the Environment."

9. The National Academies, "New Dietary Guidelines Issued for Cats and Dogs," September 8, 2003. Available at: www.nationalacademies.org.

10. E. E. Calle, C. Rodriguez, K. Walker-Thurmond, and M. J. Thun, "Overweight, Obesity, and Mortality from Cancer in a Prospectively Studied Cohort of U.S. Adults," *The New England Journal of Medicine* 348(2003):1625–1638.

    Hill et al., "Obesity and the Environment."

11. Koplan and Dietz, "Caloric Imbalance and Public Health Policy."

12. M.-P. St-Onge and S. B. Heymsfield, "Overweight and Obesity Are Linked to Lower Life Expectancy," *Nutrition Reviews* 61(2003):313–316.

13. Ibid.

14. J. Albu, D. Allison, C. N. Boozer, S. Heymsfield, H. Kissileff, A. Kretser, K. Krumhar, R. Leibel, C. Nonas, X. Pi-Sunyer, T. VanItallie, and E. Wedral, "Obesity Solutions: Report of a Meeting," *Nutrition Reviews* 55(1997):150–156.

15. Wickelgren, "Obesity."

16. M. E. Barker, M. Tandy, and J. D. Stookey, "How Are Consumers of Low-Fat and High-Fat Diets Perceived by Those with Lower and Higher Fat Intake?" *Appetite* 33(1999):309–317.

    K. D. Brownell, "Dieting and the Search for the Perfect Body: Where Physiology and Culture Collide," *Behavior Therapy* 22(1991):1–12.

    R. Pingitore, B. L. Dugoni, R. S. Tindale, and B. Spring, "Bias against Overweight Job Applicants in a Simulated Employment Interview," *Journal of Applied Psychology* 79(1994): 909–917.

17. R. C. Klesges, M. DeBon, and A. Meyers, "Obesity in African American Women: Epidemiology, Determinants, and Treatment Issues," in *Body Image, Eating Disorders, and Obesity: An Integrative Guide for Assessment and Treatment*, ed. J. K. Thompson, Washington, DC: American Psychological Association, 1996.

    J. D. Williams, C. Achterberg, and G. P. Sylvester, "Target Marketing of Food Products to Ethnic Minority Youth," in *Prevention and Treatment of Childhood Obesity*, eds. C. L. Williams and S. Y. S. Kimm, New York: New York Academy of Sciences, 1993.

18. T. M. Cutting, J. O. Fisher, K. Grimm-Thomas, and L. L. Birch, "Like Mother, Like Daughter: Familial Patterns of Overweight Are Mediated by Mothers' Dietary Disinhibition," *American Journal of Clinical Nutrition* 69(1999):608–613.

    T. T. Foch and G. E. McClearn, "Genetics, Body Weight, and Obesity," in *Obesity*, ed. A. J. Stunkard, Philadelphia: W. B. Saunders, 1980.

    J. O. Hill and E. L. Melanson, "Overview of the Determinants of Overweight and Obesity: Current Evidence and Research Issues," *Medicine and Science in Sports and Exercise* 31(1999):S515–S521.

19. R. Gurney, "The Hereditary Factor in Obesity," *Archives of Internal Medicine* 57(1936):557–561.

20. A. J. Stunkard, T. T. Foch, and Z. Hrubec, "A Twin Study of Human Obesity," *The Journal of the American Medical Association* 256(1986):51–54.

21. A. J. Stunkard, T. l. A. Sorensen, C. Hanis, T. W. Teasdale, R. Chakraborty, W. J. Schull, and F. Schulsinger, "An Adoption Study of Human Obesity," *The New England Journal of Medicine* 314(1986):193–198.

22. C. Bouchard, A. Tremblay, J.-P. Després, A. Nadeau, P. J. Lupien, G. Thériault, J. Dussault, S. Moorjani, S. Pinault, and G. Fournier, "The Response to Long-Term Overfeeding in Identical Twins," *The New England Journal of Medicine* 322(1990):1477–1482.

23. C. Bouchard, "Human Variation in Body Mass: Evidence for a Role of the Genes," *Nutrition Reviews* 55(1997):S21–S30.

    A. G. Comuzzie and D. B. Allison, "The Search for Human Obesity Genes," *Science* 280(1998):1374–1377.

    I. S. Farooqi, J. M. Keogh, G. S. H. Yeo, E. J. Lank, T. Cheetham, and S. O'Rahilly, "Clinical Spectrum of Obesity and Mutations in the Melanocortin 4 Receptor Gene," *The New England Journal of Medicine* 348(2003):1085–1095.

    S. B. Roberts and A. S. Greenberg, "The New Obesity Genes," *Nutrition Reviews* 54(1996): 41–49.

24. L. Sjöström, "The Contribution of Fat Cells to the Determination of Body Weight," in *Symposium on Obesity: Basic Mechanisms and Treatment*, ed. A. J. Stunkard, Philadelphia: W. B. Saunders, 1978.

    L. Sjöström, "Fat Cells and Body Weight," in *Obesity*, ed. A. J. Stunkard, Philadelphia: W. B. Saunders, 1980.

25. Ibid.

26. J. Marx, "Cellular Warriors at the Battle of the Bulge," *Science* 299(2003):846–849.

27. Koplan and Dietz, "Caloric Imbalance and Public Health Policy."

28. R. A. Hegele, "Lessons from Genetic Studies in Native Canadian Populations," *Nutrition Reviews* 57(1999):S43–S50.

29. E. Jéquier, "Energy Utilization in Human Obesity," in *Human Obesity*, eds. R. J. Wurtman and J. J. Wurtman, New York: New York Academy of Sciences, 1987.

    E. Ravussin and E. Danforth, "Beyond Sloth—Physical Activity and Weight Gain," *Science* 283(1999):184–185.

30. Jéquier, "Energy Utilization in Human Obesity."

31. D. L. Elliot, L. Goldberg, K. S. Kuehl, and W. M. Bennett, "Sustained Depression of the Resting Metabolic Rate after Massive Weight Loss," *American Journal of Clinical Nutrition* 49(1989):93–96.

    R. E. Keesey and S. W. Corbett, "Metabolic Defense of the Body Weight Set-Point," in *Eating and Its Disorders*, eds. A. J. Stunkard and E. Stellar, New York: Raven Press, 1984.

    S. N. Steen, R. A. Oppliger, and K. D. Brownell, "Metabolic Effects of Repeated Weight Loss and Regain in Adolescent Wrestlers," *The Journal of the American Medical Association* 260(1988):1–50.

32. H. T. Edwards, A. Thorndike, and D. B. Dill, "The Energy Requirements in Strenuous Muscular Exercise," *The New England Journal at Medicine* 213(1935):532–535.

    E. T. Poehlman and E. S. Horton, "The Impact of Food Intake and Exercise on Energy Expenditure," *Nutrition Reviews* 47(1989):129–137.

33. C. Bouchard, A. Tremblay, J.-P. Després, G. Thériault, A. Nadeau, P. J. Lupien, S. Moorjani, D. Prudhomme, and G. Fournier, "The Response to Exercise with Constant Energy Intake in Identical Twins," *Obesity Research* 2(1994):400–410.

34. P. Hubert, N. A. King, and J. E. Blundell, "Uncoupling the Effects of Energy Expenditure and Energy Intake: Appetite Response to Short-Term Energy Deficit Induced by Meal Omission and Physical Activity," *Appetite* 31(1998):9–19.

    P. Verger, M. T. Lanteaume, and J. Louis-Sylvestre, "Free Food Choice after Acute Exercise in Men," *Appetite* 22(1994):159–164.

35. R. E. Andersen, C. J. Crespo, S. J. Bartlett, L. J. Cheskin, and M. Pratt, "Relationship of Physical Activity and Television Watching with Body Weight and Level of Fatness among Children: Results from the Third National Health and Nutrition Examination Survey," *JAMA* 279(1998):938–942.

    C. S. Berkey, H. R. H. Rockett, A. E. Field, M. W. Gillman, A. L. Frazier, C. A. Camargo, and G. A. Colditz, "Activity, Dietary Intake, and Weight Changes in the Longitudinal Study of Preadolescent and Adolescent Boys and Girls," *Pediatrics* 105(2000):854–862.

36. R. C. Klesges, M. L. Shelton, and L. M. Klesges, "Effects of Television on Metabolic Rate: Potential Implications for Childhood Obesity," *Pediatrics* 91(1993):281–286.

37. W. H. Dietz, "Childhood Obesity," in *Human Obesity*, eds. R. J. Wurtman and J. J. Wurtman, New York: New York Academy of Sciences, 1987.

38. Jéquier, "Energy Utilization in Human Obesity."

    J. A. Westrate, T. Dopheide, L. Robroch, P. Deurenberg, and J. G. Hautvast, "Does Variation in Palatability Affect the Postprandial Response in Energy Expenditure?" *Appetite* 15(1990):209–219.

39. Keesey and Corbett, "Metabolic Defense of the Body Weight Set-Point."

40. J. A. Levine, N. L. Eberhardt, and M. D. Jensen, "Role of Nonexercise Activity Thermogenesis in Resistance to Fat Gain in Humans," *Science* 283(1999):212–214.

41. Ravussin and Danforth, "Beyond Sloth."

42. J. M. Slattery and R. M. Potter, "Hyperphagia: A Necessary Precondition to Obesity?" *Appetite* 6(1985):133–142.

T. A. Spiegel, J. M. Kaplan, A. Tomassini, and E. Stellar, "Bite Size, Ingestion Rate, and Meal Size in Lean and Obese Women," *Appetite* 21(1993):131–145.

L. Spitzer and J. Rodin, "Human Eating Behavior: A Critical Review of Studies in Normal Weight and Overweight Individuals," *Appetite* 2(1981):293–329.

43. "Errors in Reporting Habitual Energy Intake," *Nutrition Reviews* 49(1991):215–217.

J. Fricker, D. Baelde, L. Igoin-Apfelbaum, J.-M. Huet, and M. Apfelbaum, "Underreporting of Food Intake in Obese 'Small Eaters,'" *Appetite* 19(1992):273–283.

44. A. H. Lichtenstein, "Dietary Fat: A History," *Nutrition Reviews* 57(1999):11–14.

45. H. A. Jordan and T. A. Spiegel, "Palatability and Oral Factors and Their Role in Obesity," in *The Chemical Senses and Nutrition*, eds. M. R. Kare and O. Maller, New York: Academic Press, 1977.

A. Sclafani and D. Springer, "Dietary Obesity in Adult Rats: Similarities to Hypothalamic and Human Obesity Syndromes," *Physiology and Behavior* 17(1976):461–471.

46. H. A. Raynor and L. H. Epstein, "Dietary Variety, Energy Regulation, and Obesity," *Psychological Bulletin* 127(2001):325–341.

47. N. C. Howarth, E. Satzman, and S. B. Roberts, "Dietary Fiber and Weight Regulation," *Nutrition Reviews* 59(2001):129–139.

S. B. Roberts, "High-Glycemic Index Foods, Hunger, and Obesity: Is There a Connection?" *Nutrition Reviews* 58(2000):163–169.

48. M. G. Tordoff and M. l. Friedman, "Drinking Saccharin Increases Food Intake and Preference—IV. Cephalic Phase and Metabolic Factors," *Appetite* 12(1989):37–56.

J. R. Vasselli, "Carbohydrate Ingestion, Hypoglycemia, and Obesity," *Appetite* 6(1985):53–59.

49. A. Drewnowski, "Intense Sweeteners and the Control of Appetite," *Nutrition Reviews* 53(1995):1–7.

"Saccharin Consumption Increases Food Consumption in Rats," *Nutrition Reviews* 48(1990):163–165.

50. J. F. Wilson, "Preschool Children Maintain Intake of Other Foods at a Meal Including Sugared Chocolate Milk," *Appetite* 16(1991):61–67.

51. J. Fricker, D. Chapelot, P. Pasquet, R. Rozen, and M. Apfelbaum, "Effect of a Covert Fat Dilution on the Spontaneous Food Intake by Lean and Obese Subjects," *Appetite* 24(1995):121–138.

T. V. E. Kral, L. S. Roe, and B. J. Rolls, "Does Nutrition Information about the Energy Density of Meals Affect Food Intake in Normal-Weight Women?" *Appetite* 39(2002):137–145.

J. Louis-Sylvestre, A. Tournier, D. Chapelot, and M. Chabert, "Effect of a Fat-Reduced Dish in a Meal on 24-H Energy and Macronutrient Intake," *Appetite* 22(1994):165–172.

B. J. Rolls, E. A. Bell, V. H. Castellanos, M. Chow, C. L. Pelkman, and M. L. Thorwart, "Energy Density but Not Fat Content of Foods Affected Energy Intake in Lean and Obese Women," *American Journal of Clinical Nutrition* 69(1999):863–871.

M. Yao and S. B. Roberts, "Dietary Energy Density and Weight Regulation," *Nutrition Reviews* 59(2001):247–258.

52. A. Himaya and J. Louis-Sylvestre, "The Effect of Soup on Satiation," *Appetite* 30(1998):199–210.

H. R. Kissileff, L. P. Gruss, J. Thornton, and H. A. Jordan, "The Satiating Efficiency of Foods," *Physiology and Behavior* 32(1984):319–332.

B. J. Rolls, I. C. Fedoroff, J. F. Guthrie, and L. J. Laster, "Foods with Different Satiating Effects in Humans," *Appetite* 15(1990):115–126.

53. J. Rodin, "Current Status of the Internal-External Hypothesis for Obesity," *American Psychologist* 36(1981):361–372.

54. Ibid.

55. N. E. Rowland and S. M. Antelman, "Stress Induced Hyperphagia and Obesity in Rats: A Possible Model for Understanding Human Obesity," *Science* 191(1976):310–312.

56. S. M. Antelman and A. R. Caggiula, "Tails of Stress Related Behavior: A Neuropharmacological Model," in *Animal Models in Psychiatry and Neurology*, eds. I. Hanin and E. Usdin, New York: Pergamon, 1977.

D. M. Marques, A. E. Fisher, M. S. Okrutny, and N. E. Rowland, "Tail Pinch Induced Fluid Ingestion: Interactions of Taste and Deprivation," *Physiology and Behavior* 22(1979):37–41.

57. M. B. Cantor, S. E. Smith, and B. R. Bryan, "Induced Bad Habits: Adjunctive Ingestion and Grooming in Human Subjects," *Appetite* 3(1982):1–12.

58. C. Ferber and M. Cabanac, "Influence of Noise on Gustatory Affective Ratings and Preference for Sweet or Salt," *Appetite* 8(1987):229–235.

    A. McCarron and K. J. Tierney, "The Effect of Auditory Stimulation on the Consumption of Soft Drinks," *Appetite* 13(1989):155–159.

    T. C. Roballey, C. McGreevy, R. R. Rongo, M. L. Schwantes, P. J. Steger, M. A. Wininger, and E. B. Gardner, "The Effect of Music on Eating Behavior," *Bulletin of the Psychonomic Society* 23(1985):221–222.

59. I. C. Federoff, J. Polivy, and C. P. Herman, "The Effect of Pre-Exposure to Food Cues on the Eating Behavior of Restrained and Unrestrained Eaters," *Appetite* 28(1997):33–47.

60. C. G. Greeno and R. R. Wing, "Stress-Induced Eating," *Psychological Bulletin* 115(1994): 444–464.

61. Cantor, Smith, and Bryan, "Induced Bad Habits."

    T. W. Robbins and P. J. Fray, "Stress-Induced Eating: Fact, Fiction or Misunderstanding?" *Appetite* 1(1980):103–133.

62. M. G. Lowe, "The Role of Anticipated Deprivation in Overeating," *Addictive Behaviors* 7(1982):103–112.

63. C. P. Herman, D. A. Roth, and J. Polivy, "Effects of the Presence of Others on Food Intake: A Normative Interpretation," *Psychological Bulletin* 129(2003):873–886.

64. J. Polivy, C. P. Herman, J. C. Younger, and B. Erskine, "Effects of a Model on Eating Behavior: The Induction of a Restrained Eating Style," *Journal of Personality* 47(1979):100–117.

65. S. J. Goldman, C. P. Herman, and J. Polivy, "Is the Effect of a Social Model on Eating Attenuated by Hunger?" *Appetite* 17(1991):129–140.

66. M. Macht and G. Saelens, "Emotions and Eating in Everyday Life," *Appetite* 35(2000):65–71.

    R. Plutchik, "Emotions and Attitudes Related to Being Overweight," *Journal of Clinical Psychology* 32(1976):21–24.

67. A. J. Stunkard and T. A. Wadden, "Restrained Eating and Human Obesity," *Nutrition Reviews* 48(1990):78–86.

    R. J. Tuschl, "From Dietary Restraint to Binge Eating: Some Theoretical Considerations," *Appetite* 14(1990):105–109.

68. American Psychiatric Association, *Diagnostic and Statistical Manual of Mental Disorders* (Rev. ed.), 4th ed., Washington, DC: APA, 2000, p. 589.

69. M. D. Marcus, "Binge Eating and Obesity," in *Eating Disorders and Obesity: A Comprehensive Handbook*, eds. K. D. Brownell and C. G. Fairburn, New York: The Guilford Press, 1995.

70. American Psychiatric Association, *Diagnostic and Statistical Manual of Mental Disorders*, p. 785.

71. M. R. Lowe and K. L. Eldredge, "The Role of Impulsiveness in Normal and Disordered Eating," in *The Impulsive Client*, eds. W. G. McCown, J. L. Johnson, and M. B. Shure, Washington, DC: American Psychological Association, 1993.

    B. T. Walsh and M. J. Devlin, "Eating Disorders: Progress and Problems," *Science* 280(1998): 1387–1390.

72. R. J. Wurtman and J. J. Wurtman, "Carbohydrates and Depression," *Scientific American* 260(January 1989):68–75.

73. G. S. Birketvedt, J. Florholmen, J. Sundsfjord, B. Østerud, D. Dinges, W. Bilker, and A. Stunkard, "Behavioral and Neuroendocrine Characteristics of the Night-Eating Syndrome," *JAMA* 282(1999):657–663.

    A. Stunkard, "Two Eating Disorders: Binge Eating Disorder and the Night Eating Syndrome," *Appetite* 34(2000):333–334.

74. Ibid.

75. P. M. Whitaker-Azmitia and S. J. Peroutka, eds., *The Neuropharmacology of Serotonin*, New York: New York Academy of Sciences, 1990.

76. S. L. McElroy, H. G. J. Pope, P. E. J. Keck, and J. I. Hudson, "Disorders of Impulse Control," in *Impulsivity and Aggression*, eds. E. Hollander and D. J. Stein, New York: Wiley, 1995.

    Wurtman and Wurtman, "Carbohydrates and Depression."

77. D. M. Garner, "Defining Socially and Psychologically Desirable Body Weights and the Psychological Consequences of Weight Loss," in *Obesity Treatment: Establishing Goals, Improving Outcomes, and Reviewing the Research Agenda*, eds. D. B. Allison and F. X. Pi-Sunyer, New York: Plenum, 1995.

78. D. Grady, "Exchanging Obesity's Risks for Surgery's," *The New York Times* (October 12, 2000):A1, A26.

     J. G. Kral, "Surgical Interventions for Obesity," in *Eating Disorders and Obesity: A Comprehensive Handbook*, eds. K. D. Brownell and C. G. Fairburn, New York: The Guilford Press, 1995.

79. G. A. Bray and D. S. Gray, "Obesity. Part II—Treatment," *Western Journal of Medicine* 149(1988):555–571.

80. J. F. Munro, l. C. Stewart, P. H. Seidelin, H. S. Mackenzie, and N. G. Dewhurst, "Mechanical Treatment for Obesity," in *Human Obesity*, eds. R. J. Wurtman and J. J. Wurtman, New York: New York Academy of Sciences, 1987.

81. J. E. Brody, "Stomach Balloon for Obesity Gains Favor amid Concerns," *The New York Times* (April 29, 1986):C1, C6.

82. R. B. Hogan, J. H. Johnston, B. W. Long, J. Q. Sones, L. A. Hinton, J. Burge, S. A. Corrigan, "A Double-Blind, Randomized, Sham-Controlled Trial of the Gastric Bubble for Obesity," *Gastrointestinal Endoscopy* 35(1989):381–385.

83. "Brain, Food," *Scientific American* (November 1991):124.

84. R. W. Foltin, T. H. Kelly, and M. W. Fischman, "The Effects of D-Amphetamine on Food Intake of Humans Living in a Residential Laboratory," *Appetite* 15(1990):33–45.

     S. Heshka and S. B. Heymsfield, "Pharmacological Treatment of Obesity," in *Eating Disorders and Obesity: A Comprehensive Handbook*, eds. K. D. Brownell and C. G. Fairburn, New York: The Guilford Press, 1995.

85. D. Canedy, "Almost Anyone Can Easily Get Pill Meant for the Truly Obese," *The New York Times* (May 11, 1999):A1, C10.

     D. Grady, "History Counsels Caution on Diet Pills," *The New York Times* (May 25, 1999):F8.

     S. G. Stolberg, "F.D.A. Approves Fat-Blocking Anti-Obesity Drug," *The New York Times* (April 27, 1999):A1, A19.

86. G. Kolata, "How Fen-Phen, a Diet 'Miracle,' Rose and Fell," *The New York Times* (September 23, 1997):F1, F6.

87. D. J. Morrow, "Fen-Phen Maker to Pay Billions in Settlement of Diet-Injury Cases," *The New York Times* (October 8, 1999):A1.

88. "Diet, Neurochemicals, and Mental Energy," *Nutrition Reviews* 59(2001): S22–S24.

89. P. J. Rogers, "Food Choice, Mood and Mental Performance: Some Examples and Some Mechanisms," in *Food Choice, Acceptance and Consumption*, eds. H. L. Meiselman and H. J. H. MacFie, London: Blackie Academic & Professional, 1996.

90. Wurtman and Wurtman, "Carbohydrates and Depression."

91. J. E. Brody, "Panel Criticizes Weight-Loss Programs," *The New York Times* (April 2, 1992): D22.

92. J. Dwyer, "Sixteen Popular Diets: Brief Nutritional Analyses," in *Obesity*, ed. A. J. Stunkard, Philadelphia: W. B. Saunders, 1980.

93. J. Eisenstein, S. B. Roberts, G. Dallal, and E. Saltzman, "High-Protein Weight-Loss Diets: Are They Safe and Do They Work? A Review of the Experimental and Epidemiologic Data," *Nutrition Reviews* 60(2002):189–200.

     G. D. Foster, H. R. Wyatt, J. O. Hill, B. G. McGuckin, C. Brill, B. S. Mohammed, P. O. Szapary, D. J. Rader, J. S. Erdman, and S. Klein, "A Randomized Trial of a Low-Carbohydrate Diet for Obesity," *The New England Journal of Medicine* 348(2003):2082–2090.

94. D. A. Anderson, J. R. Shapiro, J. D. Lundgren, L. E. Spataro, and C. A. Frye, "Self-Reported Dietary Restraint Is Associated with Elevated Levels of Salivary Cortisol," *Appetite* 38(2002): 13–17.

     M. W. Green, A. D. Jones, I. D. Smith, M. R. Cobain, M. G. Williams, H. Healy, P. J. Cowen, J. Powell, and P. J. Durlach, "Impairments in Working Memory Associated with Naturalistic Dieting in Women: No Relationship between Task Performance and Urinary 5-HIAA Levels," *Appetite* 40(2003):145–153.

95. H. A. Guthrie, *Introductory Nutrition*, St. Louis: Mosby, 1975.

96. B. J. Rolls, "Impact of Sugar and Fat Substitutes on Food Intake," in *Eating Disorders and Obesity: A Comprehensive Handbook*, eds. K. D. Brownell and C. G. Fairburn, New York: The Guilford Press, 1995.

97. C. De Graaf, J. J. M. M. Drijvers, N. J. H. Zimmermanns, K. H. Van het Hof, J. A. Westrate, H. Van den Berg, E. J. M. Velthuis-te Wierik, K. R. Westerterp, W. P. H. G. Verboeket-van de Venne, and M. S. Westerterp-Plantenga, "Energy and Fat Compensation during Long Term Consumption of Reduced Fat Products," *Appetite* 29(1997):305–323.

R. W. Foltin, M. W. Fischman, C. S. Emurian, and J. J. Rachlinski, "Compensation for Caloric Dilution in Humans Given Unrestricted Access to Food in a Residential Laboratory," *Appetite* 10(1988):13–24.

98. L. Abadallah, M. Chabert, B. Le Roux, and J. Louis-Sylvestre, "Is Pleasantness of Biscuits and Cakes Related to Their Actual or to Their Perceived Sugar and Fat Contents?" *Appetite* 30(1998):309–324.

99. P. Kähkönen and H. Tuorila, "Effect of Reduced-Fat Information on Expected and Actual Hedonic and Sensory Ratings of Sausages," *Appetite* 30(1998):13–23.

A. Westcombe and J. Wardle, "Influence of Relative Fat Content Information on Responses to Three Foods," *Appetite* 28(1997):49–62.

100. A. Drewnowski, "Sensory Properties of Fats and Fat Replacements," *Nutrition Reviews* 50(1992):17–20.

101. A. Drewnowski, "The New Fat Replacements: A Strategy for Reducing Fat Consumption," *Postgraduate Medicine* 87(1990):111–114, 117–118, 121.

102. S. N. Gershoff, "Nutrition Evaluation of Dietary Fat Substitutes," *Nutrition Reviews* 53(1995):305–313.

103. M. Burros, "Consumer Group Cites Illnesses in Urging Ban of Fat Substitutes," *The New York Times* (July 2, 1996):C8.

104. M. Nestle, "The Selling of Olestra," *Public Health Reports* 113(1998):508–520.

105. M. I. M. Maas, W. P. M. Hopman, B. van Gelder, M. Jacobs, A. F. J. De Haan, M. B. Katan, and J. B. M. J. Jansen, "Does Intraduodenal Administration of Sucrose Polyester (Olestra) Cause Satiation?" *Appetite* 33(1999):195–208.

106. W. J. Pasman, W. H. M. Saris, M. A. J. Wauters, and M. S. Westerterp-Plantenga, "Effect of One Week of Fibre Supplementation on Hunger and Satiety Ratings and Energy Intake," *Appetite* 29(1997):77–87.

B. Rolls and R. A. Barnett, *Volumetrics: Feel Full on Fewer Calories*, New York: HarperCollins, 2000.

107. A. Drewnowski, "Energy Density, Palatability, and Satiety: Implications for Weight Control," *Nutrition Reviews* 56(1998):347–353.

108. G. A. Leveille, "Adipose Tissue Metabolism: Influence of Periodicity of Eating and Diet Composition," *Federation Proceedings* 29(1970):1294–1301.

D. P. Speechly and R. Buffenstein, "Greater Appetite Control Associated with an Increased Frequency of Eating in Lean Males," *Appetite* 33(1999):285–297.

109. K. D. Brownell, "Exercise in the Treatment of Obesity," in *Eating Disorders and Obesity: A Comprehensive Handbook*, eds. K. D. Brownell and C. G. Fairburn, New York: The Guilford Press, 1995.

110. C. H. Folkins and W. E. Sime, "Physical Fitness Training and Mental Health," *America Psychologist* 36(1981):373–389.

W. Hollmann and H. K. Strüder, "Exercise, Physical Activity, Nutrition, and the Brain," *Nutrition Reviews* 54(1996):S37–S43.

111. P. M. Dubbert and J. E. Martin, "Exercise," in *Handbook of Behavioral Medicine for Women*, eds. E. A. Blechman and K. D. Brownell, New York: Pergamon, 1988.

112. R. M. Lampman, J. T. Santinga, P. J. Savage, D. R. Bassett, C. R. Hydrick, J. D. Flora, and W. D. Block, "Effect of Exercise Training on Glucose Tolerance, in Vivo Insulin Sensitivity, Lipid and Lipropotein Concentrations in Middle-Aged Men with Mild Hypertriglyceridemia," *Metabolism* 34(1985):205–211.

113. K. D. Brownell and A. J. Stunkard, "Physical Activity in the Development and Control of Obesity," in *Obesity*, ed. A. J. Stunkard, Philadelphia: W. B. Saunders, 1980.

J. S. Stern, "Is Obesity a Disease of Inactivity?" in *Eating and Its Disorders*, eds. A. J. Stunkard and E. Stellar, New York: Raven Press, 1984.

114. J. E. Brody, "Panel Urges Hour of Exercise a Day; Sets Diet Guidelines," *The New York Times* (September 6, 2002): A1, A18.

J. M. Jakicic, B. H. Marcus, K. I. Gallagher, M. Napolitano, and W. Lang, "Effect of Exercise Duration and Intensity on Weight Loss in Overweight, Sedentary Women," *JAMA* 290(2003):1323–1330.

M. L. Klem, R. R. Wing, M. T. McGuire, H. M. Seagle, and J. O. Hill, "A Descriptive Study of Individuals Successful at Long-Term Maintenance of Substantial Weight Loss," *American Journal of Clinical Nutrition* 66(1997):239–246.

115. K. D. Brownell, R. Y. Cohen, A. J. Stunkard, M. R. J. Felix, and N. B. Cooley, "Weight Loss Competitions at the Work Site: Impact on Weight, Morale and Cost Effectiveness," *American Journal of Public Health* 74(1984):1283–1285.

116. B. Kanner, "Return to Slender," *New York* (February 7, 1994):16, 19.

117. J. R. Garb and A. J. Stunkard, "Effectiveness of a Self-Help Group in Obesity Control," *Archives of Internal Medicine* 134(1974):716–720.

J. D. Latner, G. T. Wilson, A. J. Stunkard, and M. L. Jackson, "Self-Help and Long-Term Behavior Therapy for Obesity," *Behaviour Research and Therapy* 40(2002):805–812.

A. Stunkard, H. Levine, and S. Fox, "The Management of Obesity: Patient Self-Help and Medical Treatment," *Archives of Internal Medicine* 125(1970):1067–1072.

118. R. B. Stuart and C. Mitchell, "Self-Help Groups in the Control of Body Weight," in *Obesity*, ed. A. J. Stunkard, Philadelphia: W. B. Saunders, 1980.

119. C. S. W. Rand, "Treatment of Obese Patients in Psychoanalysis," in *Symposium on Obesity: Basic Mechanisms and Treatment*, ed. A. J. Stunkard, Philadelphia: W. B. Saunders, 1978.

A. J. Stunkard, "Psychoanalysis and Psychotherapy," in *Obesity*, ed. A. J. Stunkard, Philadelphia: W. B. Saunders, 1980.

120. G. T. Wilson, "Behavioral Approaches to the Treatment of Obesity," in *Eating Disorders and Obesity: A Comprehensive Handbook*, eds. K. D. Brownell and C. G. Fairburn, New York: The Guilford Press, 1995.

121. Spiegel, Kaplan, Tomassini, and Stellar, "Bite Size, Ingestion Rate, and Meal Size in Lean and Obese Women."

M. R. Yeomans, R. W. Gray, C. J. Mitchell, and S. True, "Independent Effects of Palatability and Within-Meal Pauses on Intake and Appetite Ratings in Human Volunteers," *Appetite* 29(1997):61–76.

122. M. L. Skender, G. K. Goodrick, D. J. Del Junco, R. S. Reeves, L. Darnell, A. M. Gotto, and J. P. Foreyt, "Comparison of 2-Year Weight Loss Trends in Behavioral Treatments of Obesity: Diet, Exercise, and Combination Interventions," *Journal of the American Dietetic Association* 96(1996):342–346.

123. Wilson, "Behavioral Approaches to the Treatment of Obesity."

124. W. G. Johnson and L. J. Torgrud, "Assessment and Treatment of Binge Eating Disorder," in *Body Image, Eating Disorders, and Obesity: An Integrative Guide for Assessment and Treatment*, ed. J. K. Thompson, Washington, DC: American Psychological Association, 1996.

125. L. H. Epstein, B. E. Saelens, M. D. Myers, and D. Vito, "Effects of Decreasing Sedentary Behaviors on Activity Choice in Obese Children," *Health Psychology* 16(1997):107–113.

T. N. Robinson, "Reducing Children's Television Viewing to Prevent Obesity," *JAMA* 282(1991):1561–1567.

126. I. Vuori, "Peak Bone Mass and Physical Activity: A Short Review," *Nutrition Reviews* 54(1996):S11–S14.

127. R. J. Shephard, "Habitual Physical Activity and Academic Performance," *Nutrition Reviews* 54(1996):S32–S36.

128. www.handango.com.

129. S. M. Garn and W. R. Leonard, "What Did Our Ancestors Eat?" *Nutrition Reviews* 47(1989): 337–345.

130. M. Konner, "What Our Ancestors Ate," *The New York Times Magazine* (June 5, 1988):54–55.

131. K. D. Brownell and K. B. Horgen, *Food Fight: The Inside Story of the Food Industry, America's Obesity Crisis, and What We Can Do about It*, Chicago: Contemporary Books, 2004.

"Filling the World's Belly," *The Economist* (December 13, 2003):3–6.

M. Nestle, *Food Politics: How the Food Industry Influences Nutrition and Health*, Berkeley: University of California Press, 2002.

132. Brownell and Horgen, *Food Fight*.

Nestle, *Food Politics*.

133. D. A. Galuska, J. C. Will, M. K. Serdula, and E. S. Ford, "Are Health Care Professionals Advising Obese Patients to Lose Weight?" *JAMA* 282(1999):1576–1578.

C. C. Wee, E. P. McCarthy, R. B. Davis, and R. S. Phillips, "Physician Counseling about Exercise," *JAMA* 282(1999):1583–1588.

134. K. D. Brownell and J. Rodin, "The Dieting Maelstrom: Is It Possible and Advisable to Lose Weight?" *American Psychologist* 49(1994):781–791.

A. K. Lindeman, "Quest for Ideal Weight: Costs and Consequences," *Medicine and Science in Sports and Exercise* 31(1999):1135–1140.

D. D. Stallone, "The Influence of Obesity and Its Treatment on the Immune System," *Nutrition Reviews* 52(1994):37–50.

S. C. Wooley, "Maelstrom Revisited," *American Psychologist* 50(1995):943–944.

135. K. D. Brownell and J. Rodin, "Medical, Metabolic, and Psychological Effects of Weight Cycling," *Archives of Internal Medicine* 154(1994):1325–1330.

136. Brownell and Rodin, "The Dieting Maelstrom."

Wooley, "Maelstrom Revisited."

137. J. P. Kassirer and M. Angell, "Losing Weight—An Ill-Fated New Year's Resolution," *The New England Journal of Medicine* 338(1998):52–54.

138. Brownell, "Dieting and the Search for the Perfect Body."

M. Meece, "Mind-Set: Only the Svelte Need Apply," *The New York Times* (March 22, 2000):G1.

Chapter 11: Drinking Your Life Away

1. "Good Soldiers," *The New York Times* (February 16, 1991):9.
2. M. Wines, "Vodka and Water, a Deadly Mix," *The New York Times* (July 4, 1999):2.
3. M. Dayagi-Mendels, *Drink and Be Merry: Wine and Beer in Ancient Times*, Jerusalem: The Jewish Museum, 1999.
4. B. L. Vallee, "Alcohol in the Western World," *Scientific American* (June 1998):80–85.
5. D. F. Musto, "Alcohol in American History," *Scientific American* (April 1996):78–83.
6. American Psychiatric Association, *Diagnostic and Statistical Manual of Mental Disorders* (Rev. ed.), 4th ed., Washington, DC: APA, 2000.
7. "Alcohol Consumption," *The New York Times* (October 19, 1992):B1.
8. L. Reisberg, "Student Stress Is Rising, Especially among Women," *The Chronicle of Higher Education* (January 28, 2000):A49, A52.
9. H. Wechsler, G. W. Dowdall, G. Maener, J. Gledhill-Hoyt, and H. Lee, "Changes in Binge Drinking and Related Problems among American College Students between 1993 and 1997: Results of the Harvard School of Public Health College Alcohol Study," *Journal of American College Health* 47(1998):57–68.
10. A. L. Klatsky, "Drink to Your Health?" *Scientific American* (February 2003):75–81.
11. S. Glautier, K. Clements, J. A. W. White, C. Taylor, and I. P. Stolerman, "Alcohol and the Reward Value of Cigarette Smoking," *Behavioral Pharmacology* 7(1996):144–154.

P. Hudson, "The Medical Examiner Looks at Drinking," in *Drinking: Alcohol in American Society—Issues and Current Research*, eds. J. A. Ewing and B. A. Rouse, Chicago: Nelson-Hall, 1978.

S. H. Mitchell, H. de Wit, and J. P. Zacny, "Effect of Varying Ethanol Dose on Cigarette Consumption in Healthy Normal Volunteers," *Behavioural Pharmacology* 6(1995):339–365.

Vallee, "Alcohol in the Western World."

12. "Pulse: Drinking and Driving," *The New York Times* (July 12, 1992):B7.
13. J. Bogaisky, "Binge Drinking by College Women Is Found Surging," *The Chronicle of Higher Education* (June 15, 1994):A32.

    H. Wechsler, C. Deutsch, and G. Dowdall, "Too Many Colleges Are Still in Denial About Alcohol Abuse," *The Chronicle of Higher Education* (April 14, 1995):B1, B2.
14. American Psychiatric Association, *Diagnostic and Statistical Manual of Mental Disorders.*
15. Vallee, "Alcohol in the Western World."
16. Y. M. Ibrahim, "Guinness and Grand Met in $22 Billion Deal," *The New York Times* (May 13, 1997):D1, D10.

    R. P. Keeling, "Drinking in College: The Politics of Research and Prevention," *Journal of American College Health* 47(1998):51–55.
17. P. Rosenzweig, *The Book of Proverbs*, New York: Philosophical Library, 1965, p. 15.
18. Ibid., p. 47.
19. Ibid., p. 28.
20. W. Shakespeare, *Macbeth* in *The Complete Works of William Shakespeare*, ed. W. A. Wright, Garden City, NY: Garden City Books, 1623/1936, p. 1035.
21. B. Critchlow, "The Powers of John Barleycorn: Beliefs about the Effects of Alcohol on Social Behavior," *American Psychologist* 41(1986):751–764.
22. W. H. George and G. A. Marlatt, "Alcoholism: The Evolution of a Behavioral Perspective," in *Recent Developments in Alcoholism*, vol. 1, ed. M. Galanter, New York: Plenum, 1983.

    G. A. Marlatt, B. Demming, and J. B. Reid, "Loss of Control Drinking in Alcoholics: An Experimental Analogue," *Journal of Abnormal Psychology* 81(1973):233–241.
23. J. G. Hull and C. F. Bond, "Social and Behavioral Consequences of Alcohol Consumption and Expectancy: A Meta-Analysis," *Psychological Bulletin* 99(1986):347–360.
24. C. S. Lieber, "The Metabolism of Alcohol," *Scientific American* 234(March 1976):25–33
25. American Psychiatric Association, *Diagnostic and Statistical Manual of Mental Disorders.*

    M. McGue, "The Behavioral Genetics of Alcoholism," *Current Directions in Psychological Science* 8(1999):109–115.
26. N. K. Mello, "Some Aspects of the Behavioral Pharmacology of Alcohol," in *Psychopharmacology: A Reviews of Progress, 1957–1967*, ed. D. H. Efron, Washington, DC: U.S. Government Printing Office, 1968.
27. D. Goldberg, "Red Head," *The Lancet* 1(May 2, 1981):1003.

    D. E. Johnston, Y.-B. Chiao, J. S. Gavaler, and D. H. Van Thiel, "Inhibition of Testosterone Synthesis by Ethanol and Acetaldehyde," *Biochemical Pharmacology* 30(1981):1827–1831.

    J. B. Knowles, S. G. Laverty, and H. A. Kuechler, "Effects of Alcohol on REM Sleep," *Quarterly Journal of Studies on Alcohol* 29(1968):342–349.

    V. C. Taasan, A. J. Block, P. G. Boyson, J. W. Wynne, C. White, and S. Lindsey, "Alcohol Increases Sleep Apnea and Oxygen Desaturation in Asymptomatic Men," *The American Journal of Medicine* 71 (1981):240–245.
28. P. M. Suter, E. Häsler, and W. Vetter, "Effects of Alcohol on Energy Metabolism and Body Weight Regulation: Is Alcohol a Risk Factor for Obesity?" *Nutrition Reviews* 55(1997):157–171.

    M. S. Westerterp-Plantenga and C. R. T. Verwegen, "The Appetizing Effect of an Apéritif in Overweight and Normal-Weight Humans," *American Journal of Clinical Nutrition* 69(1999): 205–212.
29. Westerterp-Plantenga and Verwegen, "The Appetizing Effect of an Apéritif in Overweight and Normal-Weight Humans."
30. B. J. Bushman and H. M. Cooper, "Effects of Alcohol on Human Aggression: An Integrative Research Review," *Psychological Bulletin* 107(1990):341–354.
31. C. M. Steele and R. A. Josephs, "Alcohol Myopia: Its Prized and Dangerous Effects," *Psychological Bulletin* 45(1990):921–933.
32. S. E. Burian, A. Liguori, and J. H. Robinson, "Effects of Alcohol on Risk-Taking during Simulated Driving," *Human Psychopharmacology* 17(2002):141–150.

    K. Fromme, E. Katz, and E. D'Amico, "Effects of Alcohol Intoxication on the Perceived Consequences of Risk Taking," *Experimental and Clinical Psychopharmacology* 5(1997):14–23.

33. D. M. Lovinger, G. White, and F. F. Weight, "Ethanol Inhibits NMDA-Activated Ion Current in Hippocampal Neurons," *Science* 243(1989):1721–1724.

34. H. Moskowitz and J. T. Murray, "Decrease of Iconic Memory after Alcohol," *Journal of Studies on Alcohol* 37(1976):278–283.

    R. S. Ryback, "The Continuum and Specificity of the Effects of Alcohol on Memory," *Quarterly Journal of Studies on Alcohol* 32(1971):995–1016.

35. S. L. Assefi and M. Garry, "Absolut® Memory Distortions: Alcohol Placebos Influence the Misinformation Effect," *Psychological Science* 14(2003):77–80.

36. M. K. Jones and B. M. Jones, "The Relationship of Age and Drinking Habits to the Effects of Alcohol on Memory in Women," *Journal of Studies on Alcohol* 41(1980):179–186.

37. K. R. Ridderinkhof, Y. de Vlugt, A. Bramlage, M. Spaan, M. Elton, J. Snel, and G. P. H. Band, "Alcohol Consumption Impairs Detection of Performance Errors in Mediofrontal Cortex," *Science* 298(2002):2209–2212.

38. J. R. Wenger. T. M. Tiffany, C. Bombarier, K. Nicholls, and S. C. Woods, "Ethanol Tolerance in the Rat Is Learned," *Science* 213(1981):575–577.

39. B. Remington, P. Roberts, S. Glautier, "The Effect of Drink Familiarity on Tolerance to Alcohol," *Addictive Behaviors* 22(1996):45–53.

40. S. E. Taylor, "Asymmetrical Effects of Positive and Negative Events: The Mobilization-Minimization Hypothesis," *Psychological Bulletin* 110(1991):67–85.

    S. Siegel, "Morphine Analgesic Tolerance: Its Situation Specificity Supports a Pavlovian Conditioning," *Science* 193(1976):323–325.

    S. Siegel, R. E. Hinson, M. D. Krank, and J. McCully, "Heroin 'Overdose' Death: Contribution of Drug-Associated Environmental Cues," *Science* 216(1982):436–437.

    R. L. Solomon, "The Opponent-Process Theory of Acquired Motivation," *American Psychologist* 35(1980):691–712.

41. Siegel et al., "Heroin 'Overdose' Death."

42. R. E. LaPorte, J. A. Cauley, L. H. Kuller, K. Flegal, J. S. Gavaler, and D. Van Thiel, "Alcohol, Coronary Heart Disease, and Total Mortality," in *Recent Developments in Alcoholism*, vol. 3, ed. M. Galanter, New York: Plenum, 1985.

    D. H. Van Thiel and J. S. Gavaler, "Myocardial Effects of Alcohol Abuse: Clinical and Physiologic Consequences," in *Recent Developments in Alcoholism*, vol. 3, ed. M. Galanter, New York: Plenum, 1985.

    D. H. Van Thiel, J. S. Gavaler, and D. C. Lehotay, "Biochemical Mechanisms Responsible for Alcohol-Associated Myocardiopathy," in *Recent Developments in Alcoholism*, vol. 3, ed. M. Galanter, New York: Plenum, 1985.

43. Lieber, "The Metabolism of Alcohol."

44. Siegel, "Morphine Analgesic Tolerance."

    Siegel et al., "Heroin 'Overdose' Death."

45. R. O. Deems, M. I. Friedman, L. S. Friedman, S. J. Munoz, and W. C. Maddrey, "Chemosensory Function, Food Preferences and Appetite in Human Liver Disease," *Appetite* 20(1993):209–216.

    C. S. Lieber, "The Influence of Alcohol on Nutritional Status," *Nutrition Reviews* 46(1988): 241–254.

    Lieber, "The Metabolism of Alcohol."

46. Lieber, "The Metabolism of Alcohol."

47. G. Freund, "Neurobiological Relationships between Aging and Alcohol Abuse," in *Recent Developments in Alcoholism*, vol. 2, ed. M. Galanter, New York: Plenum, 1984.

    C. J. Golden, B. Graber, l. Blose, R. Berg, J. Coffman, and S. Bloch, "Difference in Brain Densities between Chronic Alcoholic and Normal Control Patients," *Science* 211(1981):508–510.

    G. Goldstein and C. Shelly, "A Multivariate Neuropsychological Approach to Brain Lesion Localization in Alcoholism," *Addictive Behaviors* 7(1982):165–175.

    R. E. Tarter and C. M. Ryan, "Neuropsychology of Alcoholism: Etiology, Phenomenology, Process, and Outcome," in *Recent Developments in Alcoholism*, vol.1, ed. M. Galanter, New York: Plenum, 1983.

48. S. J. Nixon, "Neurocognitive Performance in Alcoholics: Is Polysubstance Abuse Important? *Psychological Science* 10(1999):181–185.

49. M. S. Albert, N. Butters, and J. Brandt, "Memory for Remote Events in Alcoholics," *Journal of Studies on Alcohol* 41(1980):1071–1081.

C. Ryan, "Learning and Memory Deficits in Alcoholics," *Journal of Studies on Alcohol* 41(1980):437–447.

H. Weingartner, L. A. Faillance, and H. G. Markley, "Verbal Information Retention in Alcoholics," *Quarterly Journal of Studies on Alcohol* 32(1971):293–303.

50. "Liver Transplants Good for Brains," *Science* 255(1992):1638.

51. S. Y. Hill and C. Ryan, "Brain Damage in Social Drinkers? Reasons for Caution," in *Recent Developments in Alcoholism*, vol. 3, ed. M. Galanter, New York: Plenum, 1985.

52. J. C. Crabbe, J. K. Belknap, and K. J. Buck, "Genetic Animal Models of Alcohol and Drug Abuse," *Science* 264(1994):1715–1723.

53. D. R. Petersen, "Pharmacogenetic Approaches to the Neuropharmacology of Ethanol," in *Recent Developments in Alcoholism*, vol. 1, ed. M. Galanter, New York: Plenum, 1983.

54. J. A. Ewing and B. A. Rouse, "Drinks, Drinkers, and Drinking," in *Drinking: Alcohol in American Society—Issues and Current Research*, eds. J. A. Ewing and B. A. Rouse, Chicago: Nelson-Hall, 1978.

55. R. Plomin, M. J. Owen, and P. McGuffin, "The Genetic Basis of Complex Human Behaviors," *Science* (1994):1733–1739.

56. K. J. Buck, P. Metten, J. K. Belknap, and J. C. Crabbe, "Quantitative Trait Loci Involved in Genetic Predisposition to Acute Alcohol Withdrawal in Mice," *The Journal of Neuroscience* 17(1997):3946–3955.

57. M. A. Schuckit and V. Rayses, "Ethanol Ingestion: Differences in Blood Acetaldehyde Concentrations in Relatives of Alcoholics and Controls," *Science* 203(1979):54–55.

58. M. A. Korsten, S. Matsuzaki, L. Feinman, and C. S. Lieber, "High Blood Acetaldehyde Levels after Ethanol Administration: Difference between Alcoholic and Nonalcoholic Subjects," *The New England Journal of Medicine* 292(8)(1975):386–389.

59. M. A. Schuckit, "Low Levels of Response to Alcohol as a Predictor of Future Alcoholism," *American Journal of Psychiatry* 151(1994):184–189.

60. H. Begleiter, B. Porjesz, B. Bihari, and B. Kissin, "Event-Related Brain Potentials in Boys at Risk for Alcoholism," Science 225(1984):1493–1496.

J. Polich, V. E. Pollock, and F. E. Bloom, "Meta-Analysis of P300 Amplitude from Males at Risk for Alcoholism" *Psychological Bulletin* 115(1994):55–73.

61. C. R. Cloninger, M. Bohman, S. Sigvardsson, and A.-L. Von Knorring, "Psychopathology in Adopted-Out Children of Alcoholics: The Stockholm Adoption Study," in *Recent Developments in Alcoholism*, vol. 3, ed. M. Galanter, New York: Plenum, 1985.

K. S. Kendler, C. A. Prescott, M. C. Neale, and N. L. Pedersen, "Temperance Board Registration for Alcohol Abuse in a National Sample of Swedish Male Twins," *Archives of General Psychiatry* 54(1997):178–184.

McGue, "The Behavioral Genetics of Alcoholism."

62. K. Blum, J. G. Cull, E. R. Braverman, and D. E. Comings, "Reward Deficiency Syndrome," *American Scientist* 84(1996):132–145.

63. H. J. Edenberg, T. Foroud, A. Goate, J. Rice, T. Reich, C. R. Cloninger, J. I. Nurnberge, T.-K. Li, P. M. Conneally, J. A. Tischfield, R. Crowe, V. Hesselbrock, M. Schuckit, B. Porjesz, and H. Begleiter, "Genetics of Alcoholism," *Science* 282(1998):1265.

C. Holden, "New Clues of Alcoholism Risk," *Science* 280(1998):1348–1349.

E. P. Noble, "DRD2 Gene and Alcoholism," *Science* 281(1998):1287–1288.

64. American Psychiatric Association, *Diagnostic and Statistical Manual of Mental Disorders*, p. 701.

65. Ibid.

M. D. Chutuape and H. de Wit, "Preferences for Ethanol and Diazepam in Anxious Individuals: An Evaluation of the Self-Medication Hypothesis," *Psychopharmacology* 121(1995): 91–103.

V. Hesselbrock, R. Meyer, and M. Hesselbrock, "Psychopathology and Addictive Disorders: The Specific Case of Antisocial Personality Disorder," in *Addictive States*, eds. C. P. O'Brien and J. H. Jaffe, New York: Raven Press, 1992.

C. X. Poulos, A. D. Le, and J. L. Parker, "Impulsivity Predicts Individual Susceptibility to High Levels of Alcohol Self-Administration," *Behavioural Pharmacology* 6(1995):810–814.

R. E. Vuchinich and C. A. Simpson, "Delayed Reward Discounting in Alcohol Abuse," in *The Economic Analysis of Substance Use and Abuse: An Integration of Econometric and Behavioral Economic Research*, eds. F. J. Chaloupka, W. K. Bickel, M. Grossman, and M. Saffer, Chicago: University of Chicago Press, 1999.

M. Zuckerman, ed., *Biological Bases of Sensation Seeking, Impulsivity, and Anxiety*, Hillsdale, NJ: Lawrence Erlbaum Associates, 1983.

66. J. C. Crabbe, T. J. Phillips, D. J. Feller, R. Hen, C. D. Wenger, C. N. Lessov, and G. L. Schafer, "Elevated Alcohol Consumption in Null Mutant Mice Lacking 5-HT$_{1B}$ Serotonin Receptors," *Nature Genetics* 14(1996):98–101.

M. Virkkunen and M. Linnoila, "Serotonin in Early Onset, Male Alcoholics with Violent Behaviour," *Annals of Medicine* 22(1990):327–331.

67. A. Heinz, J. D. Higley, J. G. Gorey, R. C. Saunders, D. W. Jones, D. Hommer, K. Zajicek, S. J. Suomi, K.-P. Lesch, D. R. Weinberger, and M. Linnoila, "*In Vivo* Association between Alcohol Intoxication, Aggression, and Serotonin Transporter Availability in Nonhuman Primates," *American Journal of Psychiatry* 155(1998):1023–1028.

68. S. H. Stewart, "Alcohol Abuse in Individuals Exposed to Trauma: A Critical Review," *Psychological Bulletin* 120(1996):83–112.

69. J. M. De Castro, "Social, Circadian, Nutritional, and Subjective Correlates of the Spontaneous Pattern of Moderate Alcohol Intake of Normal Humans," *Pharmacology, Biochemistry and Behavior* 35(1990):923–931.

P. Doty and H. de Wit, "Effect of Setting on the Reinforcing and Subjective Effects of Ethanol in Social Drinkers," *Psychopharmacology* 118(1995):19–27.

M. Lennernäs, L. Hambraeus, and T. Åkerstedt, "Shift Related Dietary Intake in Day and Shift Workers," *Appetite* 25(1995):253–265.

70. Doty and de Wit, "Effect of Setting on the Reinforcing and Subjective Effects of Ethanol in Social Drinkers."

71. D. W. Watson and M. B. Sobell, "Social Influences on Alcohol Consumption by Black and White Males," *Addictive Behaviors* 7(1982):87–91.

72. R. L. Collins and G. A. Marlatt, "Social Modeling as a Determinant of Drinking Behavior: Implications for Prevention and Treatment," *Addictive Behaviors* 6(1981):233–239.

R. L. Collins and G. A. Marlatt, "Psychological Correlates and Explanations of Alcohol Use and Abuse," in *Medical and Social Aspects of Alcohol Abuse*, eds. B. Tabakoff, P. B. Sutker, and C. I. Randall, New York: Plenum, 1983.

73. G. N. Braucht, "How Environments and Persons Combine to Influence Problem Drinking: Current Research Issues," in *Recent Developments in Alcoholism*, vol. 1, ed. M. Galanter, New York: Plenum, 1983.

T. C. Harford, "Drinking Patterns among Black and Nonblack Adolescents: Results of a National Survey," in *Alcohol and Culture: Comparative Perspectives from Europe and America*, ed. T. F. Babor, New York: New York Academy of Sciences, 1986.

74. J. B. Reid, "Study of Drinking in Natural Settings," in *Behavioral Approaches to Alcoholism*, eds. G. A. Marlatt and P. E. Nathan, New Brunswick, NJ: Rutgers Center of Alcohol Studies, 1978.

75. K. Ackroff and A. Sclafani, "Flavor Preferences Conditioned by Intragastric Infusion of Ethanol in Rats," *Pharmacology, Biochemistry and Behavior* 68(2002):327–338.

R. Mehiel and R. C. Bolles, "Learned Flavor Preferences Based on Caloric Outcome," *Animal Learning and Behavior* 12(1984):421–427.

J. Sherman, K. W. Rusiniak, and J. Garcia, "Alcohol Ingestive Habits: The Role of Flavor and Effect," in *Recent Developments in Alcoholism*, vol. 2, ed. M. Galanter, New York: Plenum, 1984.

76. W. J. Darby, "The Nutrient Contributions of Fermented Beverages," in *Fermented Food Beverages in Nutrition*, eds. C. F. Gastineau, W. J. Darby, and T. B. Turner, New York: Academic Press, 1979.

R. Passmore, "The Energy Value of Alcohol," in *Fermented Food Beverages in Nutrition*, eds. C. F. Gastineau, W. J. Darby, and T. B. Turner, New York: Academic Press, 1979.

77. H. Cappell, "An Evaluation of Tension Models of Alcohol Consumption," in *Research Advances in Alcohol and Drug Problems*, vol. 2, eds. R. J. Gibbins, Y. Israel, H. Kalant, R. E. Popham, W. Schmidt, and R. G. Smart, New York: Wiley, 1975.

M. A. Sayette, "An Appraisal-Disruption Model of Alcohol's Effects on Stress Responses in Social Drinkers," *Psychological Bulletin* 114(1993):459–476.

G. T. Wilson, "Alcohol and Anxiety: Recent Evidence on the Tension Reduction Theory of Alcohol Use and Abuse," in *Self Control and Self-Modification of Emotional Behavior*, eds. K. R. Blankstein and J. Polivy, New York: Plenum, 1982.

78. T. F. Doyle and H. H. Samson, "Schedule-Induced Drinking in Humans: A Potential Factor in Excessive Alcohol Use," *Drug and Alcohol Dependence* 16(1985):117–132.

A. L. Riley and C. W. Wetherington, "Schedule-Induced Polydipsia: Is the Rat a Small Furry Human? (An Analysis of an Animal Model of Human Alcoholism)," in *Contemporary Learning Theories: Instrumental Conditioning Theory and the Impact of Biological Constraints on Learning*, eds. S. B. Klein and R. R. Mowrer, Hillsdale, NJ: Lawrence Erlbaum Associates, 1989.

79. J. L. Falk and H. H. Samson, "Schedule-Induced Physical Dependence on Ethanol," *Pharmacological Reviews* 27(1976):449–464.

J. L. Falk and M. Tang, "Animal Model of Alcoholism: Critique and Progress," in *Alcohol Intoxication and Withdrawal*, vol. 38, ed. M. M. Gross, New York: Plenum, 1977.

80. S. I. Ornstein and D. Levy, "Price and Income Elasticities of Demand for Alcoholic Beverages," in *Recent Developments in Alcoholism*, vol. 1, ed. M. Galanter, New York: Plenum, 1983.

J. Rabow and R. K. Watts, "The Role of Alcohol Availability in Alcohol Consumption and Alcohol Problems," in *Recent Developments in Alcoholism*, vol. 1 ed. M. Galanter, New York: Plenum, 1983.

81. D. L. Brito and C. K. Strain, "A Model of the Consumption of Alcohol," in *Advances in Behavioral Economics: Vol. 3. Substance Use and Abuse*, eds. L. Green and J. H. Kagel, Norwood, NJ: Ablex Publishing Corporation, 1996.

G. M. Heyman, "Elasticity of Demand for Alcohol in Humans and Rats," in *Advances in Behavioral Economics: Vol. 3. Substance Use and Abuse*, eds. L. Green and J. H. Kagel, Norwood, NJ: Ablex Publishing Corporation, 1996.

82. R. E. Vuchinich and J. A. Tucker, "Contributions from Behavioral Theories of Choice to an Analysis of Alcohol Abuse," *Journal of Abnormal Psychology* 97(1988):181–195.

R. E. Vuchinich, J. A. Tucker, and E. J. Rudd, "Preference for Alcohol Consumption as a Function of Amount and Delay of Alternative Reward," *Journal of Abnormal Psychology* 96(1987):259–263.

83. McGue, "The Behavioral Genetics of Alcoholism."

84. Rosenzweig, *The Book of Proverbs*, p. 66.

85. K. D. Brownell, G. A. Marlatt, E. Lichtenstein, and G. T. Wilson, "Understanding and Preventing Relapse," *American Psychologist* 41(1986):765–782.

George and Marlatt, "Alcoholism."

G. A. Marlatt, "Craving for Alcohol, Loss of Control, and Relapse: A Cognitive-Behavioral Analysis," in *Alcoholism: New Directions in Behavioral Research and Treatment*, eds. P. E. Nathan, G. A. Marlatt, and T. Loberg, New York: Plenum, 1978.

86. C. Holden, "Is Alcoholism Treatment Effective?" *Science* 236(1987):20–22.

W. R. Miller and R. K. Hester, "Inpatient Alcoholism Treatment: Who Benefits?" *American Psychologist* 41(1986):794–805.

87. M. B. Sobell and L. C. Sobell, *Behavioral Treatment of Alcohol Problems: Individualized Therapy and Controlled Drinking*, New York: Plenum, 1978.

88. G. A. Marlatt, "The Controlled-Drinking Controversy," *American Psychologist* 38(1983): 1097–1110.

M. B. Sobell and L. C. Sobell, "Controlled Drinking: A Concept Coming of Age," in *Self-Control and Self-Modification of Emotional Behavior*, eds. K. R. Blankstein and J. Polivy, New York: Plenum, 1982.

89. B. Leach and J. L. Norris, "Factors in the Development of Alcoholics Anonymous (A.A.)," in *Treatment and Rehabilitation of the Chronic Alcoholic*, eds. B. Kissin and H. Begleiter, New York: Plenum, 1977.

S. Peele, "All Wet," *The Sciences* (March/April 1998):17–21.

90. C. B. De Soto, W. E. O'Donnell, and J. L. De Soto, "Long-Term Recovery in Alcoholics," *Alcoholism: Clinical and Experimental Research* 13(1989):693–697.

91. Sobell and Sobell, *Behavioral Treatment of Alcohol Problems*.

92. J. L. Chase, H. C. Salzberg, and A. M. Palotai, "Controlled Drinking Revisited: A Review," in *Progress in Behavior Modification*, vol. 18, eds. M. Hersen, R. M. Eisler, and P. M. Miller, New York: Academic Press, 1984.

Peele, "All Wet."

J. M. Polich, D. J. Armor, and H. B. Braiker, *The Course of Alcoholism: Four Years after Treatment*, Santa Monica, CA: Rand, 1980.

93. H. Rosenberg, "Prediction of Controlled Drinking by Alcoholics and Problem Drinkers," *Psychological Bulletin* 113(1993):129–139.

94. Peele, "All Wet."

L. C. Sobell, M. B. Sobell, and T. Toneatto, "Recovery from Alcohol Problems without Treatment," in *Self-Control and the Addictive Behaviours*, eds. N. Heather, W. R. Miller, and J. Greeley, New York: Maxwell Macmillan, 1991.

95. G. E. Vaillant, "A Long-Term Follow-Up of Male Alcohol Abuse," *Archives of General Psychiatry* 53(1996):243–249.

96. M. L. Pendery, L. M. Maltzman, and L. J. West, "Controlled Drinking by Alcoholics?: New Findings and a Reevaluation of a Major Affirmative Study," *Science* 217(1982):169–175.

97. M. B. Sobell and L. C. Sobell, "The Aftermath of Heresy: A Response to Pendery et al.'s (1982) Critique of 'Individualized Behavior Therapy for Alcoholics,'" *Behaviour Research and Therapy* 22(1984):413–440.

98. P. H. Abelson, "Alcoholism Studies," *Science* 220(1983):554, 556.

D. H. Barlow, A. S. Bellack, A. M. Buchwald, S. L. Garfield, D. P. Hartmann, C. P. Herman, M. Hersen, P. M. Miller, S. Rachman, and J. Wolpe, "Alcoholism Studies," *Science* 220(1983):554.

P. M. Boffey, "Showdown Nears in Feud over Alcohol Studies," *The New York Times* (November 2, 1982):C1–C2.

K. Fisher, "Debate Rages on 1973 Sobell Study," *APA Monitor* (November 1982):8–9.

K. A. McDonald, "Rutgers Journal Forced to Publish Paper Despite Threats of Libel Lawsuit," *The Chronicle of Higher Education* (September 13, 1989):A5, A12.

99. C. Norman, "No Fraud Found in Alcoholism Study," *Science* 218(1982):771.

100. K. Fisher, "'Incomplete' Report Clears Sobells," *APA Monitor* (November 1984):2.

101. Peele, "All Wet."

102. R. Finn, "Sudden Exit Still Stuns Addiction Specialist," *The New York Times* (July 26, 2000):B2.

"Manhattan: Smithers Foundation Sues Hospital," *The New York Times* (July 27, 2000):B7.

M. Szalavitz, "Drink Your Medicine," *New York* (July 10, 2000):11–12.

103. W. R. Miller, J. M. Brown, T. L. Simpson, N. S. Handmaker, T. H. Bien, L. F. Luckie, H. A. Montgomery, R. K. Hester, and J. S. Tonigan, "What Works? A Methodological Analysis of the Alcohol Treatment Outcome Literature," in *Handbook of Alcoholism Treatment Approaches: Effective Alternatives*, 2d ed., eds. R. K. Hester and W. R. Miller, Boston: Allyn and Bacon, 1995.

104. N. Heather, "Brief Intervention Strategies," in *Handbook of Alcoholism Treatment Approaches: Effective Alternatives*, 2d ed., eds. R. K. Hester and W. R. Miller, Boston: Allyn and Bacon, 1995.

105. P. M. Monti, D. J. Rohsenow, S. M. Colby, and D. B. Abrams, "Coping and Social Skills Training," in *Handbook of Alcoholism Treatment Approaches: Effective Alternatives*, eds. R. K. Hester and W. R. Miller, Boston: Allyn and Bacon, 1995.

106. W. R. Miller, "Increasing Motivation for Change," in *Handbook of Alcoholism Treatment Approaches: Effective Alternatives*, 2d ed., eds. R. K. Hester and W. R. Miller, Boston: Allyn and Bacon, 1995.

107. J. E. Smith and R. J. Meyers, "The Community Reinforcement Approach," in *Handbook of Alcoholism Treatment Approaches: Effective Alternatives*, 2d ed., eds. R. K. Hester and W. R. Miller, Boston: Allyn and Bacon, 1995.
108. Miller et al., "What Works?"
109. J. D. Duffy, "The Neurology of Alcoholic Denial: Implications for Assessment and Treatment," *Canadian Journal of Psychiatry* 40(1995):257–263.
110. C. B. De Soto, W. E. O'Donnell, L. J. Alfred, and C. E. Lopes, "Symptomatology in Alcoholics at Various Stages of Abstinence," *Alcoholism: Clinical and Experimental Research* 9(1985): 505–512.
111. R. L. Elkins, "An Appraisal of Chemical Aversion (Emetic Therapy) Approaches to Alcoholism Treatment," *Behaviour Research and Therapy* 29(1991):387–413.
    C. T. Rinmele, M. O. Howard, and M. L. Hilfrink, "Aversion Therapies," in *Handbook of Alcoholism Treatment Approaches: Effective Alternatives*, 2d ed., eds. R. K. Hester and W. R. Miller, Boston: Allyn and Bacon, 1995.
112. A. W. Logue, "Taste Aversion and the Generality of the Laws of Learning," *Psychological Bulletin* 86(1979):276–296.
113. A. W. Logue, K. R. Logue, and K. E. Strauss, "The Acquisition of Taste Aversions in Humans with Eating and Drinking Disorders," *Behaviour Research and Therapy* 21(1983):275–289.
114. C. S. Mellor and H. P. White, "Taste Aversions to Alcoholic Beverages Conditioned by Motion Sickness," *American Journal of Psychiatry* 135(1978):125–126.
115. Miller et al., "What Works?"
116. Ayerst Laboratories Inc., *Antabuse® Brand of Disulfiram in Alcoholism*, New York: Ayerst Laboratories Inc., 1986.
117. G. K. Litman and A. Topham, "Outcome Studies on Techniques in Alcoholism Treatment," in *Recent Developments in Alcoholism*, vol. 1, ed. M. Galanter, New York: Plenum, 1983, p.172.
118. Ayerst Laboratories Inc., *Antabuse® Brand of Disulfiram in Alcoholism*.
119. G. Bigelow, D. Strickler, I. Liebson, and R. Griffiths, "Maintaining Disulfiram Ingestion among Outpatient Alcoholics: A Security-Deposit Contingency Contracting Procedure," *Behaviour Research and Therapy* 14(1976):378–381.
120. George and Marlatt, "Alcoholism."
    Marlatt, "Craving for Alcohol, Loss of Control, and Relapse."
    G. A. Marlatt, "Alcohol Use and Problem Drinking: A Cognitive-Behavioral Analysis," in *Cognitive-Behavioral Interventions*, eds. P. C. Kendall and S. D. Hollon, New York: Academic Press, 1979.
121. Miller et al., "What Works?"
122. R. K. Hester and H. D. Delaney, "Behavioral Self-Control Program for Windows: Results of a Controlled Clinical Trial," *Journal of Consulting and Clinical Psychology* 65(1997):686–693.
123. Miller et al., "What Works?"
124. B. S. McCrady and S. I. Delaney, "Self-Help Groups," in *Handbook of Alcoholism Treatment Approaches: Effective Alternatives*, 2d ed., eds. R. K. Hester and W. R. Miller, Boston: Allyn and Bacon, 1995.
    Personal communication from Alcoholics Anonymous Information Office, August 1990.
125. Alcoholics Anonymous, *Welcome to Alcoholics Anonymous*, 2004. Available at: www.alcoholics-anonymous.org.
126. B. S. McCrady, E. E. Epstein, and L. S. Hirsch, "Maintaining Change after Conjoint Behavioral Alcohol Treatment for Men: Outcomes at 6 Months," *Addiction* 94(1999):1381–1396.
127. Peele, "All Wet."
    Project MATCH Research Group, "Matching Alcoholism Treatments to Client Heterogeneity: Project MATCH Posttreatment Drinking Outcomes," *Journal of Studies on Alcohol* 58(1997): 7–29.
128. D. A. Dawson, "Correlates of Past-Year Status among Treated and Untreated Persons with Former Alcohol Dependence: United States, 1992," *Alcoholism: Clinical and Experimental Research* 20(1996):771–779.
    Peele, "All Wet."
129. Peele, "All Wet."

130. L. A. Rone, S. I. Miller, and R. J. Frances, "Psychotropic Medications," in *Handbook of Alcoholism Treatment Approaches: Effective Alternatives*, 2d ed., eds. R. K. Hester and W. R. Miller, Boston: Allyn and Bacon, 1995.

131. M. Linnoila, M. Virkkunen, A. Roy, and W. A. Potter, "Monoamines, Glucose Metabolism and Impulse Control," in *Violence and Suicidality: Perspectives in Clinical and Psychobiological Research*, eds. H. M. van Praag, R. Plutchik, and A. Apter, New York: Brunner/Mazel, 1990.

132. D. Johnson, "Reversing Reservation's Pattern of Hard Drink and Early Death," *The New York Times* (December 23, 1997):A16.

133. J. Flaherty, "Ad Campaign Focuses on Binge Drinking by College Students," *The New York Times* (September 8, 1999):B12.

L. Reisberg, "Colleges Step up Efforts to Combat Alcohol Abuse," *The Chronicle of Higher Education* (June 12, 1998):A41–A42.

Wechsler, Deutsch, and Dowdall, "Too Many Colleges Are Still in Denial about Alcohol Abuse."

K. Zernike, "New Tactic on College Drinking: Play It Down," *The New York Times* (October 3, 2000):A1, A20.

134. S. T. Walters, "In Praise of Feedback: An Effective Intervention for College Students Who Are Heavy Drinkers," *Journal of American College Health* 48(2000):235–238.

135. K. Bourke, "NIAAA Launches College Age Initiative," *APS Observer* (January 1999):1, 10, 28.

136. W. R. Miller and S. A. Brown, "Why Psychologists Should Treat Alcohol and Drug Problems," *American Psychologist* 52(1997):1269–1279.

137. D. Hawks, "Prevention and the Locus of Control: Internal, External or Somewhere in Between?" in *Self-Control and the Addictive Behaviours*, eds. N. Heather, W. R. Miller, and J. Greeley, New York: Maxwell Macmillan, 1991.

Musto, "Alcohol in American History."

M. Kuo, H. Wechsler, P. Greenberg, and H. Lee, "The Marketing of Alcohol to College Students: The Role of Low Prices and Special Promotions," *American Journal of Preventive Medicine* 25(2003):204–211.

138. M. Massing, "Strong Stuff," *The New York Times* (March 22, 1998):36–41, 48, 58, 72, 73.

Chapter 12: How Sweet It Is

1. D. Grady, "New Fronts in the War on Diabetes in Adults," *The New York Times* (September 7, 1999):F1, F9.

2. J. Marx, "Unraveling the Causes of Diabetes," *Science* 296(2002):686–689.

D. M. Nathan and R. Frishman, *Diabetes*, Boston, MA: Harvard Medical School Health Publications Group, 1999.

3. D. Grady, "More Bad News for a Fattening America," *The New York Times* (August 27, 2000):2.

4. J. Adler and C. Kalb, "An American Epidemic: Diabetes," *Newsweek* (September 4, 2000):40–47.

5. "Gene Factor Seen in Blacks' Diabetes," *The New York Times* (February 7, 1996):C9.

Marx, "Unraveling the Causes of Diabetes."

6. P. H. Bennett, "Type 2 Diabetes among the Pima Indians of Arizona: An Epidemic Attributable to Environmental Change?" *Nutrition Reviews* 57(1999):S51–S54.

Marx, "Unraveling the Causes of Diabetes."

7. Nathan and Frishman, *Diabetes*.

8. P. Björntorp, "The Importance of Body Fat Distribution," in *Eating Disorders and Obesity: A Comprehensive Handbook*, eds. K. D. Brownell and C. G. Fairburn, New York: The Guilford Press, 1995.

9. Ibid., p. 1.

10. Nathan and Frishman, *Diabetes*.

11. W. Shakespeare, *Othello* in *The Complete Works of William Shakespeare*, ed. W. A. Wright, Garden City, NY: Garden City Books, 1623/1936, p. 634.

12. K. L. Morris and M. B. Zemel, "Glycemic Index, Cardiovascular Disease, and Obesity," *Nutrition Reviews* 57(1999):273–276.

13. S. Holt, J. Brand, C. Soveny, and J. Hansky, "Relationship of Satiety to Postprandial Glycaemic, Insulin, and Cholecystokinin Responses," *Appetite* 18(1992):129–141.

14. Morris and Zemel, "Glycemic Index, Cardiovascular Disease, and Obesity."

15. J. H. Lavin and N. W. Read, "The Effect on Hunger and Satiety of Slowing the Absorption of Glucose: Relationship with Gastric Emptying and Postprandial Blood Glucose and Insulin Responses," *Appetite* 25(1995):89–96.

16. Holt et al., "Relationship of Satiety to Postprandial Glycaemic, Insulin, and Cholecystokinin Responses."

    Morris and Zemel, "Glycemic Index, Cardiovascular Disease, and Obesity."

17. J. Albu, D. Allison, C. N. Boozer, S. Heymsfield, H. Kissileff, A. Kretser, K. Krumhar, R. Leibel, C. Nonas, X. Pi-Sunyer, T. VanItallie, and E. Wedral, "Obesity Solutions: Report of a Meeting," *Nutrition Reviews* 55(1997):150–156.

    Björntorp, "The Importance of Body Fat Distribution."

    S. M. Haffner, "Are There People Who Do Not Need to Lose Weight: The Role of Body Fat Distribution and Implications from Diabetes Research," in *Obesity Treatment: Establishing Goals, Improving Outcomes, and Reviewing the Research Agenda*, eds. D. B. Allison and F. X. Pi-Sunyer, New York: Plenum, 1995.

    M. W. Schwartz, "Staying Slim with Insulin in Mind," *Science* 289(2000):2066–2067.

18. M. Wei, L. W. Gibbons, T. L. Mitchell, J. B. Kampert, C. D. Lee, and S. N. Blair, "The Association between Cardiorespiratory Fitness and Impaired Fasting Glucose and Type 2 Diabetes in Men," *Annals of Internal Medicine* 130(1999):89–96.

19. Bennett, "Type 2 Diabetes among the Pima Indians of Arizona."

    C. Gonzalez, M. P. Stern, E. Gonzalez, D. Rivera, J. Simon, S. Islas, and S. Haffner, "The Mexico City Diabetes Study: A Population-Based Approach to the Study of Genetic and Environmental Interactions in the Pathogenesis of Obesity and Disease," *Nutrition Review* 57(1999):S71–S77.

    R. A. Hegele, "Lessons from Genetic Studies in Native Canadian Populations," *Nutrition Reviews* 57(1999):S43–S50.

20. P. Tessari, "Changes in Protein, Carbohydrate, and Fat Metabolism with Aging: Possible Role of Insulin," *Nutrition Reviews* 58(2000):11–19.

21. M. Elchebly, P. Payette, E. Michaliszyn, W. Cromlish, S. Collins, A. L. Loy, D. Normandin, A. Cheng, J. Himms-Hagen, C.-C. Chan, C. Ramachandran, M. J. Gresser, M. L. Tremblay, and B. P. Kennedy, "Increased Insulin Sensitivity and Obesity Resistance in Mice Lacking the Protein Tyrosine Phosphatase-1B Gene," *Science* 283(1999):1544–1548.

22. Nathan and Frishman, *Diabetes.*

23. Gonzalez et al., "The Mexico City Diabetes Study."

    M. P. Stern, "Genetic and Environmental Influences on Type 2 Diabetes," *Nutrition Reviews* 57(1999):S66–S70.

24. J. Diamond, "Sweet Death," *Natural History* (February, 1992):2–4, 6.

    G. M. Reaven, "Insulin Resistance: A Chicken that Has Come to Roost," in *The Metabolic Syndrome X: Convergence of Insulin Resistance, Glucose Intolerance, Hypertension, Obesity, and Dyslipidemias—Searching for the Underlying Defects*, eds. B. C. Hansen, J. Saye, and L. W. Wennogle, New York: The New York Academy of Sciences, 1999.

25. Bennett, "Type 2 Diabetes among the Pima Indians of Arizona."

26. Nathan and Frishman, *Diabetes.*

27. B. J. Rolls and E. T. Rolls, *Thirst,* Cambridge: Cambridge University Press, 1982.

28. J. Rodin, "Insulin Levels, Hunger, and Food Intake: An Example of Feedback Loops in Body Weight Regulation," *Health Psychology* 4(1985):1–24.

29. P. J. Geiselman, "Sugar-Induced Hyperphagia: Is Hyperinsulinemia, Hypoglycemia, or Any Other Factor a 'Necessary' Condition?" *Appetite* 11(1988):26–34.

30. I. Ramirez and M. I. Friedman, "Food Intake and Blood Fuels after Oil Consumption: Differential Effects in Normal and Diabetic Rats," *Physiology and Behavior* 31(1983):847–850.

31. K. Ackroff, A. Sclafani, and K. V. Axen, "Diabetic Rats Prefer Glucose-Paired Flavors over Fructose-Paired Flavors," *Appetite* 28(1997):73–83.

32. R. G. Settle, "The Chemical Senses in Diabetes Mellitus," in *Smell and Taste in Health and Disease*, eds. T. V. Getchell, L. M. Bartoshuk, R. L. Doty, and J. B. Snow, New York: Raven Press, 1991.

33. H. N. Haan, "The Role of *APOE* 4 in Modulating Effects of Other Risk Factors for Cognitive Decline in Elderly Persons," *JAMA* 282(1999):40–46.

34. D. Benton, "The Impact of the Supply of Glucose to the Brain on Mood and Memory," *Nutrition Reviews* 59(2001):S20–S21.

    J. E. Morley, "Nutritional Modulation of Behavior and Immunocompetence," *Nutrition Reviews* 52(1994):S6–S8.

35. R. R. Wing, "Treatment of Obesity in the Diabetic Patient," in *Eating Disorders and Obesity: A Comprehensive Handbook*, eds. K. D. Brownell and C. G. Fairburn, New York: The Guilford Press, 1995.

36. "Lipogenesis in Diabetes and Obesity," *Nutrition Reviews* 49(1991):255–257.

    Nathan and Frishman, *Diabetes*.

    Wing, "Treatment of Obesity in the Diabetic Patient."

37. Wing, "Treatment of Obesity in the Diabetic Patient."

38. R. M. Lampman, J. T. Santinga, P. J. Savage, D. R. Bassett, C. R. Hydrick, J. D. Flora, and W. D. Block, "Effect of Exercise Training on Glucose Tolerance, in Vivo Insulin Sensitivity, Lipid and Lipoprotein Concentrations in Middle-Aged Men with Mild Hypertriglyceridemia," *Metabolism* 34(1985):205–211.

39. Nathan and Frishman, *Diabetes*.

40. A. L. Peters, "Diabetic's Olympian Triumph," *The New York Times* (October 31, 2000):F7.

41. R. M. Sanchez-Quesada, J. Ordonez-Llanos, T. Prat, A. Caixas, O. Jorba, J. R. Serra, A. De Leiva, and A. Perez, "Effect of Physical Exercise on Lipoprotein(a) and Low-Density Lipoprotein Modifications in Type 1 and Type 2 Diabetic Patients," *Metabolism* 49(2000):640–647.

42. Tessari, "Changes in Protein, Carbohydrate, and Fat Metabolism with Aging."

43. M. Wei, L. W. Gibbons, J. B. Kampert, M. Z. Nichaman, and S. N. Blair, "Low Cardiorespiratory Fitness and Physical Inactivity as Predictors of Mortality in Men with Type 2 Diabetes," *Annals of Internal Medicine* 132(2000):605–611.

    Wei, Gibbons, Mitchell, Kampert, Lee, and Blair, "The Association between Cardiorespiratory Fitness and Impaired Fasting Glucose and Type 2 Diabetes in Men."

44. S. H. A. Holt and J. B. Miller, "Increased Insulin Responses to Ingested Foods Are Associated with Lessened Satiety," *Appetite* 24(1995):43–54.

    M. McIntosh and C. Miller, "A Diet Containing Food Rich in Soluble and Insoluble Fiber Improves Glycemic Control and Reduces Hyperlipidemia among Patients with Type 2 Diabetes Mellitus," *Nutrition Reviews* 59(2001):52–57.

45. D. S. Ludwig, M. A. Pereira, C. H. Kroenke, J. E. Hilner, L. Van Horn, M. L. Slattery, and D. R. Jacobs, "Dietary Fiber, Weight Gain, and Cardiovascular Disease Risk Factors in Young Adults," *JAMA* 282(1999):1539–1546.

46. C. Senécal, A. Nouwen, and D. White, "Motivation and Dietary Self-Care in Adults with Diabetes: Are Self-Efficacy and Autonomous Self-Regulation Complementary or Competing Constructs?" *Health Psychology* 19(2000):452–457.

47. Nathan and Frishman, *Diabetes*.

48. J. Alper, "New Insights into Type 2 Diabetes," *Science* 289(2000):37, 39.

49. Elchebly et al., "Increased Insulin Sensitivity and Obesity Resistance in Mice Lacking the Protein Tyrosiac Phosphatose-1B Gene."

50. Nathan and Frishman, *Diabetes*.

51. J. E. Brody, "Small, Convenient and Flexible, Insulin Pumps Catch On," *The New York Times* (August 10, 1998):F7.

52. D. A. Galuska, J. C. Will, M. K. Serdula, and E. S. Ford, "Are Health Care Professionals Advising Obese Patients to Lose Weight? *JAMA* 282(1999):1576–1578.

    C. C. Wee, E. P. McCarthy, R. B. Davis, and R. S. Phillips, "Physician Counseling about Exercise," *JAMA* 282(1999):1583–1588.

53. Marx, "Unraveling the Causes of Diabetes."

Chapter 13: Strictly About Females

1. P. J. Brown and M. Konner, "An Anthropological Perspective on Obesity," in *Human Obesity*, eds. R. J. Wurtman and J. J. Wurtman, New York: New York Academy of Sciences, 1987.
2. S. M. Evans, R. W. Foltin, and M. W. Fischman "Food 'Cravings' and the Acute Effects of Alprazolam on Food Intake in Women with Premenstrual Dysphoric Disorder," *Appetite* 32(1999):331–349.

   C. M. Logue and R. H. Moos, "Perimenstrual Symptoms: Prevalence and Risk Factors," *Psychosomatic Medicine* 48(1986):388–414.

   P. J. Rogers and P. Jas, "Menstrual Cycle Effects on Mood, Eating and Food Choice," *Appetite* 23(1994):289.

   S. T. St. Jeor, M. R. Sutnick, and B. J. Scott, "Nutrition," in *Handbook of Behavioral Medicine for Women*, eds. E. A. Blechman and K. D. Brownell, New York: Pergamon, 1988.
3. American Psychiatric Association, *Diagnostic and Statistical Manual of Mental Disorders* (Rev. ed.), 4th ed., Washington, DC: APA, 2000.
4. "Energy Expenditure during the Menstrual Cycle," *Nutrition Reviews* 45(1987):102–103.
5. M. S. Kurzer, "Women, Food, and Mood," *Nutrition Reviews* 55(1997):268–276.

   E. T. S. Li, L. B. Y. Tsang, and S. S. H. Lui, "Menstrual Cycle and Voluntary Food Intake in Young Chinese Women," *Appetite* 33(1999):109–118.

   Rogers and Jas, "Menstrual Cycle Effects on Mood, Eating and Food Choice."
6. "Energy Expenditure during the Menstrual Cycle."

   L. A. Leiter, N. Hrboticky, and G. H. Anderson, "Effects of L-Tryptophan on Food Intake and Selection in Lean Men and Women," *Human Obesity*, eds. R. J. Wurtman and J. J. Wurtman, New York: New York Academy of Sciences, 1987.

   St. Jeor et al., "Nutrition."
7. R. J. Wurtman and J. J. Wurtman, "Carbohydrates and Depression," *Scientific American* 260(January 1989):68–75.
8. C. S. Pomerleau, A. W. Garcia, A. Drewnowski, and O. E. Pomerleau, "Sweet Taste Preference in Woman Smokers: Comparison with Nonsmokers and Effects of Menstrual Phase and Nicotine Abstinence," *Pharmacology, Biochemistry and Behavior* 40(1991):995–999.
9. T. Engen, *The Perception of Odors*, New York: Academic Press, 1982.

   R. G. Mair, J. A. Bouffard, and T. Engen, "Olfactory Sensitivity during the Menstrual Cycle," *Sensory Processes* 2(1978):90–98.
10. R. E. Frisch, "Fatness and Fertility," *Scientific American* 258(March 1988):88–95.
11. J. L. Cameron, "Nutritional Determinants of Puberty," *Nutrition Reviews* 54(1996):S17–S22.

    B. R. Olson, "Effects of Nutrition on Reproductive Capacity," in *Food Intake and Energy Expenditure*, eds. M. S. Westerterp-Plantenga, E. W. H. M. Fredrix, and A. B. Steffens, Boca Raton, FL: CRC Press, 1994.
12. J. A. McLean and S. I. Barr, "Cognitive Dietary Restraint Is Associated with Eating Behaviors, Lifestyle Practices, Personality Characteristics and Menstrual Irregularity in College Women," *Appetite* 40(2003):185–192.
13. M. E. Herman-Giddens, E. J. Slora, R. C. Wasserman, C. J. Bourdony, M. V. Bhapkar, G. G. Koch, and C. M. Hasemeier, "Secondary Sexual Characteristics and Menses in Young Girls Seen in Office Practice: A Study from the Pediatric Research in Office Settings Network," *Pediatrics* 99(1997):505–512.
14. M. May, "Battles over Body Fat," *Science* 260(1993):1592–1593.
15. R. E. Frisch, *Female Fertility and the Body Fat Connection*, Chicago: University of Chicago Press, 2002.
16. Olson, "Effects of Nutrition on Reproductive Capacity."
17. K. D. Brownell, "History of Obesity," in *Eating Disorders and Obesity: A Comprehensive Handbook*, eds. K. D. Brownell and C. G. Fairburn, New York: The Guilford Press, 1995.
18. J. E. Schneider and G. N. Wade, "Availability of Metabolic Fuels Controls Estrous Cyclicity of Syrian Hamsters," *Science* 244(1989):1326–1328.
19. Cameron, "Nutritional Determinants of Puberty."

20. P. M. Dubbert and J. E. Martin, "Exercise," in *Handbook of Behavioral Medicine for Women*, eds. E. A. Blechman and K. D. Brownell, New York: Pergamon, 1988.

   P. Ellison, "American Scientist Interviews," *American Scientist* 75(1987):622–627.

   Logue and Moos, "Perimenstrual Symptoms."

21. Frisch, "Fatness and Fertility."

   Dubbert and Martin, "Exercise."

22. L. P. Morin, "Effects of Various Feeding Regimens and Photoperiod or Pinealectomy on Ovulation in the Hamster," *Biology of Reproduction* 13(1975):99–103.

23. K. Brownell, "The Yo-Yo Trap," *American Health* (March 1988):78, 80–82, 84.

   St. Jeor et al., "Nutrition."

24. G. Miller, "Hungry Ewes Deliver Offspring Early," *Science* 300(2003):561–562.

25. K. Hawkes, J. F. O'Connell, and N. G. Blurton Jones, "Hadza Women's Time Allocation, Offspring Provisioning, and the Evolution of Long Postmenopausal Life Spans," *Current Anthropology* 38(1997):551–565.

   K. Hawkes, J. F. O'Connell, N. G. Blurton Jones, H. Alvarez, and E. L. Charnov, "Grandmothering, Menopause, and the Evolution of Human Life Histories," *Proceedings of the National Academy of Sciences* 95(1998):1336–1339.

26. M. Cooper, *Pica*, Springfield, IL: Charles C. Thomas, 1957.

   B. Knox, J. Kremer, and J. Pearce, "Food Fads during Pregnancy: A Question of Taste? *Appetite* 23(1994):288.

   P. Rosso, "Regulation of Food Intake during Pregnancy and Lactation," in *Human Obesity*, eds. R. J. Wurtman and J. J. Wurtman, New York: New York Academy of Sciences, 1987.

27. J. Le Magnen, *Neurobiology of Feeding and Nutrition*, New York: Academic Press, 1992.

28. T. Johns, "Well-Grounded Diet," *The Sciences* (September/October 1991):38–43.

   Knox et al., "Food Fads during Pregnancy."

   M. E. Mercer and M. D. Holder, "Food Cravings, Endogenous Opioid Peptides, and Food Intake: A Review," *Appetite* 29(1997):325–352.

29. E. J. Callahan and L. Desiderato, "Disorders in Pregnancy," in *Handbook of Behavioral Medicine for Women*, eds. E. A. Blechman and K. D. Brownell, New York: Pergamon, 1988.

   K. Uvnäs-Moberg, "Gastrointestinal Tract in Growth and Reproduction," *Scientific American* 261(July 1989):78–83.

30. H. A. Guthrie, *Introductory Nutrition*, Saint Louis: Mosby, 1975.

31. M. Erick, "Hyperolfaction and Hyperemesis Gravidarum: What Is the Relationship?" *Nutrition Reviews* 53(1995):289–295.

32. R. M. Nesse and G. C. Williams, "Evolution and the Origins of Disease," *Scientific American* (November 1998):86–93.

   M. Profet, "Pregnancy Sickness as Adaptation: A Deterrent to Maternal Ingestion of Teratogens," in *The Adapted Mind: Evolutionary Psychology and the Generation of Culture*, eds. J. H. Barkow, L. Cosmides, and J. Tooby, New York: Oxford University Press, 1992.

   P. W. Sherman and S. M. Flaxman, "Protecting Ourselves from Food," *American Scientist* 89(March–April 2001):142–151.

33. T. M. Bayley, L. Dye, S. Jones, M. DeBono, and A. J. Hill, "Food Cravings and Aversions during Pregnancy: Relationships with Nausea and Vomiting," *Appetite* 38(2002):45–51.

34. S. R. Crystal and I. L. Bernstein, "Morning Sickness: Impact on Offspring Salt Preference," *Appetite* 25(1995):231–240.

   S. R. Crystal and I. L. Bernstein, "Infant Salt Preference and Mother's Morning Sickness," *Appetite* 30(1998):297–307.

35. Uvnäs-Moberg, "Gastrointestinal Tract in Growth and Reproduction."

36. Ibid.

37. B. J. Moore and M. R. C. Greenwood, "Pregnancy and Weight Gain," in *Eating Disorders and Obesity: A Comprehensive Handbook*, eds. K. D. Brownell and C. G. Fairburn, New York: The Guilford Press, 1995.

38. P. J. Bradley, "Conditions Recalled to Have Been Associated with Weight Gain in Adulthood," *Appetite* 6(1985):235–241.

39. "Targeting Weight-Reduction Programs," *Nutrition Reviews* 48(1990):414–416.
40. A. P. Sisopoulos, "Characteristics of Obesity: An Overview," in *Human Obesity*, eds. R. J. Wurtman and J. J. Wurtman, New York: New York Academy of Sciences, 1987.
41. Moore and Greenwood, "Pregnancy and Weight Gain."
42. St. Jeor et al., "Nutrition."
43. T. O. Scholl, M. L. Hediger, C.-S. Khoo, M. F. Healey, and N. L. Rawson, "Maternal Weight Gain, Diet and Infant Birth Weight," *Journal of Clinical Epidemiology* 44(1991):423–428.
44. Moore and Greenwood, "Pregnancy and Weight Gain."
45. J. Mi, C. Law, K.-L. Zhang, C. Osmond, C. Stein, and D. Barker, "Effects of Infant Birthweight and Maternal Body Mass Index in Pregnancy on Components of the Insulin Resistance Syndrome in China," *Annals of Internal Medicine* 132(2000):253–260.
46. G.-P. Ravelli, Z. A. Stein, and M. W. Susser, "Obesity in Young Men after Famine Exposure in Utero and Early Infancy," *The New England Journal of Medicine* 295(1976):349–353.
47. D. M. Nathan and R. Frishman, *Diabetes*, Boston, MA: Harvard Medical School Health Publications Group, 1999.

    B. L. Silverman, L. Landsberg, and B. E. Metzger, "Fetal Hyperinsulinism in Offspring of Diabetic Mothers: Association with the Subsequent Development of Childhood Obesity," *Annals of the New York Academy of Sciences* 699(1993):36–45.
48. G. M. Shaw, E. M. Velie, and D. Schaffer, "Risk of Neural Tube Defect—Affected Pregnancies among Obese Women," *JAMA* 275(1996):1093–1096.

    M. M. Werler, C. Louik, S. Shapiro, and A. A. Mitchell, "Prepregnant Weight in Relation to Risk of Neural Tube Defects," *JAMA* 275(1996):1089–1092.
49. Columbia University College of Physicians and Surgeons, *Complete Home Medical Guide*, New York: Crown Publishers, 1985.
50. E. L. Abel, "Fetal Alcohol Syndrome: Behavioral Teratology," *Psychological Bulletin* 87(1980):29–50.

    "Fetal Alcohol Syndrome," *Science* 258(1992):739.

    E. Hunt, A. P. Streissguth, B. Kerr, and H. Olson, "Mothers' Alcohol Consumption during Pregnancy: Effects on Spatial-Visual Reasoning in 14-Year-Old Children," *Psychological Science* 6(1995):339–342.

    A. P. Streissguth, J. M. Asase, S. K. Clarren, S. P. Randels, R. A. LaDue, and D. F. Smith, "Fetal Alcohol Syndrome in Adolescents and Adults," *JAMA* 265(1991):1961–1967.

    A. P. Streissguth, F. L. Bookstein, P. D. Sampson, and H. M. Barr, "Neurobehavioral Effects of Prenatal Alcohol: Part III. PLS Analyses of Neuropsychological Tests," *Neurotoxicology and Teratology* 11(1989):493–507.

    A. P. Streissguth, S. Landesman-Dwyer, J. C. Martin, and D. W. Smith, "Teratogenic Effects of Alcohol in Humans and Laboratory Animals," *Science* 209(1980):353–361.
51. B. M. Altura, B. T. Altura, A. Carella, M. Chatterjee, S. Halevy, and N. Tejani, "Alcohol Produces Spasms of Human Umbilical Blood Vessels: Relationship to Fetal Alcohol Syndrome (FAS)," *European Journal of Pharmacology* 86(1983):311–312.
52. C. R. Goodlett, D. J. Bonthius, E. A. Wasserman, and J. R. West, "An Animal Model of Central Nervous System Dysfunction Associated with Fetal Alcohol Exposure: Behavioral and Neuroanatomical Correlates," in *Learning and Memory: The Behavioral and Biological Substrates*, eds. I. Gormezano and E. A. Wasserman, Hillsdale, NJ: Lawrence Erlbaum Associates, 1992.

    C. Ikonomidou, P. Bittigau, M. J. Ishimaru, D. F. Wozniak, C. Koch, K. Genz, M. T. Price, V. Stefovska, F. Hörster, T. Tenkova, K. Dikranian, and J. W. Olney, "Ethanol-Induced Apoptotic Neurodegeneration and Fetal Alcohol Syndrome," *Science* 287(2000):1056–1060.
53. "Fetal Alcohol Syndrome."

    A. P. Streissguth, H. M. Barr, P. D. Sampson, F. L. Bookstein, and B. L. Darby, "Neurobehavioral Effects of Prenatal Alcohol: Part I," *Neurotoxicology and Teratology* 11(1989):461–476.
54. A. P. Streissguth, H. M. Barr, F. L. Bookstein, P. D. Sampson, and H. C. Olson, "The Long-Term Neurocognitive Consequences of Prenatal Alcohol Exposure: A 14-Year Study," *Psychological Science* 10(1999):186–190.

55. P. D. Sampson, A. P. Streissguth, H. M. Barr, and F. L. Bookstein, "Neurobehavioral Effects of Prenatal Alcohol: Part II. Partial Least Squares Analysis," *Neurotoxicology* 11(1989):477–491.

Streissguth, Bookstein, Sampson, and Barr, "Neurobehavioral Effects of Prenatal Alcohol: Part III."

56. G. B. Kolata, "Fetal Alcohol Advisory Debated," *Science* 214(1981):642, 643, 645.

U.S. Department of Health and Human Services, *The Surgeon General's Report on Nutrition and Health: Summary and Recommendations* (DHHS Publication No. 88–50211), Washington, DC: U.S. Government Printing Office, 1988.

57. M. Frezza, C. Di Padova, G. Pozzato, M. Terpin, E. Baraona, and C. S. Lieber, "High Blood Alcohol Levels in Women: The Role of Decreased Gastric Alcohol Dehydrogenase Activity and First-Pass Metabolism," *The New England Journal of Medicine* 322(1990):95–99.

B. Wuethrich, "Does Alcohol Damage Female Brains More?" *Science* 291(2001):2077, 2079.

58. D. F. Musto, "Alcohol in American History," *Scientific American* (April 1996):78–83.

59. M. Barinaga, "New Experiments Underscore Warnings on Maternal Drinking," *Science* 273(1996):738–739.

J. M. Cirillo, "Differential Treatment: Considerations for the Female Alcoholic," in *Women and Mental Health*, eds. J. A. Sechzer, S. M. Pfafflin, F. L. Denmark, A. Griffin, and S. J. Blumenthal, New York: The New York Academy of Sciences, 1996.

B. L. Vallee, "Alcohol in the Western World," *Scientific American* (June 1998):80–85.

60. R. M. Gilbert, "Caffeine: Overview and Anthology," in *Nutrition and Behavior*, ed. S. A. Miller, Philadelphia: Franklin Institute, 1981.

61. B. Weiss, "Behavior as a Common Focus of Toxicology," in *Nutrition and Behavior*, ed. S. A. Miller, Philadelphia: Franklin Institute, 1981.

62. R. Martorell, "The Role of Nutrition in Economic Development," *Nutrition Reviews* 54(1996):S66–S71.

63. G. K. Beauchamp, B. J. Cowart, and H. J. Schmidt, "Development of Chemosensory Sensitivity and Preference," in *Smell and Taste in Health and Disease*, eds. T. V. Getchell, L. M. Bartoshuk, R. L. Doty, and J. B. Snow, New York: Raven Press, 1991.

L. P. Lipsitt and G. Behl, "Taste-Mediated Differences in the Sucking Behavior of Human Newborns," in *Taste, Experience, and Feeding*, eds. E. D. Capaldi and T. L. Powley, Washington, DC: American Psychological Association, 1990.

64. P. Wright, "Hunger, Satiety and Feeding Behavior in Early Infancy," in *Eating Habits: Food, Physiology and Learned Behavior*, eds. R. A. Boakes, D. A. Popplewell, and M. J. Burton, Chichester, UK: Wiley, 1987, p. 75.

65. Gilbert, "Caffeine."

St. Jeor et al., "Nutrition."

66. J. Newman, "How Breast Milk Protects Newborns," *Scientific American* (December 1995):76–79.

67. E. M. Blass, "The Ontogeny of Motivation: Opioid Bases of Energy Conservation and Lasting Affective Change in Rat and Human Infants," *Current Directions in Psychological Science* 1(1992):116–120.

68. Uvnäs-Moberg, "Gastrointestinal Tract in Growth and Reproduction."

69. R. Von Kries, B. Koletzko, T. Sauerwald, E. Von Mutius, D. Barnert, V. Grunert, and H. Von Voss, "Breast Feeding and Obesity: Cross Sectional Study," *British Medical Journal* 319(1999):1–9.

70. Wright, "Hunger, Satiety and Feeding Behavior in Early Infancy."

71. S. B. Roberts, J. Savage, W. A. Coward, B. Chew, and A. Lucas, "Energy Expenditure and Intake in Infants Born to Lean and Overweight Mothers," *The New England Journal of Medicine* 318(1988):461–466.

72. A. W. Logue, *The Psychology of Eating and Drinking: An Introduction*, 2d ed., New York: W. H. Freeman, 1991, pp. 269–270.

73. L. M. Bartoshuk and G. K. Beauchamp, "Chemical Senses," *Annual Review of Psychology* 45(1994):419–449.

Beauchamp et al., "Development of Chemosensory Sensitivity and Preference."

R. H. Porter, "Human Reproduction and the Mother-Infant Relationship: The Role of Odors," in *Smell and Taste in Health and Disease*, eds. T. V. Getchell, L. M. Bartoshuk, R. L. Doty, and J. B. Snow, New York: Raven Press, 1991.

74. L. Marlier, B. Schaal, and R. Soussignan, "Bottle-Fed Neonates Prefer an Odor Experienced in Utero to an Odor Experienced Postnatally in the Feeding Context," *Developmental Psychobiology* 33(1998):133–145.

75. J. A. Mennella and G. K. Beauchamp, "The Early Development of Human Flavor Preferences," in *Why We Eat What We Eat: The Psychology of Eating*, ed. E. D. Capaldi, Washington, DC: American Psychological Association, 1996.

   J. A. Mennella and G. K. Beauchamp, "The Human Infants' Response to Vanilla Flavors in Mother's Milk and Formula," *Infant Behavior and Development* 19(1996):13–19.

76. J. A. Mennella, C. P. Jagnow, and G. K. Beauchamp, "Prenatal and Postnatal Flavor Learning by Human Infants," *Pediatrics* 107(2001):E88.

77. L. J. Stein, B. J. Cowart, A. N. Epstein, L. J. Pilot, C. R. Laskin, and G. K. Beauchamp, "Increased Liking for Salty Foods in Adolescents Exposed during Infancy to a Chloride-Deficient Feeding Formula," *Appetite* 27(1996):65–77.

78. S. J. Cheslock, E. I. Varlinskaya, E. S. Petrov, M. M. Silveri, L. P. Spear, and N. E. Spear, "Ethanol as a Reinforcer in the Newborn's First Suckling Experience," *Alcoholism: Clinical and Experimental Research* 25(2001):391–402.

79. J. A. Mennella and G. K. Beauchamp, "Smoking and the Flavor of Breast Milk," *The New England Journal of Medicine* 339(1998):1559–1560.

80. J. A. Mennella, "Infants' Suckling Responses to the Flavor of Alcohol in Mothers' Milk," *Alcoholism: Clinical and Experimental Research* 21(1997):581–585.

   J. A. Mennella, "Short-Term Effects of Maternal Alcohol Consumption on Lactational Performance," *Alcoholism: Clinical and Experimental Research* 22(1998):1389–1392.

81. St. Jeor et al., "Nutrition."

82. Rosso, "Regulation of Food Intake during Pregnancy and Lactation."

83. K. Uvnäs-Moberg, "Endocrinologic Control of Food Intake," *Nutrition Reviews* 48(1990): 57–63.

84. "Postprandial Thermogenesis in Lactating Women," *Nutrition Reviews* 49(1991):209–210.

85. M. A. McCroy, "Does Dieting during Lactation Put Infant Growth at Risk?" *Nutrition Reviews* 59(2001):18–21.

86. Uvnäs-Moberg, "Gastrointestinal Tract in Growth and Reproduction."

87. W. Shakespeare, *Antony and Cleopatra* in *The Complete Works of William Shakespeare*, ed. W. A. Wright, Garden City, NY: Garden City Books, 1623/1936, p. 1101.

88. Ibid.

Chapter 14: When and Why Smoking Affects Your Weight

1. American Psychiatric Association, *Diagnostic and Statistical Manual of Mental Disorders* (Rev. ed.), 4th ed., Washington, DC: APA, 2000.

   C. Lambert, "Deep Cravings," *Harvard Magazine* (March/April 2000):60–68.

   P. O. Russell and L. H. Epstein, "Smoking," in *Handbook of Behavioral Medicine for Women*, eds. E. A. Blechman and K. D. Brownell, New York: Pergamon, 1988.

2. R. C. Klesges and L. M. Klesges, "Cigarette Smoking as a Dieting Strategy in a University Population," *International Journal of Eating Disorders* 7(1988):413–419.

   H. G. Pope, K. A. Phillips, and R. Olivardia, *The Adonis Complex: The Secret Crisis of Male Body Obsession*, New York: The Free Press, 2000.

   C. A. Tomeo, A. E. Field, C. S. Berkey, G. A. Colditz, and A. L. Frazier, "Weight Concerns, Weight Control Behaviors, and Smoking Initiation," *Pediatrics* 104(1999):918–924.

3. K. M. Flegal, "Trends in Body Weight and Overweight in the U.S. Population," *Nutrition Reviews* 54(1996):S97–S100.

   G. Taubes, "As Obesity Rates Rise, Experts Struggle to Explain Why," *Science* 280(1998): 1367–1368.

4. N. E. Grunberg, "Nicotine, Cigarette Smoking, and Body Weight," *British Journal of Addiction* 80(1985):369–377.

5. Flegal, "Trends in Body Weight and Overweight in the U.S. Population."

   Grunberg, "Nicotine, Cigarette Smoking, and Body Weight."

R. C. Klesges, M. DeBon, and A. Meyers, "Obesity in African American Women: Epidemiology, Determinants, and Treatment Issues," in *Body Image, Eating Disorders, and Obesity: An Integrative Guide for Assessment and Treatment*, ed. J. K. Thompson, Washington, DC: American Psychological Association, 1996.

R. C. Klesges and A. W. Meyers, "Smoking, Body Weight, and Their Effects on Smoking Behavior: A Comprehensive Review of the Literature," *Psychological Bulletin* 106(1989): 204–230.

R. C. Klesges, K. D. Ward, J. W. Ray, G. Cutter, D. R. Jacobs, and L. E. Wagenknecht, "The Prospective Relationships between Smoking and Weight in a Young, Biracial Cohort: The Coronary Artery Risk Development in Young Adults Study," *Journal of Consulting and Clinical Psychology* 66(1998):987–993.

6. N. E. Grunberg, K. A. Popp, and S. E. Winders, "Effects of Nicotine on Body Weight in Rats with Access to 'Junk' Foods," *Psychopharmacology* 94(1988):536–539.

7. R. W. Foltin, M. W. Fischman, and M. F. Byrne, "Effects of Smoked Marijuana on Food Intake and Body Weight of Humans Living in a Residential Laboratory," *Appetite* 11(1988): 1–14.

8. Grunberg, "Nicotine, Cigarette Smoking, and Body Weight."

9. J. B. Beckwith, "Eating, Drinking, and Smoking and Their Relationship in Adult Women," *Psychological Reports* 59(1986):1075–1089.

10. K. A. Perkins, J. E. Sexton, A. DiMarco, and C. Fonte, "Acute Effects of Tobacco Smoking on Hunger and Eating in Male and Female Smokers," *Appetite* 22(1994):149–158.

11. S. A. Wager-Srdar, A. S. Levine, J. E. Morley, J. R. Hoidal, and D. E. Niewoehner, "Effects of Cigarette Smoke and Nicotine on Feeding and Energy," *Physiology and Behavior* 32(1984):389–395.

12. Grunberg, "Nicotine, Cigarette Smoking, and Body Weight."

13. N. E. Grunberg and D. E. Morse, "Cigarette Smoking and Food Consumption in the United States," *Journal of Applied Social Psychology* 14(1984):310–317.

14. N. E. Grunberg, "The Effects of Nicotine and Cigarette Smoking on Food Consumption and Taste Preferences," *Addictive Behaviors* 7(1982):317–331.

15. H. B. Hubert, R. R. Fabsitz, M. Feinleib, and K. S. Brown, "Olfactory Sensitivity in Humans: Genetic versus Environmental Control," *Science* 208(1980):607–609.

16. C. S. Pomerleau, A. W. Garcia, A. Drewnowski, and O. E. Pomerleau, "Sweet Taste Preference in Women Smokers: Comparison with Nonsmokers and Effects of Menstrual Phase and Nicotine Abstinence," *Pharmacology, Biochemistry and Behavior* 40(1991):995–999.

17. A. J. Jaffe and A. G. Glaros, "Taste Dimensions in Cigarette Discrimination: A Multidimensional Scaling Approach," *Addictive Behaviors* 11(1986):407–413.

18. Grunberg, "Nicotine, Cigarette Smoking, and Body Weight."

19. K. A. Perkins, L. H. Epstein, B. L. Marks, R. L. Stiller, and R. G. Jacob, "The Effect of Nicotine on Energy Expenditure during Light Physical Activity," *The New England Journal of Medicine* 320(1989):898–903.

20. A. Hofstetter, Y. Schutz, E. Jéquier, and J. Wahren, "Increased 24-Hour Energy Expenditure in Cigarette Smokers," *The New England Journal of Medicine* 314(1986):79–82.

21. Klesges et al., "The Prospective Relationships between Smoking and Weight in a Young Biracial Cohort."

22. S. M. Hall, D. Ginsberg, and R. T. Jones, "Smoking Cessation and Weight Gain," *Journal of Consulting and Clinical Psychology* 54(1986):342–346.

R. S. Manley and F. J. Boland, "Side-Effects and Weight Gain Following a Smoking Cessation Program," *Addictive Behaviors* 8(1983):375v380.

23. M. B. Cantor and J. F. Wilson, "Feeding the Face: New Directions in Adjunctive Behavior Research," in *Affect, Conditioning, and Cognition: Essays on the Determinants of Behavior*, eds. F. R. Brush and J. B. Overmier, Hillsdale, NJ: Lawrence Erlbaum Associates, 1985.

J. Green and W. N. Tapp, "Feeding Cycles in Smokers, Exsmokers and Nonsmokers," *Physiology and Behavior* 36(1986):1059–1063.

Grunberg, "Nicotine, Cigarette Smoking, and Body Weight."

N. E. Grunberg, D. J. Bowen, V. A. Maycock, and S. M. Nespor, "The Importance of Sweet Taste and Caloric Content in the Effects of Nicotine on Specific Food Consumption," *Psychopharmacology* 87(1985):198–203.

S. M. Hall, R. McGee, C. Tunstall, J. Duffy, and N. Benowitz, "Changes in Food Intake and Activity after Quitting Smoking," *Journal of Consulting and Clinical Psychology* 57(1989):81–86.

Klesges and Meyers, "Smoking, Body Weight, and Their Effects on Smoking Behavior."

M. A. Sayette and D. J. Parrott, "Effects of Olfactory Stimuli on Urge Reduction in Smokers," *Experimental and Clinical Psychopharmacology* 7(1999):151–159.

B. Spring, J. Wurtman, R. Gleason, R. Wurtman, and K. Kessler, "Weight Gain and Withdrawal Symptoms after Smoking Cessation: A Preventative Intervention Using D-Fenfluramine, *Health Psychology* 10(1991):216–223.

24. Jaffe and Glaros, "Taste Dimensions in Cigarette Discrimination."

Hall et al., "Changes in Food Intake and Activity after Quitting Smoking."

J. Rodin, "Weight Change Following Smoking Cessation: The Role of Food Intake and Exercise," *Addictive Behaviors* 12(1987):303–317.

25. Hofstetter et al., "Increased 24-hour Energy Expenditure in Cigarette Smokers."

26. K. A. Perkins, C. Denier, J. A. Mayer, R. R. Scott, and P. M. Dubbert, "Weight Gain Associated with Decreases in Smoking Rate and Nicotine Intake," *International Journal of the Addictions* 22(1987):575–581.

Rodin, "Weight Change Following Smoking Cessation."

27. Klesges and Meyers, "Smoking, Body Weight, and Their Effects on Smoking Behavior."

Hall et al., "Smoking Cessation and Weight Gain."

28. K. Doherty, F. S. Militello, T. Kinnunen, and A. J. Garvey, "Nicotine Gum Dose and Weight Gain after Smoking Cessation," *Journal of Consulting and Clinical Psychology* 64(1996):799–807.

J. Gross, M. L. Stitzer, and J. Maldonado, "Nicotine Replacement: Effects on Postcessation Weight Gain," *Journal of Consulting and Clinical Psychology* 57(1989):87–92.

Klesges and Meyers, "Smoking, Body Weight, and Their Effects on Smoking Behavior."

29. Grunberg et al., "Effects of Nicotine on Body Weight in Rats with Access to 'Junk' Foods."

30. Gross et al., "Nicotine Replacement."

31. S. L. Frederick, S. M. Hall, G. L. Humfleet, and R. F. Muñoz, "Sex Differences in the Relation of Mood to Weight Gain after Quitting Smoking," *Experimental and Clinical Psychopharmacology* 4(1996):178–185.

32. A. J. Stunkard and T. A. Wadden, "Restrained Eating and Human Obesity," *Nutrition Reviews* 48(1990):78–86.

33. B. Hitsman, R. Pingitore, B. Spring, A. Mahableshwarker, J. S. Mizes, K. A. Segraves, J. L. Kristeller, and W. Xu, "Antidepressant Pharmacotherapy Helps Some Cigarette Smokers More than Others," *Journal of Consulting and Clinical Psychology* 67(1999):547–554.

34. National Heart, Lung, and Blood Institute, *Clinical Guidelines on the Identification, Evaluation, and Treatment of Overweight and Obesity in Adults*, 1998. Available at: www.nhlbi.nih.gov/guidelines/obesity/ob_home.htm.

35. B. Borrelli, B. Spring, R. Niaura, J. Kristeller, J. K. Ockene, and N. J. Keuthen, "Weight Suppression and Weight Rebound in Ex-Smokers Treated with Fluoxetine," *Journal of Consulting and Clinical Psychology* 67(1999):124–131

Chapter 15: We Do Not Live by Bread Alone

1. A. Waters, "How You Eat," *Chronicle of Higher Education* (June 15, 1994):B3.

2. N. R. Fitch, *Appetite for Life: The Biography of Julia Child*, New York: Doubleday, 1997.

3. E. Rozin, "The Structure of Cuisine," in *The Psychobiology of Human Food Selection*, ed. L. M. Barker, Westport, CT: AVI Publishing, 1982.

E. Rozin, *Ethnic Cuisine: The Flavor-Principle Cookbook*, Brattleboro, VT: The Stephen Greene Press, 1983.

E. Rozin, *Crossroads Cooking: The Meeting and Mating of Ethnic Cuisines—from Burma to Texas in 200 Recipes*, New York: Penguin Putnam, 1999.

4. A. Davidson, *The Oxford Companion to Food*, New York: Oxford University Press, 1999.

5. L. Abdallah, M. Chabert, B. Le Roux, and J. Louis-Sylvestre, "Is Pleasantness of Biscuits and Cakes Related to Their Actual or to Their Perceived Sugar and Fat Contents?" *Appetite* 30(1998):309–324.

6. M. Clark, "The Rich Little Secret of Top Chefs: Fat," *The New York Times* (April 28, 1999):F1, F9.

7. S. H. Katz, "Fava Bean Consumption: A Case for the Co-Evolution of Genes and Culture," in *Food and Evolution: Toward a Theory of Human Food Habits*, eds. M. Harris and E. B. Ross, Philadelphia: Temple University Press, 1987.

8. R. W. Apple, "New Math: A Chef Adds Science to the Saucepan," *The New York Times* (May 31, 2000):F1, F6.

9. S. H. Katz, "Food Behavior and Biocultural Evolution," in *The Psychobiology of Human Food Selection*, ed. L. M. Barker, Westport, CT: AVI Publishing, 1982.

10. L. L. Birch, J. Billman, and S. S. Richards, "Time of Day Influences Food Acceptability," *Appetite* 5(1984):109–116.

11. P. Huyghe, "An Acquired Taste," *The Sciences* (November/December 1992):8–11.

12. Ibid., p. 8.

13. C. Nemeroff and P. Rozin, "Sympathetic Magic in Kosher Practice and Belief at the Limits of the Laws of Kashrut," *Jewish Folklore and Ethnology* 9(1987):31–32.

14. R. K. Oniang'o and A. Komokoti, "Food Habits in Kenya: The Effects of Change and Attendant Methodological Problems," *Appetite* 32(1999):93–96.

15. L. E. Grivetti, "Food Prejudices and Taboos," in *The Cambridge World History of Food*, eds. K. F. Kiple and K. C. Ornelas, New York: Cambridge University Press, 2000.

16. N. Hrboticky and M. Krondl, "Acculturation to Canadian Foods by Chinese Immigrant Boys: Changes in the Perceived Flavor, Health Value and Prestige of Foods," *Appetite* 5(1984): 117–126.

   M. Krondl, N. Hrboticky, and P. Coleman, "Adapting to Cultural Changes in Food Habits," in *Malnutrition: Determinants and Consequences*, eds. P. L. White and N. Selvey, New York: Alan R. Liss, 1984.

   P. Saran, *The Asian Indian Experience in the United States*. Sahibabad, India: Vikas House, 1985.

17. A. Brillat-Savarin, 1825, quoted in *The Oxford Dictionary of Quotations* (Rev. ed.), 4th ed., ed. A. Partington, New York: Oxford University Press, 1996, p. 141.

18. Rozin, "The Structure of Cuisine."

   Rozin, *Ethnic Cuisine*.

   E. Rozin and P. Rozin, "Culinary Themes and Variations," *Natural History* (February 1981):6, 8, 12, 14.

   P. Rozin, "Human Food Selection: The Interaction of Biology, Culture and Individual Experience," in *The Psychobiology of Human Food Selection*, ed. L. M. Barker, Westport, CT: AVI Publishing, 1982.

19. C. Stallberg-White and P. Pliner, "The Effect of Flavor Principles on Willingness to Taste Novel Foods," *Appetite* 33(1999):209–221.

20. Rozin, *Ethnic Cuisine*.

   Rozin, *Crossroads Cooking*.

21. M. Burros, "Vietnam: A Taste Trip from North to South," *The New York Times* (May 4, 1994):C1, C6.

   M. Burros, "As Cultures Meet in South Africa, So Do the Cuisines," *The New York Times* (January 31, 1996):C4.

22. C. Claiborne, "Cajun and Creole: French at Heart," *The New York Times* (April 1,1987):C1, C6.

   R. Sokolov, *Fading Feast*, New York: E. P. Dutton, 1983.

23. B. Greene, "Cajun Country," *Cuisine* (September 1979):42–54.

24. P. Rozin, "Getting to Like the Burn of Chili Pepper: Biological, Psychological, and Cultural Perspectives," in *Chemical Senses: Vol 2. Irritation*, eds. B. G. Green, J. R. Mason, and M. R. Kare, New York: Marcel Dekker, 1990.

25. C. E. Martin, "Appalachian House Beautiful," *Natural History* 91(2)(1982):4, 6–8, 10,12, 14–16.

   A. C. Revkin, "Need Elephant Repellant? Try This Hot Pepper Brew." *The New York Times* (June 20, 2000):F3.

   UDAP Industries, *Pepper Power*, December 3, 2003. Available at: www.udap.com/faq.htm.

26. K. F. Kiple and K. C. Ornelas, eds., *The Cambridge World History of Food*, New York: Cambridge University Press, 2000.

27. B. G. Galef, "Enduring Social Enhancement of Rats' Preferences for the Palatable and the Piquant," *Appetite* 13(1989):81–92.
28. P. Rozin and K. Kennel, "Acquired Preferences for Piquant Foods by Chimpanzees," *Appetite* 4(1983):69–77.
29. M. J. Caterina, A. Leffler, A. B. Malmberg, W. J. Martin, J. Trafton, K. R. Petersen-Zeitz, M. Koltzenburg, A. I. Basbaum, and D. Julius, "Impaired Nociception and Pain Sensation in Mice Lacking the Capsaicin Receptor," *Science* 288(2000):306–313.
30. L. M. Bartoshuk, "Psychophysical Advances Aid the Study of Genetic Variation in Taste," *Appetite* 34(2000):105.

    B. J. Tepper, "PROP Taster Status Is Related to Fat Perception and Preference," in *Olfaction and Taste XII: An International Symposium*, ed. C. Murphy, New York: New York Academy of Sciences, 1998.
31. R. J. Stevenson and M. R. Yeomans, "Does Exposure Enhance Liking for the Chili Burn?" *Appetite* 24(1995):107–120.
32. Rozin, "Human Food Selection."

    Rozin, "Getting to Like the Burn of Chili Pepper."
33. H. Lawless, P. Rozin, and J. Shenker, "Effects of Oral Capsaicin on Gustatory, Olfactory and Irritant Sensations and Flavor Identification in Humans Who Regularly or Rarely Consume Chili Pepper," *Chemical Senses* 10(1985):579–589.

    Rozin, "Getting to Like the Burn of Chili Pepper."

    B. J. Tepper, "6-N-Propylthiouracil: A Genetic Marker for Taste, with Implications for Food Preference and Dietary Habits," *American Journal of Human Genetics* 63(1998): 1271–1276.
34. P. Rozin, M. Mark, and D. Schiller, "The Role of Desensitization to Capsaicin in Chili Pepper Ingestion and Preference," *Chemical Senses* 6(1981):23–31.
35. Rozin, "Human Food Selection."
36. P. Rozin, D. Reff, M. Mark, and J. Schull, "Conditioned Opponent Responses in Human Tolerance to Caffeine," *Bulletin of the Psychonomic Society* 22(1984):117–120.
37. J. Billing and P. W. Sherman, "Antimicrobial Functions of Spices: Why Some Like It Hot," *The Quarterly Review of Biology* 73(1998):3–49.

    P. W. Sherman and S. M. Flaxman, "Protecting Ourselves from Food," *American Scientist* 89(March–April 2001):142–151.
38. S. D. Coe and M. D. Coe, *The True History of Chocolate*, New York: Thames and Hudson, Ltd., 1996.

    Davidson, *The Oxford Companion to Food.*
39. J. G. Brenner, *The Emperors of Chocolate: Inside the Secret World of Hershey and Mars*, New York: Random House, 1999.
40. C. M. Gibb, P. T. G. Davies, V. Glover, T. J. Steiner, F. C. Rose, and M. Sandler, "Chocolate Is a Migraine-Provoking Agent," *Cephalalgia* 11(1991):93–95.
41. P. Rozin, E. Levine, and C. Stoess, "Chocolate Craving and Liking," *Appetite* 17(1991):199–212.

    H. P. Weingarten and D. Elston, "Food Cravings in a College Population," *Appetite* 17(1991):167–175.

    D. A. Zellner, A. Garriga-Trillo, E. Rohm, S. Centeno, and S. Parker, "Food Liking and Craving: A Cross-Cultural Approach," *Appetite* 33(1999):61–70.
42. M. M. Hetherington and J. I. MacDiarmid, "'Chocolate Addiction': A Preliminary Study of Its Description and Its Relationship to Problem Eating," *Appetite* 21(1993):233–246.
43. M. Guiliano and E. Guiliano, "Chocolate, Chocolate, Chocolate!" *Quarterly Review of Wines* (Autumn 2002): 92–95.

    K. Shaw, "A Club with a One-Track Mind: Chocolate," *The New York Times* (October 6, 2002):1, 7.
44. S. Lazarus, J. F. Mammerstone, and H. H. Schmitz, "Chocolate Contains Additional Flavonoids Not Found in Tea," *The Lancet* 354(1999):1825.

    K. W. Lee, Y. J. Kim, H. J. Lee, and C. Y. Lee, "Cocoa Has More Phenolic Phyto-chemicals and a Higher Antioxidant Capacity Than Teas and Red Wine," *Journal of Agricultural and Food Chemistry"* 51(2003):7292–7295.

D. Rein, T. G. Paglieroni, D. A. Pearson, T. Wun, and H. H. Schmitz, "Cocoa and Wine Polyphenols Modulate Platelet Activation and Function," *Journal of Nutrition* 130(2000): 2120S–2126S.

J. F. Wang, D. D. Schramm, R. R. Holt, J. L. Ensunsa, C. G. Fraga, H. H. Schmitz, and C. L. Keen, "A Dose-Response Effect from Chocolate Consumption on Plasma Epicatechin and Oxidative Damage," *Journal of Nutrition* 130(2000):2115S–2119S.

45. P. J. Geiselman, C. F. Smith, D. A. Williamson, C. M. Champagne, G. A. Bray, and D. H. Ryan, "Perception of Sweetness Intensity Determines Women's Hedonic and Other Perceptual Responsiveness to Chocolate Food," *Appetite* 31(1998):37–48.

P. Rozin, "Sweetness, Sensuality, Sin, Safety, and Socialization: Some Speculations," in *Sweetness*, ed. J. Dobbing, New York: Springer-Verlag, 1987.

46. B. L. Gelb, *The Dictionary of Food*, New York: Ballantine Books, 1978.

E. L. Gibson and E. Desmond, "Chocolate Craving and Hunger State: Implications for the Acquisition and Expression of Appetite and Food Choice," *Appetite* 32(1999):219–240.

47. J. E. Brody, *Jane Brody's The New York Times Guide to Personal Health*, New York: Avon Books, 1982.

A. Drewnowski, "The Science and Complexity of Bitter Taste," *Nutrition Reviews* 59(2001):163–169.

P. M. Fedorchak, J. Mesita, S. A. Plater, and K. Brougham, "Caffeine-Reinforced Conditioned Flavor Preferences in Rats," *Behavioral Neuroscience* 116(2002):334–346.

G. K. Mumford, S. M. Evans, B. J. Kaminski, K. L. Preston, C. A. Sannerud, K. Silverman, and R. R. Griffiths, "Discriminative Stimulus and Subjective Effects of Theobromine and Caffeine in Humans," *Psychopharmacology* 115(1994):1–8.

48. T. G. Benedek, "Food as Aphrodisiacs and Anaphrodisiacs?" in *The Cambridge World History of Food*, eds. K. F. Kiple and K. C. Ornelas, New York: Cambridge University Press, 2000.

Coe and Coe, *The True History of Chocolate*.

49. E. Tomaso, M. Beltramo, and D. Piomelli, "Brain Cannabinoids in Chocolate," *Nature* (August 22, 1996):677–678.

50. D. Lester and D. Bernard, "Liking for Chocolate, Depression, and Suicidal Preoccupation," *Psychological Reports* 69(1991):570.

G. F. Michell, A. H. Mebane, and C. K. Billings, "Effect of Bupropion on Chocolate Craving," *American Journal of Psychiatry* 146(1989):119–120.

M. Schuman, M. J. Gitlin, and L. Fairbanks, "Sweets, Chocolate, and Atypical Depressive Traits," *The Journal of Nervous and Mental Disease* 175(1987):491–495.

51. M. Harris, "India's Sacred Cow," in *Issues in Nutrition for the 1980s: An Ecological Perspective*, eds. A. L. Tobias and P. J. Thompson, Monterey, CA: Wadsworth, 1980.

C. Henderson, "The Great Cow Explosion in Rajasthan," in *Advances in Historical Ecology*, ed. W. Balée, New York: Columbia University Press, 1998.

D. Jacobson, "A Reverence for Cows," *Natural History* (June 1999):58–63.

S. E. G. Lea, "Correlation and Contiguity in Foraging Behavior," in *Predictability, Correlation, and Contiguity*, eds. P. Harzem and M. D. Zeiler, New York: Wiley, 1981.

K. N. Nair, "Animal Protein Consumption and the Sacred Cow Complex in India," in *Food and Evolution: Toward a Theory of Human Food Habits*, eds. M. Harris and E. B. Ross, Philadelphia: Temple University Press, 1987.

A. Roosevelt, "The Evolution of Human Subsistence," in *Food and Evolution: Toward a Theory of Human Food Habits*, eds. M. Harris and E. B. Ross, Philadelphia: Temple University Press, 1987.

52. K. Hill and A. M. Hurtado, "Hunter-Gatherers of the New World," *American Scientist* (September/October 1989):436–443.

53. W. Arens, *The Man-Eating Myth: Anthropology and Anthropophagy*, New York: Oxford University Press, 1979.

54. D. R. Harris, "Aboriginal Subsistence in a Tropical Rain Forest Environment: Food Procurement, Cannibalism, and Population Regulation in Northeastern Australia," in *Food and Evolution: Toward a Theory of Human Food Habits*, eds. M. Harris and E. B. Ross, Philadelphia: Temple University Press, 1987.

G. Kolata, "Anthropologists Suggest Cannibalism Is a Myth," *Science* 232(1986):1497–1500.

P. Villa, C. Bouville, J. Courtin, D. Helmer, E. Mahieu, P. Shipman, G. Belluomini, and M. Branca, "Cannibalism in the Neolithic," *Science* 233(1986):431–438.

55. A. Defleur, T. White, P. Valensi, L. Slimak, and E. Crégut-Bonnoure, "Neanderthal Cannibalism at Moula-Guercy, Ardèche, France," *Science* 286(1999):128–131.

Y. Fernández-Jalvo, J. C. Díez, J. M. B. De Castro, E. Carbonell, and J. L. Arsuaga, "Evidence of Early Cannibalism," *Science* 271(1996):277–278.

C. G. Turner and J. A. Turner, *Man Corn: Cannibalism and Violence in the Prehistoric American Southwest*, Salt Lake City: The University of Utah Press, 1999.

T. D. White, "Once Were Cannibals," *Scientific American* (August 2001):58–65.

56. P. Y. Bullock, "Evidence of Cannibalism," *Science* 277(1997):1745b–1746b.

J. A. Darling, "Mass Inhumation and the Execution of Witches in the American Southwest," *American Anthropologist* 100(1999):732–752.

A. Gibbons, "Archaeologists Rediscover Cannibals," *Science* 277(1997):635–637.

57. M. J. Kohn, "You Are What You Eat," *Science* 283(1999):335–336.

58. J. M. Diamond, "Archaeology: Talk of Cannibalism," *Nature* 407(2000):25–26.

C. Holden, "Molecule Shows Anasazi Ate Their Enemies," *Science* 289(2000):1663.

R. A. Marlar, B. L. Leonard, B. R. Billman, P. M. Lambert, and J. E. Marlar, "Biochemical Evidence of Cannibalism at a Prehistoric Puebloan Site in Southwestern Colorado," *Nature* 407(2000):74–78.

J. N. Wilford, "New Data Suggests Some Cannibalism by Ancient Indians," *The New York Times* (September 7, 2000):A2, A22.

59. N. J. Richardson, R. Shepherd, and N. A. Elliman, "Current Attitudes and Future Influences on Meat Consumption in the U.K.," *Appetite* 21(1993):41–51.

M. L. S. Santos and D. A. Booth, "Influences on Meat Avoidance among British Students," *Appetite* 27(1996):197–205.

60. M. A. Amerine and E. B. Roessler, *Wines: Their Sensory Evaluation*, San Francisco: W. H. Freeman, 1976.

J. Durac, *Wines and the Art of Tasting*, New York: E. P. Dutton, 1974.

B. Ensrud, *Wine with Food: A Guide to Entertaining through the Seasons*, New York: Congdon & Weed, 1984.

61. Amerine and Roessler, *Wines*.

62. Ibid.

63. Ibid.

64. A. V. Cardello, "The Role of the Human Senses in Food Acceptance," in *Food Choice, Acceptance and Consumption*, eds. H. L. Meiselman and H. J. H. MacFie, London: Blackie Academic & Professional, 1996.

65. Amerine and Roessler, *Wines*.

66. Ibid.

67. J.-X. Guinard, A. Souchard, M. Picot, M. Rogeaux, and J.-M. Sieffermann, "Sensory Determinants of the Thirst-Quenching Character of Beer," *Appetite* 31(1998):101–115.

68. Amerine and Roessler, *Wines*.

69. D. A. Norman, *Memory and Attention*, New York: Wiley, 1969.

70. Amerine and Roessler, *Wines*.

71. A. C. North, D. J. Hargreaves, and J. McKendrick, "In-Store Music Affects Product Choice," *Nature* 390(1997):132.

72. G. Meredith, 1859, quoted in *The Oxford Dictionary of Quotations* (Rev. ed.) 4th ed., ed. A. Partington, New York: Oxford University Press, 1996, p. 458.

73. E. R. B. Lytton, 1860, quoted in *The Oxford Dictionary of Quotations* (Rev. ed.) 4th ed., ed. A. Partington, New York: Oxford University Press, 1996, p. 458.

Author Index

Subject Index